No-One Likes Us, We Don't Care

No-One Likes Us, Us,
We Don't Care

a UKIP memoir by

Paul Oakley

Published by New English Review Press
a subsidiary of World Encounter Institute
PO Box 158397
Nashville, Tennessee 37215
&
27 Old Gloucester Street
London, England, WC1N 3AX

Cover Art and Design by Kendra Mallock

ISBN: 978-1-943003-25-9

First Edition

NEW ENGLISH REVIEW PRESS
newenglishreview.org

Thanks to Nathan Virica for his help with the text.

Contents

CHAPTER ONE

From Tory Scum to UKIP Fascist

U PON COMPLETING MY FOURTH TERM as prime minister, David Starkey shall be commissioned to write the official biography. That work will set out my life story in full. Until that day some background is necessary to explain how it was possible for a Conservative Party stalwart like me to overturn his convictions so comprehensively.

Incredible as it may sound, one day I decided to flip from the hard right of the Tories and join the UK Independence Party instead. Here is the story of my journey.

In 1992, the notorious pro-EU member of parliament, Kenneth Clarke, addressed a fringe event at the Conservative Party Conference. After that meeting, the bright-eyed chairman of Shrewsbury Young Conservatives set fire to a European Union flag in the street outside. That handsome young man was your Dear Author, and I'm very proud to have been the very first person ever to have burned that rag.

Then, in the midst of the British Parliamentary rebellion against the 'Treaty on European Union', more commonly known as Maastricht, I spent some weeks running errands for Bill Cash MP in his Great College Street office. He and his fellow 'bastards' were doing their best to kill this latest manifestation of EU federalism. If Prime Minister John Major fell in the process, well, that was just too bad. The whole exercise was a waste of time, though, as the Treaty was approved and, more importantly, I couldn't persuade Cash to call for outright withdrawal from the EU itself. And yes, you did read that correctly.

At the tail-end of that internship came the Young Conservative Conference. Dangerously, it was held in Southend, the constituency of proud EUphobe, Sir Teddy Taylor MP. As such, Conservative Central

Office were categorically not going to allow any debate on the party's European policy. However, the final session before close of conference on Sunday was to be a balloted motion chosen by delegates. So on Saturday morning, a group of us decided to work very hard from the moment the hall doors opened, not by listening to any of the speeches on the bloody 'Traffic Cones Hotline' or 'Citizens' Charter', but by talking to as many attendees as possible.

Either:

'Could you vote for us to debate this motion congratulating John Major on his foreign policy?'

'Absolutely. It's about time this party began to back the Prime Minister.'

Or:

'Could you vote for us to debate this motion congratulating John Major on his foreign policy?'

'You must be joking. He's betraying us in Europe.'

'That's precisely the point. Do help yourself to one of these little stickers.'

The stickers in question featured the EU flag. With a big red line through it. They fitted nicely onto a blank white space on the conference photo pass and looked very official indeed as the press began to query.

The motion was selected. Overwhelmingly. Party officers became uneasy as far more delegates put their names forward to argue against it than for it. I, too, put my name down—to back it. Head Office was grateful for every supporter they could get so I was duly-approved. By the time they found out that the speech wasn't an endorsement at all it would be too late.

I sought out Sir Teddy.

'Do you have a spare copy of the Maastricht Treaty please? One that you don't need returned?'

After telling him why, he laughed.

Sunday morning arrived and the debate began. One by one, the Majorettes did their best from the podium. One by one, delegates got rid of them by stamping their feet in unison and shouting 'Off! Off! Off!' I'd been lurking near the exit at the side of the hall. My name was announced for three speeches hence, so I slipped off to the bar for a single pint even though it wasn't yet noon.

National YC Chairman, Andrew Rosindell, sent someone to fetch me. Gulping the last of the beer I headed back to the hall which was suddenly quiet as people were knackered with all that be-stomping and be-booing.

I began.

'John Major deserves our full support for his European policy.'
I stopped. The quiet continued, but only for a moment.

'Rubbish!'

'UnSound!'

'You traitorous shit, Oakley!'

The Chairman calmed the hall down. I cocked my head to one side.

'Only joking.'

I started again. And the subsequent national and international
press headlines concentrated on the following words:

'John Major wants us to be at the heart of Europe. Well, it's
about time that we were at the throat of Europe.

'This is a copy of the Maastricht Treaty. It's harder to get
hold of than the 'Satanic Verses' in Iran.

'And I hope that the Prime Minister has the courage to do
this.'

I'd then torn the treaty in twain, holding the pieces in the air for the
inevitable photographs.

Yet, although your Dear Author received the only standing ovation
of the conference, two aspects of that speech still leave a sense of sadness
to this day.

Firstly, the Conservative Party filmed all debates which were then
sold as premium-priced VHS tape souvenirs. Mysteriously, the entire
footage of this one has been 'lost' by them.

Secondly, it was tinged with the sexual harassment which is endemic in the Tory Party. Fortunately, this debate was held on the Sunday morning when all were about to disperse. Had it been listed but 24
hours previously, there's no doubt I'd have been molested that very evening by a number of predatory young women. Several of them admitted
this in the months thereafter. The choicest of strumpets, too. What a
lucky escape. Harrumph.

In 1996 there was an unveiling of a memorial to A E Housman in
Westminster Abbey. Former student of Housman, Enoch Powell, was
undertaking the dedication. I hadn't seen Powell since the previous year
when I'd invited him to address the students at Bar School on the threat
of EU federalism. We'd had a pleasant lunch afterwards in Lincoln's Inn
during which we'd disagreed about Friedrich Nietzsche but concurred
in our view that Parsifal was Wagner's finest opera. Physically frail then,
he was still mentally incisive.

The intervening months had been cruel and Enoch had to be assisted to the Abbey lectern by his wife Pamela and a nurse. His oration was incoherent.

Afterwards, the Housman Society had a reception on the terrace of the House of Commons. Powell was enthroned on a white plastic chair looking across the Thames. I stood over him and tried to exchange pleasantries.

'He can't hear very well, I'm afraid,' said Pamela Powell.

Things became very Quentin Durward. I got down on one knee and thanked him for all his work fighting the European project.

'I make this pledge to you, sir. There will be many of us carrying on this battle after your death.'

He said nothing but beamed.

In 1997, I was elected chairman of the Greater London Young Conservatives on a jihadist anti-EU platform. By this time it was difficult to defend the Tory party which bowed to Brussels and sweated with sleaze. I was particularly angered by a scandal which hit the tabloids during that year's general election. The Tory MP for Beckenham, Piers Merchant, was exposed as having had an affair with 'night club hostess' Anna Cox. He was married and 30 years her senior.

On reading this the whole newspaper was crumpled up and stuffed into the wastepaper bin, squashed down with my furious foot.

Get your own mistress, pal. Anna's my bit on the side.

We'd first met while campaigning for Michael Portillo in Enfield Southgate and she'd asked if I would give her a pearl necklace. I never did. However, amongst other things I did take her backstage to a Stranglers gig at the Royal Albert Hall, a gift more valued than gold by all young women.

Election night '97 was spent at Conservative Central Office with my actual girlfriend, Justine Lovatt, who worked in the research department. Crates and crates of Heineken lay in the corridors and went unquaffed as the results came in. I thought it was great that John Major was reaping the rewards of Maastricht. In the inevitable blood-purge of the party which would follow, every pro-EU MP would be banished and I'd claim the safe seat which was richly-deserved.

I and Justine left Smith Square as the sun was rising, but before Major's public admission of defeat. We didn't want to hear his excuses. There was a crowd of hard-left Tony Blair supporters outside whom we'd been strictly instructed to ignore. They jeered and hooted at the two of us.

'You'll be sorry,' I shouted back.

And they were.

When William Hague replaced John Major as Tory leader, one of his first steps was to abolish the Young Conservatives as we'd become much too anti-EU for his taste. Sound. So, I lay low for a while, simply standing as a council candidate a few times in Lefty areas. I finally got around to taking the Tories' Parliamentary Assessment Board in Milton Keynes in November of 2002. Christina Dykes, Director of Candidates, wrote on 13th January in the new year to say there'd been a pass.

'You did well in the exercises and the assessors were pleased with your overall performance. However, they did feel you should work at your presentation. Your quick wit sometimes made you seem aggressive – that is something of which you should be aware.'

Brilliant in all respects then.

At the 2005 general election under Michael Howard's leadership I stood for the forlorn hope seat of St Helens North and garnered a result of 7,410. Despite our efforts, some wankers called 'UKIP' had put up a candidate too and had the audacity to steal 1,165 of my votes, pushing we Conservatives into third place behind the Lib Dems.

Then David Cameron was elected party leader. He introduced an 'A-List' of politically-correct candidates. I was interviewed for this by Nigel Evans MP and wore a pink shirt and pink tie to look like one of them metrosexuals. That didn't work and my application to be a Cameron Cutie was rejected.

I tried for numerous constituency vacancies thereafter but was only shortlisted by the EU-realists of Rochester and Strood and by Slough which was chaired by a mate from the anti-EU 'Bruges Group', Robert Oulds. Rochester selected Mark Reckless and he went on to win the election in 2010. This was a hoof to the head for Tory central office as Mark was solidly anti-EU. Indeed, the branch had been placed into 'Special Measures' specifically to stop his selection. Slough chose Diana Coad. Also One Of Us, she didn't win the election.

Despite applying for many more seats, I ended up with nothing and the thing that probably did it for me was the Freedom Association. One of their campaigns was 'Better Off Out' which, as you may suspect, made the case for Britain leaving the EU.

TFA Director Simon Richards asked if I'd manage 'BOO'. I thought it best to check with Davina Merison and Gareth Fox of the candidates' department. They passed the decision on to John Maples MP whom

Cameron had just appointed party Deputy Chairman.

'Definitely not,' Maples told me. 'And if you're selected for another seat you'll have to disavow your support for this campaign.'

Dream on old son.

My last Tory conference was in 2010. It had, for many years, been held in cheap and cheerless Blackpool and Bournemouth but Cameron corporatized the event and moved it on rotation to Birmingham and Manchester. It seemed as though those latter conferences had coincided with a euthanasia policy for older party members. As there's no such thing as a B & B at fifteen quid a night in these cities, many elderly activists had foregone their autumn jaunts to the seaside. They were replaced with blank-eyed spads[1] with clipboards whom nobody knew.

It was Birmingham that year. I booked into the hotel just before midnight and then headed to the secure zone. The very first person whom I saw on arriving at the bar was Lucy Bostick. She looked very ticked-off, but not with me.

Here is the best-ever and most insightful quote of all time from Miss Bostick:

'This place,' she said. 'Is full of cunts.'

After that well-deserved Tory loss in the 2010 election, those on the candidates' list had to reapply; my interview was on 21st February 2011. It was held by a 'Party Professional' and a 'Senior Party Volunteer'. The former was a fat little schoolboy who plainly didn't like me and the latter was a crinkle-eyed branch chairman who clearly did.

It seemed to go fine but the results of the assessments were held back for yonks. This might have been through incompetence. It might have been through cynicism, knowing full well that those who weren't re-adopted would probably sod off entirely, thus denying the party much-needed campaigners.

In the interim, candidate selections for the Greater London Authority took place. I applied for the Greenwich & Lewisham superseat and also for the separate London-wide top up list. In respect of the former, the final hustings was upstairs in the Mitre pub in Greenwich on the evening of 2nd March 2011. I gave a chest-thumping performance and came second behind Alex Wilson whose branch was hosting the event and whose members were the majority of voters. That was exactly

---

1 Spad is shorthand for Special Adviser. These are youngsters who head straight from university to become a staff member for a politician. They then invariably slink into a 'safe seat' and get elected without having done a proper day's work in their lives.

where I wanted to come. The Tories couldn't win the seat and I certainly couldn't be arsed giving up every weekend for the next 14 months campaigning for a lost cause. Naturally, I hadn't said that to the selectors.

I contacted Hugo Mann at the Candidates' Department the following day to tell him the result. The sift for the capital's top-up list was still pending and this placing in Greenwich and Lewisham had to be a silver star. Eventually, on 18th March, he got round to sending me this bland missive.

'I regret to advise you that you have not been shortlisted for interview on this occasion.

'We had a record number of applications for the London wide list this time, the majority of which were from applicants of a uniformly high standard.

'On behalf of the selection panel, I would like to take this opportunity to thank you for taking part in the process.'

Not even a first interview? Feedback was demanded. Even I wouldn't expect to be adopted as of right, but this was surprising given the Greenwich and Lewisham placing. Having heard nothing, he was chased three times over the next three weeks. Tumbleweeds.

Sun-Tzu wrote this:
'Treat your men as you would your own beloved sons. And they will follow you into the deepest valley.'

Tory Head Office has always disagreed with Sun-Tzu.

You can see where this is leading.

So, Oakley., having failed to get anywhere under David Cameron's Conservatives, you contemplate running off in a sulk.

Yeah? And?

There were also two bad angels on my shoulders in the shape of UKIP activists 'Uncle' Mick McGough and Tim Aker whom I regularly bumped into at EU-realist events. Both whispered of the good things that awaited if I moved over to the Dark Side. As their party was only at around 2% in the opinion polls, it wasn't that attractive. At first.

On 14th May 2011, the Taxpayers' Alliance was holding a Westminster demonstration, the Rally Against Debt. This was a counterblast to the various Leftard demos which had taken place calling for imaginary public spending cuts to be reversed. The evening before there was a meeting at TPA HQ in Tufton Street. They'd got out the waterpaints and were making up posters. Best one: 'I don't consent to being stimulated'.

Back from the post-meeting pub, I called UKIP leader Nigel Farage who would be speaking.

'Can I have a word with you tomorrow?'

'Sure.'

The next day proved the point that we swivel-eyed right wingers were not used to having demonstrations. There were far fewer of us than you'd expect at a pinko parade. Nonetheless, there were some interesting speakers in the shape of Harry Cole, Jacob Patch and Martin Durkin. There were also some uninteresting ones. Tory MP Bill Cash gave one of the most tedious speeches in all recorded history. The hugely-overrated Priti Patel MP mumbled quietly for about a minute. But Farage, as ever, was outstanding.

Afterwards, the Westminster Arms. I had my quick, quiet word with Nigel except that it turned into a long conversation and various pals ambled up to eavesdrop.

'You can stay where you are and fester,' said Farage. 'Or come over to us for some fun.'

Sod it then. I'm doing it.

This could have been carried out discreetly, but instead I demanded silence from the mob and gave a shouty speech while gesticulating in the direction of Millbank and Tory head office.

> 'I wouldn't normally endorse sharia law, but in these circumstances it is apposite.
> 'Conservative Party! Hear me!
> 'I divorce you.
> 'I divorce you.
> 'I. Divorce. You!'

This email went to Tory HQ that same evening. Many congratulatory beers having been purchased for my delectation that afternoon, it's surprisingly polite.

> 'Please do not worry about the issue of feedback now. As someone who has passionate conservative convictions and is not a Cameroon nihilist, I am resigning from my 20+ year membership of the Conservative Party and have joined the UK Independence Party. I look forward to standing as a

hard-fighting candidate against "David Cameron's Conservatives" in numerous elections in the future.'

There was no reply. Incidentally, I still haven't heard back as to
whether I'd been reappointed to their candidates' list. Perhaps I'm still
on it after all.

CHAPTER TWO

Year Zero

Sunday 15th May 2011

A BLOKE CALLED GAWAIN TOWLER, who introduces himself as the UKIP press officer, gets in touch for an interview which, rightly, becomes the lead item on the party website. 'Why I Jumped Tory Ship for UKIP':

'In a barnstorming impromptu speech Paul Oakley renounced his Tory Party membership and handed Nigel Farage his first year's subscription.'

The core reason was this:

'I figuratively nodded in agreement with each and every UKIP policy at the time of the 2010 election apart from the burka ban. By contrast, the Tory manifesto was the political equivalent of an Elvis Presley film soundtrack LP. I really wanted to like it because of who had produced it but in my heart of hearts knew that it was vacuous dross.'

And – in fact – that sums it up fairly well.

Thursday 19th May 2011

Gaucho Grill in the City. I'm looking for Lucy Bostick in the dim interior and then spot her in a booth at the back. Lucy's been turned too.

She kisses both my cheeks and whispers in my ear.

'Told you it was worth coming.'

Indeed she did, and indeed it is, because the leader of UKIP is buying us steaks.

'Glad you could make it, Paul,' says Farage. 'Can I introduce you to a few people? These are my sons and this is Steve Crowther, the chairman of the party.'

By the Lord Harry. This is nice.

As an ambitious Tory candidate I'd interacted with Leader David Cameron too, of course. On one occasion I'd attended an event hosted by 'Women to Win' at Millbank. Dave had acknowledged my presence as he ascended the stage for his speech with a friendly frown and by flicking his head sharply to one side a couple of times. It was easy for him to see me straight away because I was sitting on a reserved front row seat, surrounded by all the birds who were being plugged at the presentation.

Another time, at a candidates' drinks party, I'd barged past him with a gentle shove to the ribs and a ''scuse me mate'. Gentleman that he is, Cameron had graciously made way.

So tonight's event is nothing unusual for me.

Nigel's sounding me out. I might be a spy from the Conservatives, having been given the mission of destroying UKIP through deep cover. Never, ever trust a defector.

We exchange background details. He was a City metals trader and although once a Tory, hadn't sought elected office. Bravely forthright and willing to champion unspeakable causes, he knew that he couldn't have advanced far.

'No, they'd never have touched someone like me. Apart from everything else, I was Enoch Powell's driver for a time. They wouldn't have stomached that.'

Outstanding! At last, a politician who doesn't contort himself like a Bateman caricature if one dares to use the 'E' word.

'Nigel,' I pledge (albeit without getting down on one knee this time), 'you will have my complete loyalty in this cause.'

Friday 20th May 2011
Winston McKenzie has invited me to tea at the Croydon Park Hotel. This is directly opposite the local Court and I've stared at it balefully on numerous occasions before heading inside for hearings because it has an EU banner perpetually planted on one of the flagpoles outside.

I've heard of Winston. He has immense experience as a political activist, having first been Labour before switching to the Lib Dems. And then standing as an Independent in the Brent East by-election. And then joining Veritas. And then leaving Veritas to stand as an Independent in a Croydon Council by-election. And then re-joining Veritas. And then leaving them to become a Tory. And then departing from the Conservatives after he failed to be selected as our nominee for London Mayor. And then standing as an Independent anyway in that election. And then setting up his own movement, the Unity Party. And finally joining UKIP in 2009.

He's with his partner Marianne, the former wife of Tory Peer Peter Bowness, who is lovely. It really is sweet of them both to welcome me into the party in this way.

'Anything I can do for you, anything at all – just give me a call,' says Winston.

It's been a privilege to meet him. I pay for the teas, of course.

Monday 23rd May 2011

Nigel has collated some of us for a video shoot outside the House of Commons to make the case against EU bailouts for Portugal, Ireland, Greece and Spain.

We carry pails to represent the handouts needed by the PIGS. He gives a short speech and then we all have to sing:

'There's a hole in my bucket, Dear Liza, Dear Liza. . .'

Good fun, but very silly. Sadly – as nobody has the slightest interest in hearing our message, stunts like this are essential in order to raise our profile.

Even sillier, whoever has chosen the take which is uploaded to Youtube has picked one in which a noisy police helicopter is flying overhead. Amateurish.

Tuesday 24th May 2011

Uncle Mick McGough is having me speak at one of his 'Freedom in the City' events. These are a thinly-covered front for Provisional UKIP. Today's event is taking place at the Counting House pub and I'm standing in for journalist Jon Gaunt who's backed out.

John Moran, early founder of UKIP and a major donor, is unimpressed with the switch as he tells Mick at the bar beforehand, and within my earshot.

'Why's this Tory speaking? He's got nothing to say that I want to hear.'

There is, however, a good turnout with considerable laughter at my poor-quality jokes. I recount the history of the 1975 EEC referendum and its litany of dirty tricks, unequal funding and straightforward cheating. This is precisely what will happen if Cameron allows this generation its own vote.

'A referendum on EU membership may go against us. If it does, that will not settle the matter.

'Like unto Arnold Schwarzeneggar's Terminator, we can't be bargained with. We can't be reasoned with. We don't feel pity, or remorse, or fear. And we absolutely will not stop. Ever. Until our EU membership is dead.'

Accept an adverse referendum result with good grace? You must be joking.

Monday 13th June 2011

There's a website called 'Junius on UKIP'. The identities of those operating it are a mystery but they plainly have inside information about the party. Its thrust is anti-EU but equally anti-Farage. Today, they've published a still taken from the 'hole-in-my-bucket' video shoot the other day.

It features John Moran, David Coburn, Steve Woolfe, Nigel, Winston and me. The strapline is:

'Would you trust ANY of these men with your money? We thought not!'

Steve Woolfe is very pissed off and calls me as soon as he's seen it.

'Can't we sue? They're accusing us of outright dishonesty.'

I'm not convinced it's worth it. It'll cost us if we do and, to be honest, if we start to get our message across we'll be facing much worse than this.

I tell him that I'll have words with a particular solicitor though.

Thursday 23rd June 2011

Woolfie chases me about the prospective libel action against Junius.

'Paul - any news on your colleague looking at the case?'

Ah.

'Sorry - not heard anything.'

That's because I haven't actually been in touch with the solicitor yet. I do give the guy a quick call however and he agrees. No point. Get over it.

Tuesday 28th June 2011

Lisa Duffy, Party Director, is keen for me to pass the candidate assessment procedure. Her encouragement is gratifying and, indeed, a novelty to me.

It's being held this afternoon at the Ilford office of Gerard Batten, UKIP's London MEP.

It has been ages since I did any criminal work at the Bar so haven't had the displeasure of visiting Ilford to go to the Magistrates' Court for some time. The intervening years have not been kind. It's clear that the town has become even more of a shithole than it previously was as I head towards Batten's HQ in Clements Road. Why on earth is his base here? Has to be cheap I suppose. There can't be any other reason.

On being buzzed in, I see a familiar face in the waiting room. Dressed in a tan safari suit with a floppy-brimmed hat and ebony cane, it is Winston McKenzie. Very Daktari. He's here for the same reason as I. We wish each other good luck.

The policy section is taken by George Curtis, a member of the NEC[1]. I'd been meaning to read the full 2010 UKIP election manifesto before today which is some 400 pages in length. Unfortunately, I couldn't spare the motivation to do so in the end. I know some of the answers and the others can be worked out; what would the libertarian position be?

The public speaking session is in exactly the same format as the one used by the Conservatives. The applicant is placed alone in a room with a bigwig and a slew of newspapers. Said bigwig chooses a story from said pile and asks you to give a speech to them on that subject as if addressing a packed room. Hugely artificial.

As far as the Tories go, the idea is to disconcert the applicant a wee bit by picking a subject that they may not be interested in. When I'd taken their Board, Mark Field MP had given me the subject of 'domestic violence'. As it happens, that issue's a bugbear of mine. The police don't take it nearly seriously enough and there aren't enough prosecutions of this form of torture in the home. I'd finished off that assessment with passionate words:

'Let's hand down some proper sentences and knock this problem on the head.'

Oops.

---

1 National Election Commission

This time, Pete Reeve asks me about council house shortages. That isn't hard at all. Prioritise local residents with multi-generational links to an area. Duh.

Finally, media is being run by Stuart Gulleford, press officer to Stuart Agnew MEP. It's filmed for picking over later by a full panel. Gulleford takes a Paxman-esque role. In the kindliest possible way, I'm not taking any of his rubbish and box away his barbs. However, I do mess up a pre-prepared soundbite which contained too many 'Ps' when I wrote it down in my little red speechbook beforehand.

It ends. In all, not bad. Winston's still being assessed so I go home without the chance of a debrief with him.

CHAPTER THREE

Never, Ever Trust a Defector

Tuesday 12th July 2011

I FIRST MET DAVID COBURN in 2007, also the first time I heard Nigel Farage speak. It was a thinly-attended meeting, but that doesn't matter as it gives me the same street-cred as having been at an early Sex Pistols concert.

Farage had been speaking about the possibility of an EU referendum. He said that if this were lost, he'd accept the result and retire from politics.

I heckled.

'I wouldn't.'

Someone else heckled too.

'Nor me. I'd break out the Lee Enfields.'

This came from a portly Pict standing to my right. We looked at each other and high-fived.

That man Coburn is now chairman of UKIP London and he's started selecting people to stand in next year's elections in the capital. It's already been leaked that I've passed the candidates' assessment so he's invited me and other contenders for the mayoral nomination to be inspected by the Regional Committee at a pub called the Old Doctor Butler's Head.

I'm not keen to go as it's likely to run over time and make me miss the Freedom Association's monthly pub quiz. Coburn's unimpressed with this reticence.

'My meetings run like a 1930s Italian Railway! It's in your interest to be there, if you follow my drift.'

He then points out that whereas I'm free to attend the quiz as planned, an appropriate round for that event would be this:

'Question: Why did Paul Oakley fail to be candidate for London Mayor?

'(A) He is talented, good looking and has the body of a Greek god,

'(B) He gives Cicero a run as an orator,

'(C) He missed an opportunity to shmooze the Chairmen of every London UKIP Committee.

'See you there.'

He does, and I and the other mayoral applicants give our schpiel. Not very interesting. What's more, there are only about 8 committee members there from the whole of London.

Winston McKenzie has come too. He must have passed the candidates' assessment because he's going for the nomination as well. But at one point McKenzie says something that I don't quite catch. Then a fellow called Peter Staveley, Croydon chairman, says something else which can't be heard either. Winston retorts.

'What the fuck did you say? What the fuck did you say?'

McKenzie rounds his shoulders and clenches his fists. There's plainly some history there.

There follows a review of our policy priorities for the election. I'm only really interested in an exit from the EU and still think the abolition of the Greater London Council on April Fool's Day, 1986, was one of Mrs Thatcher's greatest achievements.

However, we'll have to say something in our manifesto. Lawrence Webb, who works for Gerard Batten, wants us to focus on the proposed Low Emission Zone in the capital. The LEZ will penalise drivers of older vehicles and, in particular, ice cream vans. It's desperate stuff and there is much, much discussion of it. I can't help thinking of my favourite ever question on the Reeves and Mortimer 'Shooting Stars' quiz.

'Name a famous Les.'

'Les Dawson?'

'No. Martina Navratilova.'

Wednesday 20th July 2011

Party Director Lisa Duffy sends me formal feedback from the parliamentary testing. 'A's for everything, apart from one section.

'You should be very proud of this assessment,' her letter concludes.

I am nothing of the sort. A 'B+' for media? This'll teach me not to conjure up tongue-twister soundbites on paper without trying them out loud beforehand.

Friday 22nd July 2011

A bloke called Damian Wilson has arranged for each mayoral candidate to produce a video. The films will be shot at 32 Smith Square. Now, I haven't been inside that building for quite a while. It was, famously, Conservative Central Office until they moved out to Victoria Street in 2004 and then, later on, to 30 Millbank. I'd gotten happily boozed-up at this old CCO building on many occasions, and had undertaken political campaigning there too.

I certainly haven't been back since the EU itself invaded the premises in 2010 having brazenly purchased the lease on the open market. That was really rubbing the noses of Tory Eurosceptics in their own insignificance.

However, as UKIP has elected representation in the European Parliament they're also entitled to office space within. Backatcha, federasts.

I've heard that security at the building has been upgraded since the Tory eviction and on arriving, there are indeed a metal detector and a scanning conveyor belt to be seen. Both are covered in plastic sheeting and non-operational.

Not that I'd ever contemplate such a thing... but...

I'm waved through by security and meet Wilson who takes us to the roof terrace. I've never been up there before. There's a wonderful view over Westminster. We need several takes, not least because there are birds twittering in the background while they enjoy the summer sun. Can't have that on the soundtrack as it makes me seem cuckoo.

We deal with City Jobs and The Lez, because I have to, but then move on.

'We've got the Olympics next year. We're stuck with them now even though they're a colossal waste of taxpayers' money. But my first decree as Mayor of London would be to reopen the VIP road lanes to all traffic. As far as I'm concerned, if these Olympic "dignitaries" have to be somewhere punctually, then they can simply get up earlier.'

I also pledge to donate half my £140K Mayoral salary to Help for Heroes. We won't win so I won't have to. But I would if we did.

Tuesday 9th August 2011

Last Thursday, police in Tottenham shot dead a man called Mark Duggan. Although there are questions which the Met need to answer about this, large parts of London are using his death as an excuse for destructive self-enrichment.

David Coburn tells me he's been affected in West London.

'Had my van turned over onto its side by the great unwashed last night. I was going to go after them with my grandfather's sabre before realising I was outnumbered 60 to 1. Teddy was pushed out of the bed in favour of the sabre and Crawford spent the night with my Zulu *assegai*. Truly terrifying. Zero law and order in Notting Hill.'

We, too, have been having problems in South East London, not least at a half-way house for youths leaving local authority homes opposite my own. A string of unfamiliar vehicles have been turning up at all hours and boxes of electrical items unloaded into the property.

Coburn is grimly concerned.

'Looking for an iPad if your neighbours have a good night tonight! Booyakasha!'

Wednesday 10th August 2011

Tim Aker is being my fearless cameraman today. I'm doing a piece to camera about the riots. We drive to Woolwich where there's been trouble at one end of the High Street and park round the back of Wilkinson's as it's free for an hour. We walk down Wilmount Street to reach the shops and as we come to the front of Wilko itself see that the place has been burnt out. Temporary fencing has been erected and firemen are running in and around the place.

I pity the poor shop workers who are now out of a job because of this sheer, fucking greed.

So – the video is shot with some anger.

'This is Woolwich. I've got some things to say about the riots. If you were involved in them, if you *are* involved with them or if you're thinking of getting involved with them you are nothing but a Greedy Little Scrote.

'If you know anyone who's been involved in the rioting, stop them. I'm only disappointed that there aren't enough prison spaces to bang them all up.'

Michael Heaver is particularly pleased when he sees it on Youtube. "Greedy Little Scrote" he repeats to me with a smile for some months afterwards.

Monday 15th August 2011

In line with the baffling trend across all parties to institute 'open primaries', UKIP has set up a web page allowing anyone and everyone to help choose their favourite mayoral candidate. This polling will be used to add weight to the actual members' votes before the party makes its final choice.

I always thought such primaries are a loopy idea because enemy parties could organise and install some nutjob or other as the candidate for their rivals. Yet it's the modern thing to do, allegedly.

Needless to say, I cheat by voting for myself on both my home and work computers, each of which have different IP addresses. I also go against the spirit of the exercise by asking Tory mates for their backing. They've complied, and I've been leading, very slightly, on the poll for several days.

That has changed all of a sudden as Winston McKenzie streaks ahead.

Coburn's perplexed.

'Marianne must be back from her holiday. Anyone know what happened to PC World in Croydon?'

I keep an eye on the site for half-an-hour or so and watch Winston receive over 100 votes.

Suddenly, the page is 'down for maintenance'. Lisa Duffy explains why.

'It's possible to place multiple votes from a single PC while browsing in private mode. We're keeping it down until this issue can be resolved.'

The issue is irresolvable apparently because the page stays down. Forever.

Tuesday 16th August 2011

Huzzah! I get a review on the 'Snipe' website which has assessed all the UKIP mayoral videos.

'Paul Oakley seems dull, his slow monotonous speech redeemed only by his impressive eyebrows. He sparks briefly into life but on the whole this is uninspiring stuff. Rating 7/10'

At least the writer rates me higher than all of the other candidates. Apart from Winston McKenzie, whom he describes as 'hilarious.'

Sunday 21st August 2011

Lewisham Conservatives have invited me to their summer barbecue in spite of everything. How lovely they are. I have an enjoyable afternoon. The speaker is Beckenham MP, Bob Stewart. I don't attempt to seduce any of them to the Dark Side and, in turn, they do not try to entrap me into Tory clutches again.

Equally, I don't take part in the raffle. There'll be no funding of enemy campaigns by me!

Wednesday 24th August 2011

Although the ballot papers have gone out a couple of weeks before, there are hustings to help choose our candidate for mayor at the Butler's Head this evening. It's a bit queer to have such an event after most members have already voted, but – hey.

All the applicants attend. That is: Lawrence Webb, Winston McKenzie, David Coburn, Mick McGough, Michael Corby and, of course, your Dear Author.

We're ranged along a trestle table which blocks access to the toilets. Party Chairman Steve Crowther, Director Lisa Duffy and Steve Woolfe observe us from the corner opposite. The rest of the room is full. Every seat is occupied and many are standing.

Hustings are what I do best and always have, ever since student days. You don't need to have gone to public school and Oxbridge University to excel at them. Natural talent is just as good and I have it.

I say stuff like this.

'Never. Ever. Trust a defector from another party. Except in my case of course.

'Contrary to what you say, I'm not pally with any of the city boys who caused the crash. The only city worker I know is Steve Woolfe. Although he's a very wicked man it's not all his fault.

'If they can elect a Monkey as mayor of Hartlepool they can elect an Oakley as mayor of London.

'It's courteous to pay tribute to the qualities of every other candidate at events such as this. And with that in mind I say – You Shall Not Pass!'

I have the room in my hands. Some of the younger members are 'BeTweeting' (whatever that may be) about my brilliance. That's about all I can remember about my own speechifying. Can't recall anything the others said as they're all boring. Although Coburn is quite good from time to time.

However, none of that matters as the whole thing's being filmed by a veteran member who's going to put the footage online.

Seriously. I'm on fire this evening.

Monday 5th September 2011

Lisa Duffy gives me a call. The results of the ballot for mayoral candidate are in. Of the six who put their names forward, I'm first - if the list's read out in reverse order.

Arsefleas.

Lawrence Webb will be standing.

CHAPTER FOUR

Infighting. Metaphorical—and Real

Thursday 8th September 2011

S O – THIS IS IT! My first conference for any political party apart from the Tories. At the Congress Theatre in Eastbourne no less, which brings back happy memories of past Young Conservative events in the town. There's one big difference however. There are hardly any people there although, allegedly, this is the best-attended UKIP conference ever. I do so approve of spin.

Sweetly, I've already become a Party Grandee and been asked to judge the Young Independence public speaking competition. The younglings try their best but largely read from sweaty pieces of paper with shaky legs. They just need a bit of practice.

Obviously, I tell them otherwise and we decamp to a nearby trendy bar.

Within that bar there is a small fish tank. Within that tank there is a single fish. That Fish is one of the ugliest things we've ever seen. It is of a mouldy mud hue with a bright pink face, protruding forehead and strange green eyes. It weighs about 9 lbs and is sorely cramped within its prison. We all feel sorry for That Fish.

Friday 9th September 2011

Nigel Farage gives his keynote speech at noon. Temporarily, Lord Pearson had taken over the leadership from Nigel while he battled Commons Speaker John Bercow MP for Buckingham in last year's general election. So this is his first oration as party leader since he was previously party leader.

Farage attacks all the old parties and especially mine.

'If you're a patriotic eurosceptic Conservative voter under David Cameron, your party has ceased to exist. If you want to vote for what you believe in, you must come and vote UKIP. It's as simple as that.'

Testify!

The speech has been timed to hit the national lunchtime news. Unfortunately, the sole camera crew present is from the BBC. Even more unfortunately, they only bother broadcasting it on the Parliament Channel. Even then, not live. They're just not interested in what we have to say.

Nigel's played off stage to the uplifting anthem that is 'Tubthumping', some rot about getting up after being knocked down.

The composers of that ditty, Chumbawumba, are at the rubbish end of the punk scale. Furious at the co-option of their work, these passionate anarchists immediately threaten the party with their wrath. With a lawsuit. Through Her Majesty's Court Service. Yes, really.

Yet, that's the full extent of the press coverage we receive, and then only in the gossip columns.

Saturday 10th September 2011

Conference draws to a close with a magnificent ball. Entertainment after the meal is a casino and a mechanical bucking bronco. I have a go at the latter and am thrown off almost immediately. Party Chairman Steve Crowther does rather better because he's taken his jacket off which allows him to stay in the saddle for almost a minute. Unfortunately, the effort expended leaves him with a damp shirt through which the outline of his nipples may be seen. Lovely.

'Go on,' I say to Farage. 'You've got to have a shot.'
He turns to me with a frown.

'No way. You're aware I've been in a plane crash aren't you?'

I was, but didn't know that it had left him with a long term injury. His neck had been fractured. I'd no idea. Bloody hell.

Tuesday 13th September 2011

The Freedom Association are having another quiz tonight at the Old Star Pub by St James' Park tube. Our team, 'That Fish', doesn't win. It's a fix; the questions were too difficult.

Afterwards we congregate outside. There are about twenty activists in all, Sound Tories and Kippers united and brothers in arms.

I speak to the UKIP member who'd filmed the mayoral hustings the other night. He'd posted coverage of his favoured of the seven on the internet.

'Just wondering why you didn't you upload the full footage of all the candidates?'

'No need. And I deleted yours. Your performance was poor. I'm not going to help any ex-Tory.'

He smiled at me. At least, I think it was meant to be a smile.

Now. Not that I'm a hippy or anything, but people do have an aura. Mine, of course, is black, but with a hint of cooling, midnight blue. And a go-faster stripe.

This person's aura is also black. But of a brownish-yellow hue. Not as gothic as grave liquor, more like a nappy change four tables away from you in the McDonalds outside Birmingham New Street station.

A nasty piece of work, he is previously renowned for posting some racially-robust comments on the internet as an evening had drawn to its end.

I call him some Saxon epithets and walk off, ensconcing myself within a ring of half a dozen decent chaps and chapesses instead.

Whilst there, I see another fellow facing me from over the shoulder of Lucy Bostick. Also a UKIP member, I haven't talked to him tonight but have known him for years as a stalwart of the cause. He doesn't speak to me now either.

Huh? What was that?

At the very moment I finally compute that this guy has just punched my left eye, he hits me again. Harder this time and right on the nose. Blood trickles down the back of my throat.

Oh, I understand that straight away and something else is about to happen when I get my hands on him. Except that Chad Noble, Tim Aker, Lucy, Dan Heaton and Big John Boulton from the Tories manage to keep a hold of me. Just.

The assailant scurries off to the Underground and disappears.

Wednesday 14th September 2011

My phone starts ringing just after 7 am. Although I'm feeling sorry for myself, nobody else is. Steve Crowther, Lisa Duffy and Stuart Gulleford all need to speak to me about last night.

I had called the police who'd taken several statements. Once home, I'd photographed time-stamped selfies of my poor face, bloody shirt and unmarked hands (both, and both sides).

Obviously, I'd decided to press criminal charges against him. But the consensus is that this might, in fact—would—reflect badly on the party.

Will I have a think about it? Sure.

The skin at the bridge of my nose has been cut into a lightning bolt by the second punch and I visit my GP who tells me that nothing can be done to rectify this. I'm now uglified forever. So what to do?

The geezer in question isn't really a wicked fellow. What he just did was definitely out of character. He might be convicted of assault and battery. This will affect the rest of his life and I'm not sure that's fair.

I call DS Worthington who's the officer in charge.

'I want to drop the matter please.'

'Are you certain? Are you being threatened in any way?'

'No, honestly, everything's fine.'

'Do you need counselling?'

I laugh inside.

'No, I'm definitely OK. Please close the file.'

You may have noticed that the ruffian's name hasn't been mentioned. It won't be because this would undermine my previous conclusions.

On the other hand, he hasn't called me to apologise as a gentleman would. So I'll sue the beggar instead. Of the variety of solicitors who send me instructions as Counsel, two are utter bastards. In a good way. They are Paul Verlander of Carpenter and Co and Simon Mcilwaine at Ormerods.

Eeny, meeny, miny mo. It's a difficult choice but I decide on Verlander and give him a call.

Monday, 26 September 2011

The Freedom Association are back at the Old Star for another event less than a fortnight after my clobbering at the very same venue. Will there be flashbacks? Nightmares? Emotional Trauma? 'Course not. I happily head over because the scheduled speaker is David 'Campbell' Bannerman MEP.

Ten days after my own journey from Tory to UKIP, he went in the other direction after falling out, again, with Nigel Farage. He is thus a foul traitor and a man of weak moral fibre. There are several rude questions to him and Sean Howlett gets dangerously close to his personal space at one point.

The consensus amongst attendees at the bar afterwards is correct: UKIP got the best deal in this hostage exchange.

Saturday 3rd December 2011

Andrew Charalambous is the UKIP candidate for the parliamentary by-election in Feltham. This is the first one I've been involved in since leaving the Conservatives. Emmett Jenner from Bromley UKIP picks me up in his car and we drive to west London. As we approach the town centre there are immense UKIP billboards with Andrew's immense face on them in prime positions.

There's an office plastered with more posters at the end of the high street. We pick up a bunch of leaflets and head out to the entrance of the main shopping mall with a wallpapering table. The take-up from voters isn't especially thrilling.

At lunchtime more people appear and start setting up their own table not ten yards from us. Looking at them as they do so, we assume that HMP Wandsworth is having an open day. Realising that this would be silly, we then conclude that they're Labour activists.

Sean Howlett goes over to have a collegiate talk with one of them. The object of his enquiry, an obese blob in his early sixties, squares up to Sean who re-squares back.

'You racist bastards.'

Howlett flicks the vees behind his back as he returns to us.

It's not Labour after all, but the British National Party. We decide to pack up as we don't want to be anywhere near these people.

So we hit the residential streets instead. No canvassing, just leafleting. As there are about a dozen of us available, this seems to be a wasted opportunity, as I tell Nigel.

'Haven't we got any polling data? Electoral registers? That sort of thing?'

'No,' says Farage with a sigh. 'We've got nothing at all. But we're hoping to build up a basic database from this election to use in the London Mayoral campaign. It's not ideal, I know.'

Not the slightest bit ideal and not what I'm used to from Tory campaigning either. We'll have to set up a professional strategy as soon as possible or we'll waste our chances to maximise our vote in this and every future election.

Thursday 15th December 2011

Despite the crap campaign, Charalambous performs rather well in Feltham. The Labour nonentity has won and the Tory is second. Andrew holds on to his deposit in fourth place on 1276 votes and 5.5% and is only just behind the Lib Dem whose support has collapsed. We've leapfrogged the BNP who are in their death throes.

This augurs well for the future, but only if we get our act together.

Tuesday 6th January 2012

Unorthodox in all senses, Bromley UKIP branch always have their Christmas dinner after Christmas. The Old Jail in Westerham lies down a rural road and is a pub of the type featured in the opening minutes of *An American Werewolf in London*. It's cosy, seating about thirty, and has an excellent range of real ales. Most importantly, it's within walking distance of Nigel's house.

The result of the UKIP members' ballot of prospective GLA List candidates has just been announced. Although the choice of mayoral candidate was decided solely by members' votes, this isn't the case for the list. These will be the candidates who have a chance of victory as the election's decided by a proportional representation. Perhaps that's the reason why the activists aren't being given the final choice about that ranking.

The members have already voted and I'm pleased at my placing even though it's only an indicative poll and not binding on the National Executive Committee. It's this.

1 David Coburn (310)
2 Lawrence Webb (308)
3 My Good Self (257)
4 Steve Woolfe (251)
5 Helen Dixon (200)
6 Elizabeth Jones (190)

I've driven to the pub clad in jeans and sweatshirt with 48 hours-worth of beard. After the meal Nigel wants a private word outside. More importantly, he wants a fag. He looks at me with disapproval.

'Couldn't you have worn a suit?'

But that's not his main line of enquiry.

'Do you actually want to be a member of the London Assembly?'

The term of office for GLA members will overlap the next European Elections as he reminds me. We need to maximise the number of our elected representatives in all public bodies to push the referendum message.

'No way. I want to be an MEP.'

'Okay,' he nods, 'that's what I wanted to know.'

Emmett Jenner wanders up for a chat with Farage, probably about the same thing. I go back inside to enjoy a frugal single pint before driving home.

Wednesday 18th January 2012

It's the night before the UKIP NEC interviews the shortlisted GLA Candidates. David Coburn wants a word. Same question as Nigel had asked. Almost.

'Do you actually want to be a member of the London Assembly sweetie?'

'Not really', I say. 'It's not much of a step-up from being a councillor and my ambitions are higher than dealing with dogshit and wheelie bins.'

He laughs.

'There's more news you know. Rumours are that Farage still wants Woolfie to be at the top of the list. But I want to knock him off.'

Oo-er missis. There'd been a public bust-up between Steve and Nigel outside the Westminster Arms some weeks ago. Rumours were that the leader was demanding Woolfe become an Assembly Member and other rumours are that Steve's not interested because he wants to be an MEP.

Davy does want it. A revelation as I'd always assumed he'd aspired to the European Parliament too. But he takes the view that his self-evident flamboyance would be an excellent means to raise the profile of UKIP in the capital. I agree.

'I'll back you, David. No problem.'

'So', he says, 'what do you want me to do for you in return?'
I'm surprised at this.

'Nothing. Nothing at all.'
He's surprised at that.

Thursday 19th January 2012

The Surya nightclub in King's Cross is owned by Andrew Charalambous. I'm not a fan of discotheques and it's strange to be arriving at one at 9.30 on a rainy January morning. Today is the grilling by the UKIP National Executive Committee for the final order of the London List.

I don't recognise most of the twenty-or so NEC members and party officials milling around but do know Steve Crowther and have heard of Paul Nuttall MEP and, naturally, Nigel. The candidates are all there at the same time and there's a real sense that we're going to tackle this battle together.

The interviews are in the basement. The quizee is given a lone, spotlit seat in front of the line of interrogators. As I sit down they're discussing matters amongst themselves and not paying a lot of attention to me.

How dare they. This goes on for some time. Psy-op?

'So,' I interject with a raised voice. 'When did you last see your father?'

Some of the committee laugh at my posh reference but most stare blankly back.

The main questions cover the issue of me being a Tory fifth-columnist. I parry with ease and take the opportunity to 'big-up' Coburn as the best choice for the top of the list. I'm also quite open about the fact that I don't want to be in a position to get elected.

You just know when an interview goes well and this one went incredibly well. Very much hope I'm on-course to remain in third place.

Friday 20th January 2012

The order for the top-up list for the London Assembly is announced.

1 Steven Woolfe
2 David Coburn
3 Lawrence Webb
4 Helen Dixon
5 Elizabeth Jones
6 Paul Oakley

Hmm. Well at least I'm definitely not at risk of being elected.

Can't quite work out how I cocked up so speak to Coburn about it.

'You and me both honey!' he says.

He has a scandalous explanation.

'Do you think there's a whiff of the unspeakable vice of the Greeks?'

I've no idea what he's on about.

'Are you saying that our friends indulge in intemperate fiscal impropriety?'

He isn't sure.

'At my school we were never told what the unspeakable vice was, but I understand a certain chumminess was involved.'

Another top-end candidate isn't pleased by Woolfe's premier placing either, according to Davy.

'Captain Mainwaring is livid and Mrs Mainwaring took it badly. Expect potential repercussions from that quarter.'

Work it out for yourself who the Mainwarings are.

Wednesday 23rd January 2012

Lawrence Webb writes to the Party Chairman to say that he's stepping down from his role as London Regional Organiser. However:

'I would stress,' he states, 'that my decision was in no way influenced by the NEC's decision to adjust the results of the members' ballot.'

So there.

CHAPTER FIVE

UKIP: Pied Piper of Conservatives

Wednesday 1st February 2012

JOURNALIST SIMON HEFFER delivers a speech to the Bruges Group at the Royal Overseas League. Usual slew of questions at the end, including one asking him to disclose his favoured EUsceptic successor to David Cameron as Tory leader.

'I can't tell you that because my endorsement would mean the death of their chances.'

Friday February 3rd 2012

As well as the important top-up list which might get one or two Kippers elected to the GLA, there are also the unimportant superseats to consider. We won't win any of them.

Lisa Duffy isn't keen for me to go forward for Greenwich & Lewisham.

'Would you be prepared to stand anywhere else?" she asks. "I have another who would stand in Greenwich due to their work but I have vacancies in North East, Enfield and Haringey, Merton and Wandsworth or South west.'

Bollocks to that. I know beggar all about these other areas and am certainly not going to traipse halfway across London for the inevitable mass of hustings and press interviews.

Greenwich and Lewisham it must be, or I'm not standing at all. I'm given my choice. UKIP have handled this issue far better than the Tories would have done.

Tuesday 7th February 2012

Nigel Farage is handed the Freedom of the City of London with a short ceremony at the Guildhall. It's more low-key than I'd expected, but pleasing to witness nonetheless.

Afterwards, we go to the pub, of course, and I get to have a proper chat with Paul Nuttall MEP for the first time. As a consequence of an administrative error at Head Office, my telephone number has been wrongly-listed as his on the contact database. This means that I've been receiving odd calls from his staff and journalists from time to time.

'Probably explained by UKIP's "skinhead problem",' he says. 'We do look a bit alike. And there are also far too many Pauls in our Party.'

'And Peters, I've noticed.'

'Well, at least you don't have a bit on the side so there will be nothing more embarrassing to come out of it,' he says.

Friday 10th February 2012

Lots of London members are annoyed at Steve Woolfe's placing on The List.

Lawrence Webb has discovered that Steve had been elected as a Tory councillor for Colwyn Bay's Rhiw ward in 2006. Having failed to turn up to any meetings for over six months, he resigned. That might not bode well for his attendance on the GLA if he gets in.

Many rumours are spinning around that this is a taste of future 'fixing' of MEP candidacies. Lucy Bostick is especially worried about my own ambitions.

'This autocracy is a disgrace, and it stitches up your prospects quite a lot. There will be winnable places further down the lists but the fact that we can't have a fair chance of selection is horrifying. Isn't that partly why we left the Tories?'

I'm not so bothered and have already worked out what will happen with my infallible political nous.

'Don't get drawn into the rumour mill. As you know, Woolfie is certain to be parachuted into London and I have apparently decided to stand as his wingman.'

Monday 13th February 2012

Janice Atkinson has had an idea for a fundraising event for the London campaign.

'I have spoken to the *Daily Star's* Garry Bushell who is happy to take part in a fundraiser, something along the lines of "An evening with

. . ." We just have to let him know what we would like him to do.

'He also has a punk and ska band but thought that some of our more genteel members may not like it. Although we could do this via Andrew Charalambous' club and we might get a bigger audience.'

Outstanding idea! Bushell's band put on a great live show. Nobody else agrees and the idea's dropped, even though Janice doesn't get 'round to telling the others the name of his group.

But. . . 'UKIP presents The Gonads'. It might not have been such a good idea after all.

Wednesday 15th February 2012

Spread-betting Tycoon and former Tory donor, Stuart Wheeler has invited me to supper at his Mayfair penthouse. He's just been appointed UKIP Treasurer. The guests include Tomas Slivnik, Simon Heffer and retiring Conservative MEP Roger Helmer. We speak freely.

Obviously, I need to know who Heffer would back as the best Tory Leader after his cryptic Bruges Group speech the other night.

'Oh, that would be Owen Paterson.'

Although sound on most things, Paterson is an enthusiast for genetically modified crops. I'm unimpressed.

Matters move on to Rupert Matthews, who was right behind Helmer on the Tory MEP list at the last EU election and had just failed to get in. When anyone stands down as an MEP, the next person on their party's list should automatically take their place. However, that can only happen if the party approves the replacement. Roger, having just turned 68, told the Tories some months ago that he'd be standing down. With that in mind, Rupert, a fierce proponent of EU withdrawal, should rightfully be his replacement.

Not if Sayeeda Warsi has her way. Having herself been appointed from nowhere to the role of Conservative Party Chairman, she's hoping to reject Matthews and give his post to another "A" list nonentity in a similar manner.

The consensus is that Warsi's a disgrace. I recount my own experiences of being sidelined for Tory vacancies as an out-and-proud EU-phobe. As Matthews is a brother-in-arms on this issue, there's no way he'll be heading to Brussels.

'Roger,' I ask. 'Can't you persuade Rupert to come over to UKIP? I had a drink with him the other day and he's very down about it. He's thinking of giving up politics completely which would be a terrible shame.'

Helmer says nothing.

Friday 17th February 2012

My Mum taught me to be good-mannered, so I wrote a thank-you letter to Stuart Wheeler and sent it first class. I've now received his reply, also first class.

'It was very good to see you. I was only sorry that you did not come higher up in the ballot for the London Assembly position.'

What a gentleman. Old-school. Sensible.

Saturday 18th February 2012

UKIP London are having a mini-conference at the Royal National Hotel. Lawrence Webb and all we assembly candidates are addressing the members. Several can't make it though and have sent apologies. One of the absentees is that person with the shite-black aura who doesn't like me because I'm ex-Tory. He's in Venice and has gone to considerable effort to organise a video presentation so that he can speak to members whilst standing against an agreeable backdrop.

Knowing this, someone asks Steve Crowther if he's set up the appropriate technology at this end.

'Ha!' he replies. 'Of course not' - and walks off.

The common theme from the other candidates as they each orate is that we might, just might, get one person on to the GLA. Or maybe two if we're very lucky.

I'm not having that when it gets to my go.

'Who are these pessimists who say we're only going to get a couple of Assembly Members? What rubbish. We're all going to be elected.'

And it's nice to be nice about Mayoral candidate Lawrence Webb. So I am.

'Most important of all, we have to replace the Liberal Democrats as the third party. Why is the Evening Standard giving column inches to their dullard Paddick while ignoring our man Webb when they're both polling 5%?'

'Lawrence Webb.' I turn to him. 'We charge you with this quest. Destroy Brian Paddick. It is your destiny!'

Then, questions. Someone who seems to like athletics asks if I'd truly close the Olympic dignitaries' 'Zil' lanes.

'I'd go further. Those people will be required to ride on the roofs of our trains. This will add to the international flavour of the games and also free up seats for our hard-pressed commuters.'

A bloke comes up to me afterwards with a smile.
'You know, you're almost as good a speaker as Farage!'

Cheeky git.

Monday 20th February 2012

We're having a fundraising launch for the London campaign at Porters in Covent Garden. Lucy Bostick and Steve Woolfe have rounded up some likely donors from their links in the City of London. Good food and good drink has been put on. We, as candidates, are to be frugal with our own consumption of the same and are instead to chat and chuckle with the targets to get them to open their wallets.

As the evening ends, we believe that we have done well.

Wednesday 22nd February 2012

We have not done well. Coburn has bad news about Monday.

'We lost money on the Porters launch and we must make sure this does not happen again. These events are fundraisers, not upper class soup kitchens.'

Thursday March 1st 2012

UKIP Conference is at the Embassy Theatre in Skegness. It's been organised by Chris Pain, the local chairman, who's a top chap. Haven't been to Skeggy for years and am disappointed to see that the ocean view is now ruined by dozens of wind turbines. It's also freezing cold and there's no breeze at all so those silly windmill things are standing completely still and generating no power whatsoever when such power is most needed.

There's also a dead whale on the beach. It stinks and is thus a metaphor for the collapsing Conservative Party.

Friday March 2nd 2012

Wasn't going to bother with the conference Gala Dinner but am glad that I have. Everyone's munching on their starters when the hum of conversation slowly dies to silence.

Nigel Farage is walking through the dining room with Tory MEP Roger Helmer and they sit next to each other at top table.

Crivvens – what can this mean?

:o)

Saturday March 3rd 2012

Nigel introduces a young lady called Alexandra Swann to the conference hall. She's just defected from the Tories.

'Until very recently she was the National Deputy Chair of Conservative Future. I'm very pleased to say. That the Swann. Has migrated to UKIP. Alexandra – you're welcome.'

We do indeed make her welcome and she giggles delightfully through her speech. I'm huddled next to Davy Coburn and we're enjoying her oratory until she says this.

'I didn't come to criticise Cameron. I think he's doing whatever he can in a terribly difficult situation.'

Do what?

'Oh well,' whispers Davy to me. 'At least she's got a nice pair of legs. That's something I suppose.'

She finishes her speech and walks off, using those same lovely legs to do so, and then we come to the real meal of the morning. Everybody's already guessed what that is as Nigel speaks from the rostrum.

'When Steve was planning this conference I did say to him – "I want you to leave me a slightly longer slot than normal because I'm hoping to have a guest speaker." In fact the next speaker ladies and gentlemen, I've hoped to have along as a guest speaker for many, many years.

'I believe that this is in fact a very big moment for UKIP and I want you please to give a huge, huge welcome to our newest member - Roger Helmer!'

Immediate, immense standing ovation from the hall.

'Now,' says Roger. 'You could say that I had to come to the UKIP spring conference because of course the Conservative spring conference was cancelled owing to lack of interest.'

Or, perhaps, the typical lack of interest from the Tory party in their hard-working activists and, in particular, Rupert Matthews.

Sayeeda Warsi will be furious. Magnificent!

Unfortunately, there's a thin media presence at the conference once more and this fine story doesn't get the coverage it deserves.

CHAPTER SIX

London Calling. Or not.

Saturday 24th March 2012

MILLWALL FC ARE AT HOME TO LEEDS. Technically, the stadium is outside the boundaries of the superconstituency in Greenwich and Lewisham where I'm supposed to be campaigning for my own election. But there's no branch in the area yet, hence no footsoldiers. Even if there were, there's no way we'd have enough bodies to cover an area formed of five parliamentary seats. With this in mind we're promoting Lawrence Webb alone at today's match. As lots of locals from the wider reaches of London will be attending the Den, efforts made here will count.

Association football enthusiast Paul Nuttall MEP supports the idea of leafleting fixtures. So we've had 1,000 flyers promoting Lawrence printed up and will harass the crowds in the hour or so before 3 pm. The time window's narrow. There's no point being there before the fans start arriving or after kickoff. We should get rid of a fair few, and if not we can hit Crystal Palace at a later date to hand out the rest.

I've promoted the event to the entire London membership of UKIP. There are four main avenues to the Den and we need a mass of people to achieve maximum coverage.

I'm outside South Bermondsey station at half past one with two boxes of leaflets stuffed into a brace of UKIP satchels. They're quite heavy, and I'm relieved when Steve Woolfe arrives and takes one off my shoulder. We wait, and then Young Independence member Alexander Balkan sidles up. He's a tall lad, but only 15. We wait for a few more minutes for the rest of the activists to appear. But they do not. It's just we three.

'Happy with each of us taking one approach?' I ask.

They are.

'We'll keep in touch by phone, and Alex – if you get any trouble from the fans, just call me and Steve and we'll rush over to help you right away.'

It is, after all, The Famous Millwall. Leeds are renowned for their own hooligan contingent as well.

We head off in separate directions. Within half an hour we're meeting up again. We've got rid of the lot, the Lions fans actually asking for them. We couldn't pass them out quickly enough and only one or two have been cast aside.

Nobody else may like Millwall, but after today, UKIP certainly does.

Sadly, they suffer an undeserved 1-0 loss to the away team.

Sunday 25th March 2012

The London Chairman is pleased with our efforts.

'Well done Messrs Oakers, Balkan and Woolfe. I thought Gawain was turning up with his children when they finished chimney sweeping? Obviously good to target footer but some members a bit nervous about violence despite me telling them that footballers are a bunch of pansies kissing and cuddling each other in front of thousands of blokes.'

Coburn's wrong. They loved us – in a blokey way. And we'll be back.

Wednesday 28th March 2012

London Elects, which is in charge of the GLA poll, publishes the list of nominated candidates. To my surprise I'm not standing for UKIP after all. Indeed, there are no candidates whatsoever for our party.

London Elects are oafs and idiots. I contact them immediately to insist that this mistake be rectified. We've been described as 'Fresh Choice for London'.

There's to-ing and fro-ing but they're adamant. The final word is given to me by John Bennett, the Returning Officer.

'Rule 6(5)(b) of the GLA Elections Rules 2007 (SI 2007/3541) requires that the description is covered by a certificate issued by or on behalf of the party's registered nominating officer, and I am advised that the relevant certificate in relation to your candidacy states that the description to be used is "Fresh Choice for London".'

We're royally-stuffed. Whose silly fault was that then? Coburn has revelations.

'I never noticed right until I was handing in my nomination papers in Bexley. The Returning officer said that "UKIP" wouldn't be the description. I called Pete Reeve right away and he said that was rot. But I then handed my phone to the returning officer who told Pete the same thing. He giggled, and said "whoops".'

So, although it was Pete Reeve's idea, nobody else had pulled him up on it. Thus, we're all equally thick and equally guilty.

Friday 13th April 2012

I've finally completed all the administrative steps to the satisfaction of Head Office. So tonight we're having the inaugural meeting of UKIP Greenwich and Lewisham at the 241 Club in Forest Hill. What an auspicious date. I'm elected chairman, of course. This is meet and fitting.

Saturday 14th April 2012

Today's a busy day for the party. Winston McKenzie hosted a public appearance by Farage outside Reeve's furniture store in Croydon first thing. Or rather, outside the blackened hole where the shop used to be until it was burned down in the riots.

There was minimal interest but things will hopefully be better this afternoon. Crystal Palace are at home and hosting Ipswich Town.

'I hear you had a great reaction at Millwall the other week,' Nigel says to me.

'It was incredible. We've high hopes for today and 5,000 mayoral leaflets to hand out.'

News of the success we had at the Den has spread throughout the London branches. Steve Woolfe and Alexander Balkan turn up again but this time we're joined by Coburn, Janice Atkinson, Peter Staveley and many others. That's more like it. None of the fans will escape.

We get started but receive a narrow range of responses.

'Well, ok. It'll give me something to read before kickoff, I suppose.'

Or:

'No, thanks.'

Or:

'No.'

Or:

'Fuck off.'

Most leaflets are discarded in the road. We should pick them up, but technically, it's the supporters who've littered and not us. So we don't bother. Besides, we've got about three-quarters of the print run still undistributed and that's more than enough for us to be carrying back.

Nigel heads off to the Director's box where he's been invited to watch the match, and there are free tickets for the rest of us in the stands.

Palace are held to an undeserved 1-1 draw. They should have lost three-nil because they are shit.

And so are their fans.

Saturday 21st April 2012
Bromley UKIP have erected a stall under a green gazebo next to the Past Times shop. There's not a great deal of interest. Bored, Farage and I decide to go walkabout down the High Street and through the open market.

Brazen as ever, I approach the shoppers as ringmaster.

'Good morning. Can I introduce you to Nigel Farage, the leader of UKIP?'

'I'm rather busy I'm afraid.'

'Sorry, I don't buy anything off the street.'

And – regular blank stares and pretence that they haven't seen us at all.

'Relax Paul,' says a mellow Nigel. 'And don't press the point if they're not interested. No need to annoy them.'

I disagree. Don't these people KNOW who this IS?

Thursday 3rd May 2012
It's polling day for the London Mayor and Assembly elections. I could give up work today to do some last minute campaigning – but don't.

Friday 4th May 2012
The count for the Greenwich and Lewisham superseat takes place at the Excel Centre in Docklands. Labour's Len Duvall comes first with 65,366 votes. Alex Wilson, who beat me for the Tory nomination, is distant second with 27,329. There's no animosity between us and we've been chatting amicably.

Oakley, the 'Fresh Choice for London' (who/what?) candidate, receives 4,997 votes, achieves 6th place and loses his deposit. Actually, the party does as they've paid it, thankfully.

We all get to deliver a speech. Mine is concise.

'Today was just the start,' I say. 'The old parties are rightly in fear of us now. The only way is up for UKIP. Just look at how many votes we got!

'Even though we did absolutely no campaigning whatsoever.'
All the candidates, including me, rudely walk off the stage as the BNP's Roberta Woods delivers her own oration.

Come the evening, I head to City Hall for the mayoral count. Never been inside before. Given the importance of this election, and the fact that I'm hungry, one would expect some sort of agreeable buffet to be available. The assembly authorities don't stretch to this but instead have generously provided some plastic cups and jugs of water.

Each party is given a room of its own in which to discuss matters in private as the evening develops. UKIP have to share with the independent candidate Siobhan Benita. As little is known about Benita and she's rumoured to be a Blairite puppet, our conversations are guarded. Our glances towards her shapely ankles equally so.

Eventually – the result. Boris Johnson defeats Ken Livingstone.

Sadly, Lawrence Webb fails in his quest to destroy Lib Dem Brian Paddick. And the Green. And the Independent. UKIP has polled 43,274 votes or 2% and comes next to last but above the British National Party.

The winner and then the runners-up give their speeches in turn. All the candidates, except Lawrence, walk off stage as the BNP's Carlos Cortiglia delivers his own oration. Photographs of UKIP and the BNP alone together on a platform might be unwise, but Webb's a brave man.

CHAPTER SEVEN

Go Back to Your Constituencies. And Prepare for Government!

Tuesday 10th July 2012

I TAKE THE OTHER HALF to the Adam Smith Institute boat party. She wouldn't miss it for anything. I tell her.

Steve Woolfe's also there with his wife, Fiona. As the two ladies are normal people and not activists, they've much to talk about. We decide to go for dinner in Pimlico afterwards.

It's an interesting evening. As we eventually depart from the restaurant in a taxi, my better half has some observations.

'He's sounding you out.'

'What for?' I'm a bit slow when it comes to things like this.

'I think he wants the party leadership.'

'Ha! Well, he'll need to get elected as an MEP first.'

'Obviously. As will you.'

I'm certainly planning to invade the EU parliament but hadn't given a post-Farage party any thought.

'If he challenges The Dear Leader then I'll back Farage one hundred percent. If Nigel steps down at any stage I'll be going for the crown myself.'

'Thought you might say that.'

Sorry Steve.

Monday 20th August 2012

UKIP London Region Committee proclaims that a branch has

been formed covering Lambeth and Croydon North. The Chairman is to be Winston McKenzie and the Treasurer his squeeze Marianne. It's a strangely-constructed area and has eaten up a chunk of the old Croydon branch. In addition, it covers the London Borough of Lambeth plus the parliamentary constituencies of Croydon North and Dulwich and West Norwood, half of which is in the London Borough of Southwark. This contortionism allows the party to hand Winston a chairmanship. Given that he is important.

Thursday 6th September 2012

Lewisham Council announces a by-election because a Liberal Democrat in Whitefoot ward has resigned to teach in India.

Beatnik.

Lewisham already has 40 Labour councillors. There are, or were, 11 Lib Dems. The Tories are down to one as the other has recently been expelled from his party.

Peter Staveley has undertaken a post-GLA vote analysis. Even though UKIP had had a stupid name on the ballot paper, our vote in this ward had actually gone up by 1.38% on the 2008 poll.

Who knows – we might be able to nick the seat. Worth a punt anyway, so I adopt myself as the candidate.

Saturday 29th September 2012

Malcolm Wicks, the Labour MP for Croydon North, has passed away. Even though his cadaver isn't cold, Winston McKenzie is lobbying to be UKIP's candidate to replace him.

Thursday 11th October 2012

It's by-election day for Whitefoot. At the members' insistence, there'd been a photo of me on our leaflet. The one of Oakley shaking hands with Farage in front of a portrait of Field Marshall Montgomery. We've delivered to the whole ward with the help of Bromley UKIP but haven't had enough bodies to undertake a canvass.

The Lib Dems have been campaigning hard with a poster-bedecked campaign HQ and a visit from their star MP, Simon Hughes. I took great pleasure in dropping one of my leaflets through their letterbox.

However, Labour beat them and are elected with 924 votes.

Despite demanding several recounts, I get precisely 100. But do surpass the Green who has just 36.

Friday 12th October 2012

Davy Coburn is surprisingly chipper about last night's result.

'Excellent first attempt on virgin soil. I have had worse scores in Kensington. Chin up!

'UKIP teaches us all humility and a dogged determination. You are now blooded.'

Bit of a contrast to the Tories. There'd have been Serious Words if I'd done so badly for them.

Monday 19th November 2012

I'm at the Lansdowne Club in Mayfair for the Bruges Group Maastricht Dinner. This is being held in honour of the 20th Anniversary of me ripping up a copy of That Treaty. Or perhaps to celebrate the work of the Tory rebels in failing to get Maastricht squished.

It's a dull and worthy evening, addressed by Bill Cash MP, Barry Legg Ex-MP, and Mark Pritchard, soon-to-be-MP. I have the particular pleasure of speaking to Teddy Taylor and Teresa Gorman; I thought they'd both gone to the green benches in the sky.

Many fine comrades are present and the conversations are far more interesting than the speeches, and one of those in particular. I and Dan Heaton decide to have a talk with John Redwood MP about the possibility of an electoral pact between the Tories and UKIP in certain constituencies.

We are perfectly polite. He is perfectly furious.

Leaping up from his seat he wobbles his arms about.

'You people are a disgrace! You're splitting the vote and undoing all our hard work over the last two decades or more!'

'Really?' I say. 'You Tory eurosceptics have achieved nothing. Nothing at all.'

We laugh at him as we walk away.

Thursday 22nd November 2012

Ladbrokes are offering good odds that Winston will come second in the Croydon North by-election and ahead of the Tories. As there are also by-elections taking place in Rotherham and Middlesbrough, McKenzie's soaring campaign will have a positive effect on those seats too.

Saturday 24th November 2012

The Labour Party hand UKIP an incredible gift. Rotherham social services, under Director Joyce Thacker, have told a local couple that they can no longer be foster parents. They'd been caring for kids for seven years but as they're also UKIP activists that suddenly makes them unsuitable. So we're bound to benefit from a sympathy vote in all three of the seats we're currently fighting.

Monday 27th November 2012

I'm too indolent to go up to either Rotherham or Middlesbrough, but fortunately, I can help out Winston instead. He has a campaign HQ in a prime location in Norwood High Street, just yards from the train station and only a couple of miles from where I live.

I turn up at the shop and the bell over the front door jingles. His other half is busy folding leaflets.

'Morning Marianne,' I say. 'How's it going?'

'Oh, it's fine.' She seems a little subdued.

McKenzie appears.

'How are you old chap? Confident?'

'Yes, mate – and I've been getting a lot of press coverage on adoption.'

This is good! The Rotherham Effect just keeps on working!

He hands me a copy of the 'Metro' which reads thus:

Winston McKenzie, the culture spokesman for Ukip, said placing children with gay or lesbian couples was 'child abuse'.

The former boxer, who is standing in the Croydon North by-election on Thursday, told Metro: 'To say to a child, "I am having you adopted by two men who kiss regularly but don't worry about it" – that is abuse. It is a violation of a child's human rights because that child has no opportunity to grow up under normal circumstances.'

Well. The Lord giveth. And the Lord taketh away.

Having been busy offloading a large pile of McKenzie's leaflets through numerous letterboxes I'm unable to check my emails until later. An immense chain has been going back and forth between the London officers. Most are incensed by the fact that Winston was allowed to stand in the first place.

Farage isn't having it though.

'Winston is the best street communicator we have in London by a country mile.

'He has my 100% support, while many in Croydon have behaved in an appalling and prejudiced way.'

Thursday 29th November 2012

It's the day of the three by-elections. Labour come top in Middlesbrough but our Richard Elvin is second on 12%. Jane Collins does better still in Rotherham and is runner-up to Sarah Champion with 22%.

Labour win Croydon North too with just over 64%. Yet, it's the Tories who place second and not UKIP as we'd hoped. Winston just holds on to his deposit with 5.7% but does beat the Lib Dems and the Greens so it's not all bad.

Although it is, nonetheless, bad.

Tuesday 11th December 2012

Sean Howlett has arranged a Young Independence drinks party on HMS Belfast. Lord Monckton is the guest speaker and orates to us all in a mighty voice:

'Our job is to infiltrate the Conservative Party and persuade them to call for a referendum.'
Really?

'Fuck that,' says Michael Heaver into my ear.

'Yes. Fuck that,' I mutter back.

We don't give a toss what the Tories want to do. Monckton, an old Conservative himself, apparently hasn't taken it on board that UKIP are now a force in their own right.

Thursday 3rd January 2013

Gerard Batten distributes a briefing note to the London branches on what he believes ought to be the criteria for selecting our next MEP candidates.

'At least three years continuous paid-up membership of the Party in good-standing.

'To have stood in at least two public elections for the Party, at local or national level.'

Sure he does. I now comply with the latter of these but, oddly enough, don't agree.

Wednesday January 9th 2013

There's another London region meeting at the Butler's Head and Coburn has more bad news.

'You know that we managed to collate a bit of voter data from the Feltham by-election canvassing? Well, it's lost. All of it. The lone hard disk that we kept the files on has failed.'

Argh. We really do need to up-our-game.

Saturday 26th January 2013

A report from Conservative "Special Administrator" Mathew Kershaw recommends that Lewisham Hospital close its Accident & Emergency department. This is stupid.

Obviously, everyone from normal people to the sensible left to a plethora of Leftards have jumped onto this under the umbrella campaign 'Save Lewisham Hospital'. There's a march today against the plans.

Is there any particular reason why UKIP can't join them? I'd checked with the party's health spokesman, Steph Williams, who reached this conclusion.

'My suggestion would be that UKIP is seen to be supporting (but not trying to take over) a campaign like this.'

I promised Steph that we'll try very hard not to.

The branch members were to meet at the grassy knoll opposite Lewisham train station but most have cried off. Although staunchly opposed to the government's plans, they're afraid that they might be attacked by the left. A new enquirer, a chap called Peter Lello, has also expressed an interest and I finally find him amongst the multitude. Can't see anyone else, so – it's just him and me.

As many thousands have gathered for this demonstration, it takes considerable time for the march to move off. Down the High Street and past the hospital itself before meeting for a rally at Mountsfield Park.

We both proudly wear a UKIP badge but apart from some surprised looks we receive no grief at all.

Lello's a civil servant and has no previous campaigning experience save for being a volunteer on Gay Switchboard (if that even counts). He's exactly the sort of down-to-earth chap we need in the party.

Having been congregating and marching for about an hour, we felt that we'd sufficiently made our point to Health Secretary Jeremy Hunt. By sheer coincidence, our part of the march has just reached the Ravensbourne Arms so we drop out. And it just so happens that Tim Aker is in the pub too. So we could have a convivial and useful political brainstorming session.

Instead, we decide to play darts and get pissed.

Wednesday 30th January 2013

I'm at Croydon County Court just after 10 am to meet my barrister, Jamie Williams. Today's the final hearing against the malefactor who duffed me up outside the Old Star. As he hasn't bothered replying to any correspondence from my solicitors, or even filed a Defence, we're surprised to see that he's actually here in court. He is, now, apologetic. Tough.

The damages which he has to pay are £5,000 with costs at double that. This probably stings even more than my poor face did. I shall fritter his money away on lager and lapdancers.

Thursday 21st February 2013

Lewisham Council announces a by-election in Evelyn Ward. This is one of the rubbish-est parts of the borough. Literally, as it adjoins the municipal dump, furnace and recycling plant. Its residents vote Labour by compulsion even though that party always has and always will let them down.

Peter Staveley's forensic analysis of the London results from last year shows that this is one of the worst areas for UKIP. Rather than waste our limited branch funds on a load of leaflets when we'd rather be campaigning in Eastleigh, it's decided that I'll be a paper candidate.

Thursday 28th February 2013

It's polling day in the Eastleigh by-election which followed the resignation of Lib Dem Chris Huhne for lying to the Bizzies about a speeding ticket. We're hoping that our candidate Diane James will be the first UKIP MP. Loads of activists have come down. We've had a prime location shop on a corner in the town centre. There's been lots of press coverage. Fingers crossed.

I get the train back to London just after 5 pm because it's a two-hour ride and we have a branch meeting tonight at which Gerard Batten will be speaking. I'm pleased when John Moss from the Tories climbs on to the same carriage.

In early 2011 he'd been organising telephone canvassing against the Alternative Vote in that referendum. My subconscious had probably already been telling me to flee to UKIP. In any case I'd decided that I wouldn't be campaigning against proportional representation in any form and told John so. And I'd been rude about Sayeeda Warsi but he hadn't dobbed me in to the Party.

'Right John,' I exclaim. 'It won't make any difference now so you can tell me why your campaign was so crap and I'll reciprocate.'

'But our campaign was wonderful,' he replies.

'In that case, why were you lot copying us with purple leaflets?'

He smiles. 'Fair enough. And it didn't help when Maria Hutchings told the country at large that a state education wasn't good enough for her son. Worst thing was that the Merlin voter database wouldn't work and we couldn't target our pledges properly. Your turn.'

'Well I'm not impressed with Diane James at all. She's a cold fish and didn't interact like a human with any of the activists. Or the voters come to that. Anyway, enough of your moaning about Merlin. Our canvassing kit was, well, rudimentary. In fact, just a clean A4 pad. We didn't even know if the householders we knocked up were on the electoral register.'

'You're joking.'

'Nope.'

As for the Greenwich & Lewisham branch meeting? Gerard Batten forgets to turn up. On the plus side, that bloke Peter Lello who went on the hospital march with me volunteers to manage our candidates for next year's local elections. He really is far more organised than me, so it's good to have him with us. Unfortunately, all the officer posts are already filled so we'll have to call him something else. 'Campaign Co-Ordinator' sounds a bit dull.

So. 'Peter Lello – Head of my Personal Bodyguard' it is then.

Yet the evening is topped off by disappointment. The Liberal Democrats (just) hold on to Eastleigh with 13,342 votes. Diane James is second with 11,571. She barely scrapes past the Tory Maria Hutchings on 10,559.

CHAPTER EIGHT

'Get that bastard off!'

Wednesday 6th March 2013

I'VE BEEN NOTICED BY SOMEONE called Ian Dunt who's editor of the politics.co.uk website. He's interviewing Kippers, including my good self, perhaps to reinforce the Bufton-Tufton prejudice about us.

I know nothing about the bloke so ask Gerard if he's dangerous. Batten replies in rhyme.

'There was a young journo named Dunt,

'Whose style was exceedingly blunt,

'When asking a question,

'He gave no time for reflection,

'And some people thought him a bad interviewer.

'Sorry no, never heard of him. If in doubt I suggest you speak to Gawain.'

Towler tells me he's a respectable leftie so I decide to go for it and there are a couple of good bits in his copy when it's published.

'We meet in Canary Wharf, which is looking even windier and greyer than usual. Halfway through the conversation his phone goes off. "Was that the Sex Pistols?" I ask, referring to the ringtone.'

"Of course it was," he says dismissively. "Certainly not Justin Bieber".

We cover the burning issues of blazers, pints of ale, whacks of cricket bats on village greens, *A Clockwork Orange* and the Blitz spirit. And, of course, the most important point of all.

'Paul is probably the most intelligent and professional of the people I speak to. He works as a barrister and only shifted to Ukip when he was overlooked for PPC elections for the Tories.'

Three-quarters accurate, so not bad coverage from an enemy scribbler.

Saturday 23rd March 2013

UKIP Conference is taking place in the Great Hall at Exeter University. Emmett Jenner drove myself and John Gill down to the town in the back of the UKIP taxi yesterday where we alternately read newspapers and dozed off.

Fresh from the semi-success in Eastleigh, it is, truly, the best attended conference that I've ever seen. The entire rear wall of the hall is peppered with TV journalists from across the globe. Farage delivers an excellent speech, as we expect, but then there's something new.

Having finished, he walks down the central aisle to leave by the back door.

And here it is.

Several camera crews have formed into a mob in front of him, stumbling backwards as he ambles forwards while shaking hands with members and grinning non-stop.

That's it. The statesman's stroll. The media have finally realised we've arrived and so we have.

The coverage is live and then on repeat throughout the news for the rest of the day.

By late evening, we coalesce at Nigel's hotel. This isn't because Farage is the Head Vampire to whose lair we are drawn. Rather, the bar's still serving after-hours. Which amounts to more or less the same thing.

The place is solid with Kippers and also with a wholly-unconnected conference of models who're wandering in and out of the same room. Tall, skinny foals with perfect skin. As one whose preference is for 'Dove'-type ladies who won't accidentally snap in the course of a cuddle I'm not intrigued. Others are, in particular an assortment of plain and ugly young men hoping for some luck. They're mixing with them and thus with us.

Now. His Nibs doesn't mind this at all. He'll talk to anyone and is genuinely interested in what they have to say. Many of these normal people are coming up to speak to him while he enjoys a pint or two.

Then footage of an interview with Nigel appears on the overhead TV. At this, someone yells out at the top of a voice which is filled with aggression:

'Get that bastard off!'

There's a shocked silence and then we all cheer and raise our glasses to the screen. The shout came from Farage himself.

I'm at the far end of the bar with Ray Finch and a couple of others. We're in a fine mood but concerns are bubbling.

'This is no good.'

'We don't know if these people are Farage fans or not.'

'Look at them all. It would be the easiest thing in the world to stab the guy.'

'Yeah, but if anyone did try anything they wouldn't be walking away in one piece.'

'Or walking away at all.'

The consensus is that Nigel now needs professional security. This will avoid the possibility of any of us doing a ten-stretch to life for defending the King.

In any case, the zeitgeist has shifted. UKIP's time has finally come. We're now going to shake things up and people are going to notice.

Tuesday 26th March 2013

A bloke called Anthony has just joined our branch in Greenwich and Lewisham. He's coming to our AGM which is being held tonight at the Hobgoblin in Forest Hill. Although this will be his first ever meeting, he wants to stand for chairman straight away. His application is distributed to the members beforehand:

'I will promote healthy debates without any bias. And want to encourage more Q&A sessions in our meetings. I will also encourage members to stick to the party's constitution. I will also be impartial to any views that our members have. I will conduct meetings in an orderly fashion and stick to time of proceedings of meetings. I will be fair and impartial and respect everybody's views. I want to promote democracy and fairness and make our meetings warm and friendly and comfortable. I will also be open to any ideas of any future discussions and motions that will help our party go forward. I will also encourage anyone from across the political spectrum to be involved in our meetings except people that promote hate and racism. I am passionate, I am fair and love democracy. I am also impartial and welcome any views and contributions that will take our party into power in 2015. I will also be happy to discuss grievances that members have. I'd love to see a more fairer, more democratic environment. I will work hard for what I have put in my manifesto.'

My own CV for the chairmanship is also sent out. It's pretty much a summary of what you've just read over the past few pages.

The candidates speak and ballot papers are distributed. Tim Aker takes me to one side.

'I need a quick word about what you're going to do as a branch for the Euros next year.'

'Ah, but only if I win the chairmanship,' says I.

Aker tuts.

'Of course you'll win it.'

Aker's right. Obviously.

Thursday 28th March 2013

The count is taking place in Lewisham Town hall for the Evelyn by-election. David Furze from the local Conservatives gives me a call.

'Where are you?'

'At home.'

It's a chilly night after all.

'What are you doing?'

'Watching telly. And eating sweets.'

He's disappointed.

'Aren't you coming to the count?'

'Naw. Can't be bothered.'

'That's a shame. Looks like it's going to be an interesting result.'

David's right. Labour win, tediously, but they're run a close second by the candidate from Lewisham People Before Profit. Then it's the Lib Dem.

In equal last position are Paul Oakley out of UKIP and the Tories' Simon Nundy, each of whom have polled exactly 119 votes. The Conservatives worked the ward hard during the election and we not at all.

Wednesday 17th April 2013

Today is Margaret Thatcher's Funeral. I'm not nearly important enough to have received an invitation to the ceremony within St Pauls' but decide to join the crowds to watch the passing of the cortege. No chance. Admittedly, I've left it late to turn up but all vantage points from the east of Fleet Street are choc-a-bloc.

As her coffin approaches the steps to the cathedral I'm crammed into the south of Paternoster Square with hundreds of others. Many of us gravitate towards the gated opening leading to the front entrance in the hope that enough people will leave its environs to let us through. Some do leave, including a well-dressed middle-aged Englishman reciting pro-IRA slogans to himself and sporting a busted and bloody nose. Bizarre. But not enough bodies depart to allow the remaining faithful to get any closer.

We can hear that the coffin has entered the cathedral. There being even less to see now that the service has started, I walk away along with everyone else. Most go back to their jobs. I head to the Pavilion End pub. The Freedom Association has arranged a post-funeral celebration of her life.

On the way I see Rupert Matthews. Rather, I see an immense 1980s Conservative Party flag, the pole of which is being held by the man himself. This battle standard depicts the-worker's-forearm-with-the-ice-cream-cone. As it isn't the modern Crayola 'Tree' smudge, I'm not repelled and happy to catch up with him. Our chat is interrupted by a Danish film crew demanding an interview.

There's a queue to get into the pub and Simon Richards has sensibly engaged several ex-forces men as ultra-bouncers to keep out all unwanted Leftards. Downstairs there's a parade of speakers paying tribute to the Great Lady's achievements. Upstairs, the televisions carry the service behind a packed bar.

As for those attending? No Cameroon Cons. Instead, there's the rump of the Thatcherite right within the old party and those of us who carry the banner within the new. EU-loathers all.

I'm glad to see old friends like Tory councillors Simon Fawthrop and Neil Dickinson. Jonathan Bullock, previously also one of their crew, has just come over to UKIP. There are others I speak to who are considering doing likewise.

However. There's a clique present whose loyalty to the Baroness is equalled by their loyalty to the Conservative Party, no matter who is leader. They're unhappy with what they perceive as betrayal by we defectors. All in a relatively-friendly way of course.

This loyalty to that party no-matter-what is often described as its strength. I'm unconvinced. Further, the wish to worship Thatcher is an unattractive one but common in men (and almost exclusively men) who've reached a certain level of middle-age. Certainly, the anti-federalist Bruges speech of 1990 was a masterstroke, but she'd campaigned heartily to stay in the EEC in the 1975 referendum and forced through the Single European Act on a 3-line whip.

My respect for the great lady is undiminished. She remains, in my view, the greatest Prime Minister of the 20th Century. Yet, as this celebration of her life reaches an unexpected conclusion, I'm no longer a

Thatcherite.

Cheer Thatcher – vote UKIP.

Thursday 16th May 2013

Footage of Nigel Farage's trip to Edinburgh is all over the news. He was corralled in the Canon's Gait pub by nationalist socialist thugs squawking racist anti-English slogans and had to be extracted by police.

I speak to him when things have quietened down.

'Don't put this off any longer. You need bodyguards.'

'You might be right.'

CHAPTER NINE

The Lure of Brussels

Saturday 8th June 2013

THE BILDERBERG CONFERENCE is taking place in Watford and London MEP Gerard Batten has asked me if I'll be going today. He's already been, and had quite a bit of media interest. There's no way I'd miss turning up to a sinister conclave of elderly men who tweak the political agenda like puppeteers. So I go along to the UKIP Conference at the Lakeside Country Club in Frimley Green instead.

The venue's miles from anywhere and a taxi ride from Farnborough station. On arriving, it's good to see that, at last, there are six-foot, flat-nosed geezers on the door. Given the distance from the station it's unlikely that gibbering Leftards will make the trip. But there's always the off-chance.

On this occasion Steve Crowther, party chairman, will be delivering a more interesting presentation than Nigel Farage. At least for those of us who hearken to the call of serving the nation within the European Parliament.

He begins.

'Right now, I find I am one of the most powerful and therefore most popular people in the party.'

A painting of Stalin holding a smily fat cherub is flashed on the screen behind him.

'When the process is all over, and the candidates have been chosen, I will be slightly less popular.'

A grainy photograph of a shrivelled Nicolae Ceauşescu appears.

There's been lots of interest with over 300 requests for application packs. Crowther tells us that 38% are from people who've joined in the past 12 months and 10% from those who signed up in the last four weeks. He goes on.

'You will forgive me for being slightly less than thrilled about the prospect of selecting people who didn't think it worth joining the party until last Wednesday.

'I must say, I have to admire their self-confidence. I certainly wouldn't have the nerve myself.

'Equally, just because you've been a member since God was a lad, it doesn't automatically follow that you are the kind of collegiate, co-operative, hard working, conscientious and indeed sane person whom we need to make up our MEP cadre.

'Clearly, I'm not talking about anyone in this room, but I'm sure we're all thinking of a fellow member right now.'

There are other speeches but apart from Farage, none of particular interest. Further, although there's a bar at the back of the hall, this closes after lunch. The owners of the venue have not the slightest conception of the purpose of a UKIP conference.

Essentially, the time's spent gossiping. Most importantly, who's going to put themselves forward to be an MEP?

My barrister colleague Matt Richardson is a certainty though, at least until I speak to him. About 6 months ago we'd bumped into each other in Fleet Street and he'd asked if I'd be putting my name in. Yes indeed.

'So you'll be battling me in London then?' he asked.

'No way. I want to stand elsewhere. Eastern maybe.'

Yet today he says that he won't be going for it after all; Nigel's just appointed him Party Secretary.

Davy Coburn kindly gives me and Lello a lift back to London. In a three-wheeled French camionette.

Sunday 9th June 2013

I've left it to the very last hours to finalise the MEP application. This isn't through my usual laziness, but in order to glean as much as possible from yesterday's lecture by Crowther.

Paragraph T.3.7 of the UKIP Party Rules says this:

'Candidates shall, in general, be expected to stand in the region in which they currently reside (hereinafter known as their 'home region'). Any Candidate wishing to stand outside their home region, or for any additional region, must apply to the National Selection Panel for permission to do so, stating a case.'

London is where I 'currently reside'.

However. House of Commons Research Paper 09/53 on the last EU Elections says this about our London vote.
'UKIP's 10.8% was the lowest of any English region.'
And the 2011 census found this.
'While White British was the majority ethnic group in London, it had the lowest percentage of White British across England and Wales at 44.9 per cent.'
And Article 19 of the EC Treaty reads thus.
'Every citizen of the Union residing in a Member State of which he is not a national shall have the right to vote and to stand as a candidate in elections to the European Parliament in the Member State in which he resides.'
As we're leading on the issue of uncontrolled mass immigration, the uncontrollable mass of migrants in London are unlikely to vote for UKIP.
So. In response to the question 'Which UK region or regions would you aim to stand for election as an MEP in?' I list Eastern, South Eastern, South West and North West because I've links to them all.
Not that I've anything against my London home you understand. However, I do actually want to be elected.

Wednesday 3rd July 2013
I hate mornings, and haven't been interviewed for ages because, being self-employed, I'm obviously the best man for the job. But today is the formal interview for the MEP list. The slots for these last all day and applicants are given a choice of when they want to be seen. I've found out from an executive search website that the best time to be seen is first thing, before the panel has become arse-achingly bored and already made their decision. So - 9:45 it is then.
UKIP have decamped to donated offices behind Claridges in Brooks Mews. The block's shared by Max Clifford's PR firm. I pass him in the foyer on arriving but pretend not to know who he is.
The Taxpayers' Alliance Party had taken place last night. I'd been

good and left early when still only quarter-cut. Other pals hadn't and it's cruelly-pleasing to see Tim Aker looking viridescent at his desk. He's not being interviewed today.

David "Campbell" Bannerman having recently flipped back to the Conservatives after being elected as a UKIP MEP, the questions focus on one main issue: was my own manifest disloyalty solely-reserved for the Tory party or might it apply to UKIP too?

'No,' I reply. 'Like a new religious convert, my fanaticism is greater than that of long-term adherents.'

There are smiles.

'Are there any skeletons in your past which might embarrass the party?'

'Yes.'

I'd told Nigel what this was when he took me to dinner at Gaucho. It didn't bother him and it doesn't bother them.

Thursday 4th July 2013

The UKIP Bromley dinner is tonight. At Oakley House. How appropriate. It's much larger than the usual venue at the Old Jail. There's a cavernous dining room and it's completely sold out.

Farage's speech is superlative and culminates with him donning some googly-eyed comedy glasses. This is met with mighty cheers.

I'd hoped to have a quiet chat with him afterwards but there's no chance. He's surrounded by hangers-on, each trying to snatch a few words of conversation.

Instead, I introduce the missis to Christine Diamond and then Kirsten Farage. When, inevitably, I'm elected to the EU Parliament eleven months from now, the wives of the great warriors will be able to console each other as their husbands perform exploits on the continent.

Tuesday 9th July 2013

Lewisham Council put on 'local assemblies' throughout the borough which allow the councillors to interact with residents and pretend they're doing great works.

Tonight it's the turn of Downham ward at the Health and Leisure Centre. At last year's London poll UKIP had seen a 2% increase in the vote share here according to Staveley. The Conservatives have also had a good showing in this ward in the past and are desperate to take back some seats next year.

So we turn up to get a flavour of what's going on. Me, Peter Lello, Ryan Acty, Ray Adams and Ken Webb. All brazenly sporting UKIP badges.

There are also lots of Tories present. None of them are wearing party regalia but I know them by sight. Great minds think alike.

And - if looks could kill? Eeh!

Saturday 27th July 2013

Our branch have arranged to seed-leaflet Lewisham today. With perfect timing, London Region then decided that prospective MEPs would have their public speaking assessment this very afternoon in the centre of town. Uncle Mick is chairing and I tell him of the problem. I definitely don't want to cancel the action day. He emails thus:

'We'll see 8 between 10 and 12pm the rest after lunch say 1-3pm.

'We will all be bored and tired by then so I suggest you get there by 2.30 latest for the graveyard slot.'

In other words, the timing will be the exact converse of the formal interview. I'll have to do jolly well to keep the beggars awake.

The branch meets at Grove Park station at 10 and we leapfrog the leafleting. I'm trying to run through what needs to be an 8 minute speech in my mind whilst moving my lips and looking a bit of a nutter. Colleagues are chatty which doesn't help. We finish at 1 and I rush home and then out.

It's a scorching day. I don't arrive at the Conway Hall venue until nearly 2.30. Other applicants are lurking in the vestibule including Andrew McNeilis and Peter Whittle. Emmet Jenner has just spoken and Winston McKenzie is just about to. Rival candidates aren't allowed to be in the main hall when their opponents are performing so I go outside to finish putting something together. Besides, Winston's speeches tend to shake the very building in which they're delivered and peace is needed.

I'm called in. My prior experience of the Conway Hall venue was limited to possession of a bootleg LP of a performance there by the punk rock stars, Crass. Full, this would be a great venue in which to speak but there's only around 30 people in the audience, largely sitting at the back with empty seats in front. Rather than stand on the podium with the microphone I decide to pace the floor and do without.

Nowadays, most politicians and aspirants utilise the 'Tony Blair Hands' in their speeches. Palms parallel to each other and jerking up and down as if conducting a fellatrix. Not me. I prefer to shake fists. I try the apocalyptic stuff as an opener but can tell the crowd are indeed bored and sweaty with no bar to pump them up so change tack.

'The MEPs won't be there because they're wonderful, beautiful people. I'm practically perfect in every way, there's no doubt about that. But this is not how or why we're elected. We're standing on the shoulders of the activists and nobody must forget that.'

Always be nice about the members. Always.

Proceedings over, several of us go to the pub where we lie to each other about how badly we think we've done. After that, I walk via chambers to Blackfriars station to travel one stop to London Bridge and then home.

That was the intention but I wake up 40 minutes later as the train arrives at Gatwick Airport. Can't think why.

Saturday 10th August 2013

'You're not going to start banging on about Islam are you?'
Farage is driving me and his son Tom down to the coast to fish.

'Course not', I reply. 'This is a side-issue and not what we're about.' Nigel doesn't say anything but appears satisfied.

It's early, but his mobile has been buzzing perpetually since the sun rose. There are press contacts with queries. Branch officers with gripes. And now, very occasionally, calls from prospective UKIP MEPs.

On Monday, the party will publish its ranked list of those who've been sifted to stand. I hope to be one of them.

He receives another call. The person on the line is irate. Farage is placatory and noncommittal. He's using a headset so only half the conversation can be heard but I try to guess who it is. Correctly as it transpires. Not that I'm telling you who it was.

Oh, alright then. It was Steve Woolfe. Nigel hangs up:

'He's found out his placing and isn't happy. But anyway, he's just a pretty face with an unrealistic impression of his underwhelming qualities. Too bad.'
Nigel knows what the scores are. I don't and won't ask. That would be bad form; if the leader wants to say how I've done, he will.

He doesn't.

Nonetheless, on the assumption that I'm somewhere on the roll it won't hurt to remind Nigel of my links to various regions in England in some detail and with some yearning. But not London.

We arrive at the harbour and meet the rest of the crew including a couple of serious anglers who write for *Total Sea Fishing* magazine, Nigel's brother and his young son.

We cast off and cruise out for two miles. Our initial run is over some sand beds where the plaice have shoaled up. I'm hooking one-a-chuck with the aid of a spoon. This is the last remaining one of the many which I stole from my school canteen. With the handle sawn off and a hole drilled in the lip it's a good attractor.

Nigel's nephew is busy catching mackerel for us to use as bait for bass. Not 'sea-bass' you'll observe. Our friends in the American colonies have both the fresh and saltwater species of this fish but we do not. Your restaurant menu is wrong.

It's easy enough to land flatties or mackerel but bass aren't so gullible and Farage is astonishingly skilled at catching them. He pulls in eight of up to twelve pounds in weight. He beats the professional anglers. He beats his brother. He beats his son and, of course, he beats me.

CHAPTER TEN

Rats in a Sack
Some are cunning, others not so.

Sunday 11th August 2013

I RECEIVE AN EMAIL from Chairman Crowther.
'We have now completed the assessment stages for the MEP Selection process. I am pleased to tell you that you have been shortlisted, and will go into the ballot with a view to representing London.'

We'll find out exactly how well we've performed tomorrow when the ratings by the professional assessors is released. However, he also wants to speak to me.

'It has been suggested that you are acquainted with Ms Claire Khaw. Is this correct?'

It is. Both signed-up Young Tories, we'd worked together for Bill Cash during the anti-Maastricht campaign. I went to her wedding soon after but then lost contact and haven't seen her in person for many years.

With the advent of bloody Facebook she got back in touch and then went a bit queer. Joining the BNP. Posing with guns and swastikas. Calling for the killing of disabled children. She decided to endorse my attempt to be UKIP's mayoral candidate (unsolicited) and then tried to garner my support for the admission of ex-BNP members including herself to the party. She wasn't pleased with my response.

Claire's posted a rather camp photograph online of me at her wedding with the late Auberon Waugh. Someone's dobbed me in about this, with the obvious intention of damaging my MEP application. The background's explained to Steve and he has no further concerns.

I wonder who could have grassed me up.

Oh. So it was that person was it? Stab me in the front please. I don't like stealth-mode nematodes.

'Oh, and Steve,' I say. 'Really don't want to stand in London. Can you slot me in somewhere else?'

'Make your application to the NEC and we'll see what we can do.'

Monday 12th August 2013

The rankings from the assessments have come out. I'm ninth out of the 60 selected for England and first in London, above our sitting MEP, Gerard.

Lawrence Webb congratulates me, apparently genuinely, and I commiserate with him, definitely genuinely. He's in at number 36 of the 60 and sixth in London.

'Do watch your back though', he advises.

Bit strong, eh Lawrence?

I decide to call Gerard, who's miffed. There was only one point between us anyway. Part of the assessment was a media grading and he tells me he didn't have this. I said that I didn't have one either.

Then I realise I had. One afternoon I received a call from an unknown number when in the garden contemplating the leek seedlings. It was from a journalist who said he was arranging interviews with prospective UKIP MEPs and would I like to take part? You betcha. However, having been taught to be cautious, I said Head Office would need to approve it. They having done so, I texted the bloke with an acceptance but heard nothing more.

Oho. So that was it eh? I ask Crowther. He replies opaquely to say that I'd 'passed the media assessment'. So the answer's yes.

Tim Aker recommends a Facebook filleting to me, just to make sure there are no spies in the list of our 'Friends' we don't actually know. We don't want them running off to the media with screenshots of our 'late night' ramblings about Gay-Moslem-Zionist conspiracies.

And I make my application to the NEC to stand anywhere but London. They turn me down. Humph.

Following the debacle over the selection of the London List, Head Office have changed the procedure again. This time 'round it's the party members who'll have the final say on the rankings and not the NEC. It is all very confusing and inconsistent.

Surprisingly enough, I'm going to vote for myself as number 1. There's no point supporting anyone else in London as this would cancel out that vote. With this in mind, I call various pals in other regions. Various pals in other regions call me with exactly the same idea. We set up an electoral college of sorts, encouraging each other's members to mark their crosses wisely.

Come the evening, it's the London Region meeting at the Butler's Head. I'm late as usual and the agenda stalls as soon as I arrive as the committee spontaneously applaud. It is proper that they do so. I wave regally and sit down.

'Good result, Oakers,' says Chairman David Coburn. 'And you even seem to have scored better than me. Must've got their sums wrong.'

He's pulling my leg and is very gracious about the fact that my score was far better than his mere, pitiful, pathetic 75.

Monday 19th August 2013

I'm supposed to be going up to the West Midlands to speak at Bill and Star Etheridge's branch in Coseley this evening along with Ray Finch who's standing in South Eastern area. I have a court hearing in Slough but can just about do it having checked the train times.

Unfortunately, my solicitors haven't conducted the case as they should and I'm fighting back against a shoeing by three opposing counsel. As it's a complicated case the minutes tick on and on. I'm not going to make it up in time.

It's after four o'clock and in a short break in the proceedings I phone Ray to ask him to tender my apologies.

'You're not bottling it are you, you soft southern bastard?' says the Scouse git.

'Nope. I'm just leaving you more Brummie cars to TWOC. Anyway, I've got to finish burying this lot at court.'

They bury me, but I make them sweat for it.

Friday 23rd August 2013

I've been noticed by Iain Dale in his Conservative Home column as he writes about the UKIP MEP sift:

'In London, current incumbent Gerard Batten is placed second on the shortlist behind Paul Oakley – Oakley is a former chairman of the London Young Conservatives. Batten will not be happy.'

Dale's surprised that John Gaunt and James Delingpole haven't made the list, snarky about Janice Atkinson and nice about Michael Heaver and Patrick O'Flynn.

He has this to say about our London Chairman:

'Top of the Scotland shortlist is the inimitable David Coburn. A born and bred Scot, gay, and with the ability to give very good media and public speaking performances, he is the best hope UKIP have of getting a MEP in Scotland, though will Farage's recent troubles north of Hadrian's Wall provide him with a handicap?'

I'm in the middle of reading this when Coburn himself phones up.

'Ooh. Have you seen Steve Woolfe's Youtube film?'

Yup.

'I cried tears, dear,' he says.

We're both fond of Steve. But as for his video? Shot outside Parliament and Temple Church, apparently he 'has a dream' and his words are backed by a soundtrack which seems to have been lifted from 'The Mission'. The film that is, not the band.

We cackle unkindly. It's best enjoyed whilst peering over the top of a pillow clutched close to the chin.

'Have you seen Patrick O'Flynn's?' Davy asks.

Nope.

'Made me feel sick with those video effects after every few words,' Coburn tells me. 'He obviously couldn't remember more than a sentence of his lines at a time so they mashed it together from a hundred takes.'

Boringly, Patrick's been filmed outside the House of Commons too.

'When's yours going up?' I ask Davy.

'Soon. Guy Ritchie's directing. There will be bullets in the European parliament, explosions, car chases. The lot.'

Coburn knows everyone so this isn't a surprise. I'm looking forward to this, having enjoyed the early noughties gangsta style and still being an adherent of black leather coats.

He's teasing of course. When his video does appear, it's been filmed outside Parliament on College Green. As is Janice Atkinson's. As are several others.

As will be mine.

Tuesday 27th August 2013

I'm appearing in the first of a three-day trial in Birmingham County Court. Matt Richardson, a practising barrister as well as Party Secretary, will be at the same court on a different case tomorrow. He'll be representing UKIP against Mike Nattrass, one of our current MEPs, who's suing the party.

Nattrass had said he was retiring. For obscure reasons he then changed his mind and decided to reapply as a candidate but failed the assessment. He's now taking us to court because: it's so unfair.

I've arranged to meet Matt tomorrow night while my own trial is moving onwards. However, my claim settles on the first day so I'm not going to be having a pie and a pint with him after all.

Wednesday 28th August 2013

The judge at Birmingham County Court is unpersuaded by Nattrass. He loses.

Thursday 29th August 2013

I'm on the email list of Gerard Batten's staffer, Lynnda Robson, and thus receive all notifications about his activities as our sole MEP for London. I'm also on the mailing list of Christine Diamond of Bromley UKIP which leads to duplicates hitting the inbox as Christine forwards just about everything she receives from the party topdogs.

So it's surprising to receive a forwarded email from Lynnda via Christine but not the original email itself.

Then the surprise disappears. Lynnda's email says this.

'You will shortly be receiving your copy of Independence magazine in which there will be a voting form for our UKIP candidates for the European Elections next May and as a personal message from me I would like to ask you to consider voting for Gerard Batten as the Number 1 UKIP candidate.'

'In London we have several good candidates but to be sure of making Gerard No. 1 in London you have to make him your first choice in this national vote.'

She sets out various pieces of fluffery and puffery about Why Gerard Batten Is A Jolly Decent Fellow. I don't disagree with any of it, but fully agree with part T.5.9 of the Party Rules:

'No candidate or supporter shall make unsolicited contact with members by any means whatsoever for the purpose of soliciting votes except in person. This shall include, but not be limited to, contact by telephone, post, email, SMS and online messaging.'

Steve Crowther expressly reminded all the candidates about this when he told us we'd got through the assessment.

I seek the counsel of Staveley, Aker and Lello. We agree that if the ranking between myself and Gerard is close then, well, 'issues' will be raised.

This isn't on.

Saturday 31st August 2013

Peter Lello films the Westminster half of My Video. The opening line's easy.

'So here it is. The compulsory clichéd shot of the candidate standing outside Parliament.'

It takes a while to record as we don't have professional equipment and car horns beep and planes fly overhead. And worse.

'We can make sure,' I'm saying, 'that the British people are fully informed. And they can do their duty and get us out when we have a referendum. In due course. . .'

Some passing Krauts are talking loudly enough to be picked up by the microphone.

'Ja, ja.'

I suck my teeth like a yardie.

'Fucking Germans.'

Peter chuckles like Muttley.

'Are you going to put that bit in?'

'Yeah. I'll do an out-take.'

'Oh, you can imagine that can't you. UKIP MEP candidate laughing at Germans?' he says.

We don't put that bit in after all.

Monday 2nd September 2013

So. Finally I get to go up to speak to the Etheridge's branch in Coseley. Star's standing as a candidate for the council by-election. As usual, she's putting everything she has into it but this has left her exhausted. She refuses to let her disability defeat her and picks me up from the station anyway.

We drive round to The Crown. Graham Eardley's there. I and he are disappointed by his failure to pass the assessment for the MEP list. The bloke has been a brilliant cornerstone of the Bruges Group for many years.

Dean Perks has also turned up. I've never met him in person before.

'Bloody hell, you're tall,' I say to Dean.

'Bloody hell, you're short,' says the insolent UKIP PPC for Halesowen and Rowley Regis.

He's just been in trouble both with the pious pinkoes of Hope not Hate and the Tory trucklers of the *Daily Mail* for sympathising with aspects of Sharia law as a deterrent to crime. He's enjoyed the publicity as has everyone else.

There are three speakers in all and both Jill Seymour and Jim Carver from the West Midlands will also orate. Following a fine roast dinner, Bill introduces me first as I have to head back to the station soon.

'I can honestly say, this is one of the most impressive men that this party's got to offer today. Ladies and gentlemen - give a good Black Country welcome to Paul Oakley.'

A Biblical soundbite is always appropriate for opening.

'Look at our pathetic Prime Minister. The only reason he's having this referendum is to take votes away from us at the general election in 2015. In that referendum he will campaign for Britain to remain in this foul organisation. He's saying: "All these things will I give unto you if you will but bow down and vote for me." Get thee behind us, Cameron.'

The thing's being filmed by a guy who has some seriously-serious professional equipment. It's going on Youtube and will hopefully receive hundreds of hits from members across the country before they cast their votes in the rankings.

Sadly, the main microphone is right by the kitchen and the footage sounds like we're speaking inside a dishwasher. Bah. It won't be posted on the interweb after all.

Tuesday 10th September 2013

It would be entirely inappropriate for me to tell the members of my branch how to vote in the ranking of MEP candidates at tonight's meeting. So, I 'just happen' to invite Bill Etheridge and Tim Aker to be our guest speakers. It's merely a coincidence that they're standing as candidates for the West Midlands and Eastern area respectively.

Star Etheridge had wanted to come down and speak, too, as Disability Spokeswoman. She's welcome, but the meeting at the Greenwich Tavern is up a flight of stairs.

'Oh, don't worry about that," she said. "Do you mind carrying me up with Bill?'

'Not at all. You'll be like the Queen of Sheba and we'll strew your path with flowers.'

Sadly, Star's feeling a bit under the weather on the day so Bill comes alone and Tim has a hustings in Essex so has to cancel.

We need two replacement speakers at short notice. This means people who can get to Greenwich quickly. Unfortunately, I've entirely forgotten both the names and the contact details of all the other candidates who'll be standing in London. So I invite Janice Atkinson and

Patricia Cullinan who are going for South East Area instead. Fancy that.

Sunday 15th September 2013

As Davy Coburn is going to be a candidate for Scotland he asks me to come to his branch's meeting at the King's Arms in Bexley. There's about twenty people there, most of whom I haven't met before. A quick informal speech but no beers at all because I've driven down. Coburn hasn't invited and will not be inviting any other applicants for the London List to his manor. He's endorsing me and nobody else. Good man.

Wednesday 18th September 2013

This is my last invitation to address a branch meeting before conference, namely UKIP Eastbourne at the Hydro Hotel along with Janice Atkinson, Ray Finch and Nigel Jones. There's a turnout of over a hundred and I'm the last speaker. Godfrey Bloom MEP has been causing a bit of trouble recently with his silly comments so I open with this.

'Good evening everybody. I do notice that this is being filmed so in the circumstances I will be very careful not to mention "Bongo Bongo Land".'

A splendid speech by me overall, but I have to leave early to catch the last train.

CHAPTER ELEVEN

In, Out, Shake It All About

Friday 20th September 2013

THE AUTUMN CONFERENCE is taking place in London. Boo. No weekend away or boozing into the early hours then. The missis will expect me to be getting the last tube home.

Nigel calls just as I'm getting ready to head out.

'Morning. I take it you're coming?'

'Dang right. Looking forward to it. Especially after Channel 4 News.'

Last night's episode had included some guff from Michael Crick about how one of Farage's school teachers had thought he was 'Literally Hitler'. Barrel-scraping.

'Yes. I know,' says Nigel. 'Do me a favour then. There's a film maker called Martin Durkin who's making a documentary about the party. Well, actually, about me.'

'Really? That's great. We've arrived.'

'Anyway, he's interviewing a few people. Would you be happy being one of them?'

'Definitely.'

'And no messing about. This is very serious and an outstanding opportunity. They might want some more established members but I'll give his crew your number.'

I'm at Methodist Central Hall just before nine and head straight inside to pick a choice seat. Not the front row, but the second. That will avoid the possibility of my view being obstructed by the hairy arsecracks of the massed photographers who are taking up space in front of the stage.

Farage is in peak form for his speech which is laying the path for both the EU and the local elections. He is soon sweating heavily. The impression left is not of disgust as was the case when Tony Blair once took off his jacket while foolishly wearing a pale blue shirt. It is of passion.

Yet there's a warning tagged on to his words in the aftermath of the Channel 4 muckraking.

'They decided not to go for the ball but to go for the player. And I am afraid we will be subject to a whole series of smears running up to next year's elections. And the elections beyond.'

Anyway, the whole thing's been broadcast live on BBC Parliament and is certain to be the lead story on every single lunchtime bulletins. Guess where we're all going now? That's right. The Westminster Arms.

Then rumours start coming through that Godfrey Bloom's been silly again. He's called women who don't clean behind the fridge "sluts" and, if that wasn't bad enough, has thwacked Michael Crick over the head with a conference brochure after the journalist had asked him why there were no black faces on its cover.

The pub has a TV in the corner which is tuned to the news. The footage becomes non-stop UKIP. Not of Nigel's speech, but of Godders' exploits.

Just after 5 pm, Crowther exercises his emergency powers as Party Chairman and removes the whip from Bloom. Nigel comes back on stage to say some unscheduled words.

'There is no media coverage of this conference. It's gone. It's dead. It's all about Godfrey hitting a journalist and using an unpleasant four-letter word. It's gone. And we can't put up with it. . .'

There's a standing ovation.

'We cannot have any one individual, however fun, or flamboyant, or entertaining or amusing they are - we cannot have any one individual destroying UKIP's national conference. And that is what he's done today.'

Saturday 21st September 2013

Press attacks on the Party are never-ending. In the aftermath of yesterday I, too, am appalled, but not surprised, to find I've been misquoted. A journo from Short List magazine had asked for a quote and has written up as follows:

'Paul Oakley, a prospective MEP candidate, will merrily reveal "climate change policy leads to fuel poverty – elderly people die over the Christmas period because they can't afford their fuel bill. The Green Party are nan killers.'"

This is a gross slur. I had actually accused the Greens of being 'Nana killers.'

Tuesday 24th September 2013

Our branch Secretary, Ray Adams, has been looking through the membership spreadsheet which comes to us from Head Office.

'We've got a BNP infiltrator,' he tells me.

That's unfortunate, because the Party Rules ban former members of the BNP and other racist groups from joining UKIP. Rightly.

Wikileaks disclosed a BNP members' list which is available all over the internet. It's not updated for obvious reasons and the British National Party aren't going to volunteer further information about their activists. As such, it's not that easy to work out who may or may not have been a member. Ray's sleuthing is therefore impressive.

'How did you find out about him?'

'Easily enough. He stood for them during the Greenwich Council elections in 2010 and got over 800 votes.'

I speak to the Party Chairman.

Monday 7th October 2013

Votes for the ranking of the MEP candidates for London have been counted as follows.

1 Gerard Batten 26,093
2 Paul Oakley 8,627
3 Elizabeth Jones 4,667
4 Lawrence Webb 4,275
5 Alastair McFarlane 2,869
6 Andrew McNeilis 2,736
7 Anthony Brown 1,750
8 Peter Whittle 1,278

I could take issue with the rule-breaking by Gerard's team and the mass-mailing of supporters. However, this result, backed by his 9 years of proven incumbency as an MEP, is overwhelming and that'd be churlish. I decide to do nothing.

Friday 18th October 2013

Steve Crowther writes to the BNP interloper within our branch.

'Following letters sent to you by Paul Oakley, chairman of UKIP Greenwich and Lewisham without reply, we have reason to believe that you stood in the 2010 local elections in the interest of the British National Party.

'I am therefore revoking your membership of UKIP with immediate effect. Your subscription is returned herewith.'

Steve is most kind about the letters I sent out to the chap.

'Exemplary. I may use them as a model for any future cases.'

Great. We have to take this seriously.

Monday 21st October 2013

LRC meeting again. I'm not late, surprisingly enough.

'Well done, Oakers,' says chairman David Coburn. 'Almost as good a placing as me in Scotland.'

He's been ranked by members at number 1 north of the border. He'd wanted to stand in London, but Nigel had persuaded him to do otherwise and sacrifice himself. Good call, although it's doubtful he'll be elected. Party before personal ambition every time, and rightly so.

There are however some rumblings from the committee.

'When are you going to stand down as London Chairman David? You can't do both,' queries Lucy Bostick.

'Piffle,' smiles Davy. 'You're not getting rid of me that easily and I'll be back down in the smoke soon enough after the election.'

Sunday 27th October 2013

As ever on Sunday nights when facing a trial first thing the next morning, I'm prevaricating about actually doing any work. Then an intriguing email arrives.

'Please would you be kind enough to phone me when convenient.

'Perhaps you recall me as a former GLYC vice-chairman - or did you take lofty office much later?

'We may have some mutual contacts in south-east London which might make for an interesting chat.

'Regards,
'Julian Grainger'

'Glick', by the way, stands for Greater London Young Conservatives. Julian's a current Tory Councillor for Chelsfield (and Pratts Bottom). From what I've heard through Bromley Kippers, he's a good councillor even though in the wrong party. Unfortunately, the Conservatives have deselected him as a candidate for the upcoming local elections.

I give him a call.

Julian's keen to remain a councillor. We speak for 25 minutes and it's pretty obvious what he's thinking about doing although he skirts around the issue. He also forgets to mention his deselection. But I know all. And see: all.

Most interestingly, he implies that other local Tories are having similar thoughts.

I give the chairman of UKIP Bromley, Owen Brolly, a ring. Being a good-mannered sort of chap it's obvious that Owen and his branch have to handle this.

Nigel then calls.

'Keep things quiet but you've got the go-ahead to meet Grainger and start talks. The more councillors we can bring over, the better. It'll be a major media event if we can manage it.'

Friday 1st November 2013

The Partridge in Bromley serves decent real ale and this is why it's the venue for this illicit tryst. Owen Brolly and Julian Grainger are already there when I arrive.

Julian explains that he has always been a 'Eurosceptic', little realising that we don't like that term. Black-ish mark. He'll have to undergo some minor political re-education.

He touches on the possibility of other councillors coming over. There are three, and he's testing the water on behalf of them all.

'How many activists do you have?' he asks.

'Fewer than we'd like.'

'How much campaign funding is available?'

'Not a lot.'

He seems less enthused.

'Oh,' I add. 'By the way, Simon Fawthrop from your branch called me up the other day. Hadn't heard from him in ages. We had a lovely chat about nothing at all but I take it he's guessed what's going on.'

I leave them to it and catch the bus up to the Ravensbourne Arms where Tim Aker beats me at darts.

Monday 18th November 2013

It's the London Region meeting at the Butler's Head. Dull until it's over. But then, before we head downstairs to the bar, Coburn's harried by a mob led by Roger Gravett.

'You've got to step down David. There's no way you can campaign in Scotland and chair London at the same time.'

'I can be in two places at once you know. More or less. There are such things as trains and planes.'

'No. You can't. Give it up.'

I'm inclined to back Coburn and have been open about it. That's probably why I was unaware that tonight he'd be given an offer he cannot refuse.

Thursday 14th November 2013

Councillor Julian Grainger formally defects from the Conservatives to UKIP. A few photos are taken which don't interest the press.

Looks like our offer wasn't attractive to the other prospective traitors. He's come over alone.

Monday 25th November 2013

UKIP Merton are having myself and Coburn to speak. There's also someone called Suzanne Evans on the bill. She was until recently a Tory councillor but has just come to UKIP along with her colleague Richard Hilton.

As I arrive Davy's already addressing a packed hall. He's wearing his signature outfit of a white v-neck sweater and a buff jerkin.

When it's my turn I naturally express admiration for him.

'Everyone loves your medieval cricketer's costume David, but you could have worn a suit.'

Lots of audience questions afterwards.

'If we do withdraw from the EU, what will be the purpose of UKIP?' asks one.

'Oh, don't worry about that,' I reply. 'We need to get out of the dastardly UN next.'

It's very nice to meet Coburn's partner Crawford at long last afterwards as well.

Saturday 30th November 2013

Party benefactor Alan Bown is organising an action day in Folkestone. There's a local opinion poll a few days from now and he wants to maximise our results by hitting the town beforehand. Nigel, Gerard and the press will be there. Even better, Alan's going to buy everyone a pub lunch afterwards. Yes. Everyone.

I take the HS1 train from Stratford with Peter Lello. Never used it before. It is indeed a breathtaking marvel of engineering. The countryside speeds by and we're there very quickly indeed. Love it! But UKIP will still be battling against the HS2 white elephant nonetheless.

Local party members have arranged to collect incomers by car from the station. Ours doesn't turn up after half an hour and I don't have a number for them. It's blinking freezing and I can't get hold of John Moran, Gerard or Jack Duffin to see where we're supposed to go. I try Nigel and go into a grumpy explanation as to where we are, how we don't know the town and have no idea what we're meant to be doing.

Nigel's still at home.

'I'm very sorry,' he says.

'What's happened? Are you double-booked?'

'No, it's not that. I'm flat on my back being waited-on by Kirsten.' Luxuriant indolence eh? Sound! Except that it isn't.

'My spine's playing up. I've just had an operation, otherwise I'd have been there.'

The aftermath of the plane crash of course, about which the compassionate left regularly laugh. You can be sure that if this dynamo says he's in pain then it's going to be very bad indeed. The bloke nonetheless sounds sheepish about 'letting us down'. Legend.

Anyway. The stall is in fact only about a 10-minute walk away. Gerard's already there handing out leaflets. Although it's Saturday, the town centre isn't that busy, doubtless as a consequence of the brass monkeys. There's a positive takeup nonetheless. Lunch is at the Fountains Pub in Seabrook Road. Shepherd's pie, then we're back out for a bit more campaigning before it gets too dark.

Gerard leaves early as he's standing in for Nigel at a golf club dinner later that night because of the leader's indisposition. He thinks the guests will be grumpy at the late change and they probably will. Yet although he lacks Farage's star quality, Batten's very good at relating tales to make the flesh creep. They ought to be grateful.

Saturday 7th December 2013

Anarcho-punk band Conflict are playing a pop concert at the Underworld in Camden. Vegan supporters of the Animal Liberation Front and opponents of the police, their gigs are hard left, occasionally marked with violence and always a wonderful aural assault.

The bash starts at lunchtime but I've been instructed to run errands by my other half so have emailed Conflict's vocalist Colin Jordan.

'What time do the Subhumans and then you come on stage? I'm not allowed to "spend all day at some bloody punk thing".'

He replies:

'Ha ha ha, well I've bloody got to mate.

'Subhumans are on 7.45 until 8.30

'Conflict are on at 9.00 until 10.15

'Shouldn't tempt you but Subhumans have confirmed for Sunday too.'

The venue's laden with 'Class War' crusties and sold out. I make a special effort to enjoy the gig. The trouble is that if I'm elected as a UKIP MEP (and inevitably become a celebrity) I'll never be able to go to one of these live outings again or I'd be stabbed, bricked, bottled, coshed or otherwise abused. Sad, but a sacrifice worth making.

Tuesday 7th January 2014

The cold, dead hands of Davy Coburn are wrested from the chairmanship of UKIP London. Actually, he goes gracefully in the end.

I propose Peter Staveley as his replacement who receives 5 votes. Roger Gravett, Chairman of Enfield and Haringey, has 11 and thus is duly-elected.

CHAPTER TWELVE

This Thing Just Got Real

Monday 13th January 2014

JIM WHEBLE AT *BBC LONDON NEWS* has been in touch with head office about a Muswell Hill church soup kitchen which is starting up next week.

'Basically', he says, 'this has been set up to help homeless Romanians, feed them, and help them with their statutory rights and how to get a job.'

They need a party spokesman and Michael Heaver decides that the task falls to me.

I'm not a fan of *BBC London News*. I don't share its chronic obsessive compulsion about schools and the NHS which bulk out every bloody bulletin. They're not fans of The Kip either. Michael tells me this:

'Use soft language if possible - this situation isn't healthy for the UK nor for these migrants coming here and living in desperate squalor.'

It's being filmed at the BBC HQ near Oxford Street tube at teatime. It's pissing down when I get to street level and I don't have a brolly. Clearly, the PC gods who protect the Beeb don't want me in their lair.

Tuesday 14th January 2014
BBC Breakfast air the footage when I'm still in bed.

'They shouldn't be stopped from getting assistance either from the local authority that they're living in or from charities to help them. But I really would much prefer it if they hadn't come here in the first place. We've got enough of a problem with homelessness in London as it is. We don't need to add to it.'

Various pals send rude texts and emails telling me how I've put them off their breakfast. Sophie posts a screenshot on Facebook in which my golden teeth are in full view. Don't care. I've just been on the BBC. And they have not.

Tuesday 21st January 2014

I'm speaking along with Batten and this new-fangled Suzanne Evans lady at the Morden Assembly Hall.

Due to a problem on the line caused by torrential rain, I and an entire trains-worth of commuters is dumped on the platform at West Croydon station. I take the tram the rest of the way. Although having nearly been killed by them on several occasions in Croydon town centre, I've never actually ridden one before. Suzanne comes to pick me up at the tramstop. It's still pouring.

Being late, I've missed the sole demonstrator outside who left as the meeting began. Gerard's already speaking and has one of their leaflets on the table in front which I read as he carries on. It accuses UKIP of the usual things like eating babies and cheating at Hungry Hippos. Can't really recall because it goes in one eye and out the other.

Batten receives solid applause and I'm on.

'Sorry about the rain. It's probably these pesky gays again. Apologies for my tardiness too. We vow that when UKIP come to power we will ensure that the trains run on time.'

Although there are a few party activists there, the majority of those present are real people. The questions afterwards are sympathetic, except from a cluster of four sitting together who look like teaching assistants.

There are two over-utilised political catchphrases of the moment which make my teeth itch. One is used by Tories: 'hard-working families'. The other is used by lefties: 'celebrate the rich diversity'.

Behold. One of this suspicious group use the latter as an argument of sorts against our immigration stance which I and Suzanne stomp on. There's general tutting from the rest of the audience and the revolutionaries pipe down.

In refusing to own a smartphone, I'm initially unaware of a minor drama which has developed. The celebratey-lady is a local school teacher called Jackie Schneider and has been incontinently Tweeting throughout.

'58 white people listening to Merton UKIP councillor blaming spending on translation services'

'Imagine being in a room with 50 UKIP supporters foaming at the mouth about immigration #mylot'

Wednesday 22nd January 2014
Richard Hilton makes a formal complaint to Schneider's employers. This makes me uneasy. We expect the hard left to crush dissent by attacking those they disagree with at their workplace and elsewhere. UKIP ought to be better than that.

In any event, she'd also sent out these Tweets on the night itself.

'Turns out my impassioned contribution in defence of immigration hasn't persuaded UKIP audience'
'I am trying to persuade people at UKIP meeting that Immigrants are not the problem #failing'
'Perfectly safe at UKIP meeting but weary at prospect of members putting me straight once meeting finishes'
'I'm not worried about physical safety but worried I can't convince good people you are wrong!'

She was correct about all of those things. So we actually won.

Monday 3rd February 2014
The upper level of the Counting House pub in the city of London is, as we know, a UKIP lair. A launch for the MEP campaign is being held tonight.

I could just deliver a speech saying how well we're going to do and how hard we need to work and so on, but everyone else is going to say pretty much the same thing.

The Kip has been receiving a lot of adverse coverage recently as groups like Hope not Hate, Unite Against Fascism, Action 2014 and Brit Influence are trawling the net looking for off-colour quotes from our people. It's time to fight back.

'Here's something you can do,' I tell the crowd. 'Type the words "Labour", "Lib Dem" or "Tory" and "councillor convicted" into Google and see what comes up. Use what you find.'
I then set out recent infractions by several rogues.

From Labour, there is Haringey Councillor Nilgun Canver who's just been convicted of perverting the course of justice. And Councillor Geoff Hammond from Waltham Forest who has stolen £100,000 from a charity.

Then there are the lovely Liberal Democrats. Derek Osbourne, Council Leader of Kingston Upon Thames is in choky for child porn offences. And who can forget Tiverton's Kevin Wilson who's just been done for benefit fraud?

The Tories don't get off either. David Whittaker from the Isle of Wight took the view that it was appropriate to have sexual activity with a child and John Morgan of the Vale of White Horse believed it was a good idea to steal from a widow.

The crowd are chuffed and I decide there and then to use this as a party piece at all public meetings during the campaign.

'That's all folks', I conclude. 'Be great to have a beer with you all, but I'm in court in Cambridge first thing.'

I head off, wrongly assuming that everyone present knows Oakley's a lawyer. This isn't so. I'm later told that a few people thought that I, too, was facing criminal charges.

Tuesday February 18th 2014
We're having our branch meeting at The Hobgoblin in Forest Hill and choosing the UKIP candidate for Lewisham Mayor. The vote for this is on the same day as the EU elections.

There are two applicants, and the Head of my Personal Bodyguard, Peter Lello, is selected over Geoff Fleming.

I'm particularly pleased by Peter's win, but either would have been fine and neither will embarrass us with fantastical headlines in the tabloids.

Tuesday 4th March 2014
Off to Brussels today with the other top-end MEP candidates. Subsidised of course. I sit with Coburn on the Eurostar out who brings me up to speed on events north of the border. There had been sour faces at Davy's installation as the favoured choice on the list and six of the other nine applicants had stood down in protest.

Scotland chairman Paul Henke then blabbed about the background to the *Sunday Herald*. In response, Steve Crowther, as national chairman, had superbly suspended his membership: for one hundred years.

Sadly, Judge Taylor at Central London County Court has just ruled that she's unimpressed by Crowther acting in such a waggishly Neronian way. She'd overturned the suspension with £30,000 costs payable by the party on top.

'And Henke told us this morning that he's defecting to the Tories after all. The wee nyaff,' Coburn informs me.

We book into our hotels on arrival and then head directly to the EU parliament for a canteen lunch. We gorge on a variety of morsels, but have to pay for our repasts ourselves. No big deal, as it's very cheap. In fact, extremely cheap because it's heavily-subsidised. My pocket approves but my ideology does not.

By 2 pm we're settled in a conference room around a half-moon table, applicants and current UKIP MEPs alike. Nigel Farage and Stuart Agnew lead the briefing about the facilities, groups and staffing arrangements. Boring but necessary.

'What are the provisions for expenses for a UK office?' I ask.

Agnew answers.

'I'm not entirely sure but it's around £9,000 a year. Although they aren't expenses, but an allowance.'

I'm planning to have a London HQ but not just an office, rather a 'shop' which will be accessible by the public and allow them to have direct contact with their MEP. I've been looking at premises south of London Bridge station and down Borough High Street. This area is within Zone 1 so easily reachable, but it's relatively shabby so the rents are reasonable. Not quite so reasonable as the £9K limit permits however.

'Oh, we're aware of that,' Agnew tells us. 'And it's a flat rate too. Many of the east European members are able to buy their offices outright on that sort of money but it's going to be tight for you.'

Not to worry. The rest of the rent can be covered by my general MEP allowances. We'll sort it. This will be a priority for me.

An early dinner follows and the existing MEPs flit from table to table to speak to us. Nigel comes over to our Mess. A week or so ago he'd been interviewed by Andrew Neil and it had been different from all Farage's previous TV appearances. On this occasion, our leader wasn't treated as an amusing eccentric to be indulged but instead given proper cross-examination. More proof that we've arrived. Neil focussed on his failure to publish details of his expenses as he'd promised to do. Nigel floundered. Badly.

'You really need to be better-prepared in future,' I advise.

He takes that badly, too, and I receive my first ever Farage furnacing.

Wednesday 5th March 2014

It's been years since I was previously in Brussels. Last time was a freebie, jointly-organised by the European Court of Justice and Grays

Inn. It was a wonderful trip, made more memorable by a letter which one of the ECJ Judges, D A O Edward, had then written to the Deputy Under-Treasurer (Students) at the Inn. Miss Margaret Chadderton had summoned me to her office after our return to London.

'Do not sit down, Oakley,' she'd ordered.

So I remained where I was. One simply did not mess about with this stern northern Boudiccan.

'There's been a formal complaint about your scornful attitude on this trip.'

Shit.

'And what's the Inn going to do Miss Chadderton?'

Final Bar exams were coming up.

'Do? Oh, nothing. Nothing whatsoever.' She almost managed to suppress her grin. 'Be off with you and never darken my door again.'

I always admired that woman.

Anyway, the reason I'm telling you this is because Aurelie Laloux is taking us on a tour of the city today and in the many years since I was last here, the EU octopus has been growing. And growing. And growing. Back then its buildings had already occupied a significant amount of the city but now it's spread even further. There are cranes and trucks and hoardings and concrete in every direction as the EU occupies even more Brussels real estate. So that's where Britain's £320 million weekly membership fees are going.

May we, the humble taxpayers, cast a gaze upon the results of our compulsory largesse? We try to look through the glass window in the door to the parliament chamber. There's little to see as it's not in session but some helpful security staff head over to assist anyway.

'*Bouge-toi. C'est interdit!*'

So the answer is no.

It's permissible for us to take a peek at our own MEPs' offices though. These are allocated by the parliamentary authorities and designation reflects the regard in which each party is held by them. So UKIP rooms don't have panoramic views of the city, wood panelling or paintings on loan from the Musée Oldmasters.

That doesn't matter as I've already decided how to decorate my own office. A company has started producing posters of the covers of the 1970s war comic books, 'Commando' and one is perfect. 'The English Resistance' depicts two guerrillas despatching Wehrmacht officers with sub-machine guns.

The only reasonable areas at which to sightsee are the Grande Place and its nearby Manneken Pis, both of which we proudly pronounce in the English manner while buying our strong Trappist ales to drink in the sunshine.

And on the Eurostar home we eschew our seats and instead stand in the bar and consume its entire stock of beers.

CHAPTER THIRTEEN

Three Million Jobs, My Arse

Friday 7th March 2014

I'VE BEEN INVITED to speak to the South Hampstead High School for girls at the Jewish Community Centre. The European Movement have sourced a 'pro' speaker.

My enemy's an old fart who's far too ancient to click with these young ladies, Martyn Bond. Unfortunately, he does click with them and buys them off by handing out posters and comics depicting the wonders of the EU. He stresses the issues which always resonate with young people, namely, the ability to study on the continent and to pay reduced phone bills while there.

I disagree.

'Great that you can use the Erasmus programme. Except most of you won't. And wonderful that those mobile calls are cheap. Except EU immigration means you'll never own a home unless your parents help out. These "benefits" are "beads and firewater".'

They're not convinced and issues move on. One young meany asks what UKIP will be called if Scotland eventually leaves the Union.

'That's easy,' I say. 'We shall become the Wales, England and Northern Ireland Independence Party. Or "We-Nip" for short.'

Laughter from the hall for the first time.

Makes no difference though. There's a vote by the pupils and I lose very badly indeed.

Sunday 16th March 2014

A chap called Nick Denys is having me on his debate show, 'House of Comments'. The subject: 'What is the EU Parliament For?' The opposition are to be Annesley Abercorn (a Conservative activist whom I vaguely know) and Ivana Bartolletti from Labour who's way down on their MEP list for London.

It'll be by Skype but audio-only. It's a similar set-up to the increasingly common use of telephone hearings by the Courts. I have on occasion 'appeared' at those hearings from the comfort of my home study whilst sitting in my underpants and a dirty sweatshirt. I still manage to sound pompously professional, as will be the case today.

The debate gets going and it isn't long before Bartoletti comes up with the old myth.

'Let's not forget that 3 million UK jobs depend on Europe.'

I'm not having that and put her right. This nonsense is based on a study carried out by Professor Ian Begg at the LSE. All he'd concluded was that 3 million jobs are associated with EU demand. That's not the same as saying they'll go when we leave the European Union. He's been vocal in the press with his irritation but Bartoletti obviously hadn't heard.

The show closes with a question about our respective priorities for an alternative British budget. Abercorn wants to lower the tax burden for those on lower or middle incomes, cut beer duty and give pubs a helping hand to keep them open. So some Tories are still sensible.

Wednesday 19th March 2014

I've been invited to address a meeting of UKIP Sutton and Cheam at the Carshalton Social Club this evening but feel a Disturbance in the Force so decide to double-check the details about an hour before leaving.

'Oh. We've had to cancel it. Didn't anyone tell you?'

No. They did not. Sometimes I despair about the organisational attributes of our party. Actually, most of the time.

Tuesday 25th March 2014

The European Society at University College London have asked my good self and other would-be MEPs to a hustings on the Bloomsbury campus. Given the probability that all these youngsters will be pro-EU, I take the precaution of inviting members of our branch along too. It's an open meeting after all.

Peter Whittle's smoking outside as I arrive.

'Is there a good turnout?'

He laughs.

'No. Half the people there are from the branch.'

Indeed they are. Students obviously aren't very interested in the EU and as my lot are hardly going to throw lances of attack in my direction, the essential aggression that I require at every hustings is lacking. What a waste of an evening.

There's one good bit though and it's from the Lib Dem geezer, Jonathan Fryer, who's second on their MEP list. As the meeting's coming to a close he says this.

No - honestly, I'm not making it up.

He actually does.

What a nong.

'As far as I'm concerned, calling for EU withdrawal is Treason!'

Well, hand me a musket and call me a Minuteman.

Saturday 12th April 2014

UKIP London's election launch is at the Abbey Centre in Great Smith Street. This is a serious event aimed at the Kippers who'll be fighting for council seats for the first time in their lives. Batten, Staveley, Webb and Richard King are delivering the sermons.

Richard's is the most important. He takes the prospective candidates through the process of getting their papers signed and filed with the returning officers.

He tells of the importance of having leaflets approved by the Regional Organisers.

He describes the process of creating web pages.

And setting up email accounts.

That's because a great many of these retirees have had no reason to use the internet at any prior time in their lives. I'm absolutely serious. God bless them, but these are the people who'll be facing the greased machinery of the old parties. It'll be a revelation for them.

Whittle, Staveley and I wander over to the Westminster Arms while the event's still winding down and the conversation turns to our scrutineers in the wider world.

Back in 2012, an academic called Matthew Goodwin had co-authored an hysterical study for those tossers at Hope not Hate entitled 'From voting to violence? Far right extremism in Britain.' That work had sought to find a common thread between UKIP and the BNP on 'armed resistance'.

Whilst some of the grandpas in UKIP doubtless dream of bashing urchins over the head with a rolled-up *Daily Express*, the premise was laughable. However, Goodwin's moved on from that piece of juvenilia and, three weeks ago, published a new book on UKIP alone: *Revolt on the Right*. On the back of intriguing reviews I'd bought it in the week of release.

'Lads,' I tell them. 'We couldn't afford to pay for all the information about our target voters which we're getting for free in this book. You have to read it. Number 1 priority.'

Thanks for all your help, Matthew!

Monday 14th April 2014

In order to stand as an MEP candidate, head office requires all applicants to sign the 'MEP Charter'. Strictly confidential, it's not to be copied or circulated either inside or outside the party. It covers staffing, spokesmanships, research, campaigning and so on. Also this:

> Every candidate for election as a UKIP MEP commits that they will, if elected
>
> . . .
>
> (2) Remain a member of UKIP throughout their Parliamentary term of office, and resign their seat in the Parliament if they:
> - cease to be a member of the party
> - resign the whip or
> - are unable to continue to follow the policies of the party.

Sensible. As the election's decided on a party list system, none of the successful candidates will have any personal mandate. The voters will cast their ballot for UKIP and rightly-expect to be represented by UKIP at all times.

I've no hesitation in agreeing to this and sign. Every other candidate will have done so too.

Tuesday 15th April 2014

The emails and calls have been hailing down all day. Much of it's essential, but a lot is irritating. This is a smashing one from a student.

I would love to know how you would respond to the push

from the public to have UKIP in the live election debate. I would also like to know what effect the Maria Miller Scandal has had on UKIP. Do you believe it has helped you gain supporters? Any other opinions on the forthcoming European elections and UKIP's growing popularity would be much appreciated.

Isn't it normal to get your Mummy to do your homework rather than a complete stranger? I tell her that I'm not going to write her essay but will chat to her if she wants to come to tonight's Greenwich and Lewisham AGM. We should have had this by the end of March. Although we've been too busy campaigning, it can't be postponed any longer. All of the officers' posts are up for re-election.

Nobody wants to challenge Ray Adams as Secretary, Paul Butler as Treasurer or Peter Lello as Head of my Personal Bodyguard. But I'm to be defied for the chairmanship by that upstart Anthony. Again.

This time his challenge is irritating. I (rarely) dream of being El Presidente for life but we're in the middle of elections and a rational person might think that if an MEP candidate is hoofed from his branch chairmanship then the press will have something to say. Apparently not.

In order to get this nonsense out of the way I open the meeting and immediately move to the officer elections.

'Anthony. Would you like to speak first?'
He gripes, saying that he hadn't expected it to be the opening item and that he isn't ready.

'Tough shit, Tony', I thought to myself.

'We have to get this out of the way first before moving on to the important stuff, the councillor nominations,' I actually say.

This is probably even ruder than my internalised musing.

He addresses the meeting acutely-unprepared. There's tutting from around the room and Ken Webb sighs loudly and rolls his eyes.

It's my go. Haven't prepared anything either and speak for less than a minute: 'Steady hand on the tiller', 'changing horses midstream', that sort of guff.

Questions follow. None for me. Several for Anthony. Ray Adams' is the best.

'So why haven't you come out campaigning on any of our action days?'
Tony gulps like a tench in a landing net.

The ballot papers are handed out and collected by the committee.

I don't watch the counting of the piles of voting slips although can't help noticing that one is an actual pile while the other is a single piece of paper. Ray announces the result. My speech is short.

'I'm not taking anything for granted, but if elected to the European Parliament we'll be doing this again in a few weeks as I'll be stepping down.'

Anthony seems interested by this but he shouldn't be.

Wednesday 23rd April 2014

Gerard Batten tells me he reckons that we'll both be elected in London. Together, perhaps, with a third MEP if we push hard.

That would be Elizabeth Jones.

We need about 18% of the poll to get the pair of us in anyway. We need to take votes from elsewhere. A lot of those will be from the Tories, obviously. Labour will come top in the capital but we're also seeing signs of disaffected old-left voters considering UKIP too.

Bob Crow had sadly died last month. Harassed commuters remember him primarily for inconveniencing them as head of the RMT union. However, he was also a committed opponent of the EU and had stood at the last European elections under the No2EU standard. It's possible that some of that support will now drift towards us.

There hasn't been any news from the British National Party. Their leader Nick Griffin has just been bankrupted. The party itself has financial troubles following its failed legal fight with the Equality Commission to open up membership to non-whites. As they need a £10K deposit to put up candidates in London alone they might not have the cash to stand. Great!

And the English Democrats are unlikely to be a problem at all.

Wednesday 23rd April 2014

Claudia-Liza Armah from the new London Live TV channel has started following me on Twitter. She used to do those 30-second news updates on late night telly but now presents a proper programme. I follow back as fast as you like and she sends a direct message.

'Hi Paul. What's the best email to get you on? Would like to invite you onto London Live lunch show Headline London this Friday 25th April xx'

I'll certainly be there. But then there's a problem.

'Hi Paul. As we're nearing election period I'm afraid we can't have you on the show.

'Unless we have equal representation from other parties. If u were to come on and talk about non UKIP subjects that would be fine.

'We are planning lots of discussions on Europe during elections so it would be great to get you in for that in future! Is that ok at all? Xx'

Blast. Electoral law is designed to do-down UKIP at every turn. As for Friday, it's probably not worth having me on just for the sake of it:

'The only things I know about other than politics are punk rock & fishing. Which aren't very interesting.'

I tell the missis what's happened while I'm ironing her blouses in the bedroom and she's out of sight in the study. She informs me that I only want to do it because I fancy Claaaaudia-Liiiizaaa and instructs me to stop smiling.

I tell her that I don't and wasn't but go a bit red in the face nonetheless.

CHAPTER FOURTEEN

Swindled by the Establishment

Thursday 24th April 2014

THE OFFICIAL LIST of all MEP candidates is published by the Electoral Commission. The BNP are standing in London after all. Oh well, we'll just have to squash them too.

And – hang on. Second-to-top of the alphabetical list is something calling itself 'An Independence from Europe' and their description is 'UK Independence Now'. UKIP itself is at the very end of the list.

What the fuck?

At the 1994 EU elections, Giles Chichester was returned as a Tory MEP having polled a margin of 700 votes over his Liberal Democrat rival, Adrian Sanders. Also on the ballot paper was another candidate, described as a 'Literal Democrat.' That person had taken 10,000 votes thus denying Sanders victory. Although a Tory at the time, I still thought this a seedy way for us to win the seat. Sanders took it to the High Court but his claim was dismissed, nothing unlawful having taken place.

There followed a number of similar cases where candidates put themselves forward as 'New Labour', 'Labor Party', 'Conservatory Party', 'Conversative Party' and 'Liberal Democrat Top Choice for Parliament'.

One of the few decent things the Blair government did was to introduce the Registration of Political Parties Act 1998. The idea was to put a stop to counterfeit parties. That act was replaced by the Political Parties, Elections and Referendums Act 2000 which gave the responsibility for this process to the Electoral Commission.

Surely we can seek redress? I call Matt Richardson as UKIP's lawyer.

'We're having words with the Commission but there's nothing we can do.'

He mentions section 28A of the Act. The question of whether a proposed name is permissible or not is at the sole discretion of the Electoral Commission. There's no right of appeal. Accordingly, whoever approved 'UK Independence Now' is a moron. Or possibly something more sinister, and as the decision was taken so long ago we're outside the time limit for seeking a judicial review. There's nothing we can do.

So who are the candidates for this shiny new party? Its leader is UKIP's former MEP Mike Nattrass who's standing in the West Midlands. All of those putting their names up in London live around Slough and I know nothing about them. Their lead choice for Eastern area is that former Kipper with the skid-mark aura. A poisonous git, this is wholly-unsurprising.

Yet I'm disappointed to see Chris Pain as their top candidate for the East Midlands. I've had many a pint with him and enjoyed his company. I tell him what I think:

'"UK Independence Now"? What repugnant cynicism. Absolutely disgusting.'

He's not having it:

'I can think of actions by UKIP's leadership that were disgusting towards myself, think they stated that's Politics! Pas pour moi!'

It won't have any effect on Nigel's chance of being elected, nor will it worry those at the top of the regional lists. It certainly will affect those lower down those lists in harder areas. Mr Pain's cold revenge will hit me smack in the chops.

I'm therefore not in the best mood when meeting Peter Lello at the office of the returning officer, Malcolm Constable, in Lewisham town hall. As our mayoral candidate, Lello had already filed his nomination papers long in advance of the deadline for doing so which is going to close within minutes. He now needs to pay his deposit and also cough up for the entry in the election booklet which is going to every household.

Constable counts the cash and rises from behind his desk.

'I'll just lock this away and get you a receipt.'

As he does so, Lello's phone rings.

'Oh,' he says. 'It's Stephen O'Hare from Greenwich council.'

He engages in the usual chit-chat and then starts to frown before hanging up.

'Right. All of our Greenwich candidates have been approved to stand. . .'

'Great news,' I interrupt. 'We can relax.'

'I hadn't finished,' he carries on. 'All, that is, bar one. He just dropped off the form at the front desk and walked away. Hadn't put the electoral numbers in. Stephen would have helped him but as he didn't hang around, he couldn't.'

And the name of this person who has left the voters in one Greenwich ward without a UKIP box to tick?

Anthony.

Yeah. That one who keeps standing to be branch chairman. Dolt.

Friday 25th April 2014

There's more bad news from Gerard Batten.

'You've seen the London parties I take it?'

'Yes. What devious arseholes Nattrass and his acolytes are.'

'Got that. Thanks. But what about the 4 Freedoms party which will be at the very top of the ballot paper?'

I'd noticed them. They are, presumably, part of the European Peoples' Party or EPP. The only virtuous achievement of David Cameron was to remove the Tory MEPs from that federast group in the EU parliament. I know who these beggars are. A total contrast to the clear philosophy of UKIP.

'Yes,' says Gerard. 'But you're far too over-informed by half. You're not a normal, mainstream voter who isn't a politics-obsessive. Look at their party description. That's what's going to be on the ballot paper.'

Don't follow. Everyone knows about the EPP. Surely?

'You really don't get it, do you?' berates Batten. 'Say their acronym out loud. Go on, say it.'

I do as Gerard asks.

'What, "UKEPP"?'

Fuck.

Fuck. Fuck. Fuck. Fuck. Fuck.

'And,' he observes. 'They're only standing in London and nowhere else.'

Fuck.

Saturday 26th April 2014

Matt Pavey, one of our branch's council candidates, has featured in a *Guardian* article. I could just leave that hanging of course without telling you anything else.

So what's Matt done? He's be-Tweeted, although not 'late at night'.

'Does anyone remember the name Jean Bradley murder unsolved in Acton, London, in 1993. Anyone looking for corruption here? No, thought not.'

'Lets all take a moment to remember Jean Bradley stabbed to death on the streets of London in March 1993 and no justice #stephenlawrence.'

'Lets please take a moment to remember Penny Bell stabbed 50 times in London 1991. No justice #stephenlawrence.'

Matt lives in Downham Ward. One of the councillors there is Liberal Democrat Duwayne Brooks who's also standing for mayor. Matt's been caustic about him online, rightly pointing out that he's turned up to fewer than half of the council's meetings recently. Brooks was a friend of Stephen Lawrence and witnessed his brutal murder so this is why they're running the story.

I have to tell UKIP HQ about what's going on and head of press Patrick O'Flynn isn't happy. I speak to Matt who locks his account.

We agree that he's not to talk to the media any further even though they're certainly interested; he's already been emailed by ITV news asking if he's available.

Yeah, right.

Are the voters of his Whitefoot ward to be swayed by this outrage? We shall see.

Monday 28th April 2014

Chartered Accountants' Hall for a hustings. This is a serious professional event. It's being jointly hosted by the Law Society, the Royal Institute of Chartered Surveyors and ICAEW. I won't get away with the straightforward tub-thumbing which I normally palm off on the punters.

Apart from me, the panel is disgracefully-imbalanced as it's all-female. There's Jean Lambert of the Greens, Caroline Attfield for the Tories, mortal enemy number one, Ivana Bartoletti and mortal enemy number two, Sarah Ludford, who's already an MEP for the Lib Dems.

We're each given a couple of minutes to open. I'm before Ludford and lead with the "3 million jobs" fib which is a well-known Lib Dem argument.

Ludford, who's sitting next to me, shifts from buttock to buttock and back again as I do. Perhaps she's furious that I've taken away her party piece. Perhaps she's simply blowing off in a ladylike manner.

Either way, she doesn't mention that rubbish statistic in the course of the evening and neither does anyone else.

Apart from Ivana Bartoletti. Although, to be fair, she now says that three-and-a-half-million jobs are at risk.

Tuesday 29th April 2014

It's the annual general meeting of my barristers' set. Sir Tony Baldry, also Tory MP for Banbury, is our head of chambers. I'm one of the last to turn up and sit next to Richard Miles who's brought his basset hound along and is sitting next to the post-meeting tray of wine. He opens a bottle, pours a glass for me and takes one for himself. None is offered to anyone else.

I can't stay long and listen with half an ear to the proceedings whilst stroking the hound and then taking a second glass of wine. *Al Jazeera's* 'The Stream' is having me on as a guest shortly. I've been given the choice of appearing by Skype or in a remote studio but chose the latter as it'll avoid the possibility that I look like some weird keyboard warrior. Time to leave.

Baldry's good enough to wish me well and to ask if I'll come back to see them.

'I'm sorry to say that it looks as though you'll be elected,' he smiles.

Although I occasionally watch the electric television and have seen remote interviews, I hadn't realised how they work. On arriving at the studio I'm placed in a dark room with a camera a few feet in front of me. I can't see any other participants and can only hear them through an earpiece. The excellent backdrop through the picture window behind is of the Palace of Westminster.

Abdul Turay, a Brit who's standing for the EU Parliament in Estonia has a dig at The Kip whilst being very pleased with himself at being a candidate in his adoptive nation.

'Paul represents a party that contradicts the very fact that I'm standing for Europe in this election. Could you have imagined that this would be possible if we didn't have such a thing as the European Union?'

Am I meant to be impressed? Nope.

'If you're going to get involved in the politics of another country then you ought to become a citizen of that country. I am absolutely disgusted that people from other European countries can interfere with domestic politics. If you want to become a naturalised citizen in Estonia then good luck to you but otherwise – no.'

'What you're talking about is xenophobia!' he yells.

'Oh, give it a rest. Absolute rubbish.'

Our host chips in to pull us apart. A pity, as I like sparring with this Turay fellah.

'Paul and Abdul, I'm just going to interject for a moment because I'm going to push this conversation on a little bit.'

Amelia Andersdotter of the Swedish Pirate Party tries to give me a kicking.

'UKIP, if I understand correctly, are using their seats in the European Parliament to drain the resources that MEPs get to advance their political views.'

Oooooh. I'm not having that!

'Let's get this straight. "Europe" doesn't have any resources of its own. "Europe" is funded through taxation of the citizens who are members of the European Union. This is our money which we are going to be using to argue the case that there should be no further extension of European law within the European Parliament and at the same time making the case for getting us out.'

Then it comes to the question of a UK referendum.

'Yes,' I concede, 'there's even a possibility that we will lose a referendum in this country but we're not going to stop. We're going to carry on arguing.'

Sakari Puisto of the True Finns is on the sidelines. I'd thought he was One Of Us but am mistaken.

'We are not Eurosceptic at all if you associate it with any kind of far right party or outright leaving the Euro or leaving the EU.'

News to me. I've had the odd pint with top bloke and leader of the True Finns party, Timo Soini. He does want out of the EU. Sakari has to be dragged in to say anything. Anything at all. 'Euroseptics' are completely useless in a scrap.

Anyway, I don't need him. The hour finishes quickly. A car's waiting around the corner outside. It is: a brand new. Black. Mercedes. With tinted windows. It's taking me right to my front door.

I ask the driver to stop off at our grubby local Co-Op as I've got to pick up something for dinner. Everyone stares at this sinister chap who exits from the back of this luxury saloon and then gets back in with a couple of shopping bags. This is both pleasing and troubling to me. I must remain a Man of the People and not be seduced by these fripperies.

Thursday 1st May 2014
AFTERNOON

I decide on McDonalds for a late lunch after court and pick up a copy of the *Evening Standard* on the way. The delicious repast is spoiled by another 'UKIP Unmasked' exposé aimed at our branch. They've now focused the sights on Gary Port who's our Charlton candidate.

They say this about him.

> 'On Facebook, he lists a page about the BNP as "liked". He also "liked" a page for a group called the "South East Alliance" which contains anti-Islam material.
>
> 'Mr Port, a 35-year-old removal man, said of the BNP page: "I 'liked' it, not to join in, but to see what other groups and parties were doing.
>
> 'But he added: "If I was racist I wouldn't be doing the job I'm doing now. I do removals for council tenants and you could probably say the majority of them are ethnic".'

As you may be able to tell, Gary's a first-time candidate. I'm not pleased with the Standard as they've cooked a stew from sinew. I'm not pleased with him because he's been told that all media contact has to be cleared by me.

I tell my enforcer Peter Lello to deal with it. Peter discovers that the pro-EU Russian-owned *Standard* hasn't abided by British standards of fair play. They've gone 'round to the house he shares with his Mum who's let them in to wait for his homecoming. Sneaky dastards.

EVENING

This is an historic occasion. I'm speaking at a hustings at St Mary's church in Putney which last featured in the annals of our nation as a venue for discussions amongst Cromwellians in 1647.

The Putney and Wandsworth Societies have also invited Tory MEP Charles Tannock, Richard Davis for the Lib Dems, Bartoletti and the Green Caroline Allen. It's raining and there are no pubs nearby so I go straight in, nonetheless insolently late. The others are droning on with their openings about how things will be so much better when they're elected. Does anyone still believe that sort of shite nowadays?

On the table in front of all the candidates is a letter from a sitting MEP, I forget who, about the ownership of historic artefacts from Ethiopia/Abyssinia. I assume that one of the other donkeys on the panel had placed it there to show what Good Works their people were doing in the European Parliament. I read it, cast it down, and huff.

Anyway. My turn. I pay homage to God's Englishman and the Parliamentarians, of whom I would definitely have been one. Indeed, I would have happily placed the 60th signature on the king's death warrant in 1649. Roundhead by conviction and by haircut.

Chairman Jonathan Callaway asks each candidate to respond to questions in turn. But he also allows Tannock a final word with a right of reply. I let this go a couple of times but then raise merry hell with him when it happens for the third time.

As the evening progresses, the others gang up on me. Not that I mind.

There's an older Rastafarian in the audience who's taking photographs with a fancy camera and I assume he's from the local rag. However, he then asks a question about the return of Ethiopian artefacts and it's plain that he's the one who's left the fliers on the table. As it happens, I believe that the recognised owners of antiquities should be their nation of origin. And yes, this even applies to the 'Elgin' marbles.

An attendee asks what will we do for them in London if elected. Tannock recites a precise factlet about the number of speeches he's made in the European Parliament. He's proud of this. He's not pleased at my response.

'Nobody's noticed. And nobody cares'.

I discover afterwards that the chap with the camera is Seymour McLean who is himself an independent candidate in the local elections. He's kind enough to post a few photos of me online with the following quotes:

'UKIP winner in Putney on Parade some said, "He was full of swagger" another commented "he was calm and full of confidence under concerted attack from all the other candidates he won because he defended the attacks and did not buckle" all said well done UKIP: the Conservative MEP departed under a barrage of discontented Tory Voters.'

'Putney winners in Order: UKIP the winner 2nd Lib Dem 3rd The Green Candidate 4th the Labour and 5th the Conservative. . .'

Naturally.

Monday 5th May 2014

That chap Ian Dale off the wireless publishes his 'European Election Result Predictions: London.'

UKIP will get two MEPs apparently. Me and Gerard. I like Mr Dale.

Wednesday 7th May 2014

It is PMQs. The Right Honourable Sir Tony Baldry MP, Member of Parliament for Banbury and Head of Chambers at 1 Essex Court asks this question of the Prime Minister:

'Does my right hon. Friend agree that the policies of the UK Independence party are based on fear—fear of the world and fear of foreigners?'

And Dave answers:

'I agree with what he says about UKIP: so much of its view seems to be that we do not have a bright future in this country. I absolutely believe that we do.'

Hmm. You could have asked me at the chambers AGM Tony. The response would have been simple:

'No. No. No.'

CHAPTER FIFTEEN

Stop Them! By Any Means Necessary.

Wednesday 7th May 2014

LISA DUFFY HAD BEEN IN TOUCH a few days prior to this, our London region rally, to see if the branch had any women activists who'd like to be showcased. We did indeed - Barbara Ray, Julie Bassett, Joanne Mullins and Gillian Radcliffe.

But this morning Nigel passed the organising to Steve Woolfe, himself of mixed-race, with a view to concentrating on our BME candidates.

Leftards will be out in force so there's a charge of a fiver to get in. Many of our previous rallies have been oversubscribed and free but the anti-democratic Left have often booked seats and then failed to turn up. If they don't want to hear UKIP speak that's fine. Deliberately stopping others from doing so is not. They can still boycott their seats tonight, of course, but it'll cost them.

Somewhat like an eighties rave, the venue's been changed at the last minute from the Troxy in E1 to the Emmanuel Centre in Westminster. Approaching Marsham Street I can hear the cawing of commies ahead. They have megaphones. I bump into Amjad Bashir, MEP candidate in Yorkshire. Whilst we stroll a spotty white student calls him an Uncle Tom. Amjad ignores the little shite. I tell him to piss off.

There's a fair-sized crowd on the north side of the road held back with barriers. These, like the members of the mob, are inadequate, and a lot of the stinky rabble are milling in front of the venue itself, being just about controlled by the coppers and getting under our feet.

They're chanting ditties, the best of which is:

"U - K - I - P, UKIP you don't speak for me!"

We couldn't agree more.

A senior police officer checks my ID in a sceptical manner and escorts me in to be sure. How rude. Lisa Duffy, who's at the front desk, gives me a nice, big hug. That will do for credentials.

Uncle Mick McGough, a big lad, is standing stern at the top of the stairwell above the mezzanine entrance. Peters Lello and Staveley are with him together with Richard King, martial artiste extraordinaire. They're all noting the various attendees who are clearly not our kin.

I wander into the auditorium as the speakers have already started and stand with Ray Finch, South East Candidate, by the front of the stage. We're scanning the crowd for those who aren't True Believers and soon realise that Leftards really are fucking stupid. If they weren't so stupid they would have dressed to fit in and perhaps acted to fit in as well. Whilst the rest of the crowd cheers and gives the occasional ovation, there are a few sitting in sparse groups or alone with their arms folded, figuratively or otherwise. We eyeball them so that they know that we know.

A group of them in front of us are kids who raise a feeble fuss early on and are booted out.

There are a couple who look like lecturers at a former polytechnic who do not, in the end, cause any trouble at all after Ray and I give them Very Hard Stares.

They're also prone to premature ejaculation, certainly in the sense of protest and probably in other ways, too, for all we know. Rather than wait until Nigel comes on stage for his keynote speech, they are exploding for the less-well-known speakers and thus being 'invited' to leave earlier than they'd expected.

Winston:

'What does that say about UKIP Being racist? A black man running for the leadership? I'm black and I'm proud and I'll shout it out loud!'

A speccy Leftard with a bumfluff beard that doesn't reach his upper lip is thrown out, assisted with a solid shove from Uncle Mick.

Pauline McQueen:

'There I see. Some spoilt middle class children. Who have nothing better to do. And how dare they call us racists. When being a black Jew. And being 60 years of age. I know what racism is.'

More heckling and more evictions.

Woolfie:

'If you don't feel that you can debate the argument. And you want to be childish and immature as though you're back in a university. Well then it's your choice sir. It's your choice.'

By the time of the finale they've all been ejected or cowed as the case may be. Farage is on point.

'The reason we've taken this abuse over the course of the last few weeks, is for the first time in 100 years, a new national political party has come along that has got the establishment rattled. We've got them scared.

'Well we're not going to stand for it. The fightback begins today. We are a respectable, decent political party who, in two weeks' time, are going to cause an earthquake in British politics.'

He receives his standing ovation.

Afterwards we're expecting that the protestors will still be there but they've all buggered off, doubtless to lie to each other about how UKIP were badly shaken by their efforts. In reality, we loved the attention.

The Westminster Arms is practically UKIP-only afterwards. We're unanimous in our view that the evening was a stonking success. Even better, we've enjoyed our highest ever polling results over the last few days such that those candidates who are very far down the regional lists might get in. We speculate about this to the extreme. Uncle Mick, 5th on the list for Eastern Area, says that being elected will fulfil his dream; he'll be able to buy cheap fags from the continent on a regular basis.

Thursday 8th May 2014

We're hanging on by our fingertips to the very edge of London, here, at the Coulsdon Community Centre (the arse-end of Croydon). Another hustings. Peter Grønborg of Danish TV2 is meeting me for an interview outside first. I like the Danes. They voted against the Maastricht treaty.

Some young spy is eavesdropping while I slag off his party. He goes up to the crew when I've finished.

'Would you like a few words from a Conservative standpoint?' he pleads.

'No. Thank you,' says Grønborg.

The event has been organised by a local resident called Peter Morgan who is actually a member of UKIP Lambeth and Croydon North branch even though this is about seven miles away. Odd. Anyway, his marketing skills aren't impressive as the huge hall is populated by only about twenty people. What a waste of time.

Tory Tannock is there and grumbles at the name cards which appear in front of each speaker. They've obviously been drawn by some local primary school children.

'These things are very unprofessional,' he says to me.

'I think they're great', I say to him.

We start, and the Liberal Democrat Anuja Prashar has a go at my party immediately. How foolish.

'UKIP aren't interested in making the EU work but they're very interested in pocketing all the allowances,' she sneers.

'Really?' I reply. 'Who can forget that vote by MEPs on March 11th to increase their pay and pensions? Nearly every British party, including UKIP, voted against. The only ones in favour were the BNP. And, of course, your lot in the Lib Dems.'

She shrinks away and shuffles in her seat. Tannock leans over to my ear.

'Oh, well done,' he laughs. 'I'd forgotten about that.'

That truce is soon over. A Tory plant in the audience pushes the point.

'Why do UKIP bother putting their names forward if they're not prepared to stand up for Britain in the European Parliament?'

'Is that a joke?' I answer. 'Our MEPs can't stand up for Britain. Even if they all voted together, we're outnumbered ten-to-one. The only reason we're doing this is because the press wouldn't be interested in what UKIP have to say otherwise.'

Tannock is magnificently-pompous.

'The prestige of being a Member of the European Parliament certainly gives one a voice and I am pleased that UKIP now aspire to it. And there are many good things which one can do. . .'

He witters on about his own Great Works which are so unmemorable that I forget them all even while he's actually saying the words.

'Prestige?' This man really doesn't get it.

Sunday 11th May 2014

Richard Shaw, chairman of Hither Green Arts Society, has invited a range of local politicos to a screening of the film *Tory Boy* with its director John Walsh. Nearly 40 candidates and politicians have been asked to come, including prospective MEPs, councillors and Lewisham Mayoral hopefuls.

But in the end, only the incumbent Labour Mayor Steve Bullock, Andy Beadle of TUSC and Caroline Attfield, the Tory no-hoper for Europe, bother to turn up. We, on the other hand, present the punters with my good self, Peter Lello for mayor and Geoff Fleming as the Lewisham Central candidate which is the ward in which the screening is taking place.

If you haven't seen the film then you should. It covers the doomed general election campaign of the eponymous John Walsh in Middlesbrough in 2010 when he stood against Labour-MP-for-life, Stuart Bell. Bell had died in 2012 and Richard Elvin had come second for UKIP in the by-election. Bell was a complete shit and won't be missed and this is precisely the sort of place that UKIP needs to target.

Movie over, the candidates get to speak. I slag off the St Helens MP and defector from the Tories, Shaun Woodward. The local Labour Party don't like him because he ousted Marie Rimmer as their PPC for the seat. I don't like him because David Cameron took over his Witney constituency and then became Tory Leader. So everything that's happened since is all Woodward's fault.

Peter Lello then has a say.

'I'd like to remind everybody that a lot of the people UKIP have got are normal, everyday, working people who have full time jobs, who have families and lots of things that we've got to do. And we've had lots of abuse thrown at us. So we know all about this, being on the receiving end of dirty politics.

'If you believe in democracy you don't do that. You let people speak and you beat them on the policies, beat them at the ballot box on arguments. Not on offensive abusive comments, behaviour and threats as we saw on that video. That is not democracy.'

I tender my apologies to the room and tell everyone that we need to leave early because I'm to be interviewed by Angela Knäble from German TV.

'She'd wanted Nigel of course but has been palmed off with me.'

I leave the screening with Lello and my better half at 8.20 although Angela isn't meeting me until 9.30. So we could have stayed on for a bit to hear Steve Bullock orate. But we'd rather go for a beer in the Station Hotel.

Unfortunately, Peter is to be on the receiving end of dirty politics himself very, very soon.

Monday 12th May 2014

I don't normally like to venture into the uncivilised half of London but tonight am appearing at the Hampstead Garden Suburb Residents

Association hustings. North of the river. Gross.

The organiser David Littaur has told us about the format in advance.

'The Free Church Hall has ample room for all the candidates, both Council and MEP. Our proposal is to welcome them all.'

And they have, which was silly as that means there's about twenty people on the panel so there are only very short soundbites from all of us. The best one comes from Labour's Ivana Bartoletti:

'Four million British jobs are at risk if this country leaves the EU.'

Within the space of a month she's gone from 3 million to 3-and-a-half million to 4 million. We'll all be unemployed at this rate. What's that famous saying about a 'big lie' again?

Tuesday 13th May 2014

Gerard Batten had his window smashed in last night and I call him when I find out. He says that he and his wife heard something in the garden at midnight but thought nothing of it. Then at about 3 am they were woken by breaking glass and found a brick on the floor of their lounge.

'It's happened before,' he tells me. 'Just something that we have to expect from the hard left. I'm tempted to stay up in the front room with a golf club to hand in case they try it again.'

'A golf club's no good as there's no room to wield it indoors,' I reply. 'You'd be better off with, say, the Mauser "butcher" bayonet. Or perhaps an 1856 pioneer sidearm. You know, with the sawback?'

'Maybe, but I don't own those things.'

'Don't you? I thought everybody did.'

We discuss the possibility that I might be targeted too and agree that it'd be best to give the rozzers a call just in case.

I was junior counsel for Norfolk farmer Tony Martin in the civil claim for personal injury brought against him by Brendan Fearon (the burglar he didn't manage to kill). That case had collapsed after the claimant was filmed by *The Sun* riding a bike. Further, I have always approved of Blackstone's observations on home invasions. So I know what's legally 'reasonable'.

Don't even think about it, pinkoes.

Wednesday 14th May 2014

Peter Lello calls. The police have told him they're going to pay a visit.

Presumably it's something to do with Gerard's window. If I'm second in this pound-shop Dead Pool then Peter may be third as he has had the audacity to stand for Lewisham Mayor. As the Leftards have made clear, UKIP are 'not welcome' in any part of London.

Peter isn't sure it's anything to do with this because the tone of the officer who had called was brusque rather than victimy-supporty.

'Maybe it's the aftermath of the party conference dinner last year?' he wonders.

He'd gone to the rubber chicken meal in September. Being unsatisfied with the frugal repast, Peter had picked up some late-night chips on his way home. A dinner suit is unusual attire for that part of south-east London at any time of day and he was thumped by a piss-or-crack-head who'd demanded a share of his second dinner. Peter had righteously and rightfully thumped them back. And that was the end of that.

However, his picture has just been circulated throughout the borough in the mayoral election booklet.

'Could be they've recognised me,' he says.

'Could be,' I say. 'They might want "justice". And perhaps "one-hundred-percent-of-the-comp-en-SAY-shun".'

We leave it there.

He calls back. It's not what we thought. They're going to arrest him for a sexual assault. On a homeless Bulgarian man.

UKIP have been leading the campaign against open-door immigration from that country so this allegation is extraordinarily convenient. My first reaction is anger which is not in any degree directed at Peter.

Peter asks for my professional help. But although I often ignore Bar Council diktats, in these circumstances it wouldn't be in his interest to represent him. The Bar's independent for good reason. Besides, I don't do criminal work. Our senior clerk in chambers, Ian Hogg, knows specialist lawyers who'll help.

CHAPTER SIXTEEN

I Get Knocked Down. Yet I Get Up Again

Thursday 15th May 2014

THE OPEN RIGHTS GROUP HUSTINGS on European digital issues started twenty minutes ago. In a hackneyed cliché, it's at the Shoreditch Village Hall in Hoxton Square and is being chaired by the technical writer, Glyn Moody.

'I see that Paul Oakley's just joined us. Do you want to quickly have a word about who you are and what your party's view on the digital rights issue is?'

'Sorry I'm late. I'm a barrister and had an urgent matter to deal with. If I'd come here on time I'd have left the geezer in the lurch. I decided to help him out.'

The geezer being Peter Lello who's now in police custody and I've been working with my clerks and some solicitors to get him decent representation. I don't tell the crowd this of course.

'What I am is a supporter of Big Brother Watch and No2ID. For this reason I refuse to have a smartphone because I don't want sinister agencies in America and elsewhere spying on everything that I do.'

Lots of questions have been asked already and Moody wants me to catch up.

'What do you feel the Edward Snowden revelations mean for this country and for Europe?'

'It's very frightening indeed. I think we all hav e to take notice of the fact that nothing we do online can be considered private.'

The compere moves on.

'I'd like to ask the panel for their views on Mr Snowden himself.

Is he a hero? Is he a traitor? Should he be given asylum? Should he be given a medal?'

The question's passed straight to me. Blimey. Give me a chance to catch a breath!

'Hero.'

I hand the microphone on to the Green representative Danny Bates who agrees, but with many more words. Lib Dem Sarah Ludford believes that he's performed a useful public service and Labour's Claude Moraes obfuscates.

It's a long, long meeting. Some of the questions are very technical but I manage to bullshit. Many of the questioners are very nerdy and would have had their heads flushed down the toilets at my school. The other panellists have piles of briefing papers on their laps. I've got an *Evening Standard* with a half-finished Sudoku which I chuck on the floor.

I have to leave temporarily for another ten minutes to help with Peter's situation. On returning, we're finishing off with digital copyright and the fact that downloaded music files can't be passed on to others. My take is this.

'I very much hope that my grandchildren are going to play my punk rock LPs to death. Although the chances are that they'll probably take them down to the charity shop. But that should be their choice. That's something you can't do with digital files and I'd like to see this change.'

And - fan mah brow! Lib Dem Ludford concurs.

'I agree with that. One thing I agree with UKIP on!'

A collegiate end to the evening.

More importantly, Lello has now got decent legal representation.

Friday 16th May 2014

Gerard Batten forwards an email to me from one Sam Nicholson, 'Assistant Adviser, Guidance,' at the Electoral Commission. It says this.

'Neither the party name "An Independence from Europe" nor the description "UK Independence Now" was already on the register. Therefore we made the decision that the party name was not likely to cause voters to confuse it with another registered party.

'We also considered the test of whether the name and description could result in voters confusing them with names or descriptions that are already registered. We decided that although there are some over-lapping words, the party name and description are sufficiently different from those registered by the UK Independence Party (UKIP) to mean that in our opinion voters were not likely to confuse them with the UKIP name and descriptions.'

Sam Nicholson is a knob.

Saturday 17th May 2014

We're canvassing in Eltham West ward. This is one of our best areas and we are double-campaigning for both the EU elections and the council elections where branch treasurer Ryan Acty's the candidate.

Peter Lello has come out with us in spite of the putrid lie he's been dealing with over the past days. All the activists know about it. Every one of them shakes him by the hand or pats him on the back or gives him words of solidarity.

It's a lovely morning and as an extra treat a photographer from Getty Images is shadowing us. As Getty put it beforehand:

'There is no fuss, no lights, just a photographer and his cameras around his neck.'

That photographer is Peter Macdiarmid. We coalesce at the community centre in Nebsit Road. Macdiarmid's perplexed that we're carrying out council canvassing for Ryan and handing out MEP leaflets as an extra.

'Aren't you doing anything in your own constituency?'
He doesn't quite get it.

'My constituency covers everything from Barnet to Bromley, Romford to Richmond, and everything above, below, left, right and round and about.'

'Bloody hell. So you've got to knock on all those doors?'

'In theory - Yup.'

'Will you manage it?'

'Nope.'

The day becomes hotter. And hotter still. One resident says he'll definitely back The Kip and Macdiarmid asks if he can nip inside the hall to photograph over the voter's shoulder as he speaks to me. This he does.

The incredible Getty catalogue includes photographs of Nixon and Presley, Thatcher and Reagan, Arafat and Rabin. Now added to that catalogue is one of me talking to this London voter who's wearing nothing but his boxer shorts.

Monday 19th May 2014

I'm fond of Lewisham People Before Profit. Thoughtful lefties (and categorically not Leftards) they work hard on community projects and put up candidates in all the borough's elections.

Their chairman, John Hamilton, called a few days ago to ask if I'd speak at a hustings today. The first part of the meeting's for voters to hear from his council candidates. Then, at 8.30pm he's switching to the EU and it'll be our turn.

I'm double-booked so had proposed that Peter Lello stand in. I then discovered a Facebook page about a protest.

> 'UKIP is standing for seats within Lewisham Borough and that in itself sends alarm bells as to how confident they feel about their chances of getting elected in this area.
>
> 'Being born and raised in Lewisham- UKIP politics is not a true representation of multi cultural and diversity area it is, and this is why doing work around the UKIP is something close to my heart.
>
> 'You have the power to prevent this from happening by standing together in solidarity with all our brothers and sister regardless of culture, background and ethnicity.
>
> 'UKIP has been very clever in how they have profiled their campaign in a manner and approach which comes across humble and genuine.
>
> 'Don't be fooled by the poker face of the UKIP party and come along to stand firm and strong on Monday 19th- to say "we will not have this in our area".

How flattering! I'm definitely doing this now and elbow Lello aside. According to the page over 90 people will be attending. Given the recent hard-left violence at UKIP events I warn John Hamilton and he says he'll get in touch with the Peelers. I do likewise. But although Lewisham has an enormous new police HQ it's hard to get hold of them. Several calls aren't returned. John has had better luck and is assured that there'll be officers there.

The venue's in Telegraph Hill. The missis drives us up with our new puppy so she can walk him in the nearby park. They're not coming to the meeting in case there is indeed trouble. We run past the venue and stop some distance away so the car isn't identified for vandalism. Sure enough, there's a big noisy crowd outside. Sure enough, there are no police at all.

I'm wearing my fourth-best black suit, Dr Martens' shoes and a short-sleeved shirt with no tie. If they try anything I'll go Red Mist. I will not fuck about. Have these student hippy types considered that possibility?

The speakers have already started. The café has French doors and those outside can hear what's going on from the open air. They're yelling and lairy. There had indeed been fisticuffs just before I arrived. I walk through the mob most politely and sit on the empty chair on the low platform. It takes a moment but then the crowd realise who's turned up and there are boos and rude words. I grin and wave.

The demonstration was supposed to be about UKIP but the unwashed mob spend most of the time yelling at their enemies in the other minor parties. Don't have a clue what it's about as all Leftards look sound and smell alike to me.

I do receive a lot of grief in the course of the evening, though, and there are regular cries of 'Waycist'.

I remind them that we are the only party who refuse membership to former BNP activists and mention the interloper we'd thrown out of our own branch.

'Nothing to do with your whining,' I tell them. 'We do this because it's the right thing.'
One heckles,

'So why have you got so many then?'

'If you Guardian readers didn't shout "Racist" at us all the time then the six-fingered BNP-types might stop believing you and try to join up. Give it a rest. You're annoying us.'

Things move on to our homophobia. The Labour representative, a dickhead, chips in.

'And don't forget. UKIP doesn't even allow gay members.'

'Sorry to have to tell you this old son. But our candidate for mayor is "One Of Them".'
He mumbles and shrivels.

The meeting judders to a halt and a Caribbean pensioner indicates that he wants a private word. He's ex-British army, had served in Aden, and polite. His query's a genuine one about our immigration policy.

As we're speaking, eight or so of the demonstrators crowd round and start regurgitating the usual catchphrases. I neither cower nor sob as they'd probably hoped.

A hand grabs my shoulder from behind and its owner says,

'I tell you what. I'm definitely voting for you.'

The freedom fighters don't like that.

Having had it made clear that they will be having UKIP in their area after all, the demonstrators drift away.

Peter Lello, Ken Webb, Hugh Waine and Ryan Acty come to drag me off and we head to Skehans pub, bouncing like Scousers.

Tuesday 20th May 2014

Someone posting as ALB writes this about last night's event on the Socialist Party website:

> 'This turned out to be an introduction to Lewisham local politics for the two of us who went. Lewisham is a Labour stronghold with three other parties vying to take them on: Lewisham People before Profit, a sort of radical residents association who organised the hustings, the Greens and SPEW as TUSC.
>
> 'The European election hustings took place after. Represented were the Greens, No2EU, the Animal Welfare Party, the National Health Action Party, us and UKIP. The local SWP turned up to protest about UKIP being invited and a scuffle broke out. What's wrong with these idiots?
>
> 'The UKIP representative, Paul Oakley, was a smooth operator who was not intimidated by the SWP disrupters. In fact, ironically in view of UKIP's political pitch, he was the only career politician there, dressed in a suit. A former chairman of the Greater London Tories, he is No 2 on the UKIP list for London and stands a good chance of getting elected a MEP and so moving further up the greasy pole.'

I hope so, too.

Wednesday 21st May 2014

It's the last day of campaigning. We're handing out Peter Whittle council leaflets at Mottingham station. Kirsten Farage phones up for Lawrence Webb's number and then Nigel wants a word. He's happily exhausted and in an end-of-term mood. We discuss the campaign.

'Do you think there's anything we could have done better?' he asks. The only thing was that interview on LBC with whining Trot James O'Brien. He'd tried to give Farage a hard time but our man had held his end up until the last moments when press head Patrick O'Flynn had foolishly interrupted to say the interview was over. The intervention was not down to Nigel at all.

'It looked liked you'd Got Your Dad on O'Brien.'

'Yes. Patrick can be a bit of an idiot. Do you want to go fishing on Saturday?'

'Of course.'

Rush-hour having died down, we retire to the Royal Tavern in Sidcup Road and Peter Lello calls. *The Daily Mirror* have been trying to contact him but he's made sure he's not contactable.

'They're outside my flat now. And they're running the sexual assault story.'

I call O'Flynn, who's unsympathetic.

'What is it with your branch? I've had quite enough of hearing about south-east London.'

'Maybe so. But it's bollocks and I'm not going to cast him to the wolves.'

Ringing Nigel again, he's not that bothered.

'They've gone with that one, have they? We'd found out that there were about six stories the *Mirror* were thinking of running. It won't make any difference now.'

'I'd be grateful if you didn't disown Lello.'

'We've no intention of doing so.'

Thursday 22nd May 2014

Today is EU and council Election Day. I don't normally read the *Daily Mirror*. Obviously. But this morning a man who I'm proud to have as a colleague and to call a friend is on the front-page of the London edition. They're trying to cause the party maximum damage as people head to the polls. There's also something odd about their story.

'UKIP candidate Peter Lello has been held over an accusation of sexual assault on a homeless Bulgarian man'

The police never divulge the nationality or residential status of such victims so this means that either a rogue copper or the poor, devastated, complainant himself have been speaking to the rag. The article goes on:

'Civil servant Mr Lello is running to become mayor in Lewisham, South London, against Duwayne Brooks, the friend of murdered teenager Stephen Lawrence.'

Peter's standing against six other candidates and has no policy platform whatsoever against Brooks or his connection with Stephen Lawrence. Nonetheless, according to the *Mirror* he is plainly a pervert, a hypocrite, a racist (twice-over) and probably cheats at bingo too, for all we know.

I've always believed that sexual offence suspects should have their anonymity protected until such time as they are convicted. People being as people are, there are always suspicions that there's no smoke without fire. Lives are destroyed by the lack of this fireguard. As and when suspects are actually convicted, the floodlights should be trained on them. But not until then.

And to scarify an innocent man in order to damage his party's chances in an election? This is filthy journalism.

Peter isn't going to hide away. He's gone to vote and bumps into Ray Woolford, the local People Before Profit candidate, at the polling station.

'Stitch-up', said Ray.

Ray's right.

I vote too. The staff in my polling station hand over the EU ballot paper properly. That is, fully opened out. As there are 17 parties standing, it's a lengthy piece of paper. The two counterfeit UKIPs are at the very top and UKIP is at the very end.

Given the immensity of the London constituency, there's not a lot that can be done today. Our leaflets are out and we've spoken to the punters. Matt Pavey decides to annoy the residents of Whitefoot by driving 'round the ward and berating them with a loudspeaker but that's pretty much it.

I relax and watch daytime TV, but jump with a start at lunchtime as a single immense thunderclap comes from a clear sky. Very Wagnerian.

As the afternoon progresses, calls start coming in to party officers right across the capital about several polling stations. They include the Greenleaf centre in Waltham Forest, Globe Town and Poplar in Tower Hamlets, Hanwell, Southwark College Ward, the Ridgeway Church in E4, Wood Street in Walthamstow, All Saints School in Carshalton, the Holy Trinity Church, Wimbledon, South Norwood, Waddon and others. And these are only the ones I've been told about.

The problem's simple. Voters who've been acute enough not to be taken in by the fake UKIPs have been complaining that, after all the fuss we've made, we aren't even on the ballot paper. They'd wanted to vote for us but couldn't.

Those who are even more astute have reported that they received a folded ballot paper which was creased in a particular way. The last inch of the sheet was turned backwards. Sharply. That last inch just happens to display the UKIP option.

Gerard confirms that his own was handed to him first thing in this way.

'I didn't think much of it at the time but I'm thinking about it a lot now.'

An email is sent out by Patrick O'Flynn to all London activists:

'There have been some instances reported from London of ballot papers being folded as they are handed to voters. If you have any concerns about folded papers, please contact your regional sub-agent or Lisa Duffy with details of the polling station address and the council.'

So we keep an eye open, but it's still going on into the evening. Paul Butler calls me at 5.30 pm to say that he'd fielded four complaints about his own polling station at the church in Westmount Road. On the back of this he'd spoken to Stephen O'Hare at Greenwich council who assured him that the problem would be dealt with. But it hasn't been dealt with so I call O'Hare too. He disagrees.

'I believe that, following our corrective action and borough-wide communication earlier today, this was an isolated exception to the process of fully-unfolded ballot paper issue elsewhere in Greenwich.'

Maybe it has been resolved and maybe it hasn't, but how much damage has been done in the intervening hours?

The folding is magnificently-malevolent. Although UKIP activists will scrutinise every vote at counting stations around the capital later on, there's no way we'll be able to tell whether papers had been handed out like that or simply creased up in this manner to fit into the ballot box. Or even if the voter would have wanted to back us at all.

We'll never know which federasts or leftards are responsible yet I can't help but admire the brilliance of this plan and bear them no ill will. Honestly. I merely hope that, when they have gone to meet their maker, their mortal remains lie undiscovered in their homes for some weeks until their neighbours complain of the stench.

Lisa Duffy calls with an update.

'London,' she says, 'is an absolute nightmare compared to the rest of the country.'

Thanks, Lisa! That's very reassuring.

Friday 23rd May 2014

Lewisham council are renowned slowpokes when it comes to vote counting.

The 2010 poll had been my last stand as a Tory for the ward of Lewisham Central. As should be done, the ballots were taken to be sifted that same evening at Sedgehill School. By sun-up the count was still going on and I walked home, knackered. Some hours later it was announced that I'd polled precisely 777 votes and was thus the Neighbour of the Beast.

Anyway, back to 2014. This time the local election count is at the London Regiment barracks in Wat Tyler Road, right in the middle of Blackheath, and it starts at lunchtime with a view to finishing at a reasonable hour. Let's see if they manage it this time. The nearest pub, the Hare and Billet, is a 10-minute walk away. Great.

The missis is going to drop me off. I've just had all five of my black suits cleaned and will be wearing the second-best one this afternoon. Having nearly reached the venue, I suddenly realise, with horror, that something is very wrong.

The dry cleaners have hung the trousers for one suit with the jacket of another and I've put on this mismatch. Idiots! I'll be a laughing stock because the weaves of each are subtly-different.

'We need to go home for me to change. Right now.'

'Don't be silly,' she says. 'Nobody will notice.'

'Of course they will!'

We turn around. On eventually getting back to the venue I bump into an old pal and Tory candidate for Mayor, Simon Nundy. We chat about the campaign and I ask what his first thought was about the allegation against Peter Lello.

'Fit-up,' he says.

So that's two Enemy Activists who can see sense.

Peter's proudly there too, as our own mayoral candidate. He's not going to hide away from anyone.

Despite the amenable hour, Lewisham polling staff are as slow as usual. It's tea time before the mayoral result is announced. Labour's Bullock is the overwhelming victor with more than half the votes. Simon Nundy is far-away runner-up with just over 8,000. Peter Lello is second to last on 5,684 or 7.87% but retains his deposit. John Hamilton of People Before Profit is slightly ahead of him. It might have been the other way round were it not for those vermin at the *Mirror*.

Eventually, the lazy sods start work on the councillor votes. Predictably, the Labour candidates win all three vacancies in every single seat but UKIP are doing very well indeed.

Matt Pavey is fourth in Whitefoot with 743 votes.

In Downham Massimo DiMambro would also have been fourth on 853 were it not for the fact that Duwayne Brooks, being famous, just sneaks ahead for the Lib Dem ticket.

Peter Lello is also fifth in Grove Park with 838 votes and is only just pipped by one of the Tories. The other parties are nowhere.

It gets to midnight and they haven't even started counting my ward, Forest Hill. Sod this, I'm going home.

Saturday 24th May 2014

I check the council website for the Forest Hill result first thing. UKIP are in equal last position with People Before Profit, both of us polling 378. Don't give a toss because I'll be going to the European Parliaments in Brussels and Strasbourg instead of the town hall in Catford.

The postman then arrives with a letter from the Electoral Commission about the MEP expense returns. They have their revenge on me for saying they're not fit for purpose by calling me a girl.

It's addressed to 'Paula' Oakley.

Sunday 25th May 2014

The count for the Euros is tonight at City Hall.

We've got some blokes coming round to the house to put up plasterboard and skim a wall first thing tomorrow morning. Being both tight-fisted and an enthusiast for destruction, I'm pulling down the old lath and plaster myself. It's a filthy job. It's also a filthy-hot day which makes it worse. The lumps of plaster are left in bags in the front yard in one pile and the wooden laths in another. An enterprising young east European, who had been driving past, says he'll take it away for a tenner. I'm sure it'll be disposed of in line with the relevant EU regulations. He takes the cash and the bags of plaster and says he'll come back for the wood but doesn't. He and his kind shall rue the day when we come to power.

I look like a warrior in sweaty grey woad when it's time to stop although the task's not quite finished. I play the Stranglers' version of 'Walk On By' several times while cleaning up. This was the second single I ever bought at the age of 9 and it remains number 1 in my all-time hit parade. This shows excellent taste at a tender age, not perpetual childishness in middle-age.

Best black suit, new white shirt, polished shoes, black-ish tie and skull cufflinks on. It turns out that the trains aren't running because of engineering works. Again. This means a cab which gets me there more-or-less promptly. As things turn out, I could easily have walked from home and still arrived in plenty of time for the result.

On arrival I'm immediately pulled to one side by *BBC London* for a panel interview with an earpiece in a side room. There are various bods in the studio who ask why UKIP haven't done so well in the council elections. Yet we have.

Finished, and a chap from LBC says that Iain Dale would like an interview if I get in. This is within Gerard's earshot and tactless.

All of our posse are wearing UKIP rosettes but I'm sporting the discrete plastic 'enamel' badge. Tony Brown kindly offers his spare instead.

'Certainly not,' I reply. 'Rosettes are a lower decoration. Mine has the status of the Knight's Cross of the Iron Cross.'

Tony stuffs his hand to his mouth and sniggers.

The BNP's Carlos Castenada, or whatever he's called, tries to engage some of our lads in conversation. They're minded to oblige but I usher them away on the pretence of having to discuss weighty matters of state. There are far too many camera phones and pinkoes in here for us to engage in social intercourse with that lot.

The missis sits quietly to one side. BBC coverage is running on a couple of large TVs. We all hoot and huzzay as the regional results amble along. There's extremely good news again and again as many of our candidates who fall far down their respective lists or in hard territory are elected. Ray Finch (fourth in South-East), Tim Aker (third in Eastern), Jonathan Arnott (first in North East), Nathan Gill (Wales), Margot Parker (East Midlands), Bill Etheridge (West Midlands), Steve Woolfe, and Mike Hookem. Seven of them are women, all of whom have got there under their own power without any Tory-style positive discrimination (which has given that party only six).

Davy Coburn and I swap calls through the evening. His count isn't finished as they're still waiting for ballot boxes to arrive from the highlands and islands. As he puts it:

'Like the Diva with the beard, my Eurovision entry comes in most dramatically on Monday as the Western Isles quite rightly keep the Sabbath and all Europe waiting.

'There is much we can learn from the Islanders correctly putting God and their consciences before the European oligarchic monstrosity.

An example to us all."

Nonetheless, enough votes have already been counted to show that Scotland has its first UKIP MEP.

We cheer as the Lib Dems are wiped out again and again and those who've turned up to City Hall begin to drift off as the evening goes on.

Yet not much is happening here. Every single London council has finished and forwarded their final voting tallies. Apart for Tower Hamlets that is, which is under the leadership of Lutfur Rahman. What the heck are they playing at?

Kirsten Farage texts me at 1.33: 'You got two! Well done!'

This rouses me from a half-doze on an uncomfortable seat to speak to my henchmen. News to them as there's been no movement at all. Kirsten's just overheard a rumour at their own count.

It's getting later and later and I'm getting tireder and grumpier. The missis goes out to find an all-night shop for something to eat and I start to finalise my winner's speech. This will express gratitude to the police and council counters as it must.

'Except,' I shall say: 'No thanks at all goes to Tower Hamlets borough. What utter incompetents they are.'

Then I'll move on to the beef of the oration which will start with a direct and unattributed quote from a 1980s horror film. When the liberal media find out where it comes from, and they shall, they'll wee their pants in self-righteous condemnation. That will be the opening gift to them of my reign.

It approaches 3 am, the demons' hour of legend, and there's a commotion by the offices. Peter Staveley's beckoned over with his counterparts from the other parties. After a few moments he comes back. The results are about to be disclosed. The rest of our retinue follows him to huddle around Barry Quirk the Returning Officer.

I decide not to join them and walk outside to the amphitheatre. This is to take some air and to look at the sky. Also, my womens' intuition has manifested itself again.

Peter Lello breaks from the group and comes over.

'No,' he says.

Gerard Batten will remain the only UKIP MEP for London.

Monday 26th May 2014

Bank Holiday today, but I'm not feeling festive at all. Up at 6 to finish destroying the wall before the plasterers arrive at 7 and scoped out with fatigue and fury.

Gawain Towler rings.

'What do you want, loser?' I ask and we cackle.

He says UKIP were 21,705 votes short of having a second London MEP. 'An Independence from Europe' robbed up to 26,675 votes and 'UKEPP', 28,014. That is, 54,689 overall and taking no account of the unmeasurable effect of folded ballot papers either.

In South West region the former of those bootleg UKIPs had stolen up to 23,169 of Gawain's votes, condemning him to remain Party Press Officer for the foreseeable future.

He warns that a journalist at *The Times* is about to call and she duly does. I'm very pleased with the soundbite.

'Mike Nattrass,' I say, 'has joined the pantheon of federast villains. Not as important as Delors, Heath or Barroso however. More like something that has stuck to the bottom of David Cameron's shoe.'

Her piece is printed but she doesn't use it. Rats.

Kirsten texts to say that the celebration will be at the Intercontinental Hotel from 3 to 6.

The plasterers don't leave until after 4. And there's no blasted trains. Again. I'm definitely going to the party though because it mustn't look like I'm overcome with envy.

I arrive at half-five just as it's winding down. Lisa Duffy gives me a hug, looking quite tearful. That might be because of me. Or it might be because she's injured her ankle which is strapped up.

Janice Atkinson is there. Jane Collins. Bill, with Star, Nathan Gill and Tim Aker. In fact, a good whack of our new MEPs.

Gawain orates a merry diatribe about the pair of us being thwarted with his arm around my shoulder to hold himself up. He falls over nonetheless. But you haven't gotten rid of us yet.

CHAPTER SEVENTEEN

Never, Ever, Ever Trust a Defector

Thursday 29th May 2014

WE'RE CRACKING ON WITH THE ASSESSMENTS for the 2015 Parliamentary candidates right away. Having groomed Peter Whittle, he's keen to put his name forward for one of our branch's seats. We'll be very glad to have him.

'I would be thrilled to be Eltham candidate, and would get going immediately,' he says. 'Is the 7th at my place OK for you drinks-wise?'

It sure is. And he commiserates again.

'Everybody's really upset about the result. Oh, except for that awful woman Elizabeth Jones.'

Do tell.

'She's put a photograph of me and her at the count online. She's written below that this was "a pleasing result for those in the know" and "you have no idea how happy the London result made me".'

Charming.

Thursday 5th June 2014

Gobby Tory MP Patrick Mercer resigned his Newark seat after saying that racial abuse was an acceptable part of army life. Today is the by-election. As a contrast to mentalist Mercer, UKIP are putting forward Roger Helmer as our candidate.

Duly-discharged from the 10.08 King's Cross train along with a morass of Conservative activists and MPs who've been whipped to attend, I stroll to the UKIP office in the town centre. The sad and sorry Labour HQ is unmanned as I pass it.

I'm sent to the Charles Street polling station first of all along with Sarinder Joshua Duroch. He's just written a book: *Enoch, I am a British Indian*. Duroch is an interesting fellow to listen to, particularly if one is enthralled to know how fascinating and important he is. Unfortunately, there are no canvass cards so we can do little except nod 'hello' to the residents who've come to vote.

Newark is soaked with the history of the English Civil War and lunch is in the Prince Rupert ale house. Although named for the Stuart fop who rose against our sovereign parliament, the route to the pub runs brazenly past the Tory HQ and is the obvious choice for the Kipper tavern.

More polling station work in the afternoon and a local activist drops me at the 12th century St Mary and All Saints church in Hawksworth. It's a twenty minute drive away along the A-road because the constituency is geographically immense.

On arrival, I'd expected to be taking over from someone else. The whole point of being a teller is to mark off those people who have voted and then cross-refer the list to canvassing returns. This means that a party can 'knock up' its supporters as the day draws to an end. It also requires a full canvass to have been undertaken and activists outside the polling station from the moment it opens at 7 am until close of voting.

There is no other activist present. There are no polling cards. There has been no full canvass.

The staff inside are kind enough to give me a chair to place at the front door. Fortunately, it's not raining. Further, the church itself is beautiful and I occupy some of the time by looking at the gravestones, many of which record the sad deaths of Georgian infants. Unfortunately, the area is out in the sticks and voter turnover is very, very slow.

I expect to do a couple of hours here and then move on somewhere else. I've also told the campaign HQ that I'm booked on the 6.55 pm return train to London. More importantly, Simon Richards of the Freedom Association has invited me for a quick drink in the town centre.

It gets later and later. I call the HQ several times.

'Yes, we're sending someone to bring you back.'

'Honestly, they're on their way.'

'They still haven't arrived? I'll chase them for you.'

Eventually, a car rolls up at 6.30. Nobody's taking over the task and I have to run for the train when we reach the station.

The result? The Tory wins with a majority of 7,403 over Roger Helmer who's in second place. On the plus-side, Cameron visited the town four times and their vote fell by nine percentage points. Farage only turned up twice and the UKIP vote rose by 23.

However, we really need to sort out our by-election campaigning. Today was pretty much a waste of my talents and, presumably, those of other activists. This isn't good enough.

Thursday 26th June 2014

A lunch date with the party chairman in Middle Temple Gardens. Crowther commiserates with me, again. Things are getting towards that stage when it isn't clear whether the bereaved should be given the usual condolences or whether sufficient time has passed for him to have gotten over it.

I have gotten over it. Just about.

He gives further feedback on the assessment process. Apparently, I came across as balanced and stable during the psychometric testing, unlike some others. It probably doesn't breach any doctor/patient confidentiality because Steve isn't a doctor and UKIP candidates aren't patients, but he's walking a tightrope when he confides this.

'Quite a contrast to some others. One on the London list was borderline psychotic, but fortunately that candidate didn't have a hope of being elected.'

However, there's more to this meeting as Crowther confirms.

'Would you like to be a Regional Organiser? It's in my gift and London needs sorting out. There won't be much available in the way of remuneration though.'

I would. And as the party's skint, again, Steve will be getting a bargain as I decide that it won't cost him anything. Although there's always the risk that you get what you pay for.

Saturday 19th July 2014

Another old Tory mate, Hugh O'Leary, has reached his fortieth birthday. His wife has invited the missis and me to a barbecue at their home in Greenwich. It's a double celebration because Hugh's other half has had some good news in the past few days.

She's just been appointed Secretary of State for the Environment. For she is the Conservative MP for South West Norfolk, Liz Truss.

The other guests regard me with only a modicum of suspicion, and there's an outstanding hog roast. Disappointingly, there's no cheese to be had.

Jackie Doyle-Price is there. We'd been surprised and chuffed when she'd scraped in to become Tory MP for Thurrock in 2010 by 92 votes. She'd also been good enough to act as one of my referees for the last tranche of Tory parliamentary assessments. I rate her highly and hope she goes far.

Jackie is in - a state of refreshment. She takes me to task about her prospective UKIP opponent for the seat who's already been working hard to take it from her at the next election.

'That bloody Tim Aker. What the hell is he playing at? He's going to damage me and let Labour back in.'

I like Jackie a lot but UKIP and an exit from the EU even more. Sorry old lass, but I'll have to back Tim. There's no pleasure in saying so however.

Wednesday 23rd July 2014

I'm 'working at home', still in a bit of a brown study after being robbed of the MEP-ship. And then discover from the internet that second-wave punk band the UK Subs are recording their new LP about 300 yards from our home.

Work is suddenly finished. The studio's behind the kebab shop and I'd never previously had an inkling it was there.

Vocalist Charlie Harper is outside. He's now 70 years old and exactly the sort of friendly, angry old man that I plan to be. He invites me in and writes some lyrics to a new song called 'Heathens' on a page of a notepad. And he asks me to take part in the recording by 'singing' those words as a backing vocalist. This is far cooler than anything you did today.

Thursday 31st July 2014

The Electoral Commission publish a report about the EU elections. Their self-serving observations include these.

Other party names and descriptions

'A significant number of people, including representatives from UKIP, strongly felt that An Independence from Europe and 4 Freedoms (UK EPP) had chosen names and descriptions that were intended to confuse voters. As of 8 July we had received more than 260 complaints from people who said that the names and descriptions of these parties had confused voters who had intended to vote for UKIP, and should not have been registered. . .

'A number of complaints alleged that these two parties had deliberately chosen names that would get them to the top of the ballot paper, while UKIP was placed at the bottom. . . .

'In the light of the experience at the May 2014 elections there is a case for reforming the rules on party descriptions...

Ballot papers for the European Parliament elections

'At the 2009 European Parliamentary elections ballot papers which had been pre-folded by the printer were being handed to voters folded in polling stations in some areas in a way that could have obscured the last line of the ballot paper, which included the candidates for one particular party. . .

'We received approximately 50 tweets from voters during the course of the day covering a total of 22 local authorities, almost half of which were in London who had the longest ballot paper. . . In addition, we received 75 emails and 5 telephone calls on the subject of folded ballot papers. . .

'We also received a complaint from UKIP who (because party names are listed alphabetically on the European Parliamentary ballot paper) were concerned that they would not be visible to voters on a folded ballot paper, and therefore disadvantaged. . .'

Ya think?

Tuesday 26th August 2014

Nigel Farage defeats rivals Piers Wauchope, Peter Bucklitsch and Elizabeth Jones and is adopted as the UKIP Prospective Parliamentary Candidate for Thanet South.

Thursday 28th August 2014

There's a press conference at the Emmanuel Centre. That Tory MP Douglas Carswell walks on to the stage.

'I'm today leaving the Conservative Party and joining UKIP. This hasn't been an easy decision. I've been a member of the Conservative Party for all my adult life. It's full of wonderful people who want the best for Britain. My local Conservative Association in Clacton is thriving. It brims with those that I am honoured to call my friends. The problem is that many of those at the top of the Conservative Party are simply not on our side. They aren't serious about the change that Britain so desperately needs.'

Honourably – he's standing down and calling a by-election. Top bloke.

Saturday 30th August 2014

Clacton, for the by-election. It's not far as the crow flies but the blasted train journey has taken an absolute age.

Yet, there's good news at long last; we've got proper polling information to work with and a canvassing database. Quite a difference from our previous by-elections. This efficiency is down to Douglas Carswell. Hope he wins and helps professionalise the party.

As for the place? Haven't been here for years but it's like my hometown of Southport. That place is full of elderly scousers who've gone to the seaside to die. This one's stuffed with old cockneys with the same plan.

It's nice here. Think I'll head back up some time just for fun.

Tuesday 2nd September 2014

Mark Webber has asked me to come to the AGM of Tower Hamlets branch at the Royal Duchess pub. No particular reason, save that he thought it might be a nice idea, what with me being a new Regional Organiser and everything.

We don't have a private room in the pub, just a corner in the main bar. Mark introduces me in a fit and proper manner, that is, effusively. For I am Very Important.

A few minutes into the meeting I have to take a phone call so wander outside. A young woman follows and, when I've finished, asks for advice.

She says that she's a school teacher, Oxford graduate, and has just defected from Labour. She's keen to be a parliamentary candidate and was previously being lined up to stand for Labour in Manchester. She seems to know little about UKIP policy and you can sense a bit of the careerist about her. Which is strange, as, presumably, a northwestern candidacy for Labour would be far more likely to result in a successful outcome than a UKIP one anywhere in the country. At all.

'I want to speak at conference in a couple of weeks. And can you arrange for me to meet Nigel?'

Perhaps. Especially as she's playing with her hair throughout our conversation and looking up with huge puppy eyes from beneath thick, wavy lashes. Petite and curvy, just how I like 'em.

I feel a disturbance in my underpants. But also in The Force. Even if I did not greatly-fear my other half, there's something odd about this one.

'What's your name?'

'Natasha. Natasha Bolter.' She gives me her mobile number.

Friday 5th September 2014

A radio debate between UKIP's Elizabeth Jones and a lefty called Helen Pattison has been aired. In the middle of the discussion Jones cuts off her tiresome opponent by screeching at the top of her voice.

'Will you SHUT UP!'

This certainly worked because Pattison does precisely that. Perhaps we should all emulate this tactic. Or maybe not.

Tuesday 16th September 2014

UKIP Greenwich and Lewisham are choosing our Eltham candidate for next year's general election. This is by far the best chance of our five seats and we'll be focussing most campaigning activity there.

We're on the second floor of the Greenwich Tavern which is furnished with soft sofas and lit with low bulbs. It's quite romantic, really.

There are two applicants. Peter Whittle has indeed put his name forward and there's also a chap from Tunbridge Wells called Chris Hoare. He's actually succeeded in being elected as a Kent county councillor for the party which isn't something we're used to boasting about in south east London.

As chairman, I decide to break the party rules by having both candidates address the branch together rather than being kept in separate rooms. Gladitorial is always best and there might be sparks! As it happens, there are none, and they're both persuasive and professional.

Thirteen votes for Whittle and six for Hoare. Even though Chris has faced the mountain of locality despite his excellent attributes, Peter had the edge. He's definitely one to watch.

Friday 26th September 2014

Party conference is at Doncaster race course. Tanks on the lawn of Labour Leader Ed Miliband. It really is very rude of us to hold the event in the heart of his constituency and I strongly approve.

Jane Collins MEP is debut speaker at the unhealthy hour of 9.55 am. I only catch the end because she's employment spokesman and I'm not very interested in employment issues. Yet – she doesn't deal with her brief at all and instead directs her ire to the child grooming scandals in

Rotherham and its environs. All of which happened under the gaze of a Labour council and Labour MPs. The scalps of Shaun Wright, the police and crime commissioner, and Joyce Thacker, head of childrens' services, have already been taken.

'However,' Jane says, 'there are many others that still have questions to answer, and possibly charges to face.

'This includes the three Labour MPs for the Rotherham area. I am convinced that they knew many of the details of what was happening.

'I am now calling for criminal charges to be brought against those who it can be proved knew about the abuse, who failed to act - because in failing to act they aided and they abetted the perpetrators and they are just as guilty.'

Crikey! Rather strong that. Presumably it's been cleared by Patrick O'Flynn as Head of Press, so it'll be ok.

The main session is chaired by General Secretary Roger Bird and there's a Big Media Event: a defector is to speak. Although it's no big deal really. We all know who it is already because she's listed in the conference agenda.

'She went to a local comprehensive school and nowadays teaches in east London. She got five A-grade "A" levels and went on to read PPE at Wadham College, Oxford. Now, I was particularly pleased to hear this because it means that I am no longer the only Oxford PPE-ist in UKIP and therefore Nigel will have to stop making jokes about PPE-ists. So I'd like you all to put your hands together to welcome: Natasha Bolter.'

Given her background, Bolter's speech is somewhat lacking in content. And timing. And delivery. Perhaps she's just a bit nervous. But there is this:

'The women in UKIP have flourished equally alongside our male counterparts. We are seen for our intelligence and aptitude. We are seen for our hard graft. We are respected for our contribution. I want to be a candidate for UKIP and campaign to win, but I want to be selected on merit.'

That's entirely in line with our party's disdain for positive discrimination. Her merits are many and hopefully she'll be A-rated by the candidates' department.

Speech over, Barry Cooper entices me for a coffee which we take to the very top row of the grandstand. We can see right across the racecourse from the pinnacle of our temporary temple and also view the temptations beneath.

There are very many women within UKIP, all of them elegant and attractive, albeit mostly of mature age. So it's a novelty to have a delightful lady of younger years within our midst. Miss Bolter is to be seen below with a crowd of male admirers. They must have been greatly-moved by her speech.

'Gawain seems keen,' observes Barry.

'Is he single?'

'Don't know at the moment,' he replies.

'Roger Bird is certainly congratulating her effusively. Is Suzanne Evans still tupping him?'

'No idea,' he says.

Saturday 27th September 2014

Nigel's second address to conference is at 2.30. I've had two big glasses of red wine over lunch with Peter Whittle so am mildly dozy. The congregation seems subdued, too, as I amble my way near to the stage and sit on the front row.

There's polite, but not overwhelming, clapping for the Dear Leader. He seems downcast.

'I booked a half-hour slot today for me to speak. But I'm done now. So you could, if you like, go for a cup of tea.'

Is that supposed to be it? Make an effort, man!

Then he continues.

'Or, alternatively, you could stay and listen to a guest of mine who's coming to speak for us this afternoon. I would like you please to give a warm welcome to somebody who's not a member of our party. He's a member of parliament for the Conservative Party. But he's coming to have a chat to our conference this afternoon. And I think it'll be interesting to hear what he's got to say. Don't you?'

I'm wide awake now. Who on earth could it be? We don't have long to wait as Mark Reckless, the MP for Rochester and Strood, strides past our row from stage right. A Mexican wave of sorts emerges as we rise to our feet in turn when we all realise who it is.

Reckless ascends the podium and stands behind the lectern as the applause swells. He stares at the audience with wide eyes, stiff-necked and bearing a rictal smirk. Relaxed he is not. The applause starts to die down.

'Today, I am leaving the Conservative Party. And j. . .'

The applause cranks up again very fast and very hard and he can't finish the word, let alone the sentence.

Bunch of oiks that we are, the hall resonates with a spontaneous hooligan chant:

'UKIP - UKIP - UKIP - UKIP - UKIP'

Mark's grin is natural enough now.

Tuesday 30th September 2014

I'm being interviewed on London Live about the swathe of defections to UKIP along with that Ian Dunt fella from politics.co.uk. It's in the old *Daily Mail* building at Northcote House.

'So, Paul Oakley,' Claudia-Liza Armah puts it to me. 'Boris Johnson has just said that anyone who would consider leaving the Conservatives for your party is "utterly nuts". What are your thoughts?'

'Well, he's wrong about that and most other things. This is a big kick in the teeth for Johnson's party.'

'It is,' interjects Dunt. 'The pressure UKIP are placing on the Tories is a big problem for Cameron ahead of the general election but there's unlikely to be a flood of defectors.'

'That's jolly unfair,' says I. 'There's going to be loads more.'

Interview over, the two of us leave together to go to the Tube and Dunt has a grump.

'I like the coverage you get on London Live but I wish they'd start paying interviewees to attend.'

Silly chap. What greater payment could one desire than to meet Claudia-Liza?

Thursday 9th October 2014

UKIP's new starlet Douglas Carswell wins the Clacton by-election with 21,113 votes or 59.7%. Tory Giles Watling is second with 24.6% and 8,709. Labour's Tim Young is a distant third with 3,957.

CHAPTER EIGHTEEN

Winston Makes a Nuisance of Himself

Tuesday 14th October 2014

STEVE CROWTHER ASKS ME TO LOOK at a letter of complaint from a Peter Kirby. He's a member of the Lambeth and Croydon North branch which is chaired by Winston McKenzie.

'And please keep it to yourself,' he says.

The letter concerns a meeting of the branch which is taking place tomorrow.

'In discussion with another branch officer we have concluded that it is desirable to have a representative from Party HQ present at the meeting.

'My seven years as an auditor has taught me that where misappropriation of money is suspected it is important to retain the element of surprise. Accordingly it is important that there should be no prior knowledge in the branch that this issue is coming up at the meeting. There may of course be a reasonable explanation.'

Crowther wants me to turn up. Just to keep things courteous.

Wednesday 15th October 2014

The Lambeth and Croydon North meeting is taking place at an office by Norwood Junction railway station. We haven't told any of the officers that I'm coming because, as a Regional Organiser, we don't have to. It's hard to find the place as it's within a darkened courtyard and up a narrow flight of stairs. On arriving, there's an altercation.

Winston McKenzie is refusing entry to both Peter Kirby and Peter Morgan whom he has blocked in on the stairwell.

'You are not coming in, either of you. I'm chairman and I decide who gets to attend.'

Erm, not quite correct, Winston.

I ask the Peters to stay where they are and guide McKenzie into a stationery cupboard for a private conversation, closing the door behind us.

'It's that Peter Morgan,' he tells me. 'He keeps sending mental Tweets on behalf of the branch objecting to the 20 mph speed limits in Croydon. And I get abused in the street about it. Me!'

Really? That's it? He doesn't mention any particular problem with Kirby.

I remind him that the party rules allow him to exclude members if they're being disruptive within a meeting but this mighty power doesn't extend to keeping anyone out just because he doesn't like them.

He calms himself and after receiving assurances from the two men that they'll behave, we all move to the meeting room. Business drags on and on in spite of the fact that a young member, Lianne Bruney, has been delegated by Winston to be timekeeper. These rules apply to every-one apart from Winston who pretends not to hear the alarming beeps from her iPhone when he is speaking.

The officers give their reports except for Treasurer Marianne Bow-ness, who's absent, according to Winston, 'for obvious reasons'. It's not obvious to anyone else though. He reads out a report from her stating that the balance in the bank account is £368.90.

At this, Peter Kirby stands up.

'I have to raise an extremely important issue.'

He throws and passes photocopies of bank summaries to all the mem-bers. His hands are shaking.

'Where's that cash payment of £1,000? It doesn't appear on any of these documents as a credit!'

McKenzie stands up himself.

'Marianne's not here to defend herself. I will not permit you to comment on the finances of the branch without her present.'

'But the complaint isn't about her,' replies Kirby. 'It's about you.'

Winston winds himself down and says that he'll ask Marianne for an updated statement at the next meeting.

Kirby's unimpressed.

'You've committed a crime! You did not pay in that £10,000 donation! Where is it?'

'What £10,000?' yells McKenzie. 'You need medication!'

'I'm sorry,' says Kirby. 'I meant to say £1,000. But in any case, it was handed over to you and has now disappeared.'

None of the members are happy about this. They decide to call an Emergency General Meeting and ask that I chair it.

Thursday 16th October 2014

I speak to McKenzie about last night's meeting and the need to arrange the EGM as a priority.

'Look, it's all a plot,' he says. 'Peter Kirby and Peter Morgan are the ringleaders but the branch has been infiltrated by Labour who see me as a threat.'

'Who's infiltrated it?'

'That Lianne Bruney. And her mum, Amaising Coborne. And Robert Anderson. And they're just the ones I know about.'

Unfortunately, there are many more members than this who have issues with McKenzie.

'Winston. If you have proof that Croydon Labour Party can be arsed to organise something like that then please forward the evidence right away. Otherwise, I couldn't care less if members have a history with other parties. I'm former Tory Scum myself, you know.'

No evidence is forthcoming.

Wednesday 22nd October 2014

My Lib Dem solicitor mate, Gordon Dean, is very pleased that I've taken his advice and put my name in for the parliamentary vacancy in Great Yarmouth. He has an office there. He won't be so pleased when I win that selection and make him put me up in his home for the duration of the campaign. Serves him right.

The reason I'm applying is that Survation have said that this is one of UKIP's eight best chances for victory in the country so it's been picked by the party as a target seat. Back in March the incumbent candidate, Councillor Matt Smith, was charged with electoral fraud so has had to step down. Nice lad, but a bit of a silly sod.

I'm one of the five shortlisted candidates for tonight's selection at the Rumbold Arms. Proceedings are being overseen by Eastern Area Chairman, George Konstantinidis and by the Head of Candidates himself, David Soutter. It's that important.

Disappointingly, the evening is to be run to the Rule Book so none of the candidates will see how the others perform. I've mugged up on facts about the locality but haven't written a speech and will just go off the cuff with a few vague ideas that are milling around.

There was of course the news story from earlier today. Former Radio 1 DJ Mike Read and party member had released a single which reached No 2 in the download charts. Sung in a cod-Jamaican accent, there's been uproar so he 'deleted' it this morning. That'll do.

'Have any of you bought Mike Read's "UKIP Calypso"?'
One or two hands are raised.

'I am disgusted.

'Not because it's a little bit racist. Although it isn't.

'Not because it's a little bit rubbish. Although it is.

'But definitely because he's caved in to the liberal media and withdrawn the song from sale.'
I sweep my arm towards the UKIP backdrop.

'We are the party of purple and gold. And these colours don't run.

'Great Yarmouth needs a nasty piece of work to stand up to these *Guardian* readers. And that person is me.'

Riding the wave of smiles and applause that this elicits, I coast easily through the remainder of the speech and the questions, one of which picks on the fact that I'm a fancy-London-counsel interloper.

'I do a lot of legal work in this part of the world. There might even be some of my clients in this room. Unless, of course, your claim was lost. In that case you're mistaken. It wasn't me but someone else.'

Boringly, the branch selects the local councillor, Alan Grey. From what's been said elsewhere, his surname's apt.

Soutter has some advice in the bar afterwards.

'Don't speak with your hands in your pockets. Churchill could get away with it, but you can't.'

'Ah. I keep my hands in my pockets because it stops me shaking my fists and poking the air.'

'Remove them forthwith. Some of the greatest public speakers waved their hands a lot. From Lloyd George to Tony Blair to Margaret Thatcher. And Bill Etheridge's friend.'
David is referring to Herr Hitler. He's not really Bill's pal of course but Etheridge had once been foolish enough to describe him as a skilled orator in a lecture to our youth wing.

But what other winnable seats are open?

'Consider Portsmouth South. Sittingbourne and Sheppy. South

Basildon and East Thurrock. The London list is wide open but your talents are noted.'

Well, that's interesting. The candidate for South Basildon until five days ago had been local councillor Kerry Smith. Head Office had deselected him, the rumour being that they want a big fish for the seat. Nice to hear that I'm considered to be such a leviathan.

I'm staying in the town overnight and a couple who are branch members are good enough to give me a lift to the hotel.

'You were outstanding,' says the missis. 'But we really just wanted someone local. You'd have been much more of a Westminster MP.'

Well, technically, all MPs are 'Westminster MPs' but I know what she meant and it was kind of her to say so.

Wednesday 29th October 2014

Hustings tonight for our parliamentary seat of Greenwich and Woolwich. There are only two candidates, Ryan Acty from our branch and Ronie Johnson, a seasoned Kent activist. Ronie decides to stand down in favour of Ryan, who's thus adopted.

So that's our two Greenwich seats covered. There's been little interest so far in the three Lewisham vacancies. This is troubling. The whole point about early adoption is that we can then carry out seed-leafleting to puff our 'parliamentary spokesman'. This avoids the recurring refrain from voters that 'we only see you at election time.'

Monday 3rd November 2014

The South Basildon vacancy's advertised by Alex Peers of the candidates' department. I express my preliminary interest straight away.

'I'll put you on the list,' he says.

'Thanks Alex. I'll punt them a CV and statement when they give me more details.'

The hustings is scheduled for 10th December.

Friday 7th November 2014

The Party Chairman has some interesting news.

'While you're embroiled in the Croydon North and Lambeth imbroglio, we are now certain that their member, Peter Morgan, is a current and active member of the Conservative Party.'

Morgan is also the controller of dozens and dozens of UKIP Croydon Twitter accounts covering each and every branch in the ward. Lots of rubbish is therefore Tweeted in our name and a brand new account for @CroydonUKIP has just come to light. Its avatar is a rather good drawing of Nigel with the heading 'He fights for you'.

Yet he fights for us in the uniform of a WWII Wehrmacht officer apparently.

So who's responsible for this idiocy? It will be either Winston as branch chairman or Peter Morgan. I email them both. McKenzie responds straight away to deny it's his handiwork but Morgan doesn't reply at all.

Wednesday 12th November 2014

Although he's forgotten to get back about the Feldwebel Farage account despite several reminders, Peter Morgan finds the time to send me an incontinent statement of evidence for Winston's EGM which is some three-and-a-half-thousand words in length. By contrast, Peter Kirby's is a concise 650. Give me strength.

Mick McGough, an accountant, has been auditing the paperwork. It's a tortuous tangle but early indications are that the figures do indeed add up.

Maybe so, but I've been fielding a swarm of calls and emails from members who are generally concerned about McKenzie's leadership. Even if he's exonerated, that bad blood won't go away. I give him a call and then Steve Crowther.

'Just spoken to Winston. We had a friendly chat but he won't consider standing down as chairman to concentrate on being a parliamentary candidate. Because he is a fighter.'

Crowther's unimpressed.

'He's a myopic fighter, actually.'

True. It'll be unfortunate if the party leadership have to dust off their grey suits.

Thursday 13th November 2014

Mick McGough reaches his conclusions as auditor of Winston's branch.

'I have found no evidence to suggest funds have been used other than on appropriate branch expenses.'

Having said that, Mick observes that the paperwork is a complete mess and this needs to be resolved.

'I suggest,' he concludes, 'that more openness and team working should avoid problems in future.'

Friday 14th November 2014

Steve Crowther suspends Peter Morgan from the party for failing to reply to our queries about the Sven Hassel-esque Twitter account.

He won't be attending the Lambeth EGM as a consequence. Good. Even if he isn't a Tory after all, he's certainly a pain in the backside.

Wednesday 19th November 2014

The Emergency General Meeting is today. There's one primary item on the agenda.

'That branch members do vote by secret ballot on the question of whether they are satisfied or not satisfied that a cash donation of £1,000 forwarded by Peter Kirby to Winston McKenzie has been properly accounted for.'

There are also five additional motions of censure against both Marianne and Winston. These have been added at the insistence of members. The signatories include Bruce Machan and Ace Nnorom who are our parliamentary candidates for Streatham and Vauxhall, respectively, so this is heavy. Although how they reckon that we'll have time for this on top of everything else it's hard to guess.

This is a closed meeting and every attendee has to prove he (or she) is a local Kipper. Peter Staveley's turned up with the latest database to avoid any doubt.

'You're not a member,' says Winston to recent recruit Marcia Simpson-James.

'Yes, I am,' she replies, taken aback. 'Here's my membership card.' McKenzie clasps it and scrutinises it.

'Just be careful,' he non-apologises. 'Or I'll report you to Nigel Farage.'

Eh?

Verifications concluded, the members take their seats but there's some rumbling towards the back.

'Mr Chairman,' says one of them. 'This gentleman behind me is a journalist.'

There's a youngish guy in a black coat browsing his phone.

'You, Sir,' I demand. 'Are you a member of this branch?'

He pauses for a couple of seconds to carry on observing the screen before looking up and acknowledging the question.

'No.'

He turns his head back down.

Insolent dog.

'Then please get out. Now.'

'But I'd like to watch what's going on.'

Sure he would. I'll call the peelers if need be although that would delay the start of the meeting. It might be quicker to ask 'Champ' McKenzie to lamp him.

'Leave. Immediately.'

He does so, grudgingly.

Peter Kirby starts as complainant.

'What happened to the £1,000 cash? It wasn't paid into the bank account.'

'Why wasn't this donation reported to the branch?'

'Why didn't you write a thank-you letter to the donor? That was very rude of you, Winston.'

McKenzie responds.

'I can only describe these as malicious, breath-taking allegations of fraud and theft.

'The £1,000 never was missing, or we could never have paid for the Local Elections this year.

'And I phoned the guy to thank him. Twice. So I didn't need to write a letter.'

Treasurer Marianne Bowness is a little more focussed.

'I was faced with unprecedented family ill-health and turmoil and made the conscious decision not to bank the £1,000. It wasn't practical for me at the time, taking into consideration the impending elections. That cash was required for urgent bills.

'In mitigation, I've had a tremendously emotional period of family problems. But I've allowed due protocol to lapse, in that I did omit to declare to Head Office the donation and for this I certainly do apologise.'

She becomes rather upset and is comforted with a nice hug by one of the ladies in the audience.

So – it's really that simple. This donation wasn't properly-recorded but it certainly wasn't purloined as some had thought. Unfortunately for Winston, other issues are raised by members as well. Like a loss-making branch fish-and-chip supper. Then there were the cash-in-hand payments to a couple of security men when McKenzie's 'Croydon Carnival' was faced with threats of leftard thuggery. Also, payments for Winston's 'Commonwealth Expo' booklets which were said to have wrongly gone through the branch. Oh – and a lack of actual invoices for leaflets. Of course, we don't have time to make findings on these and they're irrelevant even if true.

My views are kept private.

'Peter. Winston. Marianne. Do any of you want to add further comments or have you said everything you want to?'

Thankfully, they have. We proceed to a secret ballot. The papers are then unfolded in front of both the complainant and the respondents and counted under three pairs of eyes.

Eight members are not satisfied but eleven are, so Winston and Marianne are both safe for the moment.

We finish just after 11 pm. Four. Hours. Lawks, that was draining. And the pubs are now shut.

CHAPTER NINETEEN

A Bird is Rogered

Thursday 20th November 2014

IT'S POLLING DAY IN ROCHESTER and Strood. I arrive by train at about 4. While wandering through the town to the campaign office at the bottom of the High Street there are many clumps of Labour activists to be seen. I don't usually bother marking myself out until doing actual door-knocking, but pin my UKIP rosette on immediately and look haughtily at the Trots. I can't see any Tories mind you.

The campaign office, organised by Matt Luck, is choca with Kippers both inside and spilling out into the street. I spy Tim Aker MEP, click my heels and bang my right fist atop my heart.

'Axis of Evil!'

He repeats the salute.

'All Hail the Axis!'

Even though he's been a MEP for some months now, it's displeasing to see that he's still wearing those shabby black shoes of his with the turned-up toes.

'Tut tut Aker. As a gentleman you should be wearing a fine pair of brogues like mine.'

I indicate my new, highly-polished, footwear. He is impressed.

'Are they Doctor Martens?'

'Yes.'

'Oh,' he changes his mind. 'You're even less stylish than me, then.'

The activists are allocated their maps. We're given a villagey area with narrow roads and lots of parents taking their children off to the Brownies or whatever. The response is positive and we stop shortly after

8 pm.

I'd planned on heading back home but there's a party for the activists and we might just take a look. A handful of us grab a minicab and head across to the Tap 'n' Tin nightclub in Railway Street.

Frisked by the bouncers, we head in. There's a small dance floor and a smattering of raggedy half-pissed blokes leering at an even smaller number of 'Ten-to-Two' lassies. Oh dear. They're playing some banging Techno, but even that's not an excuse to stay.

We refresh our plans to head back home and start to walk out.

'Leaving already?' asks one of the doormen. He'd only waved us through some forty seconds earlier after all.

'Yes. We all, er, need to have an early night.'

'No you don't. Come with me.'

He guides us back through the dance floor and then opens a side door.

There's a huge room, flanked with TV screens showing the by-election coverage and packed to the gunnels with Kippers. The bar is free and there's a buffet with pork pies. We'll stay after all.

To cap it off, Mark Reckless is victorious with 16,867 or 42.1%. Tory Tollhurst polls 13,947. The victory isn't as decisive as Carswell's but he can build on it before the general election.

Monday 1st December 2014

Winston emails me, without explanation, some photographs which show the entrance to the offices used by his branch. There's a banner which says:

'What goes around comes around'

'#ukipstinks'

'#actuplondon'

'Solidarity on World Aids Day'.

There's also a small hillock of horse manure on a carpet offcut which has been draped with a red ribbon.

He then calls almost immediately.

'This is victimisation! The poofs did it! They're attacking me because of my Christian views!'

I try to calm him down.

'No. I'm not having it,' he says. 'The police will be getting involved. It's not on.'

'Oh, come on old chap. It's quite funny and there's just enough fertiliser there for you to spread around your roses.'

He isn't pacified.

Thursday 4th December 2014

Alex Peers brings me up to speed on the selection for South Basildon. The candidates' department forwarded the details of interested applicants to the local officers some time ago.

'We haven't heard anything, but at this point it is obviously up to the branch to decide. We don't actually ask that they tell us who has been finalised.'

Well, they haven't got in touch with either myself or several others to ask us to forward a CV. After chasing the regional officers and David Soutter, I receive an email at nearly midnight.

'Dear Mr Oakley,

'You have failed to be shortlisted for the South Basildon & East Thurrock hustings.

'Kind regards,
'Kerry Smith
'Branch Secretary'

Kerry Smith is the bloke who was deselected for the seat back in October. In the absence of any actual application by me, presumably the branch had simply shut their eyes and stuck a pin into a list of names. Can't think of any other way the shortlist might have been arranged.

Sunday 7th December 2014

Winston McKenzie tells me the latest news after the horse manure incident.

'We called the police who in turn informed special branch, we were advised to install CCTV and have security on the door especially during meetings.

'After careful consideration and advice from the Police, who have been very specific, Barry Slayford is no longer willing to allow his premises to be used to accommodate UKIP Branch meetings.

'Any Meetings that were scheduled for December are now cancelled with immediate effect.'

Monday 8th December 2014

I'm told that Natasha Bolter won't be seeking the South Basildon nomination 'after all'. Soutter had personally fast-tracked her assessment and added her to the candidates' list so she should definitely have been going for this target seat.

Have certain people in the branch blocked Natasha precisely because of her attributes? A real shame if so; an Oakley/Bolter playoff would have been something to see.

I'd still have beaten her though, because I'm brilliant.

Tuesday 9th December 2014

Mark Webber, the chairman of UKIP Tower Hamlets, confides a few things to me first thing.

'We've had suspicions about Natasha from early on but she moved rapidly to consolidate her position within the branch and the party nationally. We've also been aware of the Roger Bird situation for several weeks but have had our hands tied to some extent because head office has been dealing with it.

'Sorry - forgot to mention - please can you under no circumstances speak to the media. I've been dealing with this since 5.30 yesterday morning so I'm a bit tired.'

He's telling me this because Natasha Bolter hasn't listened to Mark as her branch chairman and has gone to the *Times* with a story.

Roger Bird, party General Secretary, is then suspended from the Party following her allegations of sexual harassment. All such accusations must be treated seriously, but these ones are undermined immediately.

Roger runs to the *Daily Mail* himself to kiss, tell and disclose some icky text messages from Natasha.

'I love u bird and wish u let me look after u. Hope u feel better xx.'

'I love u and miss u and think u r sort of perfect...'

'I am really missing u bird...'

Atrocious spelling from a teacher. Anyway, if she has indeed been shagging Roger then her affections were misdirected. It is not he as General Secretary who decides who can stand for the Party but David Soutter, the head of candidates. Duh.

Wednesday 10th December 2014

Tonight's the selection meeting for South Basildon and East Thurrock. I won't be going, and am in a huff about this, but have heard rumours that the candidates are now these: Richard King, Ian Luder (ex-Labour), Richard Bingley (ex-Labour) and somebody called Anne Marie Waters (also ex-Labour).

However, the favourite is said to be former Tory MP Neil Hamilton. Also Kerry Smith, the man who was deselected back in October, is still interested.

Thursday 11th December 2014

Turns out that "issues" were raised last night about something called "cash for questions" and Neil Hamilton stood down for the South Basildon vacancy in favour of Kerry Smith. How lucky for Mr Smith!

The tabloids have been tackling Natasha Bolter's CV, too. Barking Council deny she's a teacher. Wadham College deny she's an alumnus. The Labour party refute the claim that she defected, but say she was thrown out after failing to pay her subs. Most unforgiveable of all, Bolter is actually 39 years of age and accordingly not a fruity young gal at all. Disgraceful. Surely David Soutter would have checked this out?

Anyway, Sir Tony Baldry, head of my chambers and Tory MP for Banbury, has kindly invited me for drinks at his Pimlico home tonight. I speak to our senior clerk Ian Hogg about it.

'What time are you finishing up? We can head over to Tony's together.'

'Tony's? What for?'

I'd assumed this was a general invitation to all members of chambers and the clerks as Baldry and his wife Pippa have been generous hosts of similar events in the past. That assumption was wrong. This is a very select guest list. In fact, I'm the only person in our set who's been asked to come.

'Oops. Forget I said anything. I'm sure there's no malice intended. Probably something to do with politics.'

It is.

The Baldry home is stuffed with MPs, cabinet ministers and a former leader. The evening is highly agreeable.

Tony taps a glass with a spoon and we fall silent.

'For those who don't know, I've decided to retire from the Commons at the next election. David Cameron has been good enough to offer me a peerage and I've accepted.'

It's sad to hear this. He's only 64 years old, in good health (albeit rather portlier than he should be) and a great asset to the House. He could comfortably sit for at least one more term and he'll be missed by me. Even if he does happen to be one of those pro-EU rotters.

As a side issue, his retirement will create a juicy vacancy in a plum seat. His majority is over 18,000. Hope his replacement's a sound EUsceptic and not some box-ticking Cameron Cutie.

Saturday 13th December 2014

Winston McKenzie had been approved to stand for UKIP before David Soutter had taken over as Head of Candidates. Given recent difficulties, Soutter has re-interviewed McKenzie with Adam Richardson and both are unimpressed.

Richardson writes a report.

'His branch is a shambles, the administration is almost as bad as the accounting and the man himself, comical and harmlessly eccentric as he may seem, is a liability. He could not resist even the lightest cross-examination.

'He takes the banner of UKIP to places it should no longer be now we are a serious party. I have no desire of hanging Winston out to dry as he is clearly well intentioned but we have moved on from needing him as a figurehead.'

Soutter has been doing even more digging through Winston's files.

'I have discovered that he is a failed candidate being rated at best B- to C. This is not acceptable.

'This man and his bizarre sidekick are a clusterfuck waiting to happen.'

Sunday 14th December 2014

The *Daily Mail* has a recording of a telephone call featuring the new South Basildon PPC Kerry Smith.

He's rude about Olly Neville,

'He's now setting up BLT UKIP on Facebook. What the old poofters call themselves. I just call it a BLT like the sandwiches.'

He is horrid about Lucy Bostick and her 'Chigwell peasants.'

He is offensive about a 'Chinky bird', who is, presumably, Claire Khaw.

'No-one, not even the BNP or National Front would touch it because of her racist views.'

He's unwise about Farage's reasons for promoting Steve Woolfe to the top of the GLA list in 2012:

'He got a nice fat envelope.'

Smith steps down. A new candidate will be chosen. I'm steering clear.

Monday 15th December 2014

The Natasha Bolter situation is dragging on and Steve Crowther informs us of the line to take.

'With reference to the reports in the press over the weekend about selection and in particular the work of David Soutter, Head of Candidates, I would like to make it absolutely clear that David has at all times worked with consummate professionalism. The press reports about him and his work are entirely without foundation.'

Wednesday 17th December 2014

Things haven't quietened down in Winston's branch in spite of his exoneration over the funds. There have been a mass of resignations and regular calls to me from irate local Kippers. On top of that, the suspended member Peter Morgan has been sending out lengthy multicoloured emails to the whole membership and has arranged an unauthorised meeting for tonight. This is in breach of his suspension, section F of the Party Rules and, indeed, the Data Protection Act. He seems to have a lot of support, irritatingly enough.

McKenzie has some excuses and demands for me.

'I know you think Peter Kirby is a "dear old man", but believe me he is complicit with Peter Morgan and a leading part of the onslaught against me. I need suggestions as to various avenues available to me under the jurisdiction of the Party. Or legally.'

More hand-holding then. Sigh.

'Winston. The very fact that your branch is falling apart under your feet is unacceptable.'

He has a solution.

'Then I will be requesting the NEC to consider how something can be set up for the future. Like a troubleshooter who can zoom in on problems and aid the status quo at a minimum.'

Sure you will. But I and others are getting tired of this.

I speak to Farage.

'Nigel, you're a fan of Winston but things are getting out of control.'

'I am a fan but there are limits.'

'Peter Morgan's the immediate wrongdoer. We could use his behaviour as the reason to suspend the committee and thus the whole branch. With party oversight we'd get it back on course.'

'Light the fuse.'

Crowther concurs and authorises me to suspend the branch, which I do, with an hour to spare before the unauthorised meeting is due to start.

In the aftermath of his silly unauthorised meetings, Peter Morgan will now be facing expulsion proceedings.

Thursday 18th December 2014

A story has appeared in the *Huffington Post*.

'Tories Demand UKIP Defector Mark Reckless Pays Back £3,000'

It goes on:

'Andrew Mackness, chairman of the Rochester and Strood constituency, told the *Medway Messenger*: "Mark Reckless and Chris Irvine his agent were approving expenditure up to two days before defection which in the least was deceitful and misleading and led to costs that the Conservative Association believe should be repaid to them.'

They're going to bring a case a case against him in the civil courts. In order to do so a party must file an official Claim Form. Bullish and lairy with the righteousness of their cause, the Tories have disclosed that Claim Form to all and sundry via the *HuffPo* website. If any question of legal privilege arose at all, they've waived it.

The case is brought by something or other which is described as the 'Rochester and Strood Constituency Conservative Association' and the entire nature of the complaint is set out in these sparse words:

'Mr Reckless was a Conservative MP for the Rochester and Strood Constituency until his defection to UKIP on 27 September 2014. His defection to UKIP resulted in unusable 2015 General Election campaign literature the Rochester and Strood Constituency Conservative Association had no choice but to later discard. This consequently incurred an unnecessary expense. Mr Christopher Irvine was Mr Reckless' Agent at the time.'

There are two problems. Firstly, the 'Rochester and Strood Constituency Conservative Association' is an unincorporated body and thus has no 'legal personality'. As far as any court will be concerned, the organisation simply doesn't exist. So it can't bring any claim against anyone.

Secondly, they don't set out the nature of the matter. Are they saying a contract's been broken? Have Reckless and Irvine fallen short of a duty of care? Is there a breach of trust of some kind? Who knows?

Rochester Tories are thus bold, brave and, indeed, courageous. As Sir Humphrey Appleby would certainly say.

Reckless has sent out an email to supporters asking for donations in response to the claim. Paying them off would certainly be one way of

dealing with it. But let's not be too hasty.
      I give him a call.

CHAPTER TWENTY

Getting Fit to Fight a General Election

Friday 19th December 2014

WINSTON MCKENZIE APPEARS on a thing called 'Chat Politics'. Goodness knows why. He's not sought Head Office permission.

It's put to him that, without Nigel Farage, UKIP wouldn't be a credible force.

'Look – Owen,' says McKenzie.

The interviewer corrects him. 'Oscar.'

'Oscar. It's the punches, man. Listen. Jesus was one man, we're his army. Farage is one man, and we're his army and that's what it's all about'.

'Jesus'? The press are circling and Soutter's going to deal with it

'The matter of his supposed passing of the assessment course gets more and more convoluted. I am told that the records at Lexdrum show a fail by a huge margin. The entry on the spread sheet shows a grade "A" candidate but no record of who passed him, when he was passed, who was the lead assessor or the marks for each section.

'He is many things but a grade "A" candidate he is most definitely not.'

Friday 2nd January 2015

It's getting so boring hearing the words 'Winston' and 'McKenzie.' His adventures are still sprinkled through the local Croydon press and occasionally the national media. The London members more generally are not happy that the smell is wafting through the capital and affecting our chances in the general election.

I consult Soutter and Crowther. We're coming 'round to the view that he ought to be pushed to resign as branch chairman. His view that he is the sole and final arbiter of this decision needs to be tackled. Otherwise, the grumbles will run.

'But he should be allowed to remain as a candidate,' I opine. 'Publicity about his exploits will be diluted in the course of the national campaign. If we ditch him, there'll be the inevitable cries of "Waycist", if not from him then from others. I'm open to being persuaded otherwise.'

Nobody does try to persuade me otherwise.

Wednesday 7th January 2015

Steve Crowther writes a friendly note to Winston. It's not very subtle.

'I want to reiterate the advice that both Nigel and I gave you which is that you should now be focusing on being a candidate rather than a branch officer.'

It's nonetheless too subtle for Winston and there's no response.

Saturday 10th January 2015

This is the last session of candidates' assessments that I'm going to attend. I've been one of the quizmasters at eleven of them over the past few months. Several hundred members have passed before our baleful gazes as we're looking to have a full national slate for the imminent general election.

There are several modules and it's possible to re-sit these if there's only been a close failure. The political knowledge section covers things like payments on foreign aid, the name of the secretary of state for something-or-other and so on. One guy failed and came back the following week. He wasn't happy with the repeat grilling.

'This isn't fair! The questions you're asking are different from last time!'

Of course they are. He fails. Again.

Then there's the personal interview. Education, work, family, previous campaigning experience and stuff like that. Pretty boring, apart from on one occasion.

'Is there anything in your background which might embarrass the party?'

'Well, I've just done three years in prison for banking fraud. Will that matter?'

It will.

The media interview is three-fold because all media scenarios are different. Local papers want to deal with local issues and an applicant who can do nothing but bang on about the EU will fail. A radio station may have audience members phoning in and some of those will be hostile and/or nutters. The scenario for national media, however unlikely, is that Nigel's too busy to attend so the candidate is stepping up instead to be scrutinised by Paxman.

This is the best section. I love cross-examining.

One young lady is very flustered by my probing.

'It's certainly true what they say about you, Paul.'

'And what do they say?'

'That you are the Simon Cowell of UKIP.'

I am indeed.

Saturday 24th January 2015

The Party issues a press statement about one of our new MEPs, Amjad Bashir.

'The allegations against Mr Bashir are of a grave nature and we will be forwarding our evidence obtained so far to the police. UKIP will not tolerate anyone abusing their positions in the party, as we have a firm commitment to differing ourselves from the existing political classes. As a result, Mr Bashir's involvement with the party was suspended today with immediate effect pending further investigations.'

Bashir immediately fucks off to the Tories. David Cameron is apparently 'absolutely delighted.' Gawain Towler in turn reckons 'the Conservatives are welcome to him'.

More important is the fact that Bashir, like all other aspirant candidates, signed the Charter by which he promised to stand down as an MEP if he ever left the party. I speak to Matt Richardson.

'Can't we sue the shit? Perhaps for breach of contract?'

'No, we've looked into it and apparently the role of an MEP is, legally, seen as personal to them as far as the EU institutions are concerned.'

Un-good. Still worth a punt I reckon. The bad publicity he'd face might be worth it even if we lost.

Yet it's hopefully not going to happen again.

Wednesday 18th February 2015

Tonight our branch is choosing candidates for Lewishams West and Penge, East and Deptford. We're not going to win any of them but we're likely to do from best to worst in that order.

Although the borough used to have Tory MPs including Colin Moynihan and John Maples, locals are now riddled with Stockholm Syndrome. They consistently vote overwhelmingly for Labour MPs who consistently let them down.

The applicants include Massimo DiMambro from our own branch. There are also Mick Greenhough, Dan Tubb and Owen Brolly from Bromley and a bloke we don't know who lives in Dartford called Gary Harding. The branch also received a form at the last minute from a chap called Hugh Rosen from Fulham.

We're on the first floor of the Greenwich Tavern and the meeting's busy. I rule that all of the candidates will battle in front of each other and the members will then allocate each one to the seat they feel is appropriate.

Lewisham West goes to Gary Harding, Hugh Rosen wins Lewisham East and Massimo's given the dog turd of Lewisham Deptford.

None of the Bromley Boys are chosen although they'd all have been fine. Having said that, there's considerable irritation amongst the members that Mick Greenhough turned up in, and wore throughout, a tatty old coat. Shades of Michael Foot at that Remembrance Day Service. There are a few rude and funny comments which, hopefully, don't get back to him.

Friday 20th February 2015

Another meeting of Winston's suspended branch has been arranged for the 24th February. This has been set up by we Regional Organisers as the members need to get back on track with the election imminent. This meeting will take it out of suspension, but will also require elections to the committee and, obviously, for chairman.

McKenzie doesn't like the idea and emails Farage, copying-in Crowther, Soutter and myself.

'Guvnor,

'I appeal to all concerned that the Branch EGM for 24/02/15 be cancelled.

'I have it on good authority that both the Croydon Advertiser together with the Croydon Guardian are about to ridicule me on front page exposes, based on the information that will be pledged at this particular meeting, following on from the continuous ridicule of on-line media, Inside Croydon.

'I have the support I need, in particular with the national media who are following my campaign in light of the racism slurs made against our Party.'

And that's precisely the point, isn't it?

Sunday 22nd February 2015

I've told our three Lewisham candidates that we need to send a press release to the *News Shopper*. The chaps have been asked to send me 50 words setting out who they are and what they'd do for the voters. Plan is to collate these into a single release. Know it doesn't sound a lot, but on past experience this rag's unlikely to give us the three-page spread we deserve.

Guff duly-received from Gary and Massimo, but nothing from Hugh. I chase him.

Monday 23rd February 2015

Hugh Rosen finally replies. His boss has refused to allow him to stand for UKIP. Would've been nice if he'd checked that before putting his name forward, especially at the last minute.

We're now stuck with a vacancy in Lewisham East.

I then receive a terse email from Soutter.

'Mole Valley have requested you. Please contact Rob Burberry.'

So it looks as though the Lewisham East candidacy won't be falling to Oakley.

Tuesday 24th February 2015

The Lambeth meeting is being chaired tonight by me, again, with my lovely assistant Peter Staveley. Winston and Marianne have, at the last moment, decided they won't be standing again for the committee. Call a ticker-tape parade!

Emmanuel Ehirim is voted in as the new chairman and Peter Kirby as treasurer.

Thank goodness all this nonsense is behind us. Mother Hen that I am, I guide Winston over to Kirby at the close of the meeting.

'Can I ask you two gentleman to shake hands and bury this?' McKenzie stretches out his palm with a smile.

'I will never, ever shake hands with you,' is Kirby's response. 'You're a crook.'

Oh well.

Wednesday 25th February 2015

Michael Foulston, UKIP Agent for the Mole Valley seat, sends me a formal notification.

'Time constraints will prevent the branch from meeting before we invite you to be our candidate for the General Election so, by way of this email, I am inviting you to fill that position on our behalf, subject to the NEC approving my action. I feel that I am on safe ground in making this offer as you have been highly-recommended to us.'

And with that, I'm adopted as a Parliamentary candidate. What good taste the branch has. We agree to meet on 5th March when Bob Cane will give a tour of the constituency.

This isn't a target seat and UKIP won't be elected, but the party's wish is my command.

Saturday 28th February 2015

It's the Margate conference and it's bloody freezing. I arrive on a fairly-early train. There are rumours of a hard-left demonstration so the party badge is pinned on as soon as I step on to the platform. On leaving the station there is indeed one of them handing out leaflets. It is that co-loured-haired crone once famed for abusing Farage from the audience in an episode of *BBC Question Time*. Nobody else though. Lazy beggars.

This isn't just an event for the usual socialising. We desperately need a candidate for Lewisham East. Having made various enquiries, nobody's interested so I intend to find Mick Greenough and twist his arm to stand for us after all.

Naturally, I come across Peters Lello and Whittle in the hall. We have a coffee and then decide to wander outside to see if any pinko pro-testors have turned up.

They haven't, but an impressively-camouflaged Humvee is parked up the road. It's the Britain First "Mystery Machine" and they're here to protect us. Uninvited, we may add. We walk back inside as it's still icy.

A gruff-voiced Estuary-English speaker is addressing Conference from the podium. It is Kellie, formerly Frank, Maloney the boxing pro-moter and one-time UKIP London mayoral candidate. She's apologising for once saying that she wasn't prepared to campaign for the party in Croydon as there were too many gays there.

'Not very convincing,' observes Lello.

'What, her apology?'

'Who says I was talking about the speech?'

Bitch!

Eventually, I find Mick Greenough and put on my best salesman's patter and try to persuade him that our people honestly and truly believe he's our only hope for an historic victory in Lewisham East. Mick, however, has got the 'ump.

'Can't do it. I've decided to stand in Aberdeen instead,' he sniffs.

Most people are leaving from the rear of the Winter Gardens as the Leftards have now congregated at the front. Moreover, as it's only just turned 1 pm, we've all been ordered to spend the afternoon campaigning for Nigel in Thanet South where he's now the PPC. It's easier for us to be collected in convoy from the back of the conference hall anyway.

We lurk about waiting to be picked up and decanted to far flung areas of the seat. There are lots of us and few cars. This takes some while. It's also cold, damp and lunchtime.

I turn to the Two Peters.

'Pub?'

'Pub.'

'Pub.'

We force ourselves to walk a couple of hundred yards from the Winter Gardens. Exhausted, and having reached The Hoy alehouse by the seafront we stop for well-deserved refreshment before continuing our arduous trek to the train station. The place is quiet.

I, Whittle, Lello, Jamie Ross-McKenzie and a couple of others are seated at a table in the middle of the pub. We've just started on our second round and the place is starting to fill up. Behind us there's now a larger group of twenty or so. I have my back to them but incrementally become aware of their traditional deformities and odours.

They are Leftards.

They have overheard our conversation.

They will have worked out who we are.

Is there going to be a problem? This is a broadly-gay contingent of Kippers so the philosophical contradictions of the Trots might give them pause for thought. In any case, if they do want trouble they'll be proceeding on the stereotypical assumption that these homos will be a soft touch. How very foolish. Gays are often gym rats. And, obviously, men.

As Davy Coburn regularly reminds everyone:

'I may be a poof but I'm not a pansy.'

Sadly, our particular posse is entirely composed of willowy and blubbery aesthetes. And I myself have not lifted Extremely Heavy Weights for some time because of a rotator cuff injury.

I mention my observations to the guys.

'Probably wise if we pipe down with the UKIP stuff gentlemen.' Then a lyric by The Jam floats into the subconscious. Something about alehouses, a West London prison and a surfeit of right-wing gatherings.

Why? Because a different cluster of a dozen blokes has coalesced on the other side of the bar. They're looking at the commies. Our group is stuck between the two forces.

I don't really need to have a wee but head off to the gents anyway and as I return question one of the new gang.

'Nice pub isn't it? Are you from Britain First by any chance?'

'Certainly are mate. You lot are UKIP aren't you?'

'We are indeed. Thanks for coming out today. We're just heading off back to London.'

I get back to our table.

'Drink up chaps. We need to leave.'

We do.

CHAPTER TWENTY-ONE

Thank You, Suzanne!

Thursday March 5th 2015

BEHOLD! MY UGLY MUG IS ON THE FRONT PAGE of a newspaper for the first time ever! It's only the *Dorking Advertiser*, but a start nevertheless. Good headlines too, and both true:

'Fourth time lucky for UKIP's Mole Valley Candidate?'

'Party denies selection process has been a shambles.'

I knew that Roger Bird had initially been adopted for the seat some time ago but had stepped down after it emerged that he'd rogered that bird, Natasha Bolter. What I didn't know was that he'd been replaced by a fellow called Stephen Musgrove who'd then abandoned the role rather sharpish.

I was also unaware that Dan Tubb, one of the blokes who'd been rejected by my Greenwich and Lewisham posse on the 18th February, had then been slotted in as the candidate before levering himself out in a matter of days.

Tut!

Well, they've left the best until last.

'More from Mr Oakley in next week's edition,' the paper concludes. And there will be.

Friday 6th March 2015

Political parties must approve their candidates' general election addresses which will be sent out free of charge by the Post Office. As a Regional Organiser, I have that power of assent.

Marianne sends me Winston's draft for his seat of Croydon North.

As with myself, he doesn't have any decent photographs so that's not a concern. Yet, there's the text itself:

> 'It's all about the dump, 'bout the dump! Last year I caused controversy bringing Croydon North's plight to the attention of national media, stating "Croydon is a dump!" It's brought forth; a Rubbish Tzar and a Croydon North Streets Independent Commission actively compiling an in-depth dossier, "Clean up Croydon North"- Feb '15, with excellent recommendations. With my undoubted ability to communicate - I lit the touch-paper! Indisputable evidence was collated. Together we will improve this Borough. Next, I will tackle poverty by creating jobs!

> 'Yours, as ever WINSTON'

Harrumph. I do not approve.

Sunday 8th March 2015
Councillor Pete Reeve has heard of our problem with filling the vacancy in Lewisham East and comes up with an option – the former Labour activist, Anne Marie Waters.

I ask for the views of the branch committee and also our other parliamentary candidates. Nobody has ever met her. Except for Peter Whittle.

'I know Anne Marie well, indeed am seeing her this week. She would be an excellent candidate.'

Good. Let's sound her out then.

Monday 9th March 2015
I get in touch with Anne Marie. Is she up for it?

'Yes, very interested! Any advice or thoughts? I'm very keen and I'm grateful to Peter for his recommendation. If there's anything I can do, or anything about myself your group would like to know, please give me a shout.'

We settle on Wednesday for a chat, after the London Region meeting.

Tuesday 10th March 2015
The Mole Valley leaflets are finalised with the branch officers.

We're going to feature issues arising in Gatwick, Beare Green, Effingham Lodge and Leith Hill. They draft most of the copy as I don't even know where these places are (apart from Gatwick, obvs).

There's another issue. Mole Valley in general and Box Hill in particular are now infested with bicyclists. This is a consequence of London Mayor Boris Johnson exceeding his authority and encouraging national cycling events there in the aftermath of the Olympics. This is annoying many residents.

It's annoyed me, too, by slowing down the rightful passage of my 4WD diesel tank for a few seconds on a few occasions. How dare they!

So I've written this bit for one of the leaflets myself.

'Boris Johnson conspired with Surrey County Council to introduce regular bike competitions in the Surrey Hills. These have boxed-in locals and led to traffic chaos. If elected, I will work with the Greater London Authority to have these events moved to Uxbridge. See how he likes it.'

Johnson will probably be the new Uxbridge MP. The officers laugh and agree.

And – in other news. The party's role of Commonwealth Spokesman is abolished. This means that Winston McKenzie is now without any post. That doesn't mean he's been sacked though.

Actually, it does.

Wednesday 11th March 2015

I take the precaution of sending candidates' head David Soutter an email first thing about Anne Marie Waters.

'In general, she looks a good choice. However, her "Islamo-scepticism" does occasionally come across rather strongly. If we choose her the branch will advise her to tone down the issue. But will this be a problem as far as Head Office are concerned? If not, I think we'll invite her. Please confirm.'

There's no reply.

Come the evening, it's the UKIP London Region meeting at Brooks Mews. I've invited Anne Marie to sit in as an observer and also asked Peter Whittle to come along too. Peter Lello's entitled to be there anyway as a delegate. The four of us head to the Iron Duke afterwards to quiz her informally about the vacancy.

'You're not going to bang on about Islam are you?' I ask her.

'Absolutely not. My focus will be on winning a referendum.'

The two Peters and the lone Paul huddle together. She can string a sentence together quite eloquently. She's ex-Labour. She's a woman. And she is also a Famous Les. We're not interested in demographic tokenism but Anne-Marie's attributes kill the cliché that UKIP is just a retirement home for old Tory Boys. This might work in our favour with left-leaning voters in this left-leaning seat.

We offer her the vacancy and she accepts.

Thursday 12th March 2015

I always enjoy coming to the Medway County Court. Although it's a grotty chunk of concrete, there are excellent views over the former Chatham dockyard from the windows of the gents' toilets at the back of the building. You can see where the wooden walls of England were once constructed which allowed us to defeat Napoleon.

Today isn't for sightseeing, though. I'm appearing as Counsel for Mark Reckless and Chris Irvine in their strike-out application against the Rochester Tories' court claim. On arrival, there's a camera crew hovering. Making a wild guess that they're here for our case, I'm sorry to have to tell them that neither Reckless nor Irvine will be turning up. Not that the Defendants are being magnificent or anything, but this application is on points of law and no evidence will be heard. Disappointed, they pack up.

When I sign in at the front desk, the court usher tells me that a chap from the Press Association is also around and was wondering if he could sit in court. No problem on my part. The matter doesn't need to be heard 'in camera'.

The Conservatives are represented by one Mr Tranter who isn't a lawyer but a branch officer. He's accompanied by a chap in his 20s whose name I don't catch.

'We'd like to add another £665 to our claim,' Tranter tells me. 'We'd forgotten about the wasted postal vote letters. That will bring the total, including court fees, up to £3,862. Would you object to that?'

'You don't understand why we're here do you? I'm going to have your claim dismissed. With costs.'

We're called in before Judge Ashley. Despite running straight to the *HuffPo* when they issued proceedings, the Claimants' representatives suddenly want to make a request to the court.

'Would you mind if the press are kept out? We're acting in person and don't want to face any embarrassment.'

The Judge turns to me. 'Mr Oakley?'

'Well, it's supposed to be in open court. But I won't make a fuss either way.'

The Press Association bloke is duly-excluded.

'It's your application, Mr Oakley.'

It is, and I make the submissions. The Defendants have the right to reply. Mr Tranter begins and I start scribbling down a few notes but then realise something.

'Are you reading that out?'

'Yes. Please have a copy.' He hands one over to me.

The crux of their argument is as follows:

'Mr Reckless and Mr Irvine, in our opinion, did not exercise their duty of loyalty or use reasonable care to serve and protect the interests of the Conservative Association. They acted in their own interest, or without reasonable care, so violating their fiduciary duty and therefore become liable for the resulting expenditure.

'We can show with reasonable certainty that Mr Reckless had intended to defect to UKIP at least one month (and quite probably much earlier) before his actual publicised defection on 27 September 2014. During the weeks prior to his defection we can also show that he and his agent Mr Irvine were deliberately encouraging, assisting and/or agreeing to considerable expenditure knowing that this was a complete waste of expenditure and effort by the Conservative Association who were about to become their political opponents.'

In other words – It's so unfair! Not nearly good enough however.

Judgment is scathing:

'There are no grounds for bringing the claim in law, nor has it complied with the court rules. It was said by Mr Tranter that the association was handicapped by a lack of legal knowledge. But parties are deemed to know the law.

'The claim stands struck out and the Defendants are entitled to their costs assessed in the sum of £1,850.'

On top of this, the local Tories have also had to fork out a court fee of £185 to issue the case in the first place. So this little exercise in grandstanding has cost them a total of £2,035. Ouch!

Friday 13th March 2015

Andrew Mackness of Rochester Tories has been speaking to the press about yesterday.

'It is not a case that we have lost, the judge said it could not go forward on a technicality. It is frustrating.'

He's absolutely correct. The 'technicality' being that they had no case.

Sunday 26th March 2015

I've driven Peters Whittle and Lello and Ryan Acty down to Grays Yacht Club to help out Tim Aker in his Thurrock campaign. There's a good turnout from across London with about fifty people present. We're filling envelopes with leaflets which have been individually addressed to every voter. They're printed, but look like a handwritten note on lined paper.

They really are a brilliant personal touch and something that we ought to use in future right across the country.

Jackie Doyle-Price had better be equally ingenious for the Tory campaign or else she's out.

There's food and drink to go round too. One of the attendees is particularly pleased.

'Ooh. Ginger nuts!'

He picks up the packet, but there's a symbol on the side that he notices straight away.

'Halal-certified. I'm not eating that muck.'

Personally, I couldn't care less if these biscuits were stunned before being butchered and scoff several.

Wednesday 1st April 2015

Anne Marie wants advice.

'I've an offer of an interview with Jamie from the *News Shopper* this afternoon - any thoughts?'

I do indeed. The *News Shopper* is not to be trusted. She's to make up some excuse about being busy and get them to send their questions by email. Her draft replies are to be cast before my eyes prior to submission.

Then Peter Kirby makes another complaint about Winston for a brand new reason.

'I now ask you to remove McKenzie from the position of PPC for Croydon North. I hold signed statements from 25 branch members asking for this.'

Cheers Peter. But it's up to the Party Chairman to decide what sanction to apply, if any. Besides, the election nominations close on 9th April. If we're to act, it will have to be within the next week and that includes choosing a new candidate (and the Easter holidays). The very existence of a complaint will lead to damaging press coverage.

On the other hand, Crowther might decide not to consider the complaint until after the election itself which would be both 'unfortunate' and serendipitous.

Kirby and compatriots would be bound by the UKIP Rules:

AA.6.3 Party members shall refrain from commenting on cases in Party meetings or in public while disciplinary proceedings are pending. The Disciplinary Panel may invoke disciplinary proceedings against any member it considers to have breached this requirement.

That would zip their lips until the election is over and done with.

Saturday 4th April 2015

Kirsten Farage calls me about the new Winston thing.

'Are they absolutely mad? We can't afford this at the opening of an election. They're utterly stupid. Shut this thing down.'

I am indeed to tell them that it's being treated as a formal complaint and so write to the aggrieved parties straight away.

'The general election campaign is now in full flow. For obvious reasons, any breach of the confidentiality rules either by you as complainants or by any other party member is likely to result in the most severe of repercussions. Those repercussions may include immediate expulsion from the Party.'

I give McKenzie a call, too, because there's no doubt this will leak.

'Winston. You're not to speak to any journalist about this. In fact, don't speak to anyone at all.'

'Understood, guv'nor.'

For good or bad, Winston McKenzie will remain our candidate.

Monday 6th April 2015

Peter Kirby calls.

'It seems to me that the matter has been smartly kicked into the long grass in the hope that it will go away.'

Well-spotted Peter.

Tuesday 7th April 2015

A publication called 'Road.cc' has found out about the leaflets. They took their bloody time.

'Move Box Hill cycling events to Uxbridge, says Mole Valley UKIP candidate'

And:

'While he stops short of naming it in a leaflet distributed to local residents in the safe Tory seat, Paul Oakley's principal target appears to be the Prudential Ride London-Surrey 100 sportive and the Classic pro race that follows it.'

Yeah. What he said.

Their webpage attracts some mean comments and I'm hurt. Can't complain though as I already knew that these be-lycrad loons share the same worldview as Father Fintan Stack from 'Father Ted'. They've had their fun. And that's all that matters.

Wednesday 8th April 2015

The *London Evening Standard* have also heard of my opinions on the other kind of Boris Bikes. They, too, are horrid.

As is *The Independent*, with the headline, 'Bloody cyclists coming over here. . .'

I can't bear it!

Friday 10th April 2015

The *Surrey Advertiser* finally pick up on the Johnson bike thing. Beaten down by all this fury, I backtrack.

'In reality, I am unlikely to push for this after May 7 as our excellent Uxbridge UKIP candidate Jack Duffin will defeat the flaxen fop.'

Tuesday 14th April 2015

Hustings tonight, at the Bookham Baptist Church. Inside information is that the Green Party will be there in force to support their candidate, Jacquetta Fewster. So I've printed off the relevant parts from the 5th report of the Intergovernmental Panel on 'Climate' 'Change'. As these eleven sheets are buried within a document of precisely 1,552 pages, I'm proud of my investigatory powers.

Things focus on airport expansion to begin with. The Lib Dem is discomfited by the fact that his party compatriot Vince Cable won't tolerate this at Heathrow (where his voters live) and demands Gatwick development instead (where these voters live).

All the candidates are insistent that Heathrow's the obvious choice. I can't say anything of the kind as that would be a betrayal of UKIP's Cliff Dixon and his Hillingdon Crew who've been campaigning for precisely the opposite.

'Mr Oakley?' The Reverend Elms puts the question to me.

'Neither. Manston Airport in Kent must expand. Locals there actually want this.'

Our old London manifesto from 2012 has been useful at long last.

Then we get on to the most gassy part of the evening. 'Global' 'Warming'. Blah blah blah CO2 blah blah blah. All of them posture, even the Tory.

My turn.

'Let me read you some extracts from the IPCC report about this grave matter.'

Everyone listens with serious faces, especially the Greens (and it's fairly obvious who they are. Dirty-looking). I tie it all together.

'In other words, in spite of the scaremongering there's been no global warming since 1998 and they've no idea why. This whole theory's nonsense.'

The Kippers, and many Tories, applaud but the Greenies yelp in anger and jab their fingers at me.

'Not my words,' I add. 'This is from the Holy Book of the man-made global warming superstition.'

I waft the photocopied pages in their general direction. This makes it worse. One cheeky young lady has the audacity to consult her smartphone.

'That's not true,' she yowls. 'The report's executive summary says this.'

She reads a bit out. And I answer.

'Any executive who only looks at the executive summary will not remain an executive for very long. This is why our politicians are conning you. They haven't actually read the report.'

Fewster's keen to jump in but I don't let her.

'All attempts to impoverish us by demonising fossil fuel will fail. Think of the Icelandic volcano in 2010. Thousands of tons of gas were spewed into the air. What should we have done? Put a cork in it?'

I let Fewster have a go at last.

'Yes, but 97% of scientists agree that global warming is a serious threat to our planet.'

'Really? Name three of those scientists.'

'Um.'

Wednesday 15th April 2015

Today is the 38th anniversary of the launch of the spine-tingling

LP by The Stranglers, *Rattus Norvegicus*. It's also the launch of the spine-tingling election manifesto by The UKIP, 'Believe in Britain'. This is a magnificent omen. I drive to Essex with the bass on the stereo set to 11 while the artistry of Black/Burnel/Cornwell/Greenfield makes the car doors throb alarmingly.

It's at the Thurrock Hotel within the citadel of Tim Aker MEP. The task of compiling the policies had originally been given to Aker. For whatever reason it had then been passed to the hands of Suzanne Evans who's finally completed it. It's unclear if the launch locus shows that Timbles has been forgiven or if it's an attempt by the leadership to rub his nose in it.

On arrival, the venue's extremely busy. There are even marshals in the car park because it's nearly full with press vans and activist jalopies.

I take a chair next to Neville Watson and my phone rings almost immediately. It's Batten.

'Are you here?' I ask. 'Seats are filling up fast.'

'No,' he replies. 'I'm busy with other things today. I just wanted to tell you something.'

Oh?

'You wouldn't believe the support we're getting in Romford. I really think I can beat Andrew Rosindell.'

'Hopefully you will, Gerard. I like Andrew but Romford deserves a UKIP MP.'

'Yes,' he replies. 'But if I win that means I'll have to give up my seat in Brussels and you'll take over as the London MEP. Start making your preparations.'

That would be wonderful. However, I know perfectly well that Rosindell's a superlative campaigner. This is because I've helped him campaign. It isn't worth looking in the estate agents' windows of Brussels just yet.

Nigel opens.

'Our saving and spending commitments have been verified by the independent think-tank, the CEBR. I believe what we've done with this document is to set a new gold standard for how manifestos in this country should be produced and at the moment nobody else can match it.'

But: Farage is not to be the star of today's show.

'I can say to you today that I absolutely congratulate Suzanne Evans and her team for producing this excellent manifesto. And the fact that she has done it with all of our costings, independently-verified and backed up, says much about her professionalism.'

He hands over to Evans, who is superb. Although she was editor rather than author, this is the first manifesto ever, from any of the parties that I've been a member of, that I support in every respect.

Thank you, Suzanne.

She exits the lectern for Paul Nuttall to deal with questions. The press are disappointed that there's nothing loopy in the document so the number of hands in the air is initially sparse.

Until, that is, Christopher Hope from the *Daily Telegraph* saves the day. Hope evidently has a shrine to his hero, Michael Crick, at home. That would be one explanation for his tedious attempt to replicate the Crick/Godfrey Bloom altercation from last year.

'Are you happy that the only black face in the document is on the overseas aid page?'

Nobody thwacks him with a manifesto. Instead, an overture of sneering jeers builds to a crescendo. It is: Orchestral. He tries to carry on.

'And secondly, can I ask you. . .'

No. He cannot. He's silenced as, starting with Neville, every black and Asian activist and candidate rises to their feet and gesticulates their pride at being Kippers. There are a lot of them.

CHAPTER TWENTY-TWO

The Silence of 4 Million Voices

Friday 17th April 2015

JAMIE MICKLETHWAIT from the *News Shopper* is, for once, interested in my views on something.

'Will Anne Marie Waters or UKIP be making a statement on the *Daily Mirror* report?'

What *Mirror* report?

Oh dear. This one.

> 'Two of UKIP's election candidates have been filmed spouting anti-Islamic hate at a far-right rally.
>
> 'Magnus Nielsen and Anne Marie-Waters were guest speakers at a weekend event organised by Mothers Against Radical Islam And Sharia – MARIAS – which has close links to groups like the English Defence League.
>
> 'Ms Waters, who hopes to become MP for Lewisham East, South East London, was also filmed telling an undercover reporter "a lot of people need to be deported" and "many mosques need to be closed down".
>
> 'She said: "For a start the immigration will have to stop, the immigration from Islamic countries has to stop entirely, that is just the way it is".'

There's much frantic discussion between myself, Towler and Gill at the press office. We settle on this piece of brilliant blandness.

'Anne-Marie Waters is a well known campaigner for women's rights. She campaigns against inequality for women in British society as a whole and amongst parts of the Islamic community.'

Monday 20th April 2015

I discover that South London Anti-Fascists (who?) are organising a demonstration at the 'Mummy's Gin Fund' hustings set for 10 days' time: 'Lewisham East Says No to Anne Marie Waters (UKIP)'. Like these nobbers speak for the whole constituency. I talk to our candidate.

'Anne Marie - I suggest you tell the organisers and the police. Copy me in on correspondence to both.'

Then it's announced that Mr Justice Warby has ruled that the speech by Jane Collins to our Doncaster conference did indeed defame the Labour MPs it referred to. So it was too strong. How awful for Jane.

Wednesday 22nd April 2015

Helen, the organiser of the Lewisham, East hustings, is concerned about the planned demonstration.

'I have spoken to the local police who are using their intelligence officers to find out how much of a risk they pose, if any. I have also been in touch with the group to inform them that this is an event for women and their families and that there will be children in attendance.'

Very much doubt that the presence of kids will make any difference at all to these fascists.

Wednesday 22nd April 2015

5.31 pm. I'm trying to do some work on a case that's lain dormant for months. As I've forgotten everything about it in the interim, this is a creaky exercise. Adam Richardson breaks the tedium by calling.

'Winston's about to appear on ITV.'

Oh no.

'When?'

'Tonight. He's not cleared it with the press office. We thought you might be able to stop him.'

'What if he won't listen,' I ask, 'Does the decree come down from above?'

'If necessary.'

We hang up and Adam immediately calls again.

'Gawain's just come in. It's too late. He's in the studio.'

'Bollocks. Shall I give him a quick call anyway? Remind him of a few things?'

'Yes.'

I dial McKenzie's number. Marianne usually answers, but it's the man himself who picks up this time.

'Winston. You're at ITV aren't you? Did you clear this with the press office?'

He's tetchy.

'Yes, I did. I told Paul Lambert about it two weeks ago and he gave me a briefing.'

This is most unhelpful. I'm limited to telling him to keep his cool and do the party proud.

The programme starts at 6. Tory Andrew Rosindell is on the far left of a bench, squeezed next to Winston who is in turn jammed next to a Labour and a Liberal. They don't seem to have enough seats to go round. Rozzer's fluorescent smile suggests he's had veneers put on his teeth.

One of the issues of the week is the drowning of hundreds of migrants who are setting off in boats from Libya to reach Sicily.

Winston's incisive take is this.

'People just lost their lives. Out there in the North Sea.'

Gawain sends me a text. 'I'm behind the biggest sofa in the world.'

Thursday 30th April 2015

Towler tells me there's been a large delivery of manifestos to an address in Lewisham and the person who lives there's moaning about it. They should be grateful.

'Where?'

'Curness Street.' He gives me the number.

'I know why. That's Tim Aker's old house of ill repute.' He's now moved to Thurrock of course. 'What d'ye want me to do with them?'

'Anything you want, I guess. Might tell Heaver he needs to collect them.'

Good. As long as I don't have to do it.

At seven pm I'm outside Hither Green train station with the car to pick up Anne Marie Waters with some of the bigger lads from the branch. It's only about a half-mile walk to her intended destination in Handen Road for the 'Mummy's Gin Fund' hustings. Nonetheless, Waters isn't being luxurious and I'm not being servile. She sits in the middle of the rear seat with a bloke on either side and all of them obscured by the tinted windows.

We've informed the police but aren't expecting them to turn up. I drive slowly past the church and we see there are about twenty black clad 'hard' 'men' outside. We turn into Wantage Road around the corner before parking a fair way down it. As we disembark, a police car goes by and we flag them down. My faith in the Met is duly restored. Both officers exit their car and put their caps on.

'You're here for Anne Marie Waters, I take it?'

'Sorry, who?'

My faith in the Met deflates to its prior level.

We explain the situation. Our candidate, who's only wee, positions herself within the middle of us all and we amble around the corner.

A boy in his twenties who looks like a heroin addict is leaning against a tree as we approach. He whistles, once. We near the entrance to the church where the rest of the gaggle look at us silently.

'Racist,' mumbles one of the fascists of South London Anti-Fascists.

And that's all. What a shit demo. They might at least have made a bit of an effort.

Thursday 7th May 2015

General Election Day. In line with my pledge, I'm doing no campaigning in Mole Valley. Nor am I bothering with our seats in Greenwich or Lewisham. I collect Peter Lello at Catford Bridge station to head off to Rochester. Whittle's meeting us there.

The office at the end of the High Street has a few coming and going and it's good to see that Emmett Jenner has come separately, equally putting aside his own efforts in Bromley and Chislehurst. However, there are far fewer activists than we'd had during the by-election.

Ulrika Bergsten from *Headline News* in Sweden is filming my good self in action this day. I meet the crew with Whittle outside the office and then head off to the Cuxton committee room which is also the Reckless family home. Catriona Reckless isn't pleased to see the media and pulls me inside the house to complain. It'll slow us down, apparently, and will break electoral law. Don't see how. Anyway, I'm not sure that's the real problem.

'Where is everybody?' she asks rhetorically. 'In Thanet to have their photograph taken with Nigel, probably. They're hanging Mark out to dry.'

We're given our maps and polling lists. Spookily, these are exactly the same houses that I canvassed on polling eve on the day of the by-election back in November.

There's a lot to cover and we take a break at 3.00 and head off to the White Hart for a quick lunch. Whittle's filled with a sense of ennui.

'We're not going to hold this.'

He has me drop him back to the station.

It gets to about 6 o'clock and I head home to change into a suit, eat a pie and then drive to the count in Mole Valley.

Although I'm plainly the greatest candidate for this constituency (or indeed any other one throughout the entire United Kingdom), it's obvious that the Conservatives will hang on to the seat. The examination by UKIP activists of the piles of papers are cursory. Instead, we focus all attention on the overhead *BBC News* screen and a couple of tablets which the lads have brought along. We need to concentrate on the areas where we will actually be victorious.

The news is almost exclusively bad.

12.38 am. Isabel Hardman of the *Spectator* tweets as follows.

'Very good source tells me Farage *has* lost South Thanet. I'd be surprised if they were wrong. But we'll see.'

Presumably the announcement's imminent. Nigel's been contemplating resigning as leader if he doesn't take the seat. So I text him.

'Don't you DARE stand down if you lose Thanet.'

4.15 am. Tim Aker fails to oust Jackie Doyle Price in Thurrock. In fact, he comes third.

4.20 am. Carswell holds Clacton, but with a reduced majority.

4.40 am. I don't win Mole Valley. What a shock. Third behind that Tory (whatever his name is) and the Lib Dem Paul Kennedy, although 6 points up on 2010. On the positive side, I do jump over Labour's Len Amos. My commiserations to him are sincere because he's a decent bloke.

My speech slags off the SNP who are hoovering up seats with a fraction of the votes given to UKIP. And:

'We were sure of the win here. So sure in fact, that I was going to make an offer to buy the Conservative's house.'

Say a few goodbyes, and then drive home. There are some calls from journalists en route but I ignore them. Can't be bothered, particularly as the news on LBC is uniformly disappointing.

By 5.50 am we're nearly pulling up to our house when it's announced that Mark Reckless has lost Rochester.

And, oddly, the count in South Thanet hasn't even started yet. So how could Hardman have heard, over five hours ago, that Farage was going to be disappointed?

Friday 8th May 2015

I'm proud of the brothers and sisters in our branch.

In Greenwich and Woolwich Ryan Acty is third on 8.3%.

Peter Whittle performs magnificently in Eltham. Third place on 15% and 6,481 votes. That's significantly more than the majority which Labour's Clive Efford gets over his Tory challenger but we feel no remorse whatsoever.

Massimo DiMambro is 5th in Lewisham Deptford and just loses his deposit. Not his fault. He comes ahead of People Before Profit however.

Although it's supposed to be our best chance in the borough, Gary Harding treads water in 4th Place for Lewisham West on 7.8%. He beats the Lib Dem, but is in turn overtaken by the Green.

And – this is completely unexpected. We didn't bother with any real campaigning in Lewisham East but Anne Marie Waters comes from nowhere to grab third place on 9.1%. She performs best of all of our Lewisham candidates. Looks like the fascists of South London Anti-Fascists were wrong. Anne Marie is welcome in Lewisham.

Oh. And Gerard Batten does incredibly well in Romford by garnering support from 11,208 locals. Sadly, Rozzer of the Tories gets 25,067 and keeps his seat. I'm not going to sneak into the EU parliament after all.

All those results came in overnight. But there's a huge hole which stays unfilled almost until elevenses.

10.31 am. Thanet South is declared. Yes. 10.31. In the morning. This isn't an immense rural seat. Why the delay? Nigel Farage is beaten by Tory Craig Mackinlay by 16,026 to 18,838, yet we win control of the Council. What the hell happened?

11.24 am. Nigel holds a press conference on the cliffs of Margate outside the Botany Bay hotel.

'I don't break my word. So I shall be writing to the UKIP National Executive in a few minutes saying that I am standing down as leader of UKIP.

'I intend to take the summer off. Enjoy myself a little bit. Not do very much politics at all. And there will be a leadership election for the next leader of UKIP in September. And I will consider over the course of this summer whether to put my name forward to do that job again.'

As we've taken 3,881,099 votes nationwide Farage has nothing to be ashamed of. Although that level of support gives us just one MP, it's the British electoral system which should be retired, not Nigel.

He recommends Suzanne Evans as interim leader and she accepts. By tradition, the interim holder doesn't put themselves forward to be permanent leader because the short-term profile would give them an unfair advantage in the final battle.

CHAPTER TWENTY-THREE

Weasels Rip His Flesh

Saturday 9th May 2015

I RECEIVE AN UNEXPECTED EMAIL from the Head of Candidates.

'This is an urgent appeal to all of you to support Nigel Farage at this point in the Parties history.

'Nigel has led the party to a famous victory, we have achieved over 4,000,000 votes we have a fully elected MP and we are on course to win over 1000 council seats.

'It is vital that Nigel stays at the helm and I know you will all support this call to him to carry on the fight.

'Please email with messages of support today. This is the most important thing you can do today.

'David Soutter'

Despite his errors in both mathematics and grammar, I'm happy to comply.

Monday 11th May 2015
UKIP's National Executive Committee tell Farage to get stuffed. They won't let him stand down. Good.

Wednesday 13th May 2015
Douglas Carswell is being a git. Although our poll share entitles UKIP to some £663,474 each year in parliamentary Short Money, he's

refusing to take it. He's been justifying himself on Radio 4.

'I know that all of those people who voted for us because they want political change will recognise that here at last is a party that is prepared to actually practice what it preaches.'

Sez who? Has he actually asked them? Their tax dollars will be prised from them in any case and there is no reason why it shouldn't be spent on the cause that they are passionate about.

There's more.

Ex-treasurer Stuart Wheeler has been blabbing to the BBC's *Radio 5 Live* about Nigel:

'I don't now think he should now be leading the party but that's up to the members.'

Ex-MEP (and, indeed, ex-member) Godfrey Bloom says that Farage is:

'Clearly now an extremely tired and stressed man'.

More importantly, current MEP and current economics spokes-man Patrick O'Flynn thinks it wise to describe our leader as 'Snarling', 'Thin-skinned'. 'Aggressive.'

Mixed in with all this are two other factors. First, Suzanne Evans has refused to say she'd step aside in Nigel's favour as leader should he come back after a summer break. Secondly, many people are ticked off with the terrible twin advisers to Nigel, Raheem Kassam and Matt Rich-ardson.

As for me, I haven't got a clue what's really going on so speak to Gawain.

'Is there actually a coup? And if so, who else is involved?'

'No. It's just a bit chaotic. Although neither Steve Woolfe nor Tim Aker are answering their phones. Probably wisely.'

Later, it's the Annual General Meeting of UKIP London at Brooks' Mews. Roger Gravett has handled the last year as chairman rather well. The agenda comes to the vacancies for the new committee.

'I'll propose Roger,' I say. 'Nobody else is silly enough to want it.'

But somebody else is silly enough because John Hellings of Ber-mondsey branch also puts his name forward. I know nothing about Hellings but other delegates do apparently. Either that, or he's been lob-bying. Because he wins. Another coup.

Off to the Iron Duke afterwards and I huddle with fellow Gravet-teer Peter Lello.

'Did you have any idea that was coming?'

'None whatsoever,' he replies.

'Where's Roger by the way?'

'He headed straight for the tube home. He's quite cut up about it.'

Thursday 14th May 2015

Peter Lello is in court tomorrow morning for the purported sexual assault. What of the poor victim?

'The police can't find him,' he tells me. 'He's completely disappeared.'

There's a surprise.

And – in other news, Matt Richardson has told the NEC that he's willing to resign as Party Secretary given the criticisms that have been directed his way by the purple plotters. Protecting the King no matter what the personal cost may be. Good man.

Friday 15th May 2015

Exactly one year to the day of his arrest, Peter Lello is acquitted by a judge at the Woolwich Crown Court.

This decent, kind man has been through the mincer for the last twelve months. He's proved strong enough to break that mincer's blades, but it has hurt. None of the people who actually know him ever doubted his innocence. All this for dirty tricks.

Pink News, *The Independent* and even the *South London Press* are honourable enough to cover his exoneration. Yet there's nothing from the *Daily Mirror* which, very conveniently, broke the story on election day.

That publication is now, to me, the same as *The Sun* to a Liverpudlian.

Tuesday 19th May 2015

Patrick O'Flynn returns to his burrow with an apology.

'I would like to express to colleagues my sincere regret at going public with my frustrations about the turn of events following polling day.

'And more than that, I would like to apologise directly to Nigel for the phrase "snarling, thin-skinned and aggressive."'

In the afternoon there's the inaugural meeting of the London Management Team at Brooks' Mews. I'm pleasantly-surprised to see Mark Reckless.

'Bad luck about losing your seat old chap. Are you going to go for a by-election?'

'Maybe,' he says. 'But I've got a lot to be busy with at the moment. Nigel's just appointed me head of policy.'

Good news indeed. I do so hate to see talent go to waste.

The new London chairman John Hellings is present along with Peter Staveley. Adam Richardson is also in the room but ignoring us as he types away on his laptop.

David Soutter tells us that the entire candidates list is to be scrapped and everyone must reapply. So all the work which was carried out by we assessors is being put in the round filing cabinet. This will be a long process. On the bright side, the huge amount of necessary work will keep Soutter in a job.

Some of the candidates will be rejected though. Magnus Neillson is one. He'd signed a personal declaration at Steve Crowther's insistence that he wouldn't, well, bang on about Islam during the election but had then done precisely that. He'd taken his punishment with good grace.

I raise the issue about Anne Marie Waters in Lewisham East. Although she'd given my committee an equal assurance that she would leave the Religion of Peace alone, she'd forgotten to do so. There's no problem with her.

'Is Winston out, too?' asks Staveley.

'I can neither confirm nor deny that,' Soutter tells us.

Adam Richardson looks up briefly from his laptop.

'No,' he says. 'Winston's still on the list.'

Mark Reckless tells us his initial thoughts about the London Manifesto for next year. Thankfully, it will go further than the expansion of Manston Airport and the LEZ.

'Anyway, got to rush,' Reckless says.

He thwacks a folded copy of the *Medway Messenger* onto the table and points to the open page

'I've got to deal with this guy. He's just been elected as a councillor and has already resigned from the Group because Nigel hasn't stood down as promised.'

He rises and leaves, taking the paper with him before I've had the chance to read the piece.

'Who was that scoundrel?' I ask the remaining officers.

'That,' says John Hellings, 'was Mark Reckless. He has just lost his seat as a UKIP Member of Parliament you know.'

Really, John? Really?

Wednesday 20th May 2015

Nigel's thinking of giving Suzanne Evans the task of running the campaign for the London Mayor and Authority elections next year. How sly! If she takes the role she obviously can't be a candidate.

Saturday 23rd May 2015

The Daily Mail publishes a photograph of David Soutter 'in an embrace' with Natasha Bolter.

That explains a lot.

What a clusterfuck.

Wednesday 17th June 2015

There are rumours that Matt Richardson, thrown on the fire as a burnt offering to the Anti-Nigel plotters, has been reinstated as Party Secretary. Apparently, the NEC demanded his return.

I tender congratulations.

'Ha. So you're back with a vengeance. Excellent!'

I like his reply:

'I am pretty sure that I never left.'

CHAPTER TWENTY-FOUR

It's a London Thing

Monday 13th July 2015

Ondon Chairman John Hellings has asked to meet me and Peters Reeve and Staveley at the Local Government Association Building in Smith Square.

The meeting, to discuss the forthcoming London selections and campaign, is fairly pointless. We then head to the Civil Service Club in Whitehall where there's a room for the wider London Region Committee and, more importantly, cheap beer.

Paul Oakden tells us how the London Assembly candidates are going to be selected. Solely and entirely through assessment by party officers and with no members' vote at all. So the process is changing yet again.

He turns to Batten.

'Gerard. Can we put you down to be on this committee? You probably know the likely London applicants better than anybody else.'

Batten gives him a very mild sneer.

'Categorically not. If there's going to be no democratic input from the members, then I'm having nothing to do with it.'

Sunday 19th July 2015

Peter Kirby wants a word. He sounds ill.

'Did you know,' he asks, 'that I'm being sued for defamation by Winston McKenzie and Marianne Bowness?'

I did not. He goes on.

'I need representation and understand that you can instruct barristers directly now. I'd like you to do it.'

The request is flattering but inappropriate.

'Sorry, can't. I know both you and Winston personally.'

'Oh,' he says. 'Could you give me an idea of how much it would cost to instruct someone else?'

'You could probably get a solicitor for around £200 an hour.'

'I might just represent myself then. I will simply tell the truth and that ought to be enough.'

This isn't good. Not sure either Winston or Peter realise how much this will take out of them both. Hope they settle it, even if not in an amicable way.

Tuesday 11th August 2015

It's the Taxpayers' Alliance summer party in Tufton Street. I meet a hero author but don't realise who he is at first.

'James Bartholomew. James Bartholomew. Oh – you're the geezer who wrote *The Welfare State We're In*. Bu-rilliant piece of work.' He seems pleased.

And I scold Matthew Elliott for laziness as he's written nothing since his anti-green polemic 'Let Them Eat Carbon'.

'Ah,' he says. 'But I have.'

He takes me to his office upstairs and presents me with a new work from Business for Britain about the EU: 'Change or Go.'

'There's only a handful of hard copies available but you can have this one. It's the bible for the referendum.'

Impressively and unfortunately, it's the size of a telephone directory but full of bombs and barbs which are ideal for launching at federast fanatics.

As the evening's winding down, Lianne Bruney comes over to see me. She and her mum had, of course, been longstanding activists in Lambeth branch.

'Sorry Paul, I just need to tell you something. I'm leaving the party.'
'Why?'

'It's Winston. I've had enough of him giving us BME[1] activists a bad name.'

She's thinking of joining the Tories. I'm truly sorry to hear this.

Tuesday 18th August 2015

Rosie Beattie from Southwark UKIP wants a word.

---

1 Black, minority and ethnic.

'John Hellings was ousted as our branch chairman last night.'

The fact of his ousting is a surprise but not his lack of popularity. We Regional Organizers have received many complaints from members about rude emails and shouty phone calls from him. But people are far too sensitive in our opinions so we've done nothing about it.

'Who's taken over?'

'That would be me,' she says.

I congratulate her! She goes on.

'It was one of the weirdest meetings I've ever attended. Andy Beadle and David Kurten were refused entry by Hellings but he allowed in Elizabeth Jones who's nothing to do with the branch. And he very grudgingly let Mick McGough come in even though Mick's a member of the NEC and can go to any meeting he darn well pleases.'

Given that Beadle and Kurten were the two parliamentary candidates in the area back in May, this is indeed puzzling.

'Then we got to the vote for chairman. I put my name forward but Hellings said I couldn't and he'd be automatically re-adopted. Mick backed me and John tried to shout him down.'

Good Lord. Has Hellings no sense?

'Ha! NOBODY does that to Uncle Mick. Go on.'

She does.

'Well, then he gave Liz Jones a ballot paper and also two brand new members who aren't yet entitled to vote. I put an end to that. And then I won. Three votes to two.'

'Well done you,' I say. 'Now the question arises as to how Hellings can remain as London chairman when he's not a branch chairman.'

'It does indeed,' she responds in a smiley voice.

Wednesday 19th August 2015

After much contemplation and research, it's concluded that John Hellings can still be regional chairman. The party's branch in Harrow is officially consecrated but entirely lacking in a committee. As with any other such moribund branch, a sitting London chairman automatically becomes its notional officer. Accordingly, John Hellings is chairman of Harrow. Accordingly, John Hellings remains chairman of London.

Monday 24th August 2015

Our Head of Chambers, Sir Tony Baldry (now former) MP, has had some bad news.

Despite stepping down from his safe seat, Tony isn't to have his peerage after all. It's not a case of him having misunderstood some throwaway comment. It was certainly being lined up and he'd even had a fitting for his robes.

Gallantly, Tony has not a single bad word to say about the leader of his party even though it's obvious that he's hurt.

That reticence doesn't apply to me. Cameron is a twat.

Thursday 3rd September 2015

There's more exciting news from Rosie Beattie, the new chairman of Southwark.

'We had another meeting last night and it was unanimous. The branch has no confidence in Hellings as London Chairman and want to see a re-election for the position.'

Unfortunately, the only ways this can be done are at an AGM or by a vote of no confidence with 5 District Representatives supporting the motion. Last but not least, disciplinary action by the Party. I've no feelings about Hellings either way but it matters much that he's got up the hooters of so many activists.

The trouble is that Hellings is far too clever to get into any real trouble.

Tuesday 15th September 2015

Branch meeting at the Greenwich Tavern. We're discussing pre-ferred attributes for our GLA candidate next year.

'Who thinks we ought to have someone local?' asks Peter Lello. Every member raises a hand.

'Excellent,' says I. 'Anyone who wants to have a stab will need to go through the Head Office assessment. Who's up for it?'

Every member keeps both hands in his or her lap.

Wednesday 16th September 2015

I speak to Crowther.

'Steve. My branch want a local candidate for the GLA but nobody wants to go through the assessment. I might have to put my own name in again, but there's a "but".'

'Do tell.'

'I can't be bothered with it either. Not that I'm saying I'm brilliant or anything, even though I am. Let me stand for nomination anyway.'

'Well, alright. But you'd better not mention this to anyone else.'

Saturday 26th September 2015

It's UKIP Conference, in Doncaster once again.

Our candidates for London Mayor and the assembly are to be announced. Whittle invites me and Lello to his hotel room while he goes through the final preparations for the proclamation. Fags are smoked illegally out of the window.

Peter now being chilled, we leave and take the bus to the racecourse venue.

Party Director Paul Oakden ascends the stage to announce the results. At best, we'll only get the top two elected so those further down have no hope.

'Our eleventh list candidate is to be: Elizabeth Jones!'

Oakden begins the applause, which reaches a feebly-polite crescendo, and scans the crowd for Jones but there's no sign of her. He carries on.

10th Afzal Akram

9th Anne-Marie Waters

8th Piers Wauchope

7th Neville Watson

6th Famous Radio One Disc Jockey out of the early 1980s, Mike Read

5th Peter Harris

4th Lawrence Webb

3rd Suzanne Evans

2nd David Kurten

And then what those in the know already knew:

'I am delighted to announce that our number one list candidate and the member who is going to stand in London as our mayoral candidate for 2016 is: Mr Peter Whittle!'

Suzanne Evans will of course be disappointed with both results. Not that you'd know it. Ever-professional, she smiles broadly and applauds loudly as Whittle gives his speech.

Decree over, the candidates file away. Suzanne passes me as she heads out. There are tears in the corners of her eyes. I stop her and give her a kiss on the cheek.

'Either of you would have been excellent candidates and we'd have been proud.'

Which would've been true.

After one or two beers I head back to the hotel to change into jeans and a t-shirt, for it is the Gala Dinner tonight. Accordingly, Bill Etheridge and I are dining at the famous Shabir's curry house instead. He's also brought his new lady, Lorraine, to conference and she's joining us. I will break this fact gently, if at all, to my own missis as she's very fond of Bill's former partner, Star.

The feed is astonishingly good.

As we moan with the pleasure of repletion and undo the top buttons of our kecks, Bill notes somebody else on the other side of the restaurant. It's Douglas Carswell. He's sitting with a couple of people we don't know and leaves almost immediately without ordering anything.

Saturday 17th October 2015

Crystal Palace FC are hosting West Ham at Selhurst Park. Although we haven't forgotten our lukewarm reception there from a couple of years ago, every single vote will count in the referendum so we're going to leaflet the fans again.

There's a poor turnout from the activists but that's fine as we haven't overdone it with the supplies of literature this time. We have a fifty/fifty reception from the crowds and it becomes obvious that the Hammers fans are the more sensible of the two.

We have some competition from many more people who are giving out freebies of their own. Not politicos, but low-wage marketing assistants who've been forced to spend their Saturday dispersing mini Peperamis to the masses. As we Kippers feel sorry for them, we help them finish early by stuffing our pockets with their meaty gifts.

But then. . .

'Excuse me Sir,' comes a voice from behind me.

It is a policeman. I can tell I've officially become middle-aged because he looks about fifteen years old.

'How may I help you, officer?'

'I'll need you to stop handing out this material unless you can show me a permit.'

'I'm afraid you're mistaken. We're giving away free leaflets which we're perfectly entitled to do, with or without any permit.'

'No, you're not, sir.'

'Yes. We are. Officer. . .' I read his number out loud back to him.

'I'll check with my superiors. You can either leave or wait here for me to come back, but you're not to carry on or else I may have to arrest you.'

'Please do check, but we will be carrying on. And you'll not be arresting any of us.'

He walks away and doesn't reappear.

About half an hour before kick-off, a familiar face appears. Why, it is John Hellings, our London Chairman! He's very late but all help is appreciated, as I enthusiastically tell him.

'Ah,' he replies. 'I'm actually here to watch the match. See you at the next London meeting?'

'Yes, of course John. See you then.'

Even though he could have helped for at least ten minutes or so, he walks off. Presumably he's a Crystal Palace fan. That would make sense.

CHAPTER TWENTY-FIVE

Flying on Fumes

Thursday 29th October 2015

THE NATIONAL REGIONAL ORGANISERS' MEETING is at the Park Plaza Hotel on the South Bank. It begins at midday and is supposed to take all afternoon. I turn up at 2. No great loss as the start of the meeting is concerned with ROs reporting back about what they're doing in their part of the country. Tedious. As Party Chairman Steve Crowther has frequently said:

'People often call me up to ask if I want to know what's going on in their branches. My answer is always the same: "No".'

As I arrive, the West Midlands rep is listing the great number of public meetings which they've arranged with EFDD[1] funding. Hang on a minute. I butt in.

'Well, this is embarrassing. London can't do any more as we were told the funding's been cut.'

Lawrence Webb affirms that all £25K available has indeed been used up. Two lots on Nigel's referendum launches at the Emmanuel Centre, one lump on his upcoming public meeting at the same venue and the rest on events in Hillingdon and Hounslow.

Gerard has something to add.

'Nigel doesn't want EFDD funds spent after end of January anyway.'

This is because Wes Streeting, the new Labour MP for Ilford North and prize git, has been complaining to the EU about us using the money

---

1 Europe of Freedom and Direct Democracy Group in the European Parliament.

we're perfectly entitled to in order to spread a message which is *uncommunautaire.*

Steve Crowther winds up the meeting. The financial situation is even worse than this if we can't access more cash.

'What I'm going to say isn't to go outside the room. Like most parties, we spent more than we intended at the general election. In fact, there's no money left.'

We knew the situation was bad, but nobody had a clue we were running on fumes. He goes on.

'You know how the Treasurer's department has been in touch with the branches to ask how much they have in their bank accounts?'

There's suspicious mumbling.

'Well,' he goes on. 'This isn't something the party has had to do since the 1990s. But it might come to us plundering those accounts to fund the central party.'

Yet, there's hope according to Steve.

'Arron Banks is going to help out again. He's giving us the benefit of his business expertise. There's going to be a fundraising phone bank. Staffed with professionals, not volunteers.

'At the moment, I'm the pilot pulling back the joystick as hard as possible as we head for the trees. But we will get over those trees.'

Meeting finished, I walk to the station with Peter Staveley.

'There's more bad news,' he says. 'I've heard that Winston's been approached to appear on *Celebrity Big Brother.*'

Tuesday November 3rd 2015
Winston McKenzie is on the telly. He's leaving the party.

'I'm incensed at the present moment because where I stand in UKIP, I feel as though I've been completely ignored, racially discriminated against by people in the higher echelons of the party. I'm talking about the leader's followers.'

Surely this has nothing to do with the fact that he was turned down as mayoral candidate? In turn, that failure was probably nothing to do with the fact that his performance at the selection was abysmal.

I call him several times but the phone isn't picked up. Text messages are ignored. A contrast to the occasions when party officers have ricketed our bones into bends trying to protect him from his own idiocy.

Buh-bye then Winston.

Thursday November 5th 2015

Paul Oakden wants to set up a team with the London officers, Chris Bruni-Lowe from head office and the three lead candidates for the GLA elections, that is, Whittle, Kurten and Evans.

I put this to John Hellings but he isn't enthused.

'I can't say I relish the idea of having a talking shop with the so-called "Top 3" List candidates. In one of those candidates I see almost zero campaigning experience and no party authority whatsoever, whilst in the other two I believe they have very firm standing and experience and platforms from which to operate, but that they have no link into Party finance, administration, strategic planning or command and control.'

How peculiar.

Monday 9th November 2015

Hellings has arranged another meeting between himself and the London Regional Organisers. I suggest that this would be an ideal opportunity for Chris Bruni-Lowe to meet everyone.

John is nonetheless firm.

'Mr Bruni-Lowe is NOT invited.'

Bizarre.

Friday 13th November 2015

MORNING

'You around tomorrow?' asks Nigel.

Fishing! Yaay!

'Make it 7.30,' he says. 'Bring waterproofs.'

EVENING

Paris attacks.

Saturday 14th November 2015

It is a bloody miserable morning as Nigel drives his son Tom and myself down to Rye harbour.

'This is exactly what I said would happen months ago. When ISIS warn they'll use the migrant tide to flood Europe with half-a-million jihadists, we'd better listen.'

There are other matters arising, too.

'And we'll be stuck with the Home Secretary's snooper's bill. That will be rushed through and there's nothing we can do about it.'

He goes on.

'And the absolute certainty is that Marine Le Pen will be the next French President.'

Nigel says this with regret. There's no doubt that the Front National is replete with some nasty people even if Le Pen herself is not one of them. I am however a little surprised that multicultural Parisians would be prepared to lend her their vote.

'Don't be. The capital itself is fast becoming a migrant hub. There are pickpockets and beggars everywhere. I used to enjoy the stroll from the Gare du Nord to the Gare L'Ouest, but no longer.'

Naturally, the phone is persistent. He's not taking part in any interviews, even though a *Fox News* debate is intriguing.

'I'm giving a referendum speech in Basingstoke on Monday and they can wait until then.'

So Peter Whittle, as party culture spokesman as well as London mayoral candidate, has been delegated to speak to the media over the weekend while the leader clears his mind by focussing on fat cod from the English Channel. It's good to see that he's not just relying on the MEPs for public proclamations although it's puzzling that he hasn't gone for the obvious alternatives that are bigger names than Peter.

'Him? No. He's losing it. Look at his pallor. He's not turning up to events. I suspect there's a white powder problem.'

'Don't think so. After that MEP's dinner he tried to kick a lamp down the stairs.'

'No. You can see his hands have the shakes nearly every morning. He really needs to dry out.'

So he's given me some excellent quidnuncery and in return seeks my own views.

'What can you tell me about David Kurten?'

Kurten has a fair chance of being elected in London. I'd only talked to him at length at the Doncaster conference. He's personable though, and a good speaker. Most of all, nobody has done any bitching about him to me either in person or in a tedious bed-time email. That's all Farage wants to know.

We arrive in Rye. There are a few brave golfers facing the horizontal rain on the course next to the harbour who recognise Nigel and wave. We park and start unpacking.

'I want to show you something,' says Nigel.

He points to the nearside front wing of his car which is crumpled. I raise my eyebrow. Farage is no boy-racer.

'I'll tell you when we're on the boat,' he promises.

There are no other vessels on the water. I land a 15lb cod. Nigel and Tom pull in some big thornback rays. There are many whiting with which we could fill the boat but we're after the bigger fish so stick with the larger baits. Sadly, the weather takes a turn for the worse. The waves are rising and rising and the rain is falling and falling. I make the error of going down into the hull to pee in the toilet rather than over the side but the swaying below brings up a stomachful of vomit. Nigel and Tom rightly find my lack of sealegs amusing.

The fish aren't coming up any more so we head back. We won't fillet the catch until we've returned to harbour as we wish to retain our fingers.

We're being treated to facefulls of brine as it breaks over the bow so huddle behind the small cabin hanging on to the railings. I take the opportunity to ask Nigel about the car over the racket of the waves, rain and engine.

'Someone undid the wheelnuts.'

He must be fucking joking. Surely he's gone to the police?

'No. It was at the European Parliament and the local authorities would leak it to the press if I did.'

I still think he should. But perhaps it wouldn't make any difference if he did.

Back at Nigel's, we unpack the gear. There are towers of document boxes scratching at the ceiling.

'It never stops. I've got to go through all this which I've pulled together from various piles of papers all over the place.'

I suggest he shreds it for an easy life, but he declines as it may be useful for academic study. On this point, I recall that Matthew Goodwin is just about to publish his second work on The Kip, *Inside the Campaign*. Has he read an advance copy?

'I've a lot of time for Goodwin,' says Farage. 'He's going to be the next John Curtice, and has the added advantage of being good-looking which is always helpful for a TV talking-head.' He smiles. 'I haven't seen the full thing but it's being serialised in the *Daily Mail* this week.'

There are some additional nuggets too.

'One thing he points out about the General Election is that 2 million of our voters hadn't given UKIP their cross at the EU elections. So there are in principle 6 million party supporters out there.'

So why didn't we get them on board in May?

'Cockups through Carswell. The man has some loopy ideas and

his intellectual relationship with Tory MEP Dan Hannan is very strange indeed. A complete contrast to Mark Reckless who's a solid man.'

I'm going to be rude about our sole member of parliament. Is it fair to say that Douglas Carswell is the founder, leader and sole member of the Douglas Carswell Party?

'Precisely.'

Sunday 15th November 2015

Douglas Carswell unexpectedly adds me to the very short list of Twitter accounts he deigns to follow. Perhaps his ears were burning.

Tuesday 17th November 2015

MORNING

I managed 4 hours' sleep on Sunday night having prepped for a trial in Norwich first thing on Monday. On the plus-side I had a stunning victory. On the minus-side I didn't get back to London until 9 pm and was too late to go to Gerard Batten's public meeting at the Fairfield Halls in Croydon last night.

I call him to see how it went.

'Cancelled at the last minute', says Gerard.

Oh?

'They came up with some rubbish about the "international situation". My Lib Dem opponent Tom Brake isn't happy about it either.'

The line's beeping continuously such that I can't hear him.

'Gerard – are you in Strasbourg? There's a lot of interference.'

'No, I'm at home. Must be MI5,' he laughs.

'Oh. Fuck off MI5, then. Is it postponed or binned completely?'

'They said they'd reschedule but I'm done with them. It's a shame as we turned up anyway to tell the punters outside that it was off and there'd have been a good turnout. It's an expensive mistake as they'll be covering the wasted costs of the leaflets we produced. Stuff them. Croydon's a dump anyway.'

'Aha – so Winston was right after all?'

'Yes, McKenzie isn't wrong all the time,' he laughs.

EVENING

The party's selecting its candidate for the City and East superseat in a Stepney Scout hut and I'm chairing.

Only those members who live within the constituency boundaries are entitled to vote. We've filleted a list of the eligible and have a printout of those lucky 463.

On arrival, eleven redoubtable members have turned up along with four non-voting observers. Well, it's a filthy night after all as Storm Barney has been unleashed on London.

John Hellings and Mark Webber are outside to greet the troops. Parked right next to the venue's door is a silver Mercedes with its engine off and its headlights on. Within are four young men dressed in the garb of the Religion of Peace so I note down the number plate.

I'm not racist. But. One of the applicants tonight is Anne-Marie Waters. The shortlist hasn't been circulated but she's had many death threats. You never know.

The car drives off and I feel guilty.

Anne-Marie is first to speak.

'I ripped up my planned speech for tonight after what happened on Friday. The people in Paris were slaughtered. Not because of foreign policy or Israel, but because they are free. This is a war between democracy and theocracy.

'I'm sick of the criminalisation of those who criticise Islam. It's the ultimate appeasement. Here in East London there are Sharia Patrols and Sharia Courts and women are treated as cattle. This is the place to fight back.'

She's intriguing when talking of her personal crusade but less so when answering questions afterwards.

'Should the Garden Bridge across the Thames go ahead?'

'Er, we were discussing this before and we all agreed if we couldn't answer a question we shouldn't fluff it. I don't know.'

'Which London Airport should expand?'

'Mmm. Not sure. I probably lean towards Gatwick.'

'Can you think of one good thing mayor Boris Johnson has done for London?'

'I'm trying to think of something but I really can't. He gives a lightness to London which I suppose I like.'

Hmm. Rule number one in the aspiring politician's handbook. Always have something to say about everything, even if you couldn't actually give a monkeys.

The wind whistles through the cracks in the asbestos walls and it's Afzal Akram's turn. He's reading notes, but as a modern sort of chap these are on his smartphone. Yuck. The "speech" is basically a great big hairy Afzal Akram CV. A lot about all the good things he has done but not much about the good things he will do.

Peter Harris is next. Now. Harris was our general election candidate in Dagenham and Rainham. He'd lifted us from fifth to second place, garnering 30% of the vote and giving Labour incumbent John Cruddas a shock. He'd been by far the best-performing Kipper in London.

However. He's wearing a UKIP tie. He reads from notes set out on the table below and looks up only occasionally. He refers to 'the LibLabCon'. He tells us 'I want my country back'. Were I wearing spectacles, I would peer at him over their rims in a disapproving manner.

Yet he comes alive with the audience questions.

'Why do we want a garden bridge when we've only got a rowing boat at North Woolwich? We need more Thames crossings in the east end. And before they think of making people pay for these, let's charge tolls on Westminster and Tower bridges.'

'What do I think of Boris? Not a lot. He leased the Olympic stadium to West Ham for next to nothing. But that's fine because they're my team.'

Harris receives approved mutterings as he leaves the rostrum free for the next candidate.

Peter Muswell is a former Liberal Democrat and ex-TA member of the Parachute Regiment. A school governor, he comes from Russian, Jewish, Italian and Iranian stock and has black British grandchildren. He's multicultural London personified and also a proud Kipper, the two not being mutually exclusive.

Muswell doesn't need notes and is properly-animated.

'I met Jeremy Thorpe as a young man. He made me a cup of tea. And because of that I voted Liberal for the next three decades. But last year I saw your wonderful leader Nigel Farage debate our wonderful leader Nick Clegg. And when my leader got his arse kicked it shook me to the core.'

Harris takes the nomination. Great choice. Muswell is, rightly, a close runner-up.

We head to the pub for one drink, in my case, and John Hellings smilingly offers to buy it for me.

Even though he says that I've stabbed him in the back. The man is touched.

CHAPTER TWENTY-SIX

'North London Jewish Cunt'

Friday 27th November 2015

MICK McGOUGH IS MILDLY SADDENED that John Hellings hasn't advertised a dinner in his regional newsletter 'London Calling'. Gerard Batten was to have been guest speaker.

Hellings decides to put his riposte to Mick in writing. There are lots of good bits in it about Mick. And Gerard. And Lawrence Webb. This is just some of it.

'An avalanche of hatred and abuse, lies and cruelty and disgusting and repulsive venom and poison.

'A bitter hate-fuelled campaign by one man and his aggrieved sidekick-cum-protégé.

'His remorseless efforts to attack me and our ROs, especially Peter Staveley (not Saint Roger Gravett, God Forbid) erode and will eventually destroy this Party act-by-act with his vituperative lies and poisonous conduct.

'Batten's rubbish is not needed either. Apart from rolling in money with which to publicise his own events and having some paid staff to do his PR work for him, his knee-jerk chiming in with this poisonous individual's guff is also ill-informed and factually incorrect.'

That's told 'em.

Saturday 28th November 2015

A hustings is needed for the Bexley and Bromley superseat. As its boundaries don't correspond to parliamentary constituencies which in turn aren't commensurate with council frontiers, some of my Lewisham members can vote in the selection as well as people in Bexley and Bromley. The chairmen of all three branches must liaise.

As a result of some confusion as to who ought actually to be sending it out, the notification's a couple of days late. Steve Crowther tells me he's unconcerned.

'Don't worry. It's going ahead unless anyone complains that they've somehow been disenfranchised. And they won't.'

Julian Grainger of Bromley thus takes the lead and forwards the announcement which he's now sent to his own crew.

Tues 8th December 7:30pm for 8pm

Greater London Authority - Elections 2016

Hustings for UKIP candidate for Bexley & Bromley Constituency @ Sidcup Recreational Club, Church Ave (just north of Queen Marys Hospital)

(Bar should be open for a second 'social'!)

I send this straightaway to my squadron in the Penge and Clock House wards with an extra message.

'As you may know, because of the strange and varying boundaries in London, although you are rightly members of UKIP Greenwich & Lewisham you actually live within the GLA constituency of Bexley and Bromley. As a result, you are entitled to attend the selection meeting which will choose our candidate for next year.

'If you are free, please also consider going to their social event on the 1st as our comrades in Bromley really are a decent bunch.'

John Hellings expresses his displeasure to us all by email. Sent at 10.31 pm this Saturday night.

'I cannot call that a proper Notice of a Hustings - it is a travesty written by someone who comes across as if they are on drugs and/or are trying desperately hard to be sarcastic rather than get on and get the job done.

'I am also deeply concerned that Peter Staveley has raised the possibility that neither Bromley nor Bexley Branch Chairs have sent out Notices to their Members because they thought Head Office did so.

'For safety's sake, this Hustings is almost certainly going to have to be suspended due to astonishing neglect and/or stupidity by the three relevant Branch Chairmen.'

The neglectful and stupid chairmen are therefore myself, Julian Grainger and, of course, Catherine Reilly.

Sunday 29th November 2015
David Kurten asks for advice with his GLA nomination.

'At the moment I'm on the electoral register in Runnymede. I know I have to be on the register in London on the date of the nomination and stay on it for the duration of the term of office.

'Is it all right to go on to the register at the home of a friend or other party member in London, or do I have to be physically living at the address I am at on the register?'

I don't see this as a particular problem and there's plenty of time to sort it out.

'In broad terms you need to live or work in London but can also own property, in the area you're standing. Do you have any buy-to-let flats? If not, it would be best if you were to discuss the options with Peter Staveley. He knows all the intricacies.'

David agrees to talk to Peter and we leave it there.

Then we hear that Catherine Reilly, Bexley Chairman and potential GLA candidate, has fallen down a flight of stairs and broken her neck. She is in a coma. There's a serious chance that she will die.

John Hellings is officially an arsehole.

Monday 30th November 2015
I give Hellings a gentle nudge because we've still not had a proper meeting between London and Head Office about the GLA campaign. Two months have passed since our candidates were announced.

He doesn't take the nudging well.

'This comes out of the blue and is not, frankly, very collegiate of you as a Regional Organiser.'
I tell on him to Paul Oakden who gives his own thoughts.

'I'm frankly baffled at the hesitance to include Chris Bruni-Lowe in any planning.

'Chris will be controlling the central party budget for the GLA elections. Unless you have a stash of money sat somewhere to fight the campaign, you're going to be relying heavily on support from the central party.'

I'm baffled too. Presumably, Hellings doesn't want us to do badly?

Thursday 3rd December 2015

Many words have been spoken between the officers of south-east London about Catherine's awful condition and its consequences. The consensus is that the selection must be postponed.

I check this is fine with Crowther.

'Of course,' he says. 'What a terrible shame about Catherine. I truly hope there's a possibility of recovery.'

We don't involve John Hellings in either the discussion or the decision. The meeting's cancelled.

Friday 11th December 2015

I've snatched up a copy of the *Evening Standard* and am reading it on the tube home. Its UKIP-phobia normally manifests itself by completely ignoring the party. Not today.

'UKIP man sought false address to stand in Assembly elections.'

David Kurten sent an email to various Kippers asking for help with his accommodation issue. Do they have a room for him within London? That email's been leaked. By Someone.

Crowther must hear of this.

'No, I'm not bothered at all,' he says. 'David has been completely open with the party about his residency issues since the time of the selection. If and when he sorts this out he will be a candidate. If he can't sort it out then he won't. It's really that simple.'

'Any ideas about the identity of the leaker Steve?'

'I can't imagine! *Cui bono?*'

I've got to talk to David of course and ask him to forward a copy of the errant email which, presumably, will give a clue.

He does.

'I only sent it to 6 people. Peter Whittle, George Cottrell, Andy Beadle, Freddy Vaccha, David Soutter and Cliff Dixon.'

'The good thing is that I have found a room to rent in London from January.'

So let's have a think. Even if he were snidely-minded (which he isn't), Whittle has nothing to gain from damaging his wingman. George Cottrell isn't standing. Besides, he's made generous donations to the battle which would make it bizarre if he were to damage the campaign.

Andy and Cliff aren't candidates and are, in any event, men of honour as, indeed, is Freddy who holds the place just outside the very bottom of the list at 12th position. Even if Kurten were ousted and he bumped up, Vaccha would still have no chance of victory.

David doesn't comply with two of the Electoral Commission residency rules. However, there's one further criteria:

> 'You are, and will continue to be, registered as a local government elector in Greater London from the day of your nomination onwards.
>
> 'Unlike the other qualifications that must only be satisfied on the day of your nomination and on polling day, this is an on-going qualification.'

Nominations don't close until March 31st. David has plenty of time to fulfill this. He's done nothing wrong. Not that Iain Dale from LBC agrees. He's all over the story on his evening show, plugging his bezzy mate, Suzanne Evans, as Kurten's replacement. Nothing to do with him of course and he'll be ignored.

Sunday 13th December 2015

Hellings has some thoughts to share with the London ROs before our meeting which is to take place four days hence.

This email from him, timed at 11.43 pm, is a top-10 example of why one should hesitate before clicking 'Send' at the close of day.

> 'Some people are so dreadful one has to wonder why they joined UKIP in the first place - apparently one of Mr Gravett's close friends did so in order to have anal sex with women. Mr Gravett's friend was so liberal with his expressions of desire for anal sex with strange women that several Official Complaints against this particular sex pest will follow.
>
> 'I am sure Mr Gravett's very religious friend Andrew Price from Haringey will steer us religious folk away from the anal rape scenario of one of Gravett's and Price's closest friends, and forgive him on the altar of Christianity, whilst I am sure Price will also have a lot to say about random sexual assault against women. I look forward to Mr Gravett's explanation of this disgusting behaviour amongst his friends, Branch members and religious bigots.'

Thursday 17th December 2015

Peter Whittle speaks to me about John Hellings' continual obstruction of the campaign. As mayoral candidate he's not going to stand for it.

I call Farage.

'Hellings has no redeeming qualities at all.'

'You may be right. Fix it.'

Easy to say, but not to do.

Hellings' management meeting is at the LGA office this afternoon. This is in Smith Square. On approaching I see Steve Crowther and Damian Wilson at a table outside the MOG. They wave me over.

'Where are you off to Oakers?'

'A meeting with Hellings.' I roll my eyes.

'Don't look so glum,' says Crowther. 'Things often have a way of sorting themselves out.'

I wander off to my doom.

Hellings is contrite and apologetic to Roger Gravett during the meeting. Apparently, the cryptic references to the bumming of ladies apply to Nigel Sussman. John explains, in detail, why he believes that this is true and why he feels that this is a concern. We nod politely and Roger, being a decent man, accepts his apology.

Apart from that, the meeting's a total waste of time. Thankfully, it's over soon and I head to the Civil Service Club to meet Whittle and other serious operatives. We're going to campaign properly for the GLA, with or without Hellings.

That meeting is indeed productive, and it just so happens that our Westminster Branch are hosting a Christmas buffet at this very venue and on this very evening.

By a further coincidence, John Hellings is in attendance, as is Nigel Sussman.

As the event winds down, Hellings can't contain himself.

'Fuck off, Sussman,' he yells at the top of his shouty voice, 'You north London Jewish cunt!'

Our London Chairman is bundled out of the club by several members without further ado.

CHAPTER TWENTY-SEVEN

Banging On About Islam

Friday 18th December 2015

MORE TROUBLE. Douglas Carswell has told BBC Essex that Nigel should stand down as leader.

'Maybe you need a fresh-faced approach sometimes. You need a fresh face and an optimistic message.'

Farage fights back straight away.

'Our opinion polling shows us up 25% since the general election. We've got one person who happens to be an MP who consistently privately, and now publicly, challenges my leadership. Now look, the answer's very simple, Mr Carswell—Put up, or shut up.'

Rather a shame that the Party will only be getting rid of the small fry that is Hellings rather than the stinky old turbot that is Carswell. On that point I ask Whittle for an update.

'Do you know if Crowther's pronounced the death sentence yet?'

'A pretty ghastly night and Hellings excelled himself. I'll find out.'

'Good. Tell me when you know. Steve's got enough to deal with regarding today's treason without me pestering him too.'

'I will. And bugger Dougie.'

Saturday 19th December 2015

The Party Chairman writes to John Hellings.

'In the light of previous complaints which have been received, both formally and informally, about your behaviour, and the nature of this occurrence which could have caused very serious reputational damage to the Party, I am hereby suspending you.'

Being suspended as a member in good standing, his post as London Chairman also goes.

Wednesday 23rd December 2015

Things are moving with regards to the London Elections bank account. Then this email comes in from Suzanne Evans to all of us on the campaign group.

'Re names on the account, I know it was suggested at the meeting that it might be me, Peter and David Kurten.

'Given what has since transpired about David Kurten's address, I would feel very uncomfortable indeed were this idea to go forward. Quite how this situation came about, and what might happen with regard to it in the future, I don't know, but if we either can't trust candidates to be honest about their eligibility to stand, or they are not competent enough to check their eligibility, then I don't feel we should include them with serious matters such as signing cheques.'

Not helpful Suzanne. Not helpful at all.

Friday 1st January 2016

What a happy start to the new year. Adam Richardson, Head of Legal, confirms that Suzanne's still refusing to be a signatory to the bank account.

He's going to shake the issue by the throat.

'It's clear Suzanne's eyes are on the number 2 spot but she needs to know David isn't going anywhere. If our top three GLA candidates can't work together then we are fucked right out the gate.'

Monday 4th January 2016

Having enjoyed a traditional 1980s Christmas, that is, without the internet or social media, I catch up on several days' news on the splendid *Breitbart* site all at once. The loosening of the wheelnuts on Nigel's car has hit the press: 'UKIP "Furious" After Details Of "Assassination Attempt" Against Farage Leaked'.

I leave a message for Gawain who calls me back from the wilds of

Australia.

'It wasn't me, old chap' I tell him.

'Nobody's suggested it was. I thought you were calling about Anne-Marie Waters.'

Oh?

'She's launching Pegida UK this morning with Tommy Robinson and Paul Weston of Liberty GB.'

Pegida being the street movement originating in Germany and describing itself as Patriotic Europeans Against the Islamisation of the West.

FFS.

I call Nigel and wish him a happy new year.

'Just so you know. It wasn't me that grassed about your car.'

'Oh, don't worry about it. I've got a fair idea where it came from. I thought you were calling about our London meeting on the 14th.'

Not I.

'It's been pulled. I was going to speak with Gerard but the organisers have got cold feet.'

So that's two cancellations. Croydon and East London.

'Actually Nigel, while we're sharing bad news, what do you want to do about Anne-Marie Waters?'

'To be honest, I never wanted her standing for us at all. She's got to go although this will be down to the NEC.'

Tuesday 5th January 2016

Having spoken to a few people, the Anne-Marie situation's troubling so I talk to Crowther about it.

'Steve. Pegida isn't on our proscribed list. If it's added now then she can't be hoofed out of The KIP retrospectively. Besides, there are very many activists who sympathise. We can't afford a mass flouncing-off if we're too harsh.'

'Yes,' he replies. 'And I think we'd find ourselves on the other side of a writ if we did. I've told Nigel this. I've also told him that if we handle this badly it could tear UKIP apart.'

Wednesday 6th January 2016

Today is Peter Whittle's 55th birthday and he's having drinks at the Westminster Arms. I get there early and nurse a pint with an *Evening Standard* while waiting for the birthday boy to arrive and, more importantly, to see Anne Marie Waters who wants to speak face to face.

Nigel turns up with David Coburn, who gives me a hug as we've not seen each other for a while. He's full of salacious gossip which I won't repeat. The Dear Leader suddenly has to leave and it's only then that Anne Marie arrives.

We decant to a downstairs booth for privacy. I really don't want to read her the Riot Act.

'How is Mr Tommy Robinson? I've just finished reading his new book. It's rather good.'

She says that she too has written one and is looking for a publisher. Iain Dale's Biteback Publishing has turned her down. There's a surprise.

I broach the question about the London List.

'We need to talk about this.'

Anne Marie throws back her arms and slumps in her seat. Not in anger or despair it seems, but with a sense of relief.

'Yes – I'm happy to stand down.'

Well, that was easy.

'Brilliant! Look, there's no intention to stomp on you. It's just that if you became the story that would detract from Whittle's chances. And the two of you are close mates.'

She understands.

'Yes, I know. Look, it was just such a rush. Tommy phoned me an hour or so before the launch and asked if I'd sign up. And I just threw caution to the wind and thought "why not?" I should have given it some thought but to be honest I agree with their entire platform and would never shrink from saying so.'

Tuesday 12th January 2016

Hustings tonight for the Greenwich & Lewisham Superconstituency. Paul Oakley (your dear author) is one of the candidates. Yet there's an interloper from elsewhere who's put his name in too. Dash his insolence!

Oakley wins, but the challenger is very good indeed and will do well wherever he eventually stands.

Nonetheless – we don't like outsiders in these 'ere paaarts.

Wednesday 13th January 2016

The postponed selection meeting for Bexley and Bromley is tonight. The seat is the best chance we have of winning a superconstituency in London. Not that we will.

There are many people milling around at the bar. Sadly, that isn't our member turnout and we have only 18 in attendance. We're stuck at the back of a large room which is open to the rest of the pub and thus noisy. Not the best choice.

I'm chairing along with Peter Staveley. Chris Attard, interim Bexley Chairman, joins us. He gives an update on Catherine Reilly's condition. She's sitting up in bed with breathing devices but hasn't yet been informed of the extent of her condition. This is awful.

There are supposed to be three candidates. Ronie Johnson and Frank Gould, both of whom turned up to watch the Greenwich selection last night, are already there. Rathy Alagaratnam is also putting her name forward but hasn't arrived. We get started in the interim with both lads' opening speeches.

Still nothing from Rathy so Peter Staveley calls her. She'd been expecting to hear more from the branches about tonight and assumed she wasn't selected. We take that as a withdrawal.

The vote is 10 – 8 in Frank's favour which is a fair outcome as they're evenly matched.

Julian Grainger then wants to have an open discussion about local planning issues. Neither I nor Staveley are particularly, or at all, interested. So we leave. Politely of course.

Thursday 14th January 2016

I'm scanning my favourite news website, *Breitbart*. Anne Marie has written a piece about the desperate widows and orphans who've sought sanctuary in Europe.

'Dear So-Called Feminists – Your Open Borders Bullshit Will Ensure Thousands Of More Rapes And Sexual Assaults'
No problem with that, but there is one at the end of the article:
'Anne Marie Waters is a UKIP London Assembly Candidate.'
I call Raheem Kassam as editor of the site.

'Could you remove the tagline that she's an assembly candidate? She's agreed to step down at the NEC's request.'

'That's an outrage.'
I don't agree.

'Nigel & Steve thought it best she go. She agreed and volunteered to go gracefully. She's still a member in good standing. Rightly, in my view.'

'This is the moment I stop supporting UKIP, I think. I'll see what she has to say about it.'

Nigel needs to be informed. We can't afford to lose a sympathetic news outlet. He tuts when told.

'Doesn't Raheem realise who these people are? The former EDL head and the one from Liberty GB? Their supporters would have no time at all for people like him.'

I leave a message for Waters herself and, as if by magic, immediately receive a call from the Party Chairman.

'Have you heard from Anne Marie?' Crowther asks. 'The press office are getting calls about her.'

I bring him up to speed.

'It's probably Raheem.'

'Oh. He'll be pleased to know that Tariq Saeed will be taking her place on the list. A Moslem.'

I finally speak to the lady in question. She's already heard from Kassam.

'Raheem was quite angry but I told him that I wasn't at all. Look, I know that it would deflect from Peter Whittle's candidacy and I wouldn't want to do that to him.'

'Thanks,' I reply. 'This wasn't an easy decision for the party to make. You know that we don't hesitate to throw people out on their backside when required. And it wasn't required in your case.'

Time to see if Raheem's sulking.

'Is everything Zen and chilled? Anne Marie's confirmed that she is.'

'We'll run a story and let readers decide.'

He does, almost immediately: 'EXCLUSIVE: UKIP Drops London Assembly Candidate Anne Marie Waters For PEGIDA UK Link'.

Fortunately, most of those commenting on the piece fully-understand the dilemma. UKIP are damned if we keep her and blasted if we don't. It'll blow over.

CHAPTER TWENTY-EIGHT

Gays, 'GO' and Galloway

Tuesday 26th January 2016

OFF TO THE CIVIL SERVICE CLUB for a London campaign meeting. We discuss problems with finding suitable meeting halls at which Nigel and our top candidates will speak. Given that His Nibs will ensure there's a good turnout and the party is as skint nationally as it is in London, the idea is that box office takings will be split evenly between head office and the region.

Suzanne Evans is appalled.

'That's appalling. Doesn't he know that we need the money here to put on a good campaign?'

The rest of the room isn't so convinced.

We have, finally, a draft campaign leaflet to look at. It's passed around.

Suzanne Evans is appalled.

'Most of this stuff has nothing to do with the mayor's powers. We can't do anything about immigration.'

She promotes, once more, her idea of a 25p tourist tax on hotel rooms to fund, well, something or other. Sadly, tonight's *Evening Standard* announced that the Lib Dem mayoral candidate is herself proposing a £2 a night tourist tax. I don't bother telling Suzanne this.

In addition, there's no photograph of Suzanne on the draft about which she may also be appalled.

There's a general discussion about the *Standard*. Peter's upset about the interview with him that they've just published.

'They made me sound so boring. And, honestly I'm not. They

didn't even mention that I'm a poofter even though they seem to have at least one gay article in every issue. You might almost think they're trying to dull me down.'

Mind you, the other candidates aren't receiving a huge amount of coverage either.

Suzanne Evans is appalled.

'Why isn't the press office promoting the rest of us? They didn't even mention the two latest things about me.'

I already know what they are, but ask her anyway.

'Debrett's have classed me as one of the most influential politicians. And I had an article in the *Telegraph* this morning. Why isn't the party publicising this?'

She looks at John Gill who's running Press in the temporary absence of Gawain.

'This sidelining of me really is pathetic and has to stop.'

John looks up at the ceiling and then down at his stripy multicoloured socks and says nothing.

They really are an excellent pair of socks.

Thursday 28th January 2016

A busy and constructive campaign meeting of London Region takes place at the Novotel in Waterloo. Much of the discussion revolves around the aftermath of the John Hellings situation and his abuse of Nigel Sussman.

Afterwards, I walk to the station with Sussman. As we pass the walls of Lambeth Palace two men approach from the opposite direction.

'At least', says Nigel, 'Hellings has given me a title for my new blog. I'm going to call it: "North London Jewish Cunt".'

The two men open a side door in the walls. One of them looks at us with disapproval as they disappear inside.

I vaguely recognise him. Warble? Wobble? No - Welby.

Um-Ah!

Sussman just said the 'Cunt' word!

In front of the Archbishop of Canterbury!

Friday 5th February 2015

Roger Gravett is chairing the selection meeting for the South West constituency of the London Assembly. Richard Hendron is up against Alan Craig.

Hendron is passionate and speaks from the heart.

'We have an image problem and people believe that we're racist, sexist and homophobic. It does not help in any way shape or form putting up candidates who are openly homophobic. Candidates that call gay activists the "Gaystapo".'

'You know, I don't normally like attacking other candidates. When I discovered that I am against somebody who is overtly homophobic I am almost insulted that UKIP have allowed the man in the other room to actually be against me.'

'If we put up candidates with those kind of views. Candidates who praise the Bishop of Rochester who says homosexuals should repent and change. Candidates who attend conferences on "how to cure gays". I find that, you know, excessively offensive.'

'So all I'm saying is, the question really is: what kind of party do you want to be in?'

The audience is largely made up of those in late middle age or older. Hendron's given them a lot to think about. He is unassailable in his view that a re-examination of their core beliefs is overdue.

As for Alan Craig's speech? Boringly and predictably, he focuses on the battle to leave the EU.

The result is decisive. Richard Hendron receives two votes. As he lives in the seat one of those is presumably his own. Unless, that is, he voted in a chivalrous manner and endorsed his opponent. In any event, Craig is nominated.

Sunday 7th February 2016

Mr Hendron takes his ball home and resigns from UKIP. He speaks to *Pink News* about it.

'I have tried my hardest to fight for the party and LGBT issues but I have been met with a barrage of resistance at all levels. UKIP is not really interested in equality, the LGBT group do nothing other than tick a box for the party, they do not push for change in the party or support LGBT activists who are trying to make a change, they even refused my application to join the LGBT group stating that being gay and in UKIP does not automatically qualify you for membership of LGBT in UKIP.'

Preposterous. There is solid synchronicity between UKIP LGBT and the wider party. We all agree that Hendron's a wanker.

Monday 8th February 2016

Except – Suzanne Evans doesn't agree. She's been mouthing off to *Pink News* too.

'I've written to the Chairman and our National Executive Committee to make my personal views clear: that the views of Alan Craig should not be implicitly condoned by UKIP by making him a GLA candidate.'

'I'm confident he won't be the SW London candidate for much longer.'

That's fine, perhaps. Going public about it is not.

Thursday 11th February 2016

John Hamilton of Lewisham People Before Profit, you remember, 'the radical residents' association', has invited me to a meeting about the referendum at the Catford Constitutional Club. I've not been inside for years. It had been the local Tory drinking hole long ago when Lewisham still had some Conservative MPs.

It now looks derelict from the outside and is reached from an alleyway which is plainly used by blokes coming back from other local dives for unsavoury purposes. It pongs.

It also looks derelict from the inside, with peeling wallpaper, chipped paintwork and chairs leaking horsehair. Although Miss Havisham seems to have been commissioned as interior designer, the place is very full indeed.

Sensibly, John's booked us into a side room for privacy. As well as him there is Cheryl, her friend Alex, Peter and Pat Richardson and a couple of others.

'We'd like to work with you on the Leave side.'

Great!

'But there's a problem', Hamilton continues. 'UKIP's stance on immigration. We're very uncomfortable with this.'

'Understood,' I reply. 'When I became an EUphobe back in the 1990s, migration wasn't an issue but the arguments for withdrawal were still unassailable.'

'We have leaflets of our own and also some from anti-EU socialists,' John tells me. 'But I'm afraid we won't be able to distribute any of yours.'

'No problem. But we'll be glad to deliver anything you want to give us.'

I pretend not to notice that Alex has been sketching a cartoon of me from behind my right shoulder. It's really quite good.

Saturday 13th February 2016

I like *Russia Today*. Its news coverage is a refreshing alternative to the endemic bias of that state-owned propaganda channel, the BBC. And my hearty breakfast is rendered especially enjoyable this morning as George Galloway is interviewing Nigel Farage on his *Sputnik* show about the referendum. They agree on just about everything.

Monday 15th February 2016

The London Region meeting coalesces at the Civil Service Club to talk tactics for the two-pronged campaigning we're currently facing. And, rude as ever, we all gaily discuss our own local priorities with the colleagues we're sitting next to while the main agenda is covered in parallel. 'One Meeting'? No. Several.

Then Peter Reeve, perhaps because of his councillorship and membership of the Local Government Association, comes out with a corking suggestion.

'How about this? We step back from campaigning for the referendum until May 6th and focus solely on the London Assembly before that date.'

Attendees stop their own conversations immediately and there's complete silence for an instant before Peter is assailed from all side with shouts of disgust. Dogshit and wheelie bins or withdrawal from the EU? Priorities, old chap.

Wednesday 17th February 2016

Best check with Farage about whether it's ok to get under the duvet with the Lewisham lefties in the referendum campaign. I put it tentatively at first.

'You know how you clicked with George Galloway in the interview on RT? And you know you said that Kippers can and should be working with whichever campaign wants out, whether it's Vote Leave or . . .'

'Let me stop you there,' Nigel butts in. 'We're not going to work with Vote Leave at all. They're a Tory Boy Front. Many of them actually want to stay in a "reformed" EU or are calling for a second referendum which will have the same effect. Don't touch them. We're going to throw everything behind Grassroots Out.'

'Noted. What about respectable lefties?'
I tell him about the meeting and our regard for John Hamilton and his posse.

'What did they think of the Galloway interview?' he asks.

Nigel seems particularly interested in this. I can't give him an answer though because we met on the Thursday and his interview with the

Respect leader wasn't broadcast until Saturday.

'I'll ask them at the next meeting, but suspect they'll have approved.'

He pauses for a moment.

'Do you know? I've no problem with that. So, yes. Do it.'

Friday 19th February 2016

Tonight is the launch of the 'Grassroots Out' campaign at the Queen Elizabeth II Centre. There will be a very special guest. There's been much discussion about the identity of that person. Labour MP Simon Danczuk perhaps? Possibly even mayor of London Boris Johnson. Although I doubt that as BJ has his own career aspirations uppermost in his mind at all times.

There's significant security at the venue even extending to having a guard in each lift which transports us to the third floor.

The hall is utterly rammed with attendees and that's just at the front. The room's divided into two halves and the other section's stuffed as well.

I have never. Ever. Seen an EU-realist meeting as busy as this. Two thousand? Maybe.

There are no seats available at all. I find a space to stand which, coincidentally, is next to Lucy Bostick's chair. We haven't seen each other for over a year. She tells me the reason she's not been around is because she's left the party. I'm sorry to hear that.

Peter Bone, Tory MP for Wellingborough, opens proceedings. There are large video screens behind him but even if there were none it would be impossible to miss the foul green "GO" tie he's wearing. I want one.

'The first speaker we have tonight has just come back from Brussels. He's been batting for the British Interest. He likes to be called "Dave". . . . er.'

There are chuckles. What – THAT Dave? Can it be true? After all, he'd vowed to lead the Leave campaign if he didn't receive a respectable new deal from the EU. Naw – we wouldn't have him anyway as Bone confirms.

'It's my proud privelege to introduce the chairman of Conservatives for Britain and the GO movement's political advisory committee: David Campbell Bannerman MEP.'

There are several boos from the Kippers as Bannerman had of course defected from UKIP to the Tories. I'm one of them and Lucy thumps my leg.

'Don't do that!'

This is a light-hearted meeting with many jokes from the speakers as well as serious argument. We have Gerard Batten, Bill Cash, Ruth Lea and Tom Pursglove MP. From the left there is John Boyd, a trades unionist, and Kate Hoey MP. Representing normal people are Scott Kimber, a cabbie, Henrik Overgaard from Denmark and businesswoman Pam Watts.

It's a great meeting but it starts to drag because my foot's throbbing from a recently-broken toe and I'm still standing up. I go for a stroll to loosen my old bones and come across Gawain Towler.

'What's the remaining running order and who's the special guest?' I ask.

'David Davis, followed by Nigel.'

'Is Davis meant to be the special guest? That's a bit rubbish.'

'No, it's not him. But I don't know who as it's top secret. Genuinely.'

Farage finally comes on and is, as ever, excellent. He enters the room and finishes his speech to standing ovations before striding off. Sweating with fervour, he then returns to the stage. An encore? That's not like him and we're now running past the 9 pm advertised watershed.

There's a disturbance at the back of the room but it's impossible to see what it might be. Nigel speaks again.

'Our last speaker tonight is without doubt one of the greatest orators in this country. He's a towering figure on the left of British politics. And he's coming on to this platform today to join the Grassroots Out movement. And I want you to give a very big warm welcome. To George Galloway!'

As the young people say – O.M.G.

Galloway strides down the central aisle with several minders. There are many jeers and rudities and his bodyguards jerk their heads around like meerkats to cast baleful glances at the perpetrators.

Lucy Bostick, and several others, storm out. But most people stay and most people clap and most people cheer.

'Comrades and friends,' Galloway begins.

We like that.

'I'd like to thank Nigel Farage very sincerely for his kind words. The more generous because Nigel and I agree on hardly anything at all.'

We like that too.

'But we do agree at least on one thing. And it happens to be the most important thing, not only now, but in the lifetime of everyone in this hall and everyone in this country. It is the demand that Britain should be an independent, sovereign and democratic country. And that means leaving the European Union.'

We like that best of all.

Meeting over, it is of course time for the Westminster Arms.

I speak to Raheem Kassam.

'Did you like Galloway?'

'No. I'd no idea he was coming until I saw him in the green room just beforehand. I'm not happy.'

Journalist Harry Cole is writing something on his mobile with a hand in a sling. I ask him straight away about the most burning question of the moment.

'How did you break your wanking spanner Harry?'

'Ah,' he says. 'That's the other hand. I fell in the sea.'

'But George Galloway?'

'I'm just thinking about it. What do you reckon?'

'It's like Powell and Benn being on the same side in the 1975 referendum. Might be a good idea, might not be.'

'I may use that,' says Harry.

Many Tories whom I haven't seen for years are milling around including Adrian Lee, Chris Williams and Andrew Rosindell, Romford's MP. Rozzer grasps my hand and shakes and shakes and shakes. He introduces me to his retinue who are fellow Tories but I don't know them.

'Everyone - this guy got me into real trouble. He ripped up a Maastricht Treaty at a Young Conservative conference when I was chairman. I got hauled in to Central Office to explain myself. I thought it was great, and told them so.'

CHAPTER TWENTY-NINE

Naughty Suzanne!

Saturday 20th February 2016

DAVID CAMERON APPEARS outside Number 10 to make the announcement we've all been lusting after.

'On Monday I will commence the process set out under our Referendum Act. And I will go to parliament and propose that the British people decide our future in Europe through an in-out referendum on Thursday the 23rd of June.

'The choice is in your hands.'

Saturday 27th February 2017

Lunchtime. Llandudno conference. Nigel has another launch for 'GO'. Suzanne Evans and Douglas Carswell do likewise for Vote Leave. At the same time.

And – Suzanne has apparently told the sparse number of attendees that Farage is one of the least trusted voices on the EU. Not clever.

Friday 4th March 2016

Finally! Leaflets and freebies from the Grassroots Out campaign have been delivered to London.

I drive up to collect our branch's batch from Roger Gravett in Wood Green. His van's parked in the street and when he opens the rear doors it's jammed from floor to ceiling. I was expecting a few thousand leaflets which I'm duly-given and load into the back of the car before closing the boot.

'No', says Roger. 'There's a lot more than that.'

He hands over another box.

'What's this?'

'Helium for the balloons.'

There's that box of balloons as well. Also, one full of badges (two kinds). Clipboards. Stickers. T-Shirts (in several sizes). Flourescent green cagoules. A table cover. Bags. Beermats. A roller-banner stand.

Crikey. There's several hundred quid's-worth of merchandise here. And that's just for our branch. Someone has spent an awful lot on this campaign.

'Are there many more people coming to pick up this stuff from you today?' I ask.

'A few. And I'm going to Chingford tonight to drop off a load. Oh. And visiting the station later to hand over the Croydon allotment. Kathleen Garner and a few of her branch are coming up by train to collect.'

'By public transport? They must be mental.'

'No comment,' smiles Roger.

Saturday 5th March 2016

Here it is. The national day of action for GO. It's a miserable morning marred by freezing rain as I head to Eltham. Traffic is slow on the approach to the Clifton's roundabout on the South Circular and police are dotted all over the place. There's been a stabbing at the Esso petrol station, which isn't at all common in South London (in our aspirations).

Twelve activists have turned out at the High Street meeting point including three new lads: Nick, Richard and Paul. They've come along to help as normal members of the public and not as Kippers.

Given the filthy rain which now includes sleet, we decide that it's not balloon weather, so won't bother bringing out the helium.

So we spread out and get going. As ever, I lack the modesty or shame of my fellows and declaim a loop of catchphrases to the passers-by.

'Vote out of the European Union.'

'Say No to Brussels.'

'Three for a pound.'

Maybe not the last one. I'm getting rid of the leaflets fast. Many stop to talk. I have just two swivel-eyed pro-EU people to deal with. One glares at me and tells us that we must be mad.

'Not as mental as you. Federast.'

I'm happy to be rude when necessary.

A woman comes up to me with a smile.

'Anti-EU? Can I have one of those please?'

She takes the leaflet and walks straight to the street bin where it is deposited.

'That,' she says, 'is where this rubbish belongs.'

I tell her there's nothing that her kind can do to stop us but am smiling inside at her little exploit. I resolve to do the same myself in future when faced with enemy street campaigners.

Our mayoral candidate Peter Whittle turns up and poses for photographs. The group is positioned on the small plaza next to Delicio. I'm on the other side of the road accosting people passing Costa Coffee but notice that others have turned up to distribute leaflets of their own right next to our banner. Fair enough. Free country innit? I go over to peer at them.

'Who are you from?' I ask.

'BNP'.

He hands a leaflet in my direction which I refuse to take.

'We're on the same side,' He entreats

'Fuck that. We are not nearly on the same side.'

As this meeting has been publicly advertised on the GO website I'm suspicious that this is precisely why they're here. I'm not having it and tell the troops.

'Come on comrades, we're moving further up.'

We decant to a less-salubrious area next to Iceland. Which does of course have its own positive symbolism. Another half hour passes and we've handed out a full box of literature. Lunch beckons and it's time to pack up.

Whittle's heading down to Croydon to show his face at their own street stall which is being set up at around now. I drive him to the station and he decides to Tweet as we go.

'What shall I say?' he asks.

'Tell the world we had a great morning and shifted 2,000 leaflets.'

'Did we? I didn't think it was as many as that.'

'It was only about eight hundred actually. But nobody will ever know.'

Peter Tweets this white lie accordingly.

Thursday 17th March 2016

Disciplinary proceedings are being convened about Suzanne Evans' criticism of Craig and Kurten.

Monday 21st March 2016

Suzanne wants to finish our London Manifesto and has been rightly nagging for photos of all the candidates. If we don't get them to her by the middle of the week our pictures won't be featured in the copy.

Bah. I hate having my photo taken. Besides, now that my missis has insisted I grow my hair this means going to the barbers, which is a pain. As a consequence, it's not been touched for a couple of months and is now greebo.

'Sorry Suzanne – I've not had time to do this, not least because I need a haircut. My ugly fizzog will need to be absent from it in the circumstances.'

She laughs.

'I'm sure your hair is fine! The heat's off as I'm still awaiting a final draft of the manifesto but the sooner the better.'

Wednesday 23rd March 2016

There's grumbling from the London candidates because the manifesto still isn't ready. Surely Suzanne's finished it by now? She eventually emails us all.

'I would just like to confirm in case there is any doubt that I finished the manifesto a while ago. It's at the NEC policy subcommittee that it's stuck.'

Then it's announced that Suzanne has been suspended from the party.

Steve Crowther sends a few of us a statement at 5 pm. She's been given a caning by the NEC.

'The panel resolved to suspend her membership of the party for six months. The decision may be subject to appeal. Ms Evans sought an injunction in the High Court today to prevent the hearing, but this was unsuccessful.

As a consequence of this, she will not now be nominated as a UKIP candidate in the London Assembly elections to be held on May 5th.'

Oh – and it's said to be nothing to do with any battles between her and Nigel.

Thursday 24th March 2016

A national RO meeting which largely deals with boring administrative issues. But of course the Suzanne Evans situation has to be discussed, not least because Adam Richardson, barrister and counsel for the Party, is at the meeting. He'd represented us at court yesterday to resist her application for an injunction to prevent the party from:

'abusing the disciplinary process to stifle my progression and reduce my standing within the party.'

Adam confirms that those complaints were solely about her objections to the candidacies of notorious homosceptics Alan Craig and David Kurten. Hendron's brother, Henry, had represented Suzanne at court. It's surprising that Hendron, H, had found the time to do this because he'd just pleaded guilty to charges of possessing drugs with intent to supply at the Old Bailey. His boyfriend had died as a result. He'd had a busy day what with battling UKIP in the morning and then appearing before a judge himself that same afternoon.

I'd met Henry once before. We'd both been invited to a solicitors' party in the grounds of Wallington library. He'd spent the evening making malapert comments to and about other attendees before falling asleep in one patio chair with his feet up on another. The evening wound down. The guests drifted away. The caterers packed up. The outside lights were turned off. It would have been easy for anyone to nudge his shoulder and wake him. But nobody wanted to so we left him where he was.

Adam wasn't impressed with his opponent. He's very rude about him, and very funny.

Other Regional Organisers are keen to tell the Party Chairman about the complaints they've been receiving regarding Suzanne's suspension.

Crowther sighs.

'Look. If it's important, pass any emails on to me and I will send them in turn to the NEC who will then deal with it.'

But a query's raised.

'Who'll be chairing the NEC when it considers these complaints?'

Crowther rests his chin in his palm. He stares down at the table before him. After a period of reflection, he raises his arm slowly into the air, saying nothing.

Tuesday 29th March 2016

Off to the Old Doctor Butler's Head. Can't be bovvered with this tonight and I'm deliberately late to avoid paying the Congestion Tax too.

On arriving, there are no spaces around the table so I join the boys in the naughty corner, namely John Gill from the Press Office, Matt Luck, who's in charge of the London campaign, and Whittle.

Chairman Freddy Vaccha says something about having my good

self executed *pour encourager les autres* as I sit down.

There are 12 issues on the agenda. And 14 sub-matters.

Matt Luck is to give a briefing on the mayoral campaign and manages to push his presentation up the agenda, mentioning other commitments that evening. He says his piece and leaves.

Peter Whittle has to address the meeting too. About five minutes after doing so he taps my arm and mutters.

'Do you fancy a quick drink? I can't bear listening to all of this.'

'Sounds great, but I've got to stay.'

Peter sits back. After a couple more minutes and at an appropriate lull in the proceedings he gathers together his things.

'I'm sorry, Mr Chairman, but I'll have to bid you farewell. I'm due to be schmoozing a potential donor tonight and will have to leave you to it.'

He does too. Lucky dastard, because the next item on the agenda is:

'Round-up of branches - What do you want to share with us? GO campaign experiences?'

The multiple chairmen present will thus have the chance to tell us all, at length, about their adventures if they wish to do so. They do wish. All of them.

The meeting finally finishes at a quarter-to-ten. There is however one useful piece of information. The NEC have confirmed they've expelled former London chairman and shouty anti-semite John Hellings from the party.

Good.

Wednesday 30th March 2016

Tomorrow's the closing date for the London Assembly nominations. There are forms to hand in at each council office and deposits of £1,000 to pay. Cash or bankers' draft only. No cheques. No electronic transfers.

As UKIP Greenwich & Lewisham are temporarily without a bank account, I'll have to pay this cash from personal funds. It's the week after Easter and I'm under the impression that today is Tuesday. My local bank is closed every Wednesday, a matter which I'd forgotten until turning up at its doors.

Have to head to the Catford branch then. I don't like it. There's only one counter and the bank's full of unsavoury customers. I hand over a written note when reaching the teller:

'May I please have £1,000 cash. In fifties, preferably.'

I stuff the envelope into my pocket and then head over to Laurence House where Lewisham Electoral Services are based. I've been calling Malcolm Constable, its head, to arrange an appointment and am ticked off that he's not responded.

On arrival, I'm met by the very helpful Julie who takes us to the back office.

'Do you have all the papers? We'll need to check them,' she tells me.

'That's okay. I've already sent a scanned version to Malcolm and he says they're fine.'

'Ah,' she says. 'You didn't know. Malcolm died yesterday.'
He was only 64. He'd slipped away while watching TV and leaves two teenage children. Terrible.

As Julie takes away the forms and the money to double-check both with a colleague, I call Staveley to tell him the sad news.

He has other news. He hasn't yet filed the nomination papers for the Assembly which isn't like him at all.

He explains. There are two versions. One featuring the name of Suzanne Evans, and one without Evans and with Peter's own name taking up the absent place at the very end of the list.

Paul Oakden has required this because Suzanne's appealed to the NEC against her suspension. That appeal is being heard as we speak. If she's not successful, the latter paper will be submitted.

'Congratulations Peter,' I say. 'You'll be an excellent candidate even though you won't get elected.'

'You're correct on both points,' he replies.

CHAPTER THIRTY

London Hasn't Fallen After All

Monday 4th April 2016
Afternoon

W E'RE SELECTING OUR CANDIDATE for the Glyndon ward by-election in Greenwich tonight. All applicants have to be approved by Head Office beforehand to check that they're not a nutter. Facebook and Twitter are examined before they are given a tick.

I call Gawain to ask if he can help with an update. He can't, but offloads the latest load of grief on my ears. One candidate for the Welsh Assembly, Gareth Bennett, has proved to be, well, unhelpful. The NEC has decided to endorse him nonetheless. As a direct consequence, 16 other candidates have decided to stand down.

'This is all the fault of Douglas Carswell and Neil Hamilton,' he tells me.

Everyone knows that Carswell's Not Clubbable but it's surprising to hear that Hamilton is engaging in skulduggery too.

'They're trying to position themselves to oust Nathan Gill in Wales and then introduce a candidate to replace Farage.'

'Who?'

'Paul Nuttall.'

'But Nuttall and Nigel are tight aren't they?'

'Exactly. It's madness. And the NEC aren't helping at all.'

'Don't worry. The London candidate situation was sorted. This will be too.'

'I hope so,' says Towler.

He doesn't sound certain.

EVENING

7 pm. The meeting to select our by-election candidate is at the Greenwich Tavern. Permanent applicant for anything and everything, Anthony, is there before us.

There's no sign of his challenger, Rita Hamilton. Uh-oh.

Time marches on. The horrifying scenario of Tony being selected by default is too much to stand. To our relief, Rita finally arrives. She'd thought we were starting at half-past.

The pub's fairly quiet so we coalesce around a refectory table in the main bar. Tony decides it'll be 'ladies first' so we ask him to move away while we examine Rita. He does so and we begin, but then I notice that he's moved back to our vicinity and is lurking behind a nearby pillar within earshot.

'Tony. Could you disappear please?'

Rita's brought a ringbinder. She knows the facts about the ward. She's keen to get on the streets. She answers the questions well and is shyly reticent about the considerable campaigning she's already done for the branch.

Anthony's turn. He's brought no paperwork. He answers the questions poorly and is shyly reticent about the total lack of campaigning he's ever done for the branch.

It's unanimous. The best woman wins.

Anthony isn't happy. He's mumbling about standing as an independent. I don't bother telling him, but fighting against an official UKIP campaign would mean expulsion from the party.

Being a kindly old gentleman, I pull him to one side.

'Look, you fell down because you did nothing for the EU or council elections. Nothing for the general election. And you've not volunteered for the referendum or London mayor. We're hitting the streets this weekend. Come out, and you'll have a better chance next time.'

'OK then,' he says. 'I'll see you on Saturday morning then.'

I very much doubt that we will.

Saturday 9th April 2016

This is the action day which Whittle and Kurten have asked us to hold in Eltham. Anthony doesn't turn up.

David buys us all drinks in the Old Post Office pub afterwards. Peter isn't pleased about yet more delay in publishing the manifesto which still hasn't been signed off by the NEC.

'It's these blasted libertarians. They won't agree to anything which interferes with the market so I can't do nearly what I want to do about housing.'

He speaks, of course, of moves to restrict home ownership by foreign investors.

'It's ridiculous. When we're at hustings Sadiq-bloody-Khan is standing up for Brits more than I am.'

I'm giving Peter Lello, Hugh Waine and Jo Mullins a lift back to Lewisham. As we leave the pub we pass a plant stall to our right.

'Pansy's 2 for £1'.

I try very hard but the internal sniggering is unbearable.

'Oooh look Peter. A bargain for you, dear.'

Lello points at me theatrically with his eyes forced wide:

'Homophone!'

Monday 11th April 2016

London Region Meeting at the Civil Service Club. The manifesto has yet to be signed off. Freddy Vaccha tells us this is because Tomas Slivnik, Sark minarchist mathematician of the NEC, is still tweaking it. Still.

Freddy also tells us that we are categorically not to sign any document that Vote Leave place before us.

'They won't let you deliver any UKIP leaflet along with their literature. There's talk of suing if you do. Effectively, all the Tory boys are getting Kippers to do the grafting on their behalf while they swan off and campaign for Zac Goldsmith's battle for London Mayor.'

There's even more disturbing news.

'I've been in touch with Grassroots Out to get details of London supporters who've signed up. Can anyone guess how many we have?'

Kathleen Garner tries. Wrongly.

Freddy breaks the mild sense of anticipation.

'It's about. Eight hundred. And fifty.'

A strong sense of disbelief fills the room. After all the woman-hours of street stalls and delivering – that's it?

I ask if he could pass on the details of these people although suspect that most of them will be Kippers in any case. We desperately need more bodies to campaign and it's the same for the other branches. Even one or two new people would help.

'I'm not allowed. They made me sign a data protection form.'

'Well perhaps you could just leave the sheets lying around while you go to the bog or something.'

'I'm ahead of you, Mr Oakley. Read these.'

He hands over two pages of confidentiality clauses. One of which expressly forbids leaving-the-said-clauses-lying-around-while-you-go-to-the-bog-or-something. Or words to that effect.

He takes them back.

'I'm wondering if perhaps both Vote Leave and Grassroots Out are each enemies who have been set up to squeeze UKIP.'

I'm not so sure. In GO's case it's probably just stupidity. Can't comment about Vote Leave as I'll have nothing to do with them.

Wednesday 13th April 2016

The Electoral Commission announces once again that it's UKIP-phobic and unfit-for-purpose by designating Vote Leave as the official 'Out' campaign for the referendum.

The media says that Arron Banks is going to court to seek a judicial review. I call him and leave a message. Please don't.

Party Chairman Steve Crowther is easier to get hold of.

'Worry not,' he says. 'Both me and Nigel have told him to back off. Arron reckons a court case would postpone the referendum until October and then we'd have the benefit of a further migrant flood over the summer. But we've told him that'll just piss people off.'

'Good,' I reply. 'I'm just concerned that Vote Leave won't allow us to deliver UKIP election leaflets along with their own bumf. But - fuck them.'

'Yes, fuck them. And don't forget that UKIP has £4 million of its own to spend in the campaign. So you can just deliver our stuff and nothing else if you want.'

Tuesday 19th April 2016

London manifesto launch at the Emmanuel Centre in the morning followed by a street stall in Bromley in the afternoon. Nigel's become a rock star and is mobbed, even by a crowd of French students.

We sit in the garden of the Partridge for one beer afterwards and he's waylaid by lairy passing schoolboys who point, chant his name and demand selfies.

London chairman Freddy Vaccha is trying. To be helpful. He's standing in the street on the other side of the fence from Nigel, accosting passers-by with UKIP leaflets and directing their gaze to the leader. Give the guy a break.

Nigel looks tired. I ask if he's managed to get out to fish but he hasn't yet this year. I tell him about the Old Quarry at Betchworth and its resident pike. Next time I'm hoping to pull out a thirty-pounder.

'When are you planning on going to the lake?' he asks.

'Well, I had been meaning to head down today if it wasn't for the launch. But very soon and before they start spawning.'

'There's something primeval about hunting pike isn't there? I'd like to come but I'm not sure if I'll have a break in the diary.'

His phone rings. Yet again. And he's back with the task at hand.

Peter Whittle's also knackered. He's been up since the early hours to do an interview at 6.30 and there are more hustings tonight. We ask about his impressions of the other candidates. Caroline Pidgeon (she of 'Caroline Pidgeon's London Liberal DemocratsTM') is a bit odd. He sometimes clicks with George Galloway but sometimes Mr Galloway doesn't allow him to do so.

There's then a detailed discussion about Green Candidate Sian Berry.

'Tell me,' I ask intrigued. 'Is Miss Berry truly the MILF[1] she appears to be?'

'Funnily enough, not at all up close. It's surprising.'

'So she has a touch of Kronenbourg about her.'

Peter doesn't follow.

'Kronenbourg. 1664.'

He still doesn't get it.

'Looks 16 from a distance but 64 close up.'

'Ha. Yes indeed!'

We leave the pub. The top candidates are going to carry on campaigning. Nigel's off to Scotland to help Coburn. I'm returning to chambers.

As we part ways John Gill pulls me aside.

'Please take Nigel fishing. He's exhausted.'

Saturday 30th April 2016

Farage is undertaking a grand tour of south east London on this, the final Saturday of the mayoral campaign. He's going to Sutton and Orpington first before heading to Eltham to meet our crew. After that he's off to Dagenham for a stroll with Peter Harris.

We're hoping he'll be here on time as we're at the Den for the Millwall v Oldham match this afternoon. Kick-off is at three.

We've set up a wallpaper-paste stand in Plassey Place as usual. Defiantly, it is covered with the bright green Grassroots Out cloth and

---

1 An attractive older woman.

framed by a GO backdrop. 'Vote Leave'? Who?

I don't notice a cameraman who has set up over to one side. Peter Lello notices everything and notices this.

'Lordy, It's Richard Hendron.'

Dear me. Hendron, R. The sad-act who resigned from UKIP because we're homophobic. There can't possibly be any other explanation for his abject failure to be anointed as a candidate.

'Don't look now,' says Peter, 'but he's filming you.'

And so he is. The tripod's about three feet away from the back of my head without so much as a do-you-mind. He's using a 'London Live' camera. That channel has definitely gone downhill since the lovely Claudia-Liza went over to Sky News.

Lello texts his pals in UKIP LGBT about the incursion. Chairman Flo Lewis gives the best advice:

'Make it look like an accident.'

Nigel is now en-route. I give him a warning call.

'Oh, I know,' he says 'He's been skulking around Orpington too. The fucking weirdo.'

Nigel sweeps into Plassey Place and there's almost immediately a sounding of horns and waves from cars as well as a natural mob forming around him. We go on a walkabout up the High Street with an unshaven Peter Whittle and a late-arriving David Kurten.

Many photographs are taken both by ourselves and passers-by. Freddy Vaccha manages to feature in all of them.

Lello has a question for Farage's bodyguard.

'Do you carry firearms at these events?'

'Sadly, we're not allowed.'

'So you don't even have a gun with one bullet for Freddy Vaccha?'

'Sadly, we're not allowed.'

Unfortunately, the sunny side of the road which we chose to perambulate becomes narrower and narrower as we forge forward so we cross to the shaded and grim side of the street. At this point Hendron gulps down his metaphorical can of spinach and accosts Farage with a mild question about how we think we're going to do.

'Oh, very well. We're going to get at least two candidates elected.'

Hendron then moves to his real hobby horse and starts wittering on about the party marginalising 'diversity.' That the two UKIP men who're going to invade City Hall after 5th May are proudly gay and black respectively hasn't registered with him.

Nigel starts giving him a kindly and rational answer. I take a different view.

'Bo-ring.'

The social justice warrior cringes away.

Farage heads off and the branch packs up and zooms to SE16 in convoy. We'd hoped to be there by 1.30 which would have given us enough time to find parking around South Bermondsey but are now late. After circling for a while, one resident of the local estate is silly enough to drive off and I nab his space. We've only got 40 minutes before kick off.

There's other people handing out leaflets too. They are our brothers and sisters from Sutton Branch with a batch of Gerard Batten's literature. Great to see them. Sadly, the Sutton crew haven't developed my fairground barker skills. They hand them to people without a word. As a consequence, many of the recipients look at them, realise they're not interested, and chuck them on the pavement. The proper way of doing it is to lock your gaze on a potential victim and then yell at them that this is UKIP. This is Referendum. This is taking our country back. Then, they only take it if they actually want it.

A policeman speaks to me.

'Sir. You're making a mess with all these fliers. You need to pick them up'"

'No I don't. Those ones aren't mine. These are mine. I'm not a roadsweeper.'

'You still need to clear up this rubbish.'

'Make me.' He doesn't.

This is disturbing though. That's twice now to my knowledge that the constabulary have tried to bully the Kip while campaigning. Perhaps words have been had by senior officers to the grunts in the name of the great goddess that is political correctness. Something to explore later.

And: Millwall smash Oldham 3-0 and thus win a place in the League One play-offs.

When I arrive home there are cardboard boxes piled up at the front door. Head Office have delivered several hundred new Whittle/ Kurten leaflets and some excellent posters. Yet today was the very last Saturday before this week's poll. Although we've had some very hard working people in the branch over the last few weeks, many of the members haven't come out at all.

I make a few calls to persuade activists to take, and shift, some before Thursday. No dice. There's no way we'll be able to distribute them. Most will be binned. What a waste.

Wednesday 4th May 2016

Helen Corbett from the *News Shopper* rings me up. Local candidates are regularly called by the paper. Except, of course, if you happen to be UKIP. So I'm surprised to hear from her.

'Do you have any photos we can use?' she asks.

'Well I've got some good ones from our walkabout on Saturday with Nigel, Peter Whittle and David Kurten. I could get some of those over to you.'

'Oh no,' she says. 'We'd like some photos of you.'

'Ah. I'm not sure there are many. I'm very vain you see so don't like unflattering pictures in the media. I'll see what I can do.'

I'd almost forgotten that I'm a candidate too, for the superseat. Flicking through the shots from Saturday and excluding those of me with crows' feet, gray chest hair poking out the shirt collar, beer belly or double chin, I find a good one with me, Farage and Whittle and send it off. One.

Later, I'm returning from London and arrive at my home station at 9.30. Time to pick up a kebab from the shop which is opposite the now-unmanned ticket hall.

The Metro newspaper racks are normally empty at this time of day but not this evening. Green Party litterbugs have dumped piles of leaflets punting their campaign in each one. Disgraceful.

As a keen environmentalist, I collect them all up and drop them in the trash outside. Lewisham Council don't have street recycling bins so this means it's off to landfill or the furnace with them.

Thursday 5th May 2016

It's polling day. I'm busy drafting a tedious advice on liability when John Gill telephones.

'Peter Whittle's at a bit of a loose end. Is there anything you lot are doing today? Where he could show his face? Get some press photos? That sort of thing?'

Sorry John. We're doing nothing.

Poor Peter.

Friday 6th May 2016

Jo Mullins is excited to be coming along to her first ever election count and asks when it starts.

'Well, the ballot boxes are due to be opened at 8 am.'

She actually turns up at that time. Bless her.

We're in the same aircraft hangar at the Excel Centre as in 2012. It's needed, because they're counting all the votes for Bexley & Bromley, City and East, Lambeth and Southwark, Greenwich and Lewisham and Havering and Redbridge. All our candidates are there and many activists.

The process is supposed to be swift. Having slouched into the hall after 10, I was troubled to think that adjudication might be imminent. Not so.

Each ballot paper had been handed out to the voter fully-flat and then placed by them, flat again, in black collapsible ballot boxes. Made of corrugated plastic, they're not exactly secure. Now at the count, the papers whiz through a scanner and the unclear ballots are checked by hand and shown on a computer screen which is also visible to the political spectators.

There are a few oddities given that the voting slip offered a first and second preference for mayor. Some electors are mad. Women's Equality Party first and Britain First second anyone? There are many papers marked with both choices in the same column. Those people weren't mad, just a bit dim.

Running totals are shown on screens around the auditorium. Whittle isn't doing very well. He's definitely behind the Green and leap-frogging, and being leapfrogged by, the Lib Dem. We'd thought he'd be wandering around this and the other count stations at Olympia and Alexandra Palace. As we haven't yet seen him, I call him. He's at his office in central London as a base camp for media interviews and won't bother with the venues. Fair enough, there isn't really any point.

Bored, Roger Gravett and Peter Harris pull me aside for a coffee. We're glum. Roger has over a hundred boxes of the newest leaflets hidden in the sheds at his workplace.

'I'm well pissed off. Loads of branches haven't bothered to pick them up. What am I supposed to do with them?'

I suggest that we follow the example of 'The Great Escape' by dispersing them surreptitiously through holes cut in our trouser pockets across London.

The Britain First people Jayda Fransen and Paul Golding are suddenly seen swarming through the Excel together with minders. They speak to nobody and leave almost immediately. One of our crew is sympathetic to Ms Fransen. Insofar as he'd like to 'give her one' as she would likely 'be dirty.' Ew.

This is going on. And on. And on. My afternoon nap's overdue.

Eventually, the results are announced. Back in 2012 each candidate had the chance to speak. This time it's not permitted. Winner only, thanks.

Peter Harris isn't gruntled by this. He's polled very well in City and East and has written a speech on proper cards. That was a waste of time.

Only the Great Unmesh Desai, Labour victor, is permitted to orate. This geezer's cornucopia of clichés has obviously been practiced in front of the mirror for weeks. There's no doubt that he's a true believer: in the apparent fact that the victory was wholly a result of his own outstanding attributes.

Lawrence Webb hasn't won in Havering and Redbridge either. He's a bit down as they've also lost a council by-election. At least there's some consolation in that the Tory candidate has emerged victorious. Not that we like him, but he's beaten Ivana Bartoletti for Labour who was of course a mortal foe in the London MEP campaign. So no speech from her to be endured. Silver lining and that.

Oh – almost forgot. In Greenwich and Lewisham my vote more than doubles on 2012 to 13,686 and I sneak up to fourth place. The deposit is kept this time which is just as well because I'm the one who's paid it from my own pocket.

All done, we head to the Westminster Arms where there's a UKIP party. Money's been placed behind the bar so that activists need only show their membership cards to receive free booze. I like this. When we come to power this method of payment shall be used by all Kippers in all establishments for all products.

Then Farage receives a serenade from a lone bagpiper. As ever, this tingles the tearducts in my eyes and the hairs upon my arms. When my time to depart this earth arrives it must be with a sword in one hand and the skirl in my ears. Nigel sympathises.

I can't be bothered going on to the count at City Hall as it's a foregone conclusion. Result for first-preference votes is:

Sadiq Khan (Labour)	1,148,716	44.2%
Zac Goldsmith (Tory)	909,755	35.0%
Siân Berry (Green)	150,673	5.8%
"Caroline Pidgeon London Liberal Democrat" TM		
	120,005	4.6%

And then:

Peter Whittle	94,373	3.6%

Below UKIP are the more extreme candidates for the Womens'

Equality Party, Respect, Britain First and the BNP.

As for the London list for top-up members, this is the outcome:

Labour	1,054,801	40.3%
Conservative	764,230	29.2%
Green	207,959	8.0%
UKIP	171,069	6.5%

Below that, the order is –

Ah, who cares? The main thing is that UKIP will have two solid men on the London Assembly. Peter Whittle and David Kurten. Mint.

CHAPTER THIRTY-ONE

The Answer Is—We're Out

Monday 9th May 2016

See, The Conquering Heroes Come. Both of them. Whittle and Kurten enter the London Region meeting at the Butler's Head to cheers.

Chairman Freddy Vaccha has brought lots of sweeties to the meeting. This is good.

He's also brought a copy of every referendum leaflet which is or has been available for distribution. He proceeds to display and describe them all. This isn't good.

'Freddy, we've been delivering these for weeks. We know what they are,' say I.

He carries on.

'What's the point of this exercise?' huffs Gerard Batten.

Freddy won't be dissuaded and completes his show-and-tell. There's then a discussion about Gerard's own literature. Everyone likes Gerard's leaflet although I don't mention the unequal discards compared to UKIP leaflets at the Den nine days ago. This would be rude.

'Lawrence Webb has asked me to ask you something Gerard,' says Freddy. 'Could you please think of removing your photograph from the referendum leaflets?'

How weird. As Lawrence works directly with Batten he could have made this request in private. Nobody's sure why it's important anyway.

'I have worked bloody hard on this campaign for over twenty years,' says Batten. 'Nigel's photograph is on everything. Why the bloody hell shouldn't mine be?'

Gerard receives an impromptu round of applause for this. Only the third one I've heard in all my time at London Region meetings.

But the meeting drags on and on. I'm sitting right next to Whittle but send a text to his mobile anyway.

'As you can't use the excuse of fundraising any more, you'll have to stay to the end. Bwah-ha-ha!'

Then other things happen. Elizabeth Jones, present as a member of the NEC and not as a London rep, raises the question of regional funding. Specifically, tithes from the salaries of our newly-elected representatives which will be handed over to UKIP head office. They're not actually paid that much at around £50K gross. Unlike our people in the EU, there are no expense allowances and in any case our Assembly candidates didn't sign any Charter promising a percentage for the party.

Freddy interjects.

'This isn't really something for this meeting. Perhaps we can discuss it in private. Let's move forward.'

But Elizabeth Jones is having none of it. She carries on. And on.

David Kurten stands up silently and walks out.

I've never seen Peter Whittle angry until now. He half-rises from his chair.

'It's just bitterness on your part, isn't it, Liz? And we all know why you're bitter.'

She doesn't reply as Whittle picks up his coat and leaves.

Thursday 11th May 2016

Martin Durkin's 'Brexit – The Movie' is receiving its premiere tonight at the Odeon in Leicester Square. There's a red carpet. There are Japanese tourists taking photographs of the attendees because they assume that we must be famous. Some of us are of course, but in any case each and every activist is far more important than any luvvie Ac-Tor.

I've dressed for the occasion in black tie. The other half has a posh two-piece and pearls. Emmett Jenner is clad in a bright purple outfit with silver shoes. David Kurten is wearing an ordinary suit with his trademark too-short trousers.

I come across Peter Kirby of Croydon branch who is also correctly-attired and ask about the libel case that Winston's bringing against him. By my guesstimate the case ought to be coming on for trial about now. He talks vaguely, saying that he's not sure what McKenzie's case is.

'When does he say that you spoke the defamatory words Peter?'

'Oh, I'm not sure. Something around fifteen months ago.'

'And has he actually issued the claim against you?'

'Well no, so it's just hanging over me and not getting anywhere.'

I decide to make Kirby's evening for him.

'He had to bring the case within a year. It's now statute-barred under the Limitation Act.'

Peter breaks out a beautiful smile. It's obvious that the great grim stone which has been crushing his shoulders for months has fallen off in an instant. I'm pleased. Although he's certainly been a pain on occasion, it's not right for this otherwise fierce octogenarian to be facing that sort of stress.

The auditorium is choca. Martin Durkin stalks on stage first to thank his backers large and small. Then it begins, focussing on the issues of trade and the democratic deficit. There's nothing about immigration. The event is pure music-hall. Farage's wide-screen fizzog is cheered and cheered. Tory MEP Dan Hannan is applauded (but less so). The celluloid Douglas Carswell is greeted with polite silence. Cameron's booed and Heath given shouts of 'traitor' and 'quisling'.

It took a while for everyone to get into the auditorium in the first place and takes a while for us to leave. As people are milling outside there's foul-mouthed yelling. A middle-aged nutter with glasses and a green sports jacket is being escorted away by security guards.

'You fucking cunts! You fucking fucks! You fucking Leavers!'

His spittle-flecked exclamations are emphasised by V-signs from both hands. It isn't clear if he's tried to cause trouble within the auditorium or outside. In any case, his impotent fury at our power is a joy to see.

Sunday 15th May 2016

Sadiq Khan having sadly won the Mayoral election, he's standing down as MP for Tooting and there will be a by-election. We'll have to put forward a candidate. Tsk!

I've asked Strachan MacDonald, the local chairman, to provide the names of people who're interested. He suggests Trish Ward, Rathy Alagarathnam and Tom Blackwell. Also Elizabeth Jones.

I then receive an email which seems to be from Ms Jones' normal account. It connects to an online petition. I click the link.

Elizabeth Jones for Tooting
By: Liz Jones
Target: UKIP Party Chairman
3 supporters

'UKIP have a real opportunity to win the upcoming Tooting by-election — but only with me as the candidate. I have devoted my life and soul to UKIP for nearly a decade, I have campaigned tirelessly in London and indeed the length and breadth of the United Kingdom.

'I know what the people of Tooting want. I stood in Dartford during the 2015 general election where I obtained 20% of the vote narrowly losing to the Tory incumbent. More recently I was, overwhelmingly by the party membership, elected to National Executive Committee.

'As a highly skilled lawyer I feel that am the most competent candidate to stand for UKIP in this upcoming by-election. As a prominent NEC member I have the full support of our party leader Nigel Farage and our MP Douglas Carswell. Please support me by signing this petition.'

This is heartening. Although the consensus is that UKIP will come nowhere, Ms Jones is patently the one person who can win the seat for us. On the other hand, it's odd to see that Farage has tendered his support and even weirder that this would be done in conjunction with Carswell.

I have to speak to Nigel who categorically confirms that he has not, and will not, endorse anyone at all.

'It's not our best area by a long way is it?' He asks.

'No. And it would be helpful if we had a candidate who's unlikely to screech "shut up" in any interview.'

I tell Crowther too.

'Unbelievable,' he says. 'Although, perhaps, believable.'

Steve calls back after about an hour.

'She says it's a fake petition and she didn't post it.'

Sunday 22nd May 2016

Elizabeth Jones has been duly-selected as our Tooting candidate. I call Crowther to see if there's been any clues about the fake petition sent from a counterfeit Jones email account.

'There haven't but we've not been looking. To be honest, although I fully accept her word that she hadn't created this petition I wouldn't have been surprised if she had.'

Jones was selected because she'd had the best result from amongst her competitors at the general election. Rathy, by contrast, had lost her deposit. Not a fair comparison because Dartford was a prime chance and, well, Dulwich and West Norwood wasn't.

'Tom Blackwell came across decently but hadn't passed the candidate assessment,' Steve tells me. 'And Trish Ward is definitely one to watch although she's a new member with no track record.'

I'll tell the London officers to keep an eye on Trish and groom her. In the nicest possible way.

'But,' Steve signs off, 'Nigel says that in all his years of campaigning this is the first by-election that he couldn't care less about.'

Tuesday 7th June 2016

It's the great debate tonight at the Zion Chapel in New Cross Road. The church elders are putting on tea and buns beforehand but as they'll expect us to socialise and I still need to decide what to say, the Royal Albert pub is a better place to focus my thoughts. And have a beer.

Lello calls my phone because I'm now late. As usual. A briefing for the panellists is already ongoing. I enter the room and Pastor Max rolls his eyes and repeats what he's already said. We're only going to have a three-minute opening as there are six of us and we're not to mention facts and figures for some reason. The others seem relieved. I am not. Bah.

As seems to be common for Lewisham Labour MPs, Vicky Foxcroft has magisterially tendered her apologies for tonight and won't be making herself available to her public after all. As such, the final line up is this: John Hamilton of People Before Profit, a bloke from TUSC, and Oakley will represent the Leavers. On the Remainiac side are two Labour councillors and a Lib Dem. So, a balanced panel with five pinkoes and one UKIP.

I'm on last so can and do take the flavour of the meeting and realise that Red UKIP colours will need to be worn. There are some feeble jeers as UKIP's introduced. I point at the culprits.

'Thanks for the boos. We feed on your tears.'

The theme I take is: The School Bully.

'According to that lot, our quivering carcass of a country is only held together by EU membership. Remainers are no different from bigger boys who tell you that you're rubbish at football while demanding your dinner money. It's time to stand tall, punch them on the nose and vote Leave.'

The Lib Dem says something about his child not being able to enjoy the benefits of EU citizenship like he was able to. So what?

The Labour Councillor for Forest Hill ward, who had the audacity to be victorious over ME in the 2014 local elections, is called Maja Hilton. She's from Bosnia, or somewhere, and practically incoherent.

Labour's Joe Dromey is very tall but his political nous is inversely proportional to his height. He accuses the Trots on our side of being running mates of racists. The TUSC geezer's having none of it.

'That's fucking outrageous! I've spent years fighting racism!' In the House of God no less. The audience applaud and so do I.

Mr Dromey also decides to set out an obviously-rehearsed list of Naughty People Who Are Your Best Mates If You Want Out. Marine Le Pen because her dad's a nasty piece of work and lo the sins of the fathers shall be visited upon the children. Nick Griffin. Because he's a current big name, isn't he? The audience don't like his escapade of equivalence and neither do the rest of the panel.

There's no a vote at the end. Taking a taste of the audience reactions, they're evenly-split. Although the staunch left goes down well in this area, shiny New Labour types are less persuasive. Intriguing.

Thursday 9th June 2016

Today is the council by-election for Gipsy Hill. There's a low turnout, unsurprisingly. Labour win, obviously, and in descending order thereafter it's the Greens, Tories, Lib Dems and then Elizabeth Jones for UKIP with 73 votes.

Not that anyone really cares, but this is hopefully not a portent for next week's Tooting parliamentary election to replace Sadiq Khan.

Wednesday 15th June 2016

This contracting that I'm doing for the Financial Conduct Authority is a pain as I'm missing out on events like the Leave EU Thames Flotilla. Nigel's joining a fleet of fishermen from as far away as Scotland who are sailing up the Thames to protest about the EU decimating their industry.

My window seat on the 27th floor of 1 Canada Square does however have a glorious view of the river and – Yes! – I can see them below!

Naturally, I keep an eye on social media to see what's going on. It turns out that Bob Geldof is staging a counter-protest on the water backed by various others including Brendan, the husband of Labour MP Jo Cox.

My activism is reduced to a forlorn Tweet:

'Lacking a famine to boost his flagging career, Bob Geldof attacks struggling UK fishermen on the Thames.'

Leftards immediately start sniping at me but then photographs emerge of Geldof making rude gestures at the trawlermen. The internet bursts with fury.

Heading for the station after 6, the LED screen on the Reuters Building shows that Leave has edged ahead in the polls. Thank you! Thank you, Sir Bob!

Thursday 16th June 2016

Jo Cox, Labour MP for Batley and Spen, is murdered by a mentally-ill constituent. This is dark. Our elected representatives must be protected but it's not clear how they can be.

And the Gipsy Hill by-election did set a precedent for Tooting. Elizabeth Jones is in fifth place once more on 507 and loses her deposit. This is less than a third of the votes that had been cast for our lad Przemek Skwirczynski in the general election last year. To be fair, the party wasn't doing any real campaigning in the seat this time around. Our priority's the referendum and nothing else.

Even if we'd chosen a top quality nominee, it's doubtful the result would have been much different.

Friday 17th June 2016

I'd been planning to go to Nigel's last London referendum speech first thing but it's rightly been pulled because of the Jo Cox murder.

What, if anything, are we doing tomorrow? Street stalls as planned or not? It's the final Saturday before the referendum. Lots of people want us to carry on although I'd rather not. If head office is deciding against it they'd better tell us quick. Oakden will know.

'Steve's just about to send out an email cancelling all high street events. We can campaign discreetly but just by a bit of delivering,' he says.

I've heard differently.

'You're aware that Vote Leave are setting up stalls though? They've got a massive list of events.'

'No,' says Oakden. 'They're cancelling too. As far as we know the Remainers are doing likewise. We're concerned about the hard left attacking activists apart from anything else.'

'Oh. One more thing Paul,' I say. 'My thinking, if it's worth anything, is that we mustn't put up a candidate in the Batley by-election. It'd be disrespectful.'

'My thoughts exactly. In fact, I'd probably resign from the party if we did.'

Saturday 18th June 2016

Labour have called a council by-election in Bellingham. Inconveniently and possibly deliberately, they've timed it so that nomination papers must be handed in by June 24th. Yes. The very day after the referendum. We might as well do some quiet leafleting in the ward beforehand but we won't be delivering anything from UKIP, Leave EU or GO.

Bellingham's primarily made up of low-rise, red brick council housing. It's a nice quiet area but solid Labour. With this in mind we're distributing two leaflets. Paul Lebby has a pile of Labour Leave stuff and I have the 'Trade Unionists Against The EU' booklets with the picture of Bob Crow and Tony Benn on the front. It's not really cheating because motive for a 'no' vote is irrelevant. I do however hope that nobody stops us to chat about the specifics of either group's campaign because none of us will have a bloody clue.

Tuesday 21st June 2016

We're selecting our candidate for Bellingham this evening. Massimo DiMambro and Ed Smith are interested but then Massimo tells us his Dad's unwell so withdraws. Ed will do.

It's an informal meeting at the Ravensbourne. There's quite a few members there but also quite a few of the public so we sink into sagging Chesterfields by the back wall for some privacy.

I'd rather not have to go out myself to get the signatures but will if I must. Given other events and the fact that having a beer with the Farage entourage on Referendum Night is a much more appealing prospect, I'm pleased that John Holland offers to go round with Ed chasing the autographs.

'Don't forget,' I remind them. 'Get their signatures and nothing else on the nomination paper. Take another blank sheet with you and have them sign that with their name and address. The details on the nomination paper have to be exactly as they appear on the Electoral Register and we don't want any mistakes or it'll be rejected. I'll complete the polling numbers and hand it in. Got that?'

Wednesday 22nd June 2016

I try to call Towler about potential events on Friday (if any) after the result's announced. Donald Trump is rumoured to be in Scotland at the moment and if so he might head down to London on the 24th so I can get my photo taken with the next US President.

Gawain doesn't answer and I don't bother leaving a message. Instead, he sends me a text. Twice.

'At the Lamb at Leadenhall.'

I call to see what's going on.

'Nigel's decided to stop off for a beer. The campaign bus has broken down so we've taken it out of service. The big stickers are coming off the sides because there's no point any more.'

'Aren't we doing anything tomorrow?'

'No, and not tonight either. Channel 4 had booked him to appear in a debate with Alan Sked. But we're not going on the same platform as that fucker.'

Canary Wharf to Bank station only takes about 15 minutes and I'm at the pub before 6. Gawain has texted again in the interim.

'And everybody here in the team thinks I'm a cunt.'

This isn't true at all as I surmise at the end-of-term UKIP party outside this packed city ale house.

Steve Woolfe grabs me for a hug.

'Hoy Woolfe,' I grumble. 'You used to be sexy. What happened?'

We compare beer bellies.

Nigel's last referendum speech had been at the Emmanuel Centre earlier today and Steve had been on the platform. We're asking about the poem Steve had recited.

'I was Googling the words as you read it out,' says Gawain. 'Where's it from?'

'I actually wrote it myself,' says Steve. 'This whole thing over the last five years has been very serious. I've met a lot of good people and been moved as never before about their desire for freedom. I just had to put it into words.'

Woolfe has to leave as he's catching a train up to Chester. It's quite emotional. Although, to be clear, none of us cry like metrosexuals or nothing.

I, too, head off and walk across London Bridge. There are ever more people wearing Remainiac stickers. Something smells.

Yes. There's a group of wet Tory boys on the station concourse handing out pro-EU crap. They've stuck their stinky old 'Stronger In' posters to some bollards. This is flyposting and British Rail (or whatever it's now called) frowns on political campaigning on their property. At least they do when we try it.

'Do you want a leaflet?' one of them simpers.

I pull a couple of their posters down and crumple them up before dropping them on the ground.

'No.'

I walk onto the concourse and stare at the information boards which are showing delays.

Been there for a minute or so and a bloke moves right into my personal space.

'Why did you throw their leaflet in that man's face? That's assault.' He prounces off.

'I didn't throw anything at anyone's face. I chucked their dross on the ground.'

He prances back.

'I'm a solicitor. Are you saying I'm a liar?'

A solicitor eh? Ho ho ho. He prances off again. I snort.

'I'm a barrister. Are you saying I'm a liar?'

He turns back, looks at me and splutters.

'Well. You're drunk!'

Slightly true. Three pints.

'Well. You're a twat!'

He fucks off for the third time and I win.

Apocalyptic thunder and lightning erupts over sarf-east London at bed time. What is it with all this heavenly discomfort whenever UKIP are fighting a campaign?

Thursday 23rd June 2016

MORNING

Referendum Day! I'm woken just after 5 am by rain which sounds like BB shot on the windows. I climb down the stairs and open the back door to look outside. The pounding deluge is smashing down water to an inch of thickness on the patio slabs. I've never seen anything like it.

The news bulletins show massive travel disruption across the capital. Sensible London commuters will be leaving home earlier than usual as a consequence. That means they probably won't have the chance to vote before work. Good. The polls are showing that they're mainly Remainers.

Indeed, I have to be at Canary Wharf before 9 for a meeting myself. No chance. There's flooding at Surrey Quays and Canning Town so the rare Overground trains are packed full and moving as slowly as bloody tourists on Oxford Street.

The deluge suddenly stops as rush hour comes to an end.

Last night John Holland had been out with Ed Smith collecting the Bellingham signatures. That'll give me a comfortable amount of time to drop them off at the Council Offices tomorrow. If Lewisham Labour are hoping that the other parties will be too preoccupied to put up candidates of their own they're going to be disappointed.

At least John has taken that worry off my shoulders with his kind offer to help. We're going to have a quick meeting to make sure the form is correctly completed and then I can file it.

But John has, it transpires, completed all the details already. He's also scanned the form and emailed a copy to the Council Offices. And the names are wrong. And it describes us as 'United Kingdom Indepence Party'. I ask him to collect the signatures again.

'I shall not be able to,' he says. 'I spoke to Ed last night and he confirmed he does not wish to proceed.'

Fucking great.

EVENING

The day has been overcast throughout. As rush hour approaches again, the rain starts once more. Heavily.

Southern services, Abellio, Gatwick Express, Thameslink and South West Trains have all been affected. Tracks are flooded at Clapham Junction and Victoria. Waterloo's closed. Cannon Street was shut anyway because of signalling failures and Charing Cross and London Bridge are also disrupted. To cap it all, several Tube stations are awash including Blackfriars, Westminster, Farringdon, Tooting Bec and Lambeth North. That means many Remainers won't be able to vote after work either. What a shame.

The Overground remains open, just, and I'm able to get back to south east London reasonably quickly. It's straight to the polling station for me, dripping wet. Done.

Back home, a change into a Barbour jacket and then out to Bellingham even though I'm still moist. I have a copy of Ed's erroneously-completed form together with a chunk of the electoral register and a clipboard with a plastic cover. The signatures will be re-done even if I drown.

Fortunately, the rain stops again and remains off but I'm embarrassed to have to knock on the same doors that they'd pestered last night. Thankfully, all those who are in are merely amused by our inefficiency and glad to re-sign. There's a difficulty however. Four of the signatories aren't in or, at least, aren't answering their doors. It's getting late and I can't say I blame them. So it's a case of looking through the electoral register and picking a few listed houses at random. Most targets tell me to 'get bent' so it's nearly 10 before it's all done.

Straight to McDonalds in Catford for some well-deserved flesh. Blinking starving. What now? I'm shattered, and can't be bothered heading in to Millbank for the Arron Banks party. Besides, I have to be at the Financial Conduct Authority for nine tomorrow as usual.

Right. I have passes for the counts in both Greenwich and Lewisham boroughs so head to them both to see how things are going. Rather better in the former as it happens.

Back home at midnight. Oh, go on then. I'll just watch an hour or so of the results as they come in and then head to my pit.

Friday 24th June 2016
I don't go to bed after all. Finally, Dimbleby speaks.

'Well, at twenty minutes to five we can now say the decision taken in 1975 by this country to join the Common Market has been reversed by this referendum to leave the EU. We are absolutely clear now that there is no way that the Remain side can win. The British people have spoken and the answer is - "we're out".'

I feel no sense of relief. It might just be my womens' intuition, but I don't think this is over.

CHAPTER THIRTY-TWO

Hungry Like the Woolfe

Wednesday 29th June 2016

A CALL FROM ANNE MARIE WATERS about a matter unconnected to Brexit.

'How are things going with Pegida by the way?' I ask.

'Oh, it's all fallen apart. It turned into the Tommy Robinson show and ground into the mud. And Paul Weston of Liberty GB wouldn't work with me for reasons unknown.'

Now that is news. I hadn't heard anything about Pegida but hadn't been listening out for it either. In Germany it has become huge and shows no sign of slowing its growth. Yet it's not happening in the UK. Something about the British character perhaps.

'So, would you want to come back as a UKIP activist then?'

'I'd like that. Although I'm still going to carry on as before with the anti-jihad work.'

'Thought you might. I'll have a word with the higher-ups if you want.'

Nigel, of course, will be one of those. I give him a call and we discuss the result again.

'We might have to pay the EU some sort of subscription,' he says. 'And there might have to be some compliance with petty rules. But the main thing is that we've got the supremacy of our own law back.'

'Yup. And if we get a rough deal then five, ten, years down the line we can renegotiate.'

'Precisely right,' says Nigel.

I ask him about Anne Marie.

'To be honest,' he replies, 'I'm just going to relax for the moment. That decision should be made by others.'

'I'm going to discuss it with Crowther,' I say, 'but wanted your view in the first place. If it was a definite "No" then that would be that.'

'I'd want to know what we'd have to gain by taking her back on,' he says. However, he really doesn't seem to care whether she stands or not. I wonder why.

Monday 4th July 2016
Farage calls a press conference first thing at the Emmanuel Centre.

'I have never been, and I have never wanted to be, a career politician. My aim of being in politics was to get Britain out of the European Union. That is what we voted for in that referendum two weeks ago. And that is why I now feel that I've done my bit. That we couldn't possibly achieve more than we managed to get in that referendum. And so I feel it's right that I should now stand aside as leader of UKIP.'

He means it this time. I feel exactly the same way as I did when The Clash finally broke up.

Tuesday 5th July 2016
Any member whatsoever can put themself forward to lead UKIP and the frontrunners at the moment are Paul Nuttall, Suzanne Evans and Steve Woolfe.

Neil Hamilton's endorsing Nuttall. Given the whispers of a long-firm coup with Paul installed as interim leader before the Tory Boys replace him, this isn't good news. I like Paul a lot but not the politics of the people who are coalescing around him.

Suzanne Evans remains suspended although this will have come to an end by the time of the September vote. Much as I love her, Suzanne is one of those very Tory Boys.

So that just leaves Woolfie. For all his imperfections, there's no doubt that northern Labour seats are now open to us and Steve is a whippet-baiting black-pudding eater. Or, at least, he comes from Manchester. In any case he's eloquent and personable.

Whittle would like to have a crack but doesn't yet have national recognition. In addition, he's a soft southern poofter (which has nothing at all to do with his sexuality). He may not go down so well north of Watford, but if he runs, his national profile will rise.

I share some thoughts with him.

'What about a dream ticket with you and Steve for deputy and leader respectively. North and south and that.'

'Well, I don't know,' he says. 'Woolfie's rumoured to be luke-warm because his wife doesn't want him to do it. If you're leader it really takes over everything. Whoever gets in will have a really shitty time of it. It'll be easier for whoever steps up after this incumbent.'

Monday 11th July 2016

Nominations open for the leadership. Peter Whittle can't stand after all as the NEC has decided that all applicants must have been party members for five years. Nor, for the same reason, can Arron Banks, Suzanne Evans or Douglas Carswell.

Wednesday 13th July 2016

Drinkies with Whittle and Kurten at City Hall. The UKIP group, both of them, have been allocated a small office quadrant with an angled view to the river which is overlooked by adjacent tower blocks. Not the best part of the building, surprise surprise.

There are a few crisps, cashew nuts and sandwiches. There's a lot of cava and red wine. This isn't a huge event. Only the staff are present with a handful of others including Matt Luck who announces that he's jacking in the UK and relocating to Texas. Naturally, I have to explore with him the possibility of buying and using a number of firearms while he's there.

Whittle chats with me about the leadership. Now that he's been excluded as a candidate himself because of the five-year membership requirements, he'll need to latch on to somebody who isn't so restricted.

Not having bothered to read the rules myself, I'm disappointed to hear that the deputy's post isn't up for election and is merely an appointee of the leader. No reason why I should have known that, of course, as Farage and Nuttall have held their respective roles throughout my membership of the party.

Woolfe turns up with Nigel and Raheem Kassam. After circulating, they decamp to Kurten's office and shut the door. Matt Luck sidles in as well and I follow. I have to buttonhole Steve to press Whittle's case.

'It would be absolutely ideal,' say I. 'If we were to have a northern pie-muncher and a southern nancy on the same ticket.'

Steve's noncommittal. I can tell he's already decided to go for Nathan Gill. Much as I like Nathan, this is an opportunity lost.

Nigel, of course, gives a speech to the selected and selective crowd. He looks healthier than I've ever seen him. He's pleased that he'll no

longer be troubled by 'that woman' as a result of the membership requirements for leader. He says many other things but they're not for
public dissemination.

He does not endorse Steve Woolfe.

Thursday 14th July 2016

'Hello, Peter,' I say. 'Thanks for last night. What are you going to
do? My gut tells me Woolfie's going for Gill as running mate.'

'I think you're right. But I'm not sure what exactly I can do. I guess
just carve out my own role.'

Whittle has to hang up because he has been invited to Woolfe's
leadership launch campaign this morning. That might bode well.

He telephones me afterwards. He's been appointed Steve's campaign manager. The deputy campaign manager to be precise.

So that's it? Yes.

'He was surprisingly nervous today and I was on the front row so
could see it. But he wasn't drinking at all last night I noticed. Maybe that
shows how seriously he's taking this. We'll see.'

I tell Whittle how Nigel described Steve way back in 2013 when he'd
found out how badly he'd done in the MEP assessments. Peter chuckles.

'That sounds about right.'

Wednesday 20th July 2016

A chap called Sebastian Mann gets in touch on Twitter.

'Hi there, I'm a reporter for the *Evening Standard*. Pls can you follow me back so I can DM you for a story I'm working on?'

I do and he does,

'I was hoping to speak to you about a UKIP councillor in Bromley who some are claiming has posted offensive comments on Facebook
about Remain supporters.'

Ruh-roh.

A Googling shows he's already been in the *Kent Messenger*.

'The comments were made by Terence Nathan, the Ukip councillor for Cray Valley West.

'They read: "Time to start killing these people till article 50 is in-
voked, perhaps remainers will get the message then."'

I speak to Crowther about it first.

'He must apologise immediately and effusively. The silly git.'
I call Emmett Jenner from the man's branch in Bromley.

'Give me Terry's phone number and I will render unto him a telling off.'

'I would,' replies Emmett. 'Except that he's deaf.'

Great.

I speak to Gawain, who's blunt.

'We're not going to hang him out to dry because he said something a bit off-colour. He's apologised and that's it. The media and the police never show the slightest interest in all the promises of violence directed at Nigel'.

Pleased he's prickly. And the quote, when it appears in that day's edition of the *Standard*, is an excellent one.

'A UKIP source added: "Nigel Farage is the subject of daily personal death threats, and the police do fuck all."'

Wednesday 20th July 2016

Been trying to get hold of George Cottrell without success. His phone's dead, and then I remember he'd mentioned heading over to the US to hobnob at the Republican convention. I'd instructed him to obtain a Trump-endorsing fridge magnet for me. NRA for Trump or Bikers for Trump would be ideal.

Anyway, we need to finalise some issues about the funding for Whittle's mayoral battle. There's money left over which needs to be transferred to other UKIP campaigning. So I text George.

'Are you in the states at the convention? Just wondered if that payment was sorted ok.'

George doesn't reply.

Friday 22nd July 2016

Cottrell is arrested by the FBI as he disembarks from a plane at Chicago's O'Hare airport.

I rather wish that I hadn't sent that text to him as the Fed'ril Guv'mint will have noticed.

Sunday 31st August 2016

The leadership nominations close.

Wednesday 3rd August 2016

UKIP's National Executive issue a statement.

'By a clear majority of NEC members Steven Woolfe MEP's application was considered to be ineligible as a result of a late submission and as such he did not meet the eligibility criteria.'

I'm not happy with the NEC. His application was 17 minutes late. Yes – maybe he was in strict breach of the rules, but to adopt and adapt the procedure from the civil courts of England, he should have been asked to apply for 'relief from sanctions'. There must have been good reasons.

But, apparently not. He accepts the decision immediately and wishes the other candidates well. It's almost as though he didn't really want the leadership.

The approved candidates are accordingly these: Phillip Broughton, Lisa Duffy, Bill Etheridge, Diane James and Elizabeth Jones.

For reasons unknown, Diane James is the favourite although I certainly won't be backing that damp rag. Lisa's lovely, but she hasn't a hope. So it's a toss-up between Bill and Broughton. Let's see how this develops. If Etheridge looks as though he might overtake James then I'll definitely support him. If not, my vote's going to Broughton. He's a minnow at the moment and won't win, but I've heard good things and it's always sensible to promote the talented-but-obscure in our party.

Thursday 1st September 2016
Both Bill Etheridge and Philip Broughton go public with their disapproval of Diane James' decision to avoid every single leadership hustings. Bill in particular tells her to 'get off your throne and have a debate.'

Hustings are the bestest part of any election. If it were possible for her to fall any lower in my estimation then she would.

Friday 16th September 2016
Bournemouth conference. Diane James is elected leader.
Meh.
Her repelled reaction when Nigel tries to give her a congratulatory peck says it all. She isn't one of us.

Wednesday 5th October 2016
Our wonderful new leader Diane James has decided to stand down after 18 days.

'I have been in discussion with party officers about the role. It has become clear that I do not have sufficient authority, nor the full support of all my MEP colleagues and party officers to implement changes I believe necessary and upon which I based my campaign.

For personal and professional reasons therefore, I will not take the election process further.'

Meh. Again.

At least it gives Woolfie a chance to run once more. I'll give him a ring tomorrow and tell him to pull his finger out.

Thursday 6th October 2016

I have Tweetdeck open at all times when working at the PC as it's the best way of keeping up with breaking news. So as lunchtime approaches it's intriguing to see that 'Steve Woolfe' has started trending. It's then disturbing to see that he has collapsed, and horrifying when a photograph appears of him lying face down in the EU parliament.

I give him a call to check he's ok but it goes straight to voicemail. I also try Farage, Aker, Coburn, Etheridge and Towler. None of them pick up.

A sense of slight nausea develops. Never before have I watched rolling news coverage of a pal who may be suffering from severe injury. Or something worse. It's deeply unpleasant and not to be recommended.

Friday 7th October 2016

Steve was taken to hospital but is now awake and seems fine. Things aren't as serious as expected. In many respects they're worse. It turns out that there was a scuffle between Woolfe and Mike Hookem. The former claims to have been hit by the latter who, in turn, dismisses it as 'handbags at dawn'.

All this is said to have developed from rumours that Steve had been in talks with the Tories about defecting. That's inexcusable.

Woolfe is finished. Has to be.

Whittle calls me.

'Paul – if they reduce the period of membership that's needed to stand then I'm going for it.'

'And I'll support you if you do.'

I speak to Farage to see if it's possible to winkle out any further information.

'So, Steve must be a dead man walking?'

'I'm not pre-judging the matter,' says Nigel. 'There's going to be a full enquiry before we decide what to do. If anything.'

I pull the conversation round to Whittle's attributes. It's not very good.

'Sorry, Peter,' I later tell Whittle. 'He had many good things to say about you but won't endorse anyone. His concern is that you might not pull them in from Wales and the north. I strongly suggest that you have a word with Nathan Gill about a dream team.'

Then the Party Chairman sends out an email mid-afternoon.

'Nigel has asked that I launch an investigation to look into what actually happened in Strasbourg between Steven Woolfe and Mike Hookem. This is something we will do calmly, diligently and without undue haste. I will travel to Brussels next week to speak with those involved personally and will not engage, or allow myself to be led into speculating on a situation that I did not witness myself.

'I join with Nigel now in urging all members to do the same.'

Wednesday 12th October 2016

Being a lovely sort of chap, I tend to follow our Greenwich and Lewisham members on Twitter. As a consequence of this a Tweet from Tony is noticed. You know, the guy who's applied for more posts in the branch than he's delivered leaflets.

It says:

'I am now officially a Tory.'

Surely they're overjoyed. We are. Unfollowed.

Monday 17th October 2016

Woolfe has written an article in the *Telegraph*.

'It is with a huge amount of sorrow and regret that I am abandoning my leadership bid and resigning from the party with immediate effect.

I will remain an MEP. As an independent member of the European Parliament, I will continue to stand up for the values I hold dear – those of freedom, democracy and an independent United Kingdom.'

He too 'forgets' that he signed the MEP charter which requires him to stand down from his seat. He's depriving the next in line, Shneur Odze, from his rightful post.

Bad form Steve and deeply disappointing of you.

CHAPTER THIRTY-THREE

I'm the Leader of the Gang, I Am

Tuesday 18th October 2016

CROWTHER CALLS.

'Are you going to put your name in for the leadership?'

Who? Me?

'Nice of you to ask Steve, but nobody's heard of me outside London and half of them probably don't like me. Maybe more. I'd lose.'

'Of course you'd lose. But it would raise your national profile.'

And reduce my local profile with the missis when the £5,000 deposit was lost. Although a narcissist, I am a frugal one.

'Well, what about standing for the NEC then?' asks Steve.

'Perhaps.'

'I'm going for it.'

'But you've only just stood down as party chairman. Haven't you had enough?'

'Yes,' he says, 'but we have to keep the party on an even keel. If you sign my nomination I'll sign yours.'

Oh. OK then. Deal.

Sunday 23rd October 2016

The missis is out today and I've been instructed to clean the house. I've not had time to finish it off because Peters Whittle and Lello want to meet in the Greenwich Tavern. Accordingly, it is fully-appreciated that I'm to be in the naughty corner as I shut the front door.

It being the Sabbath, Greenwich is busy. It being the Sabbath, Greenwich's grasping Labour council is still charging full fees for street parking and there are only free slots on the other side of the park. So I'm late. They're sitting in the beer garden as I walk up behind Whittle.

'. . . and she said that he was having an affair with Nigel Farage!'

'Hello Peters. Who was having an affair with Nigel?'

'Oh, hello Paul,' says Whittle. 'You, apparently.'

He tells me where the allegation came from. When the women in question was giving Peter a lift in her car. Utter frothing loon that she is. It's very funny though.

Anyway, to business. Lello's been collecting signatures for Whittle's leadership nomination. We need seventy-five from at least ten branches. There's been a problem as several people have already committed to support Andy Beadle or David Kurten who are also going for it. It's not possible to sign more than one form so this has taken time but we're nearly there.

Peter, Peter and Paul are under no illusions as to his chances though. The top candidates will be Suzanne and Nuttall so Whittle will be squeezed between them if he stands until the bitter end. But. If he steps down shortly after nominations close and endorses Paul, he will, hopefully, be given some kind of post as compensation. Deputy Leader's the obvious choice. Even better, he'll be able to reclaim most, if not all, of his deposit.

We chortle at our cleverness as I sign his papers.

Wednesday 26th October 2016

The new Party Chairman Paul Oakden publishes his conclusions on the Woolfe/Hookem face-off.

> 'The investigation notes that Mr Woolfe has now left UKIP and so has moved beyond the reach of this investigation. Any action now taken by the party therefore would be solely applicable to Mr Hookem.
>
> 'As Chairman, I'm appalled that such a situation could arise between two of our most high profile representatives and I have strongly considered suspension as a possible course of action.
>
> 'I do however take into consideration the following:
>
> (1) 'The apology and regret shown by Mr Hookem, for agreeing to join Mr Woolfe in the anteroom.
>
> (2) 'The excellent record of Mr Hookem in representing UKIP and its values prior to this incident.

(3)   'Acknowledging that Mr Hookem, whilst foolish, was not the instigator of this incident or subsequent press coverage and as such cannot be held principally responsible for either taking place.

'In light of this, a formal reprimand will be placed on the internal record of Mr Hookem to be considered in the event of a recurrence of any infraction which might cause damage to the reputation of the party.'

'This matter is now closed.'

Monday 31st October 2016

Fishing with Farage off Dungeness for cods. Just me and him. There's a heavy swell on the water which needs a pound of lead on the line to hold it to the sea bed. I catch bugger all but he hooks some bits and, more impressively, a conger eel of about 30lbs which is too big to bring on to the boat so is unhooked in the water.

I raise the issue of an honour for him following his superb work in obtaining the referendum in the first place. And then winning it.

A peerage or a knighthood? I'm clear in my own view.

'A "K" is just a pat on the head. You deserve a seat in the Lords. Apart from anything else, it'll give you a legislative voice in the Brexit process.'

'Yes, but that would stop me from standing in any more elections for the Commons. Besides, I'm not sure I want to be an absentee peer as I'll be spending a lot more time in the States.'

Makes sense, but – still. If it was up to me there'd be an hereditary peerage for the bloke.

However. All is not perfect with the world. I'd noticed something in the car as he drove us down to the coast but pretended that I hadn't. He pulls it out of his pocket again.

'What's that?' I query.

'What's what?'

'That.'

'Ah. It's a smartphone.'

I've always admired Nigel's technophobia. Indeed, my own basic mobile is far too flash because it has a colour screen unlike the monochrome green of his elderly Nokia which he's had for years.

'It's useful for reviewing the videos that Dan Jukes shoots of me before we upload them to Youtube.'

That's as mebbe. This is letting the side down.

Tuesday 1st November 2016

Leadership hustings at the Emmanuel Centre. Raheem Kassam withdrew his own application last night and endorsed Whittle. Which was nice.

MOG afterwards. The NEC nominations close imminently and I need backers. Now, I could have done the honourable thing and approached people in advance to schmooze them and make all sorts of promises.

Instead, being lazy, I've simply crushed the papers into my pocket with the intention of pulling them out from time to time and waving them at whoever I happen to be chatting to in the pub.

McIlvenna, Lello, Craig, Dixon, Staveley, Tennant, Beattie, Beach, Whittle. Jukes and Patel are compliant. I've already got Crowther's autograph so that's the whole lot done in about 15 minutes.

Friday 4th November 2016

Peter Whittle makes his planned announcement.

'After a great deal of thought, I have decided to withdraw from the leadership contest and recommend wholeheartedly that members vote for Paul Nuttall'.

Monday 21st November 2016

Is there something in the water? Our underwhelming leader-for-18-days Diane James has also resigned from UKIP. I'm not the slightest bit disappointed, having expected no better from her.

Farage puts it best to the press.

'This is yet another act of irrational selfishness from Diane James.

'This pattern of behaviour says that is she unfit to continue as an MEP. She should do the honourable thing and resign.'

She doesn't.

Friday 28th November 2016

Back to the Emmanuel Centre for the leadership announcement. Nigel gives another farewell speech and Paul Oakden comes to the results.

'With the Labour Party now led by some random combination of Jeremy Corbyn, John McDonnell and Gary Lineker. The Liberal Democrats firmly re-establishing themselves as Supreme Champions of the Lost Cause. And the Conservatives up to their neck in the task of renegotiating our independent nationhood. This is UKIP's time. All we need now is a new leader.'

'The results of the election are: in third place, with 2,775 votes or 18.1%. . .'

I'm jotting the figures on the margin of the *Metro*. Having seen the online traffic about the candidates and calculated their level of support on the back of it, 'Suzanne' is quickly scribbled. But Oakden carries on.

'. . . John Rees-Evans.'

Oops.

'In second place with 2,973 votes or 19.3%. Is Suzanne Evans.'

'And therefore, the successful candidate and new leader of the UK Independence Party with 9,622 votes, 62.6% of the vote, Paul Nuttall!'

Photo poses on the stage with Nigel, then Nuttall takes the podium.

'I will build a team of all talents, from all wings of the party. To that end, my first appointment is my deputy leader. He is someone who has backed my campaign and bought into my call for unity from the very beginning. Ladies and gentlemen - Peter Whittle.'

I yelp 'YES' at the top of my voice. Our cunning scheme has worked.

Then – we all pile off to the MOG where our new leader buys us beers. Top lad.

And - I finally see Bill Etheridge and David Kurten standing next to each other. The resemblance is startling in the flesh. No, really.

'Clearly separated at birth,' I observe to them. 'Tweedle Dum and Tweedle Dee.'

They promise to sit on me in tandem if I don't watch it.

CHAPTER THIRTY-FOUR

Stoke Up the Boiler

Thursday 1st December 2016

THE COUNT FOR THE NEC BALLOT was due to be on 3rd December. As 91 people have put their names forward and there aren't enough volunteers to help out, Kirstan Herriott says that it'll be postponed for a week.

'Ballot papers are being held at a secure location and cannot be accessed by the party in advance. The count will take place at Derby Cricket Ground at 7.30 am.'

Given that the odds are 13:1 against being elected and being snug asleep at that time on Saturday mornings is my hobby, I hope that my attendance may be excused.

Thursday 15th December 2016

I'm elected to the NEC along with Steve Crowther, Katie Fanning, Fiona Mills, Mick McGough and Anish Patel.

Sunday 18th December 2016

David Soutter, now out-of-favour, has written a review of the newly-elected NEC for *UKIP Daily*.

'Finally Paul Oakley. I first met Oakley shortly after taking up the post as Head of Candidates. I then kept running into him at numerous branch hustings which I was required to chair because of, shall we say, little local difficulties. He was and is one of the most able candidates I have met. Why was he not selected? Because UKIP branches are still determined not to select the best candidate but the local candidate. Please do not take that as a criticism but as an observation. Oakley is a barrister and perhaps needs to chill out a little when addressing hustings meetings but he will be a real asset to the NEC.'

How insightful of him. This shall be pasted into my CV for all future selections.

Saturday 31st December 2016

The New Years' Honours List is published and, at last, UKIP is recognised. Councillor Pete Reeve receives an MBE.

My old colleague, Jasvir Degun, goes one better and is given an OBE. He's the treasurer of Vauxhall Labour Party and I tell him that even though he's a horrible lefty I'm pleased.

Nothing for Nigel though.

Thursday 12th January 2017

Anil has invited a select few to dinner at his restaurant in Covent Garden. Paul Nuttall and Peter Whittle are both taking tobacco outside as I arrive. We have a laugh about the latest satirical news story in the *Daily Mash*. It has announced that Nuttall will bring back good old fashioned white dog excrement when UKIP come to power. We resolve to adopt this as official policy.

The restaurant is busy but we're in a private room. There are about 15 of us. And, Lo: I am seated at the left hand of the Leader. Gerard Batten is to my own left.

I tell Nuttall about local unease over the proposed compulsory purchase order of the land around the Millwall ground. As Paul's great enthusiast for 'Association' 'Football' he's already heard rumblings and is happy to endorse a campaign. His proposed quote for a leaflet is scribbled on a napkin.

'We stand firmly with Millwall fans in their battle with Lewisham Council. The Den was, is, and should remain a vital part of life in Bermondsey and South East London.'

Paul's in a positive mood and starts chatting about footie more generally. Gerard knows sweet FA about it.

'Sorry,' he says. "I've got no interest in any sport. At all."

We move on to events oop north. Labour MP Andy Burnham is going to be his party's candidate for Manchester's Executive Mayor. If he wins that post, Burnham will have to stand down from Parliament and there will be a by-election for his Leigh constituency.

'I've given this some thought,' says Paul. 'Our best chance of winning a seat is definitely in the North of England. So – as and when – I'm putting my name forward.'

The voting patterns in the referendum show there's strength in his view and having our Leader in the Commons would be a great boost for Brexit.

'Hang on a moment though, Paul,' I say. 'Isn't that being a little defeatist about the chances of Shneur Odze?'
Shneur is our own candidate for Manchester Mayor.

'To be honest, he hasn't got the slightest chance. The city suffers from the same metropolitan Marxist malaise as London. Burnham will walk it. But if I win the parliamentary seat I'll have to stand down as an MEP. And then Shneur will automatically take my place.'

Brilliant! Now that would be ideal.

Friday 13th January 2017

Well, well, well. Despite last night's discussions about the Leigh constituency, Paul Nuttall might not be standing there after all. This is because Blairite Labour MP Tristram Hunt has decided to resign from his seat in Stoke-on-Trent to take up a lucrative post at the Victoria and Albert Museum.

Friday 20th January 2017

The selection of our Stoke candidate is tonight. I'm not traipsing all the way up there to watch and in any case it would have been a short meeting as Adam Richardson confirms.

'Having just left the hustings event, all candidates withdrew including the local chairman to give an endorsement to Paul Nuttall.

'It is now for the NEC to confirm this decision. Can you all please vote on this by return?

'Also please can you keep this completely confidential until the press conference tomorrow?'

I have a quick look at the political betting websites to see if there are any odds on the name of our candidate but, sadly, there aren't. No sneaky insider dealing then.

Sunday 22nd January 2017

Ray Woolford, veteran of Lewisham People Before Profit, tells me that he was interviewed by the police this morning about the Millwall compulsory purchase hoo-ha. They're speaking to several people with a view to, potentially, setting up a fraud investigation. This will be huge if they've got the evidence to do so.

Tuesday 24th January 2017

The Millwall leaflets which we've designed in conjunction with Rosie Beattie and her Southwark crew have been printed, paid for, and delivered. Both branches are going to meet at South Bermondsey station this Sunday. There's a noon kick off for the match with Gillingham.

I bully Whittle and Kurten to come along.

'I've heard that you're both keen Millwall fans and have season tickets for the Den. If I'm mistaken about this then here is an issue for you to get your teeth into.'

And, for an all-out assault we're going to liaise with People Before Profit again and plot with Ray Woolford and John Hamilton. They, too, have produced fliers which are, in fact, rather more detailed than ours. Although their members will be loath to hand out UKIP leaflets, our lot will be more than happy to distribute theirs.

Thursday 26th January 2017

At the very thought of The Mighty UKIP campaigning against them, Lewisham's Labour council have caved in and cancelled the Compulsory Purchase Order at the Den.

As such, Sunday's campaigning is pointless. Well, at least the leaflets (now useless) aren't cluttering up my own front hall and somebody else can trip over them.

Thursday 23rd February 2016

I head to Euston to get the first off-peak train to Stoke for polling day.

Oh no I don't. Weather bomb Storm Doris is exercising her charms over the Midlands. The train's cancelled. As is the next one. And the one after that. I call Oakden to tender my apologies and head back down the Northern Line.

Euston remains in chaos for the rest of the day. Perhaps this mighty tempest has been conjured up by UKIP sorcery to keep Labour voters at home and hand us victory.

So I'll have to satisfy myself by watching BBC *Question Time*. Carswell's a guest so it (might) be quite good.

It isn't.

He concedes defeat in Stoke without even being asked. Then there's a startling exchange between journalist Isabel Oakeshott and 'our' Douglas.

Isabel has this to say.

'As I was making my way up here tonight I had a very interesting tip-off, and since we're here, I thought I would ask you directly about it. David has mentioned the feud between yourself and Nigel Farage which you yourself brought up. I understand that Nigel Farage should have got a knighthood. I personally believe he deserved to get a knighthood. . .' She is interrupted by audience applause.

'And he was certainly put forward for a knighthood and it appeared that everything was going swimmingly. Until you were asked to give your endorsement to that. . .'
The screen shifts to Carswell narrowing his eyes.

' . . . and you failed to do so. Is that true?'

He replies.

'That's simply not the case I'm afraid. I would love it if I had the power to give knighthoods. I would award lots of people knighthoods. . .'
Oakeshott isn't having this.

'I didn't say that. I said you were asked to give your backing to it.'

'I've, I've, I've, I absolutely. . .'
Oakeshott continues to stab:

'So you were never asked to give your backing or give any comment or feedback on it?'

'Absolutely not at all.'
Dimbleby digs in.

'Is it in your power to give knighthoods to Nigel Farage?'

'I wish it were.'
And our host continues:

'Would you give him one if you were. . .'
Carswell's reply is: Most. Witty.

'I've often called him "Sir".'
The audience jeers.

Do. Wot?

Farage is in the States and I'm too parsimonious to make a long-distance call to his mobile. Gawain will be able to confirm if there's anything to this.

'Isabel wouldn't make that up,' he tells me. 'But I don't know.'

The Stoke result comes out later. Labour's Gareth Snell just wins with 7,853 votes. Paul Nuttall is runner-up on 5,233 and he's followed by the Tory with 5,154. The Labour vote went down by 2.2% and ours increased by 2.1%. Mistakes were made in the campaign, of course, but overall, we've not done as badly as we might have in the face of a horrid press campaign against us.

CHAPTER THIRTY-FIVE

The Execution of Douglas Carswell

Sunday 26th February 2017

ARRON BANKS HAS BEEN MUTTERING about taking over as party chairman after Stoke. The likely presence or absence of blood in such a coup cannot be ascertained. Which is doubtless why Mark Wallace of Conservative Home gets in touch about tomorrow's meeting of the NEC.

'Mr Oakley! Hope you're well? Chatting to various people anonymously about Arron's demand to become UKIP party chairman – I wondered what your thoughts were on the idea?'

Wallace is a decent fella and a gracious host of salon parties at his flat which is not so far from me in southeast London. However.

'Now Mark. You know that if I told you anything I would have my tongue torn out by the roots and buried at the low water mark. Let's just say that the meeting might be...emotional.'

'Ha! Quite. Hence the anonymity. I might use the "emotional" line if that's ok?'

Suppose so. I put the phone down and spit copiously.

I'm just getting back into brushing my teeth when Oakden calls about that very meeting. There's rumbling about moves to get him sacked. The chairman isn't asking for my backing but gets it anyway.

'By the way,' he says. 'You know how you signed the Stoke office wall with "Paul Oakley (Not Paul Oakden)"? Well I reciprocated with "Paul Oakden (Not Paul Oakley)".'

Then the curse of my-phone-number-being-mixed-up-with-Paul-Nuttall's-by-UKIP-head-office strikes again as I receive a text from Arron Banks.

'Paul. I'm still very much behind you as leader – I've sent an email to the NEC and it's over to you. We can either transform UKIP like the Five Star Movement, run it efficiently or I will focus on a new movement which will be cross-party. I'm sorry you didn't win but awful smear campaign.'

Then another one.

'PS – O'Flynn, Evans, Carswell and co only waiting to replace you with Evans you must know that. The party would love this move and we could get on with winning!'

I reply to point out his mistake.

'Whoops!' he says. 'I'll give you a shout in a mo.'

He does. We exchange thoughts about Stoke but I'm not so pessimistic as he. He has a plan for the future of the party which he'll distribute to the NEC through Mick McGough.

We then move on to Mr Carswell. Banks has been digging. He's spoken to one of our Peers, Malcolm Pearson, who'd said that he heartily recommended Nigel for a knighthood. Douglas was asked for his own thoughts by the civil service. Arron's seen an email and paraphrases, but it's something along the lines of DC believing that Farage barely deserves an MBE.

This. Will. Not. Do.

Monday 27th February 2017

I'm annoyed at having to traipse up to Manchester for today's NEC meeting. Surely, London's the most convenient venue for everyone? It certainly is for me, and that's the main thing.

There are discussions about the by-election, of course. That moves us on to Carswell. Not every member saw the Question Time appearance so I find it on Youtube and we cluster 'round the laptop. Nobody's impressed and several rude words are uttered. Both of these issues naturally move on to Arron Banks and his offer to revive UKIP.

Mick hands 'round copies of Banks' letter which reads in part:

'I wouldn't want to list the deficiencies in the party organisation as it would take too long.

'As you are aware, I have offered to take over as Chairman of UKIP in order to transform it into an efficient, professional and ultimately electable party.

'My first move would be to bring in a CEO from industry.

'The party is at a crossroads. We have to be radical to become relevant once again.'

McGough hands one to Katie Fanning, who's been idly scanning social media during the meeting.

'I don't need one thanks. Arron's already published it all over the internet.'

Kinell[1] Arron. What about some confidentiality? Anyway, the upshot is that we're going to invite both Banks and Carswell to address the NEC at imminent meetings. The former might be given a gold star, the latter six of the best, although neither outcome is assured.

Meeting over, and Nigel rings within three minutes. The guy's psychic. I bring him up to speed.

'Well,' he says. 'The NEC have no guts as far as Carswell's concerned. They've all been lobbied by him, they all think he's a good chap and in reality he's been working against us ever since the general election.'

Tuesday 28th February 2017

Farage has wasted no time in dealing with the Carswell situation. An opinion piece is published by him in the *Daily Telegraph*.

'As a party, how can we let a man represent us in the House of Commons who actively and transparently seeks to damage us?

'I think there is little future for Ukip with him staying inside this party. The time for him to go is now.'

Wednesday 1st March 2017

George Cottrell is sentenced by a US court to 8 months in prison and has to pay a $30,000 fine for wire fraud. Given time served, he's coming out straight away. The lucky little sod. I will insist that he buys me a drink when he gets back to Blighty.

Thursday 2nd March 2017

Paul Oakden sends the NEC their orders of the day just after lunch.

'The leader has now requested that the NEC do NOT engage with the media any further on the issue of Douglas and Nigel. Douglas has now given further information to Paul, in writing, on his discussions

---

1 Short for 'f***ing hell'.

relating to peerages and knighthoods — this will be shared with the NEC shortly. The leader will be speaking publicly to this matter in the near future and it is important we do not add any further oxygen to the issue before then.'

Yup. Pretty obvious. And pretty pointless as we had discussed the importance of radio silence at the NEC meeting. Why's he bothering?

Peter McIlvenna reveals the reason. He's been watching the *Daily Politics* and Elizabeth Jones has been a guest, blabbing about it. There are no disciplinary procedures being brought against Carswell that she's aware of. As yet.

Cheese 'n' crackers.

Whittle tells us more.

'I've been in touch with Paul Oakden stating that she should be banned from any future such appearances. She apparently only told the press office with 10 minutes to go before air.'

Just to make sure there can be no misunderstanding, Gawain sends out an evening email.

'Can I pass on a request from the Party Leader that nobody accept privately an invitation to appear on tomorrow's *Daily Politics* to discuss internal matters?

'If we keep hanging up dirty linen, we will never have the time to get it washed in the first place and do that we all know we must.'

Friday 3rd March 2017

Paul Oakden calls about Carswell.

'I met with Douglas on Tuesday afternoon to seek assurances as to whether there had been an attempt made to push for a Farage knighthood specifically. I can confirm that such assurances were given.'

Sounds a bit Neville Chamberlain to me.

Carswell had sent an email to that effect on 28th February. Oakden knows that I've been plotting with Arron and Nigel because I've been perfectly open about it. Nonetheless, I give him my word that the email won't be disclosed to anyone so he forwards it.

'I attached the email exchange already in the public domain, between me and Malcolm Pearson about Nigel's knighthood.

'To reiterate a point I have made in public several times before: I do support a knighthood for Nigel and did so in conversations I held through the usual channels to secure recognition for him.

'Far from being evidence of a lack of effort on my part, this email exchange confirms that I did indeed try to lobby. It is evidence that I put in a good word, at the request of Malcolm, as soon as I was asked to.

'If you look at the dates of the email exchange, you will see that I am emailing Malcolm the day that New Year's honours are made public. It was evident on that date that our efforts had been unsuccessful. I am commiserating with an old friend after it has been made clear that our efforts were unsuccessful.

'I hope that is absolutely clear.
'Warm regards,
'Douglas'

From: Lord Pearson of Rannoch
Date: 30 December 2016 at 11:58
To: Douglas Carswell
Subject: Re: Nigel's Knighthood

'Dear Douglas,

'Could you let me know how your talk with Gavin Williamson went before Christmas?
'By phone if you prefer?
'Good wishes.

'Malcolm'

From: Douglas Carswell
Date: 31 December 2016 at 09:38
To: Lord Pearson of Rannoch
Subject: Re: Nigel's Knighthood

'As promised, I did speak to the government Chief Whip.
'Perhaps we might try angling to get Nigel an OBE next time round? For services to headline writers?
'An MBE, maybe?
'Let's discuss . . . .'

So. . . Carswell isn't adding anything new to the patently-damning stuff that's already been disclosed in the press. In fact, he's referring to and relying upon it.

Naturally, I snitch to Nigel although describing Douglas' email in general terms in order to stick to the letter of the secrecy undertaking.

'I have actually seen it, you know,' he says.

'Thought you might. Anyway, I was expecting a full report from Carswell rather than a couple of lines. He's taking the same approach as seasoned gangsters in police interviews. Sticking with "no comment" to avoid self-incrimination.'

'There's a lot more,' Farage says. 'Have you read *Brexit Club* by Owen Bennett?'

I haven't yet, but it's on the Amazon wishlist.

'Read it. Especially chapter 14.'

Oh. And to round off the evening, Arron Banks has given a lengthy interview to the *Independent*. He slags off Carswell, the party, the Stoke campaign and Nuttall himself who is, he says:

'Weak, but potentially a good leader.'

Banks also says he'll definitely be standing against Carswell in Clacton when the 2020 General Election comes round.

Monday 6th March 2017

There's been a string of emails from NEC members about the Arron Banks thing, most of which I can't be bothered reading. Nor can Paul Nuttall who's taken time to set out his own view.

'I'm not having a ding dong with Arron. I actually like him a lot and think what he says has resonance. I want to bring him in and not shit him out.

'However, I do take exception to be being described as 'weak' in newspapers and also being hit with an ultimatum on the chairmanship in the media. This - as I am sure as members of the NEC will agree - should have all been done "in house".'

Tuesday 7th March 2017

Arron has a very basic printout which is said to show accessing of confidential polling data from our Caseworker system during the general election.

'The attached page is the download of Thanet South data by Carswell.

'Only three people had access to the data. Carswell, Bruni-Low and Survation.'

The information was downloaded eleven times in total on the face of the document. There are suspicions that Douglas has passed the information on to the Tory Party. If that can be proved, the man's finished within UKIP. Yet, there's no proof whatsoever.

We need much more than this. Specifically: evidence. We agree to dig further and I ask Adam Richardson if he can assist.

'I have never actually seen the Caseworker evidence and I'm not quite sure how we get it. I was led to believe that Douglas didn't download the South Thanet pledges but ALL caseworker data, but let me try and narrow in on that.

'Also, I've now looked at the document and that simply shows he logged into Caseworker's national system a few times, not that any downloads took place as has been explained to me by Chris Bruni-Low previously. But I will seek definitive clarity.

'I always was under the impression, and you know where I stand on this, that the data point was not provable regardless.'

Well, let's have a look at that data and see if that's the case.

Wednesday 8th March 2017

3 am. I close my copy of Owen Bennett's *Brexit Club* having read it in one go.

Chapter 14 speaks of a 'Tate Plot' between Douglas Carswell, Mark Reckless and Tory MEP Dan Hannan to undermine UKIP from within.

There are direct and damning quotes from Hannan but none from Carswell. Presumably, Bennett interviewed all three before writing the book. If so, there ought to be tapes or a transcript. Primary evidence in other words. If we're to destroy Douglas we need to get hold of them.

Friday 10th March 2017

We had a lengthy NEC meeting this afternoon. It's now twenty-past nine in the evening and I am reclining on the *chaise longue*, consuming a kebab and watching Gogglebox. Dan Jukes calls to find out what went on. I tell him in broad terms and then hang up. He texts straight back.

'Nigel expecting your call before 9.30.'

What, tonight or tomorrow morning? I'm not really in the mood. Besides, I've Had Beer.

No. Now apparently. He needs to know whether Arron's still going to get a proper hearing before us.

I do as I'm told.

'Nigel – there were four of us backing Arron addressing the NEC. Me, Katie Fanning, Anish. And also Liz Jones. But it's not on for him to keep gobbing off in this way about Nuttall.'

'I know. It's not good.'

'He should know when to keep his fucking mouth shut.'

'OK. I'll have a word with him.'

Sunday 12th March 2017

The *Mail on Sunday* has a startling headline about South Thanet at the time of the general election.

'Did Carswell pass confidential Ukip data about local voters to the Tories to help them defeat Farage? Astonishing claim made to police as electoral fraud inquiry grows.'

Before my Coco Pops are even finished, Adam Richardson sends round an email of rebuttal to the NEC.

'I would like to make it clear from the outset that almost all of this article is UNTRUE. Literally lies and there will be legal consequences.

'Chris Bruni-Lowe has NEVER approached the police let alone been interviewed by them. Douglas, to my knowledge, is not under investigation. No-one saw conservatives walk by at dinner. The entire thing is a fabrication and will be promptly removed.'

I give Nigel an inconvenient call just as he's about to appear on the *Sunday Politics*. All we have is the fact of Carswell looking at the data several times. We've still no idea what, if anything, he did with it. There's no dossier and, as a consequence, no case for Carswell to answer, on that issue at least.

Swiz.

Monday 13th March 2017

Arron Banks calls up to talk about the invitation to address the NEC with his reform proposals. He's been busy with his son's cross-country running over the weekend. The lad came in the top 20 of the national prep schools' championships and as a Dad he's rightly-proud. Much more important than UKIP bitching.

'What happened at Friday's meeting? I hear Bickley and Crowther were less than complimentary. . .'

I agree about Bickley, although it had to be said that Steve's motion to invite Arron to address us wouldn't have passed at all without certain stings in its tail.

He hasn't had his invitation from either of the other Pauls yet. I tell him about the strict conditions which are going to be attached to it anyway: shut up in public.

'That meeting was bloody arse-ache for those of us who do want to hear what you have to say. And your Tweets calling Paul a weak leader who couldn't knock the skin off a rice pudding didn't help.'

'But the thing about the rice pudding was directed at the whole leadership, not just Paul,' He explains.

Arron sighs.

'Having chatted with Nigel, we've pretty much given up on UKIP. The party isn't interested in winning. We'll now keep our counsel until after the May elections. Anyway, we're just heading off to California for a while to explore some opportunities.'

I remind him that Carswell's due to answer questions on March 27th and set out some thoughts about *Brexit Club*. We'll need evidence of his actual words.

'Give Owen a call,' says Arron. 'He works for the *Huffington Post* but he's ok. I'll give you his number.'

He does, and I send a text telling him nothing of these dastardly plans but simply confirming that I'm not Paul Oakden and want to speak to him. He replies straight away.

'Hi Paul. I can call you this evening around 7.30 if that's any good? Or tomorrow?'

He does neither.

Tuesday 14th March 2017

I'm perched on the bank of the Old Quarry lake in Mole Valley trying to swindle some pike into eating my deadbaits. The Joey mackerel caught on the last seafishing trip with Nigel are ideal for this and didn't die in vain. I'm enjoying the solitude when several impertinent people have the audacity to call my telephone. What are Nuttall and Banks on about? Naturally, as I refuse to own a smartphone I haven't the slightest idea.

Turns out that Paul has now written to our donor in the following terms.

'On Friday, I met with the NEC to discuss the contents of your letter. The NEC resolved to keep open their invitation to you to meet them on 27th March in London to discuss the ideas outlined in your letter. Any and all contributions to our work are welcome. However, I should make clear that, whilst

I am open to working with you on improving and enhancing our party, the Party Chairmanship is not on offer.

'In addition, whilst the NEC are keen to discuss and examine your ideas, they are concerned about continuing negative and damaging publicity flowing from this matter. Mindful of their primary responsibility to safeguard the reputation of UKIP, they have asked me to tell you that should you choose to further criticise UKIP, its leadership or the elected representatives in either the media or on social media, they will withdraw their invitation.'

On the back of that Arron won't be bothering to turn up to speak to the NEC, after all. Worse, I also lose one pike which sheds the hooks (but do catch two others, so it's not all bad).

Oh. And I leave Owen Bennett another message as he's still not been back in touch.

Thursday 16th March 2017
The Electoral Commission publishes its damning report into Tory overspending in several seats at the general election. South Thanet and its winning MP Craig Mackinlay have particular questions to answer.

UKIP Head Office wastes no time. An email is sent out inviting applications for the seat.

Nigel has to put his name forward. Unfinished business.

Saturday 18th March 2017
No contact from Owen Bennett. Nigel's batman Dan Jukes knows him personally so I ask him to give Bennett a nudge, which he does. I'm not going to chase the geezer again like some bloody groupie. Dan forwards an appropriate assurance from him.

'Hello mate, yeah sorry, been a mental week! Will call him tomorrow.'

Sunday 19th March 2017
Radio silence from Bennett. Who does this arseling think he is? JK Rowling?

Tuesday 21st March 2017
I tell on Bennett to Dan Jukes. Presumably, he must be suspicious about something or other.

'No, he's just been lazy. I've just nudged him again.'

Nigel isn't so bothered.

'The book's enough.'

Disagree. Carswell's aware that he's no longer welcome in UKIP yet refuses to take the hints. Something more forceful is needed. The trouble with Chapter 14 is there's no express self-incrimination by him. On the other hand, if Carswell was present at the same interview and failed to correct Hannan that may be enough.

Not sorry if this seems legalistic. It is. If we're to initiate disciplinary proceedings against 'our' MP then we need primary evidence. It's really that simple.

Thursday 23rd March 2017

Toby Coke has resigned from UKIP and thus from his post on the NEC too. It's all very cryptic. Something to do with candidate selection in Norfolk. How dull.

He's a perfectly-nice old duffer although I've only spoken to him a couple of times. That he's a Douglas Carswell enthusiast is his only downside.

Paula Walters will take his place as the person who just missed election to the NEC before Christmas. Never heard of her, so impossible to know if she's a Carswellite or not.

Friday 24th March 2017

I cave in and leave another message for Owen Bennett because Carswell's due before the NEC inquisitors this very Monday and the brief must be prepared. This isn't a case where it's good enough to 'read the papers on the way to court' as barristers often choose to do. He's having a drink with Dan Jukes over the weekend so perhaps I can tag along.

Guess what? No reply.

That's it. He's officially useless.

I speak to Nigel, who isn't surprised.

'Never thought he would help, to be honest. He's a journalist, not a party activist. What would be in it for him?'

'Well, perhaps an exclusive interview if we use his material to kill Douglas off at last.'

'You don't need it. Stick with the book. Even if you can't prove the plot there's no doubt that he backed Vote Leave instead of Grassroots Out to screw our chance of getting the referendum designation.'

I'm not convinced but we leave it there.

Lacking the primary evidence that we'd hoped for, I put The Chapter through the scanner and ask Oakden to email it to all attendees of Monday's meeting so they can read it in advance. I'll cross-examine Carswell on it. He probably won't like this but if he refuses to play we can draw inferences from his silence. Wherever that may take us.

Then I have an idea. If we go for a full disciplinary complaint it won't succeed because of the lack of primary evidence. Yet we shouldn't forget that Al Capone was laid low by his humdrum tax issues and not his more spectacular escapades.

Let's just pass a motion declining to renew his membership. The Party Constitution says this:

> 'The Party Chairman (or, in his absence, his designated deputy) shall, without reservation or qualification, be entitled, subject to the approval of the NEC, to refuse to renew the membership of any person and may exercise this power without giving reasons for the same, if he deems it appropriate so to do.'

There's nothing to stop the NEC from directing that the Party Chairman does so refuse. Path of least resistance. Carswell's membership doesn't expire until 1st August but if he's got any honour he ought to resign forthwith if this is passed. I send a quick email to Nigel setting out my thoughts and then head over to Woolwich.

Whittle's having a 'do' at his home in the old Arsenal buildings. I arrive at the complex fairly late to see Rosie Beattie walking towards me as she heads home. I've not yet been to Peter's new flat so ask her for directions.

'It's very easy. And if you're stuck just look up at the windows. You won't be able to miss the commodious view of David Kurten's back.'

She grins.

The site is a series of gated communities which will offer some protection when the zombie apocalypse comes. I reach Peter's block and there's a sinister young man in black holding the iron gate open while, inevitably, peering at his smartphone. It's Dan Jukes.

He's seen, and is very pleased with, my email to Nigel but hasn't grasped the simplicity of it.

'We can just show that DC's, well, obviously brought the party into disrepute and then kick him out?'

'No. We don't even have to do that. We don't have to give any reason whatsoever.'

I head into the courtyard to be shouted at by Tim Aker who is 'refreshed' and sitting next to massive ornamental cannons with a monstrous cigar. Peter Whittle, a smoker himself, has asked him to go outside to indulge. The cigar truly is immense and it's doubtful that it'll be finished any time soon, so I head inside to the flat. Gossiping's fine but there's work to be done.

There are only around twenty people left. Jamie Ross McKenzie has some useful thoughts about the replacement NEC member Paula Walters. She'll vote to remove Carswell. There follows some notional totting-up of the relative strengths on the NEC. My good self, McGough, Patel and Fanning will definitely slice him up. There are others who won't under any circumstances, and then it's a case of deciding which of the rest could be turned to the side of righteousness.

Our host chips in.

'You know, if you can't get first-hand evidence of the betrayal from Owen Bennett you can always ask Michael Mosbacher. He interviewed Douglas, too, and he condemned himself in much the same way.' Mosbacher is the co-author of The First Ever Published Book About Our Glorious Victory, *Brexit Revolt*.

'Yeah, but the trouble is the meeting's on Monday. Tick tock.'

I text Mick McGough to see if he'll be turning up to it. Guy's a globetrotter so it can't be guaranteed. He replies.

'Sadly no, but I have submitted questions for Carswell.'

Not good enough Mick. We need your vote. This whole thing is too finely-balanced without you. The motion that the membership of Douglas Carswell MP be not renewed shall have to wait.

Rats' cocks.

Saturday 25th March 2017

I'm sitting in the car on a side road in Croydon while the missis is buying essentials. It's pay-and-display and we've done neither as the Labour council would only waste our pounds on some rubbish or another. This means I'm peering left, right, centre, repeat in the mirrors to make good an escape should a parking attendant appear.

The phone buzzes with a text from Jukes.

'Carswell has resigned.'

It vibrates again and this time the culprit is Adam Richardson.

'Ding dong the prick is dead.'

How mundane.

This is as disappointing as HG Wells' *War of the Worlds*. The alien interloper ought to have been defeated in an epic battle with all guns and explosions and that. Not by germs. Pah.

Sunday 26th March 2017

Carswell and Nuttall are both guests on the BBC *Sunday Politics*. I decide to idly browse the former's Twitter feed only to find – he's blocked me. With no interaction at all. Har! Apart from the subtle chats at Peter's bash the other night, my discretion's been watertight. So could it be someone who was at that party who's told on me? Who knows?

At ten-to-four I notice a miscall from Owen Bennett who's finally decided to get in touch. I don't bother calling back. In the words of Motörhead's Lemmy:

'Too Late, Too Late'.

CHAPTER THIRTY-SIX

Brenda from Bristol is a Very Wise Lady

Tuesday 18th April 2017
MORNING

IT'S ANNOUNCED THAT THE PRIME MINISTER will make a statement at 11 o'clock.

Oakden rings me.

'It's one of three things. Either the Queen has passed away. Or there'll be direct rule in Northern Ireland as they haven't been able to form an administration. Or there's going to be an election.'

The second possibility is a serious one if it puts the Good Friday Agreement at risk. The third option is horrific as UKIP has no money and no candidates.

Hope it's the Queen.

We wait to see. It isn't.

Oakden calls again.

'Not happy at all. We've not decided how to run this yet but we might just re-adopt all the 2015 election candidates.'

Argh!

'Well that'll give us real problems,' I tell him. 'As far as Greenwich is concerned, Ryan Acty's gone AWOL. Gary Harding in Lewisham West has sodded-off to the Tories. Is Anne Marie Waters still on the naughty step or can she stand again in Lewisham East?'

'No,' says Paul. 'She can stand.'

I call her and Anne Marie is happy to put her name forward, so that's one of the five seats covered by our branch at least. We might do rather well there as she managed to increase our vote five-fold in 2015.

Peter Whittle isn't sure if he'll be our man in Eltham again.

'I don't know. I might go for Clacton, but I'm still thinking about it.'

Could be a problem there as Arron Banks then proclaims that he's interested in Clacton too. Except he's not even a current UKIP member. If he's going to be stubborn and stand no matter what then it has to be under our banner. Otherwise, if it's Banks versus an official Kipper then Carswell will slither back in, whether as a prodigal Tory or, less likely, an independent.

I text Banks to say that I'll back any attempt he makes to come back on board. No other option makes sense.

EVENING

We're having our branch Annual General Meeting at the Zion Chapel. The only candidates putting their names forward are myself for chairman, Peter Lello as secretary, and Paul Butler as treasurer.

'Does anyone else want to stand?' I ask.

David Warwicker puts his hand up.

'You know, I might just go for chairman too. Make it more fun.'

'By all means, David.'

He puts his hand back down.

'Actually,' he says. 'I've just changed my mind. You might decide to withdraw and then I'll be stranded with it.'

I might indeed. We're all re-elected *nem con*[1].

I now have to tell them that the procedure for selecting candidates has been altered. Again.

'In common with every branch in the country, we must hold a hustings at 7.30 next Wednesday, 26th April. Candidates can only put their names forward for a single seat so choose wisely. If you want to apply then that means you're going to the candidates' assessment this weekend.'

The members aren't pleased.

Wednesday 19th April 2017

Douglas Carswell has written this on his Blog.

"I have decided that I will not now be seeking re-election. I intend to vote Conservative on 8 June and will be offering my full support to whoever the Clacton constituency Conservatives select as their candidate.'

Big Feartie.

---

1 *nemine contradicente*: with no one dissenting; unanimously.

Thursday 20th April 2017

Farage announces that he won't be putting his name in again for Thanet. Or, indeed, anywhere else. He doesn't want to fester on the backbenches of the Commons when he should be putting the case for a hard Brexit across the EU. There's some sense in this, but it's still disappointing.

Saturday 22nd April 2017

Elderly punk rockers GBH are performing a pop concert at the New Cross Inn. As this is a seven-minute train journey away, I'm certainly going. As it's a two-minute walk for Peter Lello from his home he's coming too, whether he likes it or not.

Naturally, I wear a black leather jacket, black 'Hooligan Rock and Roll' T-shirt, black jeans and black DM boots. This is understated as there are far more people there with Mohican hairdos, studs, tattoos and skin diseases. Peter's never been to a punk gig before and dresses outrageously in his pale blue cagoul and grey slacks.

We mumble, very quietly, about UKIP business.

'Would you be willing to be one of our candidates old chap? There is of course the possibility that the press will have a crack at you again.'

'Well there is that, but also my job. I don't know if they'll let me stand.'

'Fair enough. But if there's any criticism of you I've already got the press release drafted:

"UKIP Greenwich and Lewisham are proud to have Peter Lello as their candidate. *The Daily Mirror* can go fuck themselves".'

Will he? He won't. Disappointing.

I get into bed at 2 am.

Sunday 23rd April 2017

I get back out of bed at 6.30 am.

Woe! Woe!

Emmett Jenner is picking me up to drive to Nottingham for the candidates' training session which starts at 10. Neither of us can be arsed but we have to go or else we won't be allowed to stand in the election. Bah.

The event is at the Jury's Inn, right next to the railway station. As we draw up we're disgusted to note that the hotel is still flying an EU flag outside.

We stand in line to register with about thirty others and I chat to

Mark Webber of Tower Hamlets.

'Have you stood as a candidate before?' Mark asks.

He gives some tips about campaigning and I smile gratefully. Suddenly, his eyes narrow.

'Oakers! It's you!'

It is indeed. He's been hoodwinked by the grizzled beard and long hair and hadn't recognised me. I ponder the possibility of carrying out an armed robbery before reverting to a normal appearance.

We start with group sessions at which we exchange our electioneering experiences. I learn nothing, but have a disagreement with another attendee over the importance of local candidates. I say it makes no difference, especially if they can't string a sentence together. He thinks it's vital. Hope his view doesn't become party policy or my chances of holding elected office are slim for so long as I reside in the Soviet borough of Lewisham.

No food is put on for us at lunchtime although bar snacks from reception are recommended. So me and Emmett head into town to find the nearest Wetherspoons.

The afternoon session's a public speaking exercise. Volunteers are sought to take a folded piece of paper from a tub and then speak for two minutes on the jocular subject written thereon. I can't be bothered with this as I have a headache and am struggling to remain awake. Even if bearing neither of these burdens, I would still not wish to play this party game for I am a bad sport.

I try to avoid the eye of Deborah who's carrying the bucket and fail. The exercise is compulsory. My subject is: 'Worms.'

Lugworms. Redworms. Lobworms. Ragworms. Brandlings. Tench. Chub. Carp. They go in thin and they come out stout. Etc.

Etc. Etc. Etc.

Many decades have passed since I was a sixth-former who might be expected to gain some knowledge from such an exercise. Seriously – bugger off and leave me alone.

Paul Oakden turns up at last and sits next to me at the back. He wants a word outside about our target seats so we leave.

'We're not going for fifteen now,' he tells me, 'just these five.'

They are Thurrock, Boston, Hartlepool, Heywood and Middleton, and Clacton.

'No Thanet South?' I ask.

'Nope. We've had some private polling done and, without Nigel as candidate, we're miles behind.'

'Well, what are you doing about Clacton if Arron still wants a go? It has to be under UKIP colours or the Tories will win.'

'Yes,' says Oakden. 'We had dinner with him and Nigel last week and Alan Bown tagged along. It got heated. And I swore.'

'But why's he bothering? Carswell's resigned so he's won without a single shot.'

'No idea. It's sad in a way that Douglas has gone. If he hadn't and Arron was our candidate I think the MP would have stayed the same.'

We head back in. The public speaking thingy is wheezing to a close. There is, however, one last piece of paper in the tub.

'Who hasn't had a turn?' demands Deborah.

Pauline McQueen turns round in her seat and points to Emmett. 'He hasn't.'

'Yes I have,' he lies. 'About twenty minutes ago.'

As Deborah's not sure whether this is true or not, he gets away with it, the spawny git. Oakden's handed the final piece of paper to undertake the exercise. He ignores the subject and brings us up to speed about our troubles instead. Oh, and there's going to be a series of policy launches, including a ban on sharia law. I interrupt.

'Paul – you can't just ban sharia courts. They arise from the Arbitration Act. If you scrap this then all forms of alternative dispute resolution will be squashed as well. It's not that easy.'

'OK. I'll have a word with Nuttall.'

An old boy sitting to my immediate left farts loudly. I hope that Oakden doesn't think it was me.

CHAPTER THIRTY-SEVEN

Clacton Carpet-Bagger

Monday 24th April 2017
MORNING

CONTEMPLATING THE TARGET SEATS. I wouldn't even think about putting my name forward for Thurrock. Aker's done lots of good work there and deserves to be the next MP. I've no knowledge of or links to the northern constituencies. Besides, the logistical horrors of standing in a faraway seat is a fresh memory from my Tory candidacy in St Helens in '05. That only leaves Clacton.

Herewith the dilemma. If Arron and Whittle are going for it then it might royally-annoy them if I do likewise. The missis certainly thinks so.

On the other hand, it gives me a good line for a speech.

'They are already established as giants of UKIP, like our own Sinatra and Presley. But tonight. At this hour. In this room. You have the chance to discover our Beatles. That is – me.'

OK, OK. That might need work but I'll go for the seat anyway.

I call Whittle out of courtesy and leave a cryptic message on his answerphone asking him to call. He doesn't get back. However, he had earlier invited me to the Marriott Hotel in the old GLC building for an announcement this morning. He didn't say what it was about. Wasn't going to bother going before but I will now. If he's proclaiming his candidacy for Clacton then at least I'll know.

As I turn up, Paul Nuttall's speaking, followed by David Kurten, Margot Parker and Peter himself. It is in fact the launch of the party's 'Integration Agenda'. A UKIP government would ban 'face coverings' in public, strengthen the law on female genital mutilation, abolish postal voting on demand and treat the 'honour' aspect of murders as an aggravating factor.

I agree with each proposal, except perhaps the burqua ban. But to announce them all at once is certainly Banging On About Islam.

My concerns about the formalities of dealing with the Moslem 'legal system' have been taken on board however as Whittle confirms in his speech:

'It is our intention to ban sharia law. To this end we would establish a legal commission to draw up proposals to disband sharia courts.'

Far better for these intricate issues to be dealt with by cold legal minds than by our lovely National Executive Committee.

The speeches are warmly-received by the cornucopia of Kippers in the room and Anish Patel in particular is ecstatic. The press aren't so chuffed. Rather than putting serious questions there are sneering Guardianista debating points, like whether the 'burka' ban would extend to beekeepers. Ha Ha bonk.

Press conference over, Gawain clears a space through the crowd for Paul Nuttall. Having had their fun on the purpose of the morning, the media hyenas re-target their nips to the question of whether Nuttall's going to stand in the election. And if so – where?

I hang around for Whittle, who's now being interviewed for Sky. Presumably by that dreadful Kay Burley as he's glunching at the camera which is facing him.

This gives me the chance to talk to Gerard Batten. Anyone would assume that he'd be huzzaying, given that he's always been robust with his Islamoscepticism. But no.

'The burka ban's a stupid idea. How on earth are they going to enforce it? Send police snatch squads into Tower Hamlets? There'd be riots.'

Towler interrupts.

'Oakley. Get into that side room with the leader. Now.'

I thought Nuttall had already left but this isn't so. His car hasn't yet arrived and he's waiting in an anteroom. The press pack are packed outside, barking questions through the closed door. I force my way through them.

The reason for Paul's seclusion is mundane and he certainly isn't hiding from the media but the tableau now looks very bad and that's what counts.

Nuttall's seated in a red leather club chair in the corner, his head resting on one hand while smiling to himself. Paul Oakden's on the phone chasing up the car and David Kurten and John Gill aimlessly hover about.

Oakden hangs up.

'The car will be here in two minutes. I need you all in a doughnut around the leader as we leave.'

'Well,' I say. 'This Kurten bloke's a huge chunk of beef but we could do with some more. Peter Harris and Roger Gravett are outside.'

John Gill fetches them both. We line up fore and aft and, as we're just about to depart, concertina doors to an ante-room off this ante-room are opened as hotel staff start to prepare the whole space for lunchtime dining.

'Perfect,' says Oakden. 'We can leave through there. And it'll be funny if we sneak out further down the corridor.'

Nuttall seems amenable but I'm certainly not.

'No way. It'll look as if we're shit-scared. Paul – never forget. You are The Bad Bootle Meff. We exit through the front door.'

We do, and the media attack straight away.

'Why aren't you standing in the election?'

'Where are you standing in the election?'

'Will Nigel let you stand in the election?'

'Are you worried that you'll do as badly as you did in Stoke?'

Paul's only response is this.

'The NEC's meeting at the end of the week. I can't say anything more than that, so let's kill it dead.'

Kill it. Dead. I dearly hope not.

AFTERNOON

The Integration Agenda certainly risks rebranding the party into one that Bangs On About Islam. And as if by magic, Anne Marie Waters sends me a message.

'Wondering if I should put my hat in for Lewisham East? I have no idea if I have a chance there, but I think with the new Sharia stuff I would be well-placed to deal with it and give knowledgeable answers. Let me know what you think.'

I do let her know. It's hers if she wants it.

Candidates are only allowed to apply for nomination in one seat. This must be done today. And I will be going for Clacton. But before I can ring Arron to tell him, the news comes in that he's been on a day trip to the town, met the councillors, and decided not to bother. He'll be backing a local candidate, Councillor Jeff Bray, instead.

Tuesday 25th April 2017

Social media sleuths have uncovered some elegant online musings which, it is alleged, are from Clacton's Mr Bray.

'just read a site that says muslims burning poppies is "disrespectful" bollocks !! disrespectful my arse. scum, if i decicrated muslim culture in Iran i would be shot. not all muslims are terrorists, but all terrerists are muslims.'

I take the opportunity to check my own Twitter feed and remove several sinewy denunciations of the religion of peace which had been posted after a variety of atrocities. Just to be on the safe side.

Wednesday 26th April 2017

Morning

Peter Whittle finally returns the call. I tell him that no disrespect to him is meant, nor is this a stab in the back, but I'm going for the Clacton nomination. Hopefully we'll remain pals, but may the best man win.

'Oh, don't worry about that, dear. I'm after South Basildon and East Thurrock.'

Ha! That poisoned chalice.

'Actually', Whittle continues, 'I'm with Paul at the moment and we're off to Brussels to read the MEPs the riot act about Monday's launch. They really do need to keep on-message.'

Well. That will be. Interesting. Some of the MEPs have already said they're furious about the announcements and, in particular, that they weren't told in advance. I wish him luck with that.

Kirstan Herriott from the candidates' department then says I've been shortlisted by Clacton branch and will be interviewed this evening.

'That's wonderful!' I exclaim. 'How many put their names in? I bet it's been a real job sifting through them.'

'Well, it was just you and Councillor Bray who applied. But you're the better candidate by far.'

Oh.

Oakden wants a word.

'Well done,' he says. 'The branch chairman has just been on to me. Nobody has the faintest idea who you are but everyone's annoyed with the Bray revelations. It may be yours for the taking.'

So now the only potential sticking point is Banks if he is still going to back Bray. We have to speak.

'Arron. This chat is entirely off the record, but I'm being interviewed for Clacton tonight. Just so that I know how to approach the hustings, can you tell me if you're still behind Jeff Bray?'

'That's good news. Well done. I'll back you instead then.'

'No, honestly, that wasn't why I was calling. I just wanted to know how best to . . .'

'No problem at all. I'll email the councillors and tell them so.'

EVENING

So I'm triple-booked. I could go to my chambers' annual general meeting.

Or my branch's candidate selection for our local seats.

Or. I could head over to Clacton.

What do you think?

I have to be at a pub called the Wick Lodge in Jaywick by 7.30 and decide to drive. Haven't done this before but getting the train up there for the Carswell by-election was a bit of a shlep. Should be easy enough. Straight through the Blackwall Tunnel and then north east. I'm too tight to pay for the Dartford crossing.

Big mistake. Traffic is heavily, heavily backed up. To make my mood even worse, I'm listening to LBC on the wireless. They're leading on plans by that vile Gina Miller woman to fund the campaigns of pro-EU candidates.

I have to call the branch chairman, Tony Finnegan-Butler, to tell him that my ETA's getting later. Then have to call again to say that it'll be later still.

I'm on the motorway when I receive another call. Oakden.

'Are you there yet?'

'Nope. Are you nagging me about being late?'

'Nope. I have a question.'

He's hesitant.

'Go on,' I say.

'We're assuming you're going to get the nomination. If you do, I've a favour to ask.'

He has some trouble formulating the words. Spit it out man!

'Would you be willing to stand down in favour of Paul Nuttall?'

Leaving me with a crappy seat somewhere else, presumably. Like Lewisham Deptford. I say nothing for a few moments while collecting some thoughts.

'Paul?' prods Paul.

'Yes. Of course,' I reply. 'More than happy to do so for the good of the party.'

And I will, without any complaint at all. But - Gah!

'Thanks,' he says. 'It might not come to that but Nuttall still has to stand in a high profile seat, even after Stoke. Or especially after Stoke.'

Once past Colchester I make good time and arrive at the pub just before 8. The car park's busy and I have to go to the very back to find a space.

On getting out a chap immediately points a microphone at my head.

'Simon Dedman, BBC Essex. Do you have any comment about your challenger, Councillor Bray?'

'Not really, I've never met the bloke.'

'But what about his decision this afternoon to step aside in your favour?'

'Has he? I'd no idea.'

'Yes, but he's changed his mind and is going for it after all.'

'Good. I always welcome a battle.'

What a strange thing to do. The man's obviously a flake and/or an idiot.

There's a welcoming committee at the door of the pub. It's reasonable to assume that they'd have started already by hearing from Bray but they haven't. A coin's tossed and my challenger decides to go first anyway. Sadly, they'll be seeing us separately as per the Party Rules so there will be no chance for me to squish him face to face.

A charming old lad called John Wrigley buys me a pint and a fellow from the local paper, James Dwan, introduces himself.

'Any thoughts for the *Gazette* about tonight?'

'Speak to me afterwards. I need to get in The Zone.'

Finding a defensive position on my own in a corner, I read my research covering the council, local schools, NHS provision and so on. Should have started studying these days in advance rather than for the first time at this very moment, but there you go.

Then I'm on. It's a large room at the back. Most seats are full although not all those attending will have the right to vote. I decide on overacting, at least to begin with.

'As I look around this room. I feel a real sense of disappointment. You were hoping to see that handsome young Paul Oakden. But you've got Paul Oakley instead.'

They laugh, obviously, at this and other quips and boo appreciatively when referring to various Enemies of the People. But there's serious stuff too. A couple of years ago Channel 5 had run a series called *Benefits by the Sea* about this very part of Clacton which is said to be the most deprived area in the country.

'I enjoy sniggering at the contestants on the Jeremy Kyle show as much as anyone. But that documentary crossed a line. Jaywick locals have been badly let down by all politicians. "Benefits Porn" isn't funny and it'll be my priority as an MP to stand up for these people.'

My performance, overall, is outstanding. But you knew that already.

I'm escorted back to the bar while the branch hold their private discussion. Having now got the chance to speak to Jeff Bray one-to-one it turns out that he's a reasonable fellow. However, the waspish words which Michael Crick once used about another election sneak into my subconscious: 'Barely councillor material.' Bray is no statesman.

The Chairman approaches us with the result. Nineteen votes for Jeff and sixteen for me. Not ideal, but respectable. Local incumbency wins out over the stranger's stardust.

I give an interview on camera for Simon Dedman. The best man won; Bray will be an excellent MP for Clacton, that sort of thing. Always be gracious.

Having said that, I can't resist having a dig at Carswell too.

CHAPTER THIRTY-EIGHT

The Suicide of Anne Marie Waters

Thursday 27th April 2017

PETER LELLO HAD STEPPED IN AS CHAIRMAN of the branch last night while I was up in Clacton. Anne Marie Waters was unanimously re-adopted as our candidate. Although to be fair, she was the only person to put her name forward.

She'd Tweeted about it:

'I'm delighted that I've been selected again to stand for UKIP in the Parliamentary seat of Lewisham East. Looking forward to campaigning!'

I re-Tweet this, as do a thousand or so others.

Tim Farron of the Lib Dems is really upset about her nomination. As are the *Guardian, Daily Mirror* and *Evening Standard*.

Who gives a toss what they think?

We do, apparently.

Come the evening, Peter Harris wants a quiet word after the London Region meeting at the Vibast Centre.

'You know we live just outside Clacton?' he asks. 'Well, we've got a massive static caravan in the garden. You can kip over in that for the campaign.'

'That's really kind Peter,' I tell him, 'but Jeff Bray won the nomination.'

'Yes,' he replies. 'I know.'

Friday 28th April 2017

The story about Jeff Bray's 'muslamic' social media posts has been picked up by many more media outlets. Rather than front it out, Bray tells the world he's been hacked. Yes. Amateur.

I'm just arriving for the NEC meeting when Davy Coburn calls.

'Will you be there? Will Whittle be there? Well, you can tell him a thing or two from me.'

Coburn is furious about Peter telling-off the MEPs.

'Who the hell does Whittle think he is?'

I have to cut him off as I'm heading inside.

Anne Marie's in reception. She'd been invited to address this meeting anyway before her adoption for the seat, or, indeed, the calling of the election. It's likely that the focus of today's discussion will shift away from its intended route. Whittle and I have a private word with her. This is branch business.

'Am I standing or am I not?' she asks.

'Well, standing as far as I'm concerned,' says I.

'That's not what Paul Nuttall stated on Radio 4 this morning. He said that I'll categorically not be a candidate.'

Hmm. A bit of *ultra vires*[1] activity on the part of Mr Nuttall there. It's the NEC as a whole which decides who can and cannot stand.

Both myself and Whittle still want her. We advise her to keep the discussion congenial and remember that there are plenty of other policies to focus on until election day. She doesn't need to, and must not, Bang On About Islam.

Paul Nuttall arrives and asks Whittle and I to come outside while he has a fag.

'I can't have her standing. She says Islam is evil.'

'Then the first question will be – why did we let her be our candidate in that same seat two years ago? And the second question will be – if you're appalled by "Islamophobia", are you going to drop Monday's policies?'

'But Paul, that's all I got in interviews this morning. Bloody Anne Marie. It's going to overshadow the campaign.'

'Give it a few days to die down and refuse to answer any more questions about her. Never apologise. Never explain.'

Nuttall isn't convinced. He's looking tired and drawn.

The meeting begins. Naturally, I'm concentrating on the agenda but Coburn sends me a string of text messages which I have to read through a cupped hand.

'Basically, the islamo-genitally-mutilatedly-obsessed-Queeny Wiffle and the former political editor of the *Beano* have just incorporated

---

1 *ultra vires*: acting beyond his authority.

Daft Duffy's failed leadership manifesto/rant as our integration policy without even telling the elected MEPs and councillors that they were launching it. Nathan was on TV at the time and just faced with it. Party run by Minger, O'Flannigan, Oakden, Waffle and Theresa May.

'They are planning to end party democracy by threatening to throw anyone out of the party who opposes policy! I thought we were a libertarian party, not the NSDAP.[2]

'Waffle tried to lecture me on Islam. I speak Arabic, have read the Koran, traded futures for the Saudis, trekked across the Sahara and also own a chunk of North Africa. This silly suburban queen has not been south of Bexley or north of Highgate. As for "culture" I have more Picasso on my walls than he has sucked cock.'

Well, he's made his position clear. I text him back eventually.

'Davy – you ought to know that I'm sitting right next to Peter.'

'Make sure he can't see,' he replies, 'or wave your cock as a distraction.'

Anne Marie is called in to speak. She doesn't take the advice which Peter and I gave her.

There's a vote. I propose her adoption and am backed by three members. The other four in attendance, including Nuttall, go the other way. Deadlock. At this, Oakden places his casting vote as chairman behind the leader's position. That's entirely the right thing to do. Never mind.

Other seats are also dealt with and Clacton comes up. Oakden properly requests that I leave the room so I sit in the waiting area with a Spink medals catalogue. I'm called back in and the meeting closes shortly afterwards. No conclusion is announced.

Elizabeth Jones is suddenly very kindly and attentive towards me. What a novel situation.

'Paul! Paul! Why don't you stand here?' She points to a map of London constituencies. 'Or here?'

I'm noncommittal.

Most of us head to Henry's Bar and I buttonhole Whittle outside.

'I infer from Mizz Jones' warmhearted concern that she's pleased I didn't get Clacton.'

'Oh, I know, the woman's utterly ghastly. But it won't be Bray either you'll be surprised to hear. Or maybe you won't.'

'Nuttall's going for it then after all? Good choice. I'll pop up there

---

2 Nationalsozialistische Deutsche Arbeiterpartei: National Socialist German Workers Party; the Nazi Party.

to help him.'

'No, he's decided to stand in Boston and Skegness.'

'So who is it?'

'Well, I shouldn't really say. It's for Oakden to tell you.'

'Do so nonetheless or I shall give you a Noogie.'

'Alright then, it's someone called Diana Coad and Nigel recommended her. I know nothing about her but apparently she owns a small business there.'

I do know her of course. She's the one who, thankfully, beat me for the Tory nomination for Slough and I successfully represented her in a libel action a few years ago. Diana's a lovely person, yet . . . we will not win in Clacton.

I send Farage a grumpy text.

'Bit ticked off to be honest about that East Coast seat. I won't make a fuss. But – hey.'

He doesn't respond.

Saturday 29th April 2017

I'm on the email list for those tapeworms of social media, Hope not Hate. They've just proclaimed the following.

'THIS ELECTION CAMPAIGN WILL BE OUR MOST TARGETED AND SOPHISTICATED TO DATE'

They are, allegedly, going to battle UKIP in seven seats. Heywood and Middleton. Thurrock. Hartlepool. Stoke-on-Trent North. Grimsby. Boston & Skegness. And Clacton.

As ever, there's the usual rider which appears in one form or another on most of their missives.

'If you'd like to support our election campaign, please donate here.'

Beggars.

Wednesday 3rd May 2017

Nominations close for the election on 11th May. Our branch isn't going to field a candidate in Lewisham Deptford after all. Having lost our deposit there two years ago even when at our polling peak, we're not going to donate another £500 to the Lewisham Mayor's champagne fund (or whatever it is this cash is usually spent on).

We won't stand in Eltham either. Whittle's vote last time was far greater than the difference between Labour victor Clive Efford and his Tory challenger. Efford's a dirty Remainer and Conservative, Matt Hartley a Brexiteer-true. We've checked. There'll be no public announcement of this, but we're going to give Hartley a free run.

So that was just two seats to fill but after Anne Marie's NEC rejection it's gone up to three. There's no time for another formal branch meeting so the committee of myself, Lello and Butler are going to interview and make our choices.

I'll probably be selecting myself for Lewisham East. Sigh.

We're having a quiet pint with a chap called Joseph Langton in the Greenwich Tavern. His CV spans Bloomberg, Barclays and the Royal Bank of Canada. He's eloquent, intelligent, appealing and, well - young. This man is no make-weight candidate but would be a superb choice for any political party to have. He won't become an MP this time, but in years to come? He's Cabinet calibre. I'm not joking.

I've put my phone on the table and it vibrates just after 8 pm.

'Apologies gents. It's the Dear Leader. I'll have to take this.'

'What does Nuttall want?' asks Paul Butler.

'Slip of the tongue. I'll tell you later.'

I head outside for privacy.

'Evening Nigel.'

'Hello Paul. Look. Clacton. I didn't know you'd put your name in. I just suggested Diana Coad as I've known her for a few years and she has local links.'

'I know her too and she's a reasonable choice. It's just that – well. As you know I never boast about my own attributes, but she's a bit staid. And I am not. Are you insistent on her being the candidate?'

'Not at all. And I wouldn't have any problem with you putting your name forward again.'

Before going back into the pub another number is called with an 01255 prefix.

'Tony. It's Paul. If you're not set on having Diana Coad I'd like you to reconsider me.'

Oh. And we snatch up Joseph Langton as our own candidate. With gratitude and relief.

Thursday 4th May 2017

I'm a speaker on some Brexit Panel thingumy at the University of East London on their Docklands campus which is being filmed by or for Channel 4. The venue, the Sportsdock, sits opposite City Airport.

While walking up to the doors the phone rings. It's Anthony Finnegan-Butler, the Clacton chairman. Can't hear a word he's saying as a plane is just taking off. Glad I'm not studying here.

'Sorry Tony, what was that?'

'I said the committee have had a meeting. We've nothing against Diana Coad but know nothing about her. She didn't apply for the seat in the first place as you know.'

'True,' I reply. 'But I do have some knowledge of Diana and she'd certainly be a safe pair of hands.'

Always be gracious, lad. Always be gracious. But – oh please. Oh please oh please oh please oh please oh please. . .

'She might well be suitable,' says Tony. 'But at least we've seen you in action at the hustings. We're offering you the nomination.'

It is grabbed.

Tuesday 9th May 2017

We may have a candidate for Lewisham East after all. Keith Forster of Bexley Branch has been to see Peter Staveley this morning and approved to stand. Now he needs his papers signed. Sadly, this will have to be without the hands-on help of the branch officers. I email him the contact details of our 26 members in the seat. They can at least sign his papers themselves and perhaps even help him out with door knocking if he struggles.

I send him a second email with a copy of the electoral register.

'My phone's collapsed under the weight,' he says. 'I might go in to the council offices and collect a paper copy.'

Staveley speaks to me.

'It would be helpful to know who is going to be Keith's election agent. If Keith is his own agent then he'll need an "office" address which isn't in his home borough of Bexley.'

It'll have to be Lewisham borough then. Easiest if I do it because I live here. So we're going to have both a paper candidate and a paper agent in Lewisham East.

CHAPTER THIRTY-NINE

It's SO Unfair!

Wednesday 10th May 2017

J EFF BRAY HAS GONE SOBBING TO THE PRESS because he's been replaced by an NEC member who's been 'parachuted in'. This bollocks is all over the place and the BBC in particular announces:

'UKIP's Clacton candidate dropped in "shambolic" move'

They also say this:

'The BBC has approached London-based barrister Mr Oakley for comment.'

Have they heck as like.

In order to dash Mr Bray's hopes once and for all, I'm outside Tendring town hall at 11 am to meet the branch committee and file my papers. This shouldn't take more than ten minutes. It certainly doesn't in Lewisham. The staff there are polite and proficient, but no extra effort is spent by them on the interaction because UKIP stand no chance of being elected.

Today however, it takes longer. There's no problem with the nomination. Instead, the council's Chief Executive, Ian Davidson, has heard of my frustrations about Jaywick and gives me a detailed briefing on local regeneration proposals. He even pulls out the architects' plans which have yet to be signed off. This lasts over an hour. He didn't need to do this and I'm grateful. The council obviously think UKIP might win. Crikey.

I'm driving back to London when the BBC finally get in touch for an interview. Boringly, they focus on what you'd expect.

'I'm not a local as you're perfectly aware. But I'm not running to be King of Clacton and won't be going in there to tell people to do what

I say. I'm going to be relying on the councillors, the activists and more importantly the local people to tell *me* what to do.'

'How close are you to Nigel Farage?'

I know exactly what they're getting at but I'm not playing that game.

'Right at this moment I'm parked up in an industrial estate in Thurrock. I've no idea where Nigel is.'

Closer to home in South East London, we've been having real trouble getting signatures for our candidates' nominations. We have sufficient members in each seat to get them done easily, but people are proving elusive. I eventually scraped together enough for Hoong Wai Cheah in Lewisham West, largely by harassing my neighbours. Anyway, that one's done.

Keith Forster struggled to get them in Lewisham East but finally managed it.

Lello's been trying hard for Langton but has to send out another pleading email after 11 pm.

> 'I'm writing to you as a UKIP member based in the Parliamentary constituency of Greenwich & Woolwich to ask if you're available tomorrow, Thursday 11 May 2017, before 3pm, and would be able to meet our prospective candidate for the coming General Election and sign his nomination form.'

Thursday 11th May 2017

Off to Catford to see Jamie Baker with the nominations for Lewishams East and West and a grand's worth of twenty pound notes in a bum bag. This must be done today and the council will gladly carry out an informal check of each signatory against the electoral roll before formal submission.

'Hoong Wai's fine,' Baker says, and picks up Keith Forster's papers. I stare at the screen as he goes through the names.

'Ah,' he finally says. 'There's a snag.'

'There shouldn't be. I'm always very careful.'

'Not your fault. The names and numbers are spot on. Only problem is, this person's already nominated the Green candidate. You can't do two.'

Stupidity or sabotage? Who the fuck knows? I speak calmly however.

'Will we need to complete the whole lot again?'

'No. I'll cross this one out and will be happy to accept a new signature on a separate sheet before you hand the thing in properly.'

You diamond, Jamie. I head out of the offices to the Broadway and make a number of calls to relevant branch members. None are picked up but I leave messages asking them to call back urgently.

Nobody does. Except, eventually, Mike Farish, who drops what he's doing straight away and heads over to sign the nomination. Another diamond. Sorted.

Peter Lello then calls from Greenwich.

'We can't do it. Nobody's got back to me. We've been reduced to knocking on random doors. We're three names short and there's not enough time before the deadline.'

He's done his best, there's no doubt about that. Yet there's also no doubt that a lot of indolent sods in the branch have just deprived the voters of Greenwich and Woolwich of a UKIP box on their ballot paper. Totally inexcusable.

Right in the middle of my very late lunch, Clacton's Tony Finnegan-Butler calls up.

'Can you ring Mark Stephenson? He's the leader of the UKIP group on Tendring council. He runs a print business in Old Road and doesn't take any nonsense. He's insisting on a chat.'

I comply. Mark's sceptical about my motivations but admits he knows nothing about me. He's equally sceptical about Jeff Bray and his motivations and knows him very well. I give him the spiel about the actual course of events rather than the imagined ones.

'There's a meeting of the councillors tonight. Be there.'

'Can't. I'm in court tomorrow. We'll have this out on Saturday if you can get your colleagues along.'

Friday 12th May 2017

I'm really not pleased with a huge lazy contingent of our membership in Greenwich and Lewisham branch and have sent out a snotty email.

'To those members who did answer our calls for teamwork – we are very grateful indeed. Thank you.

'To those who couldn't be bothered even replying – you may have saved a few minutes of your own time but have wasted many hours of both Peter Lello's and mine. I am appalled at your discourtesy and deeply embarrassed that our branch let Joseph Langton down so badly.'

A furious response is received from someone called John Lindsey who says he's resigning his membership. No idea who the geezer is as he's not done any campaigning for us to the best of my recollection. But that's usually the way of it.

> 'Any discourtesy is yours and God help the people of Clacton if they are asked to vote for you. I have copied in the editor of the *Clacton and Frinton Gazette* newspaper with my comments so he can know what their UKIP candidate's standards are.'

Shall I be apologetic and placatory? No. Rudely polite is always more fun.

> 'Thank you for your email. I stand by my observations and will naturally give your own an appropriate level of consideration.
> 'I note that you have copied in the editor of the *Gazette* and trust that this has brought you joy.
> 'Upon the resignation of a member for any reason, it is usual to express regret. Unfortunately, I am unable to do so on this occasion.
> 'Kind regards'

I don't hear back from him.

Saturday 13th May 2017

I arrive in Clacton just after lunch and head straight to Mark Stephenson's print shop. The meeting with the UKIP councillors is in the back office. There are thirteen people there in total, which means that quite a few have stayed away. The absentees include Mr Bray who's resigned from the group in a fit of pique.

They regard me suspiciously.

'Everything I'm about to tell you is confidential,' I say. 'But because it's confidential, I'm going to tell you everything.'

I've already spoken to the Party Chairman and arrange to put him on speakerphone so he can confirm what I'm saying and add to it where necessary. Oakden explains exactly how they ended up stuck with this carpetbagger.

As there's nothing more to tell, we hang up. The phone rings again immediately. It's Peter Whittle. He just wants a general chat.

'Mate,' I say, 'I'm being grilled this very minute by the Clacton councillors. Can I put you on speaker?'

He agrees.

'Ladies and gentlemen. I've got the deputy leader on the line. Say hello to everyone, Peter.'

He does, and explains his own understanding about the rejection of Bray, installation of Coad and ultimate triumph of me.

'You know, I've worked closely with Paul for over three years. He gave me huge amounts of help in my own campaigns for a council seat, for Eltham in the general election and then for the London Assembly. He always puts the party before his own ambitions. He's a really decent chap, you know? And you're genuinely lucky to have him.'

Well. My cheeks tinge and we hang up.

Councillor Andy Pemberton cracks a big smile.

'How much did you have to pay him to say that?'

He's teasing. I honestly wasn't expecting that call but am very glad that Peter made it.

Ted Whitmore comes over with his hand outstretched.

'Before this meeting I was prepared to rip strips off you. You now have my full backing.'

I look at the rest of the room.

'Is everybody satisfied?'

They are.

'In that case, how about I call James Dwan at the *Gazette* and have him take a few photos?'

They agree. Dwan duly comes over for his big scoop.

Formalities over, I have a quick coffee with him.

'Oh, by the way,' he says. 'A man in your London branch forwarded me a couple of emails from you yesterday. He's really annoyed.'

I struggle for a moment to think of who that could be and then recall it must be that Lindsey fella.

'Ah yes. And are you going to print his scathing observations? I really don't care if you do.'

'No, it's of no relevance at all up here. But your response to him made me laugh.'

CHAPTER FORTY

Let's Go to Work

Monday 15th May 2017

DELVING THROUGH RECENT EDITIONS of the *Clacton and Frinton Gazette* to tie down the local issues to put on our leaflets, a piece in the 2nd May edition about Tory candidate Giles Watling jumps out:

'I voted remain in the referendum, but above all I am a democrat,' he said.

Sadly for him, more than 70% of Clacton residents voted the other way.

I give Harry Cole of *The Sun* a call.

'Now Harry. Do you think I'm an absolute scoundrel and would be an utter disaster if elected as an MP?'

'No, not at all.'

A boon is craved.

Tuesday 16th May 2017

Harry really is a lovely fellow. It's on page 2 of today's edition:

'UKIP seat glee: hopes of holding their only Commons seat boosted after Tory candidate reveals he backed Remain.'

That's Campaign Leaflet #1 sorted out. The famous photo of Theresa May with the 'I'm In' poster from the referendum. A screenshot taken from a Youtube video of Watling which has been precisely-paused to make him look especially ugly. A couple of quotes from the *Financial Times* and *Sky News* about the threat of soft-Brexit Tories. Giles' unwise comment to the *Gazette* and a chunk from today's *Sun*.

The last two are exactly the same story of course but, like a mirror facing a mirror, its reach is, potentially, infinite. I hope.

'Don't let the Conservatives betray your vote for Brexit.'

Wednesday 17th May 2017

All campaigns need a launch. Maybe a nice conference room in the Kingscliff Hotel? Perhaps the Colvin Memorial Temple masonic lodge? Possibly even the Princes Theatre?

Stuff that. We're doing it outside the Jaywick Community Resource Centre.

Sky News, the *Washington Post, ITV,* the *Guardian, RSI Switzerland* and the *BBC* accordingly all get the chance to see this badly-neglected former holiday town. The view to the ocean across the golden sands is calmly beautiful and the chalet cottages charming, or at least, they were once. The moon-craters in the roads and the high hillocks of fly-tipping are less enticing.

Residents are surprised when we knock their doors and more so when they realise that we're not looking for freak-show footage.

'We never see politicians here,' one tells me.

'You'll get sick of the sight of me if UKIP win the seat,' I tell him.

There's a bright pride in the community. Everyone seems to know everyone else and they look out for each other because the state does not. The damage done by Channel 5 with that blasted documentary series hasn't been forgotten though.

'Get that FACKING camera off my house,' comes one yell through an open window.

Thursday 18th May 2017

The Conservative manifesto is launched. I haven't read it but am glad others have.

The Daily Telegraph:

'Middle-class pensioners to lose benefits under Tory plan to fund social care'.

The Express:

'A GUARANTEE that the state pension will rise by at least 2.5% a year is to be dropped by the Conservatives.'

The National Pensioners Convention:

'The Conservative manifesto pledge on social care offers the worst of all possible worlds for millions of older people and their families.'

Thousands of Clacton retirees will be delighted. Perhaps Theresa May has a secret crush on me. That might explain why she's working hard for UKIP to win here.

Campaign leaflet #2 is finalised on the back of this.

Friday 19th May 2017

Paul Oakden gives me a ring at 7.30 am. Nuttall was due to bring the UKIP Battle Bus to Clacton this afternoon. It was heading to Thurrock and Dagenham first of all and I was planning on meeting it en route with Peter Harris.

'Cancelled I'm afraid,' Oakden tells me. 'It was damaged overnight.'

'Oh?' My eyebrow raises. 'How?'

'Wing mirror knocked off while it was parked up.'

'Leftards do you think? It would be hard to miss the fact that it's a Kipper bus.'

'Probably not. Chances are it was clipped by another HGV as there's no other damage although we really can't say. It'll be fixed by tomorrow and we'll postpone it till then.'

Pah. What a nuisance. I'm still going to have some fun anyway and get straight on to Twitter.

'Now hear this! The UKIP Battle Bus has been mysteriously damaged overnight so will now be in Clacton at the weekend and not today.'

The press are straight on to me, just as I'd hoped. *Sky, the BBC, The Mirror, Guido, The Evening Standard, ITV* and of course the *Clacton and Frinton Gazette*. But the only quote I give is to Tom Rayner who attempts to tie me down as to whether it's being said that lefty vandals have been at work.

'I have no idea Tom. I wasn't there.'

Jasvir Degun, OBE and Labour lad, gets in touch. He's obviously been very worried about me.

'Just seen the *BBC News*. Are you sure you didn't have a go at the wing mirror yourself just to get in the press?' He chuckles.

'Naw. But between you and me I am milking it a bit.'

'I don't blame you.'

'Where are you standing?' I ask.

'Nowhere this time round. I went for retirement seats but didn't get one.'

'What a shame.'

'I know. The party owes me for it and I think they know. Hopefully I'll get a by-election soon enough.'

'Good. I'd wish you well, albeit through gritted teeth. Horrible lefty that you are.'

'Likewise, you awful right winger.'

Anyway, it's not a wasted day for publicity by any means as I'm all over *Sky News* with the footage that was recorded the other day in Jaywick. Digging at Douglarse of course.

'Douglas Carswell was always semi-detached, but this is a Brexit seat, that's the important thing.'

'Right across the political parties, Labour supporters, Tory supporters and obviously UKIP supporters in this seat wanted out of the EU, so I want to pick up on that support and get a proper UKIP MP here for the first time.'

Best of all, the footage is introduced by Claudia-Liza. Be still, o my beating heart.

Saturday 20th May 2017

It's 9 am and the Clacton Crew are at the Bowling Green Pub, waiting for Paul Nuttall to turn up. The Battle Bus is already waiting in the car park but Paul's being driven down from the north west where he's spent the night. Very early start then, poor bloke. And he's late.

As soon as he's dropped off at the door of the pub Paul's accosted by branch secretary John Wrigley.

'It's very rude to turn up this late. Some of our members have been here for an hour and it's most discourteous of you.'

Nobody's safe from a Wrigley roasting. He's given me a few and not even the leader of a national political party is safe. Nuttall takes it in good spirit, apologises, grabs John across the shoulder and invites him and his wife Joan on to the charabanc.

The famous Battle Bus is rather like something out of Spinal Tap. Low lighting, a bar and bench beds. No groupies though, sadly. We spend the short trip into town dissecting Paul's performance in the party leaders' debate two days previously. I thought he'd done well but he bashes himself up over the gaffe of calling Plaid Cymru's representative 'Natalie' on a couple of occasions.

'Gawain's asked me to Tweet a picture of my hand with "Leanne Wood" written on it in marker pen but I'm not convinced,' he says.

'Well, it would be a laugh. Although you could annoy the woman even more by referring to her as "James Woods" from now on instead.'

Disgorged outside McDonalds it takes some time to move through the media morass to reach the Moon and Starfish for a quick pint (even though it's not yet noon). Andy Pemberton leads the way and tells the staff that the two great men are coming. It's a Wetherspoons, so there won't be a problem. Besides, Farage had a photo-op in this very pub during the Carswell by-election.

Except this time there is a problem and the manageress says we're not welcome. Moon and Starfish? Chocolate Starfish more like.

Dang. We'll have to have a trip to the famous ice cream Kiosk at the pier head instead. Mike Bush, top geezer, jogs ahead to buy us both a frozen treat. I shout after him:

'Lollies Mike!'

Ice creams tend to melt and we want to avoid an Ed-Miliband-bacon-sarnie type situation. He doesn't hear and buys us both a '99'.

Photographs are taken by Getty and others but, unfortunately, we have to throw away the dissolving remainder of our cones. This is a shameful waste of food, especially when there are starving children in Newcastle.

Paul heads off and the rest of us decide to coalesce around Mark's print shop to pick up, and deliver, the big pile of leaflets inside. Trouble is, the shop's locked and we can't get hold of him.

Instead, John Rees Evans, lovely bloke, films me for one of the campaign videos he's producing for several of the 'more interesting' candidates. I really appreciate this. The theme is: 'put your money on the dark horse.' Me, in other words. I'm perfectly aware that this is a mountainous struggle.

Monday 22nd May 2017

Gawain forwards an email with a single question mark being his own contribution to the discussion.

> 'Dear Paul Oakley,
>
> 'I am writing an article for HOPE not hate about your candidacy in Clacton.
> 'Could you please confirm that you have held a personal relationship with Claire Khaw.
>
> 'Yours sincerely,
> 'David Lawrence'

Boring. Not this again. I fill Towler in on the background and tell him this.

'We never had a "relationship" in the Biblical sense if that's what's being implied and you might like to advise this weasel to be very careful what he writes.'

'Thanks for that,' says Gawain. 'What skunks they are.'
We hear nothing further from that little clump of arse fluff.

Much more importantly, there's been a bombing at the Manchester Arena at a concert by Ariana Grande. Filled with children. Twenty-two people have been murdered by Mr Salman Ramadan Abedi. Thankfully, that piece of shit died in the blast too.

Wednesday 24th May 2017

Been planning the campaign and am horrified to discover there are no hustings in the seat. At all. Not by a church, old peoples' group, school, round table or anything. Given that I reckon hustings are the bestest bit of all elections, I'm not having it and email the rest of the candidates.

'Who's up for it?'

Everyone. Apart from Tory Giles Watling, whose agent Stephen Canning replies on his behalf.

'I'm afraid we're going to decline this invitation, thank you.'

Harrumph. Taking tips from his frit leader's decision to avoid debating Jermy Corbyn it seems. We'll see about that.

Thursday 25th May 2017

The UKIP manifesto launch is taking place at the Institute of Civil Engineers in Westminster. It's been postponed from yesterday as a mark of respect in the aftermath of the Manchester atrocity.

The manifesto covers a whole range of policies, but given the evil murder of those children enjoying a bloody pop concert, fundamentalist Islam is on the agenda.

There are no 'thoughts and prayers' from Paul Nuttall.

'It's not enough to light candles or signal our upset on social media. When you are the leader of a political party you have a duty to set out how you would protect the people of your country from the threat to their entire way of life. I was criticised by certain sections of the media for calling rrrrradical Islam a cancer in our society following the Westminster attack. I make no apologies for saying this and I will repeat it today. It is a cancer which needs to be cut out.'

Michael Crick has a question when he's finished.

'Mr Nuttall. Your opening speech. Wasn't that blatantly exploiting Manchester for election. . .'

'Get stuffed,' yells I.

'Rubbish,' says someone else.

'Boo,' say many more.

Nuttall nonetheless answers politely.

'No, Michael. It certainly wasn't exploiting Manchester. What I wanted to do was to ensure that the democratic process continued because the one thing that they hate most about us is our democracy. And they want to see it destroyed. And the best way of telling them that they won't win is by getting out and campaigning and debating these issues.'

The next in line isn't raving about our smashing policies either.

'Andy Bell, Five News. Following on from that, can you confirm that you haven't added anything in to your manifesto since what happened on Monday night? That everything you've presented here was already there before the events in Manchester?'

There's a minor hint of a sneer on Nuttall's face.

'No. It went to print on Saturday night.'

In your FACE, Bell.

Laura Kuenssberg has a try.

'It sounds like you're near as dammit blaming the Prime Minister for this attack and the circumstances that led to it. . .'

Someone interrupts in a very forceful manner.

"Is that the BBC? Is that the BBC?"

This is from Robert Andersen of UKIP Lambeth. Wish he wasn't shouting at the top of his voice from right behind my ear, but he's on the money.

'Crawl back down your hole' offers Stuart Agnew MEP.

'Don't you understand English?' queries the Earl of Dartmouth.

Naturally, Crick comes to interview some of we ruffians afterwards. Andersen explains.

'Why should journalists not be shouted down? Do you have a God-given right? Are you the authority? You are part of the problem which has led to where we are today.'

Crick isn't getting it, or at least pretending not to, so I interject.

'If the media don't ask stupid, insulting questions then our people won't react in that way. Ask some sensible questions. It really is as simple as that.'

He gets it now.

We head off to the MOG where all members present of The Crew sign my copy of the manifesto. Paul Oakden has some advice.

'You need to get a wet beer glass to sign it too.'

I do just that, carefully placing a pint to mark a ring of finest English ale on the title page.

Friday 26th May 2017

After much pestering, Clacton Tory Watling has graciously condescended to address a hustings after all and a vicar in Walton-on-the-Naze, Peter Edwards, has offered his church as the venue.

'I understand this is very short notice, and I expect Mr Watling's diary is already extremely full. However, if there is any chance he might be available on one of those evenings I will invite the other candidates along.'

The rest of we candidates will be happy, nay – honoured - to fit in with Mr Watling's schedule.

Saturday 27th May 2017

I receive a wonderful pledge request in my role as an election agent. It comes from an organisation calling itself 'Lewisham Is For Europe'. The reply as follows.

'Thank you very much for your letter in which you ask the following questions of Keith Forster, the UKIP candidate for Lewisham East.

'If you are elected as MP for the constituency, we would like to know if you will:

- 'Champion the UK's membership of the EU as best for the national interest

- 'Oppose the so-called "hard" Brexit (leaving the single market)

- 'Support a referendum on any deal that emerges from negotiations, and which includes the option of remaining in the EU.'

'I would normally pass such queries over to our candidate straight away, but am sure Keith won't mind if I don't trouble him with yours on this occasion. The answers are:

- 'No.

- 'No.

- 'No.

'I take it you've never heard of UKIP. Look us up on the internet.'
Sometimes my eyes ache from the effort of rolling them.

Sunday 28th May 2017

The Clacton candidates are doing *Sunday Politics East* hosted by Stewart White. We're all at the Golf Club at 11 am, apart from the Lib Dem who, being a non-resident carpetbagger, hasn't made it in time.

Tut!

I spoke to the journo Chris Bond, who's organised it, in advance.

'If it's outside, please make sure that we're not in direct sunlight. The Missis doesn't like it when I squint into the camera and show the wrinkles.'

'OK,' she says. 'I'll see what we can do.'

It is outdoors and we are indeed facing direct sunlight. I insist on moving my seat to The Dark Side, but as the sun rolls around during the shoot, it's a waste of time.

Compere White focuses his gaze on me.

'So you're planning to be the second ever UKIP member of parliament are you Mr Oakley?'

'Second?' I reply. 'No, third. After Carswell and Mark Reckless.'

'But there's only been one. Douglas Carswell.'

'Not true. Unless I dreamed about campaigning for Reckless and then going to his victory party. Although, that's always a possibility.'

We bicker for a bit, but he's underbriefed. Why are journos suddenly forgetting about Mark? White isn't the first.

Tuesday 30th May 2017

Chris Mendes, techy chap, has finished my Clacton website and it's just gone live. It really is impressive and we receive our first email through it within the hour. Great!

But.

'Your representative for UKIP organised a press event at Lifehouse spa and hotel on the 24th April. They walked out without paying the outstanding amount, and despite several requests for payment we have not received contact back.'

There's a bill attached for £254. Beggared if I'm settling it though, so make enquiries with the branch. Mark Stephenson confirms this was something that had been booked by Arron Banks when he met with the UKIP councillors last month.

It's sorted out with Arron's team and the invoice is paid, but I've got better things to do than act as a volunteer debt collector.

Wednesday 31st May 2017

Decide to spend a couple of minutes browsing the Hate not Hope website while enjoying a cuppa. Here we are: 'UKIP racism roundup'.

Various whines about various of our candidates, then a fascinating nugget which is news to me:

'The party also deselected leading anti-Muslim activist Anne Marie Waters following pressure from HOPE not hate and other media sources earlier this month.'

Presumably in the same way as a remora steers a great white shark. The NEC hadn't noticed that this lot were squeaking about Anne Marie. A pity, as the vote on adopting her might have gone the other way if we had.

Thursday 1st June 2017

My free election leaflet is finally being posted through Clacton letterboxes. Late, late, late. Sod you, Royal Mail. But it's raised some interest as a chap called Mark Coventry gets in touch on the back of it.

'I am a professional photographer specialising in Headshots and Portraits and as I'm sure you are aware your headshot is where most people will gain their first impression of you.

'Please don't take offence as this is meant in a constructive way, but to be blunt, you look vacant and unapproachable.

'If you would like to have a headshot that does what it is meant to do, I would be more than happy to help you.'

Yeah. He's probably right. Although I'm not taking up the offer.

On a positive note, the Party have paid for two separate full page adverts in today's *Gazette*. One on the Tories breaking faith with OAPs and the other slagging off the Remainerast Tory Giles Watling.

Friday 2nd June 2017

Guess who's coming to Clacton today to endorse the first-rate UKIP candidate? That's right. Nigel. We've timed this perfectly so the coverage hits the *Gazette* on polling day itself. Aren't we clever?

As expected, an immense crowd of journalists builds around him as he arrives. Would be nice if these dastards moved away to a respectful distance as we're more interested in meeting the voters. They do, eventually, as five young boys between 8 and 12 years of age want to get their hero's autograph. They also ask for Nigel's.

Farage is talking politics to the journalists but he's talking about more important things with me.

'Have you wet a line here yet?'

'No, but I've had my new beachcaster rod in the car all week. Just not had time to go out.'

'Head towards the Jaywick beaches,' he tells me. 'There's a lot of rays feeding out that way at the moment.'

I certainly shall.

Dan Jukes is fielding all his calls as we head past the arcades. He taps Nigel's arm while he's in the middle of a walking interview.

'You need to take this.'

He does. Jukes bends towards my ear in a conspiratorial manner.

'You won't fucking believe this. That Tory MP Craig Mackinlay is going to be prosecuted for expenses offences in Thanet.'

Don't care if it does expose my yellow teeth. I can't help grinning like a chimpanzee.

Nigel hands the phone back to Dan. He seems deflated. Hopefully our candidate, Hell's Angel Reverend Stuart Piper, will be the next MP for South Thanet on the back of this. He's a great chap, but he isn't Farage.

CHAPTER FORTY-ONE

Thwarted. Again.

Saturday 3rd June 2017
DAYTIME

THIS IS THE VERY LAST SATURDAY before polling day. UKIP is flooding its best seats with activists. The London members have been strictly-told that they're to campaign only in Thurrock for Tim Aker or in Dagenham for Peter Harris. There's still a lot to do in Clacton but today I'm going to join the throng and help Harris break through from his second placing in the 2015 election.

It's a two-way struggle between him and Labour's Jon Cruddas, both of whom have been all over the media. The Tory, Julie Marson, has been invisible. Some of her leaflets have accidentally fallen out of peoples' letterboxes and into Kippers' pockets and they're laughable. On one in particular the word 'Conservative' appears just twice whereas 'Theresa May' crops up a dozen times. As the PM is now no better than a greying corpse, chained to the legs of her poor candidates, this is all to the good.

Peter Harris can and will be the next MP.

We're congregating at his business workshop in the middle of the seat. The swarm of people gradually grows and we're ready to go to work. There is Harris. There is me. There is a chap from my branch. And there is my dog.

Four of us. Four.

Facing us are scores, perhaps hundreds, of Labour and Momentum condottieri. They've infested all the streets and have a stall at the railway station. But we shall never surrender.

Peter solemnly hands over a megaphone and we climb into his car which is covered with UKIP logos. Labour are going to get a drive-by dissing from me.

'Don't vote for John Cruddas. He's a waste of space.'

'Make Dagenham and Rainham great again. Vote Peter Harris UKIP.'

EVENING
London Bridge terror attacks. Jesus.

Sunday 4th June 2014
Giles Watling sends out a missive to all his fellow-candidates.

'After last night's terrible events in London I and my team are standing down for the time being. No campaigning until further notice. How long this lasts is anybody's guess, but I sincerely hope it will not impinge on tomorrow night's hustings.'

Up to you mate. I beg to differ.

'UKIP take the view that these vermin should not be allowed to disrupt our democracy so our campaigning will continue.'

Monday 5th June 2017
MORNING
Doing some delivering, just me and the dog. Dwan calls.

'Looking for another quote from you. It's about a letter we've had from Jeff Bray.'

'Sorry James, but I'm not going to slag him off. Better things to do.'

'You might want to this time. This is my draft copy so far:

'The man who was sidelined by UKIP in favour of Clacton General Election candidate Paul Oakley has called on voters to back the Conservatives to safeguard Brexit."

The sad, sad little man.

'Well, you'll still get nothing from me because I'm far too grand to respond to such pettiness. But give me half an hour and you'll have something.'

I hang up and call Mark Stephenson. Being the leader of the UKIP group on the council he'll bash Bray up on my behalf.

'How about this?' he asks.

'I'll grant you it's an interesting letter from ex-UKIP Councillor Jeff Bray. I find myself asking if he would have made the same statement had he been the parliamentary candidate."

EVENING

The sky has darkened. We're in for very heavy weather, starting from this minute. I park the tank round the back of All Saints' Church and head to the vicarage where the Reverend Edwards resides. I have my suspicions he's a Watling supporter. Typical pinko parson.

My purple party golf brolly is open against the horizontal rain. Then:

'Yoo-hoo! UKIP! UKIP! Wooh! Woop!'

Blimey. It's a group of teenage girls and they're Kippers. A contrast to the low-IQ social justice warriors of that age and sex that I'm used to seeing in hillbilly London.

Quick briefing in the padre's parlour and then across the road to the church. It's full, despite the short notice. We've each been given a bar stool to sit on. I'm unimpressed. This will require me to stay upright at all times like a Val Doonican rather than slouch and stick my crossed legs out like a pissed-off 15-year-old boy as I prefer.

There are opening speeches and Chris Southall of the Greens tries to gang up on me. Sadly, he does it all by himself.

'And that's why,' he exclaims, 'you cannot trust UKIP on the environment.'

There is a pause. He looks at me and I look back. The pause continues. Realising it would be ill-mannered not to respond I do so eventually.

'Sorry – what was that? I wasn't listening.'

Yet the main attacks are all directed at Tory Giles Watling. That is completely unacceptable. He replies to all barbs in a sonorous RADA voice but it's clear he's not used to this. Worse, he's relying on notes. Notes! Then again, his career has been based on the comfort of scripts.

Well, at least the Reverend likes him as per my suspicions. That's why he allows Watling to drone on for as long as he likes while cutting me off after 15 seconds or so of each answer to the pre-submitted audience questions which are supposed to be directed at all candidates. And, perhaps, why he allows one question for me alone which asks for an explanation as to why I've got the audacity to stand here at all.

'Winston Churchill, Margaret Thatcher and Tony Blair had no link to their constituencies when they first stood for them. When elected, I, too, will make you proud of me.'

Neither the Lib Dem nor the Eng Dem are asked for their own excuses.

Summing up, I have some fun.

'This is a two-horse race. If you want the Tory to lose you're going to have to vote for UKIP no matter if you're a Liberal, Green, Labour or anything else. Whether you like it or not.'

That goes down surprisingly well with the lefties in the audience.

The last query of the night is from the vicar himself.

'Will the candidates tell us what their favourite biscuit is?'

Ho ho ho. I bet his sermons are a real hoot.

'I don't like biscuits,' I say.

He presses the point.

'Well, if you insist – pork scratchings. They're a bit like a biscuit. But savoury. And made from pigs.'

A crowd crush round me afterwards. A weaselly geezer stands quietly off to the side. After the melee disperses, he walks up.

'Are you Paul Oakley?'

Thicko.

'Er – yes.'

'In that case, consider yourself served.'

He hands me an envelope and scuttles off as fast as his wee legs will carry him. I'm perplexed.

'That was Richard Everett,' John Wrigley tells me.

Aha. Everett has been indignantly dessicating himself ever since the party chose a decent candidate instead of his BFF, Jeff Bray. I've been vaguely aware of tales of his furious anger but haven't paid them any attention.

I open the envelope. It's supposed to be a legal letter-before-action. As an NEC member, I am allegedly duly-served on behalf of a member of staff at UKIP Head Office who referred to Bray's 'muslamic' posts in an email. What rubbish. Were I a compassionate fellow, I would feel an acute sense of embarrassment on Mr Everett's behalf. But I am not.

I head to the Victory pub, dropping Everett's letter in the bin on the way. Going for a pint with James Dwan and his brother in order to bend their ears. In particular, is Theresa May going to visit the town before polling day? Or any other famous Tory?

'No,' says James. 'Not that we've been notified and they're too late for our deadline now, anyway.'

Another gift! So let's review everything.

- Dougie does a Hermann Göring and cheats the hangman, leaving Clacton free.

- The PM calls an unnecessary election.

- Jeff Bray is an idiot.

- Your Dear Author slips into the vacancy.
- The Tories choose a Remainer for a Brexit Central seat.
- Theresa May thinks it a good idea to mug a retirement town with a dementia tax.
- No Conservative grandee is going to bother making a trip here.
- And then, last of all, there's the name of this very ale house, Victory pub.

On the downside, Hope not Hate have been no help. If they'd produced 'Oakley Attack' leaflets Andy Pemberton was going to get hold of a big pile with the pretence of delivering them. I and Nigel would then have autographed the lot and we'd have flogged them at twenty quid apiece to benefit party funds. Yet despite their threats, these blowflies have done nothing at all in the seat that we're aware of.

Perhaps, just perhaps: Allah wills it.

Thursday 8th June 2017

General Election Day. I'm at Clacton station with Andy to meet the commuters before the first train to Liverpool Street at 5.20 am. Yes. 5.20 am. I'm never normally up at this time unless fishing tackle and open water are somehow involved.

Pemberton is both a diamond and a dynamo. While still dark, he'd scampered round the constituency with a pocketful of cable ties to fly-post UKIP corex boards to council-owned lampposts, roadsigns and fences. He also takes the lead when it comes to reaching the commuters now the sun's up. Rather than stand politely by the station entrance to engage the (very few) potential passengers, he rushes through every carriage on every train as it sits at the platform, leaving a leaflet on all the seats. The cleaners will love us.

Rush hour, such as it is, being over by 8.30, we head off to leaflet streets in separate areas. I pick up a copy of today's *Gazette* on the way to my own patch. There's a double-page spread with colour photos of Nigel's visit on Friday. Two other pics of me with stories. And a nice letter from Ian Cross describing me as an 'exceptional candidate'.

Late morning, I head to the polling station by the Sainsbury's off St John's Road to greet the voters with the dog, who is cute. This will persuade them that I, too, am lovely. My fellow-candidate, the Independent Caroline Shearer, turns up to help her Mum cast her own vote. And her Mum, Caroline tells me with a loud voice and a big grin, is giving that vote to me.

The rest of the day is spent leafleting, leafleting, leafleting. It gets to six o'clock when I'd earlier planned to pack it in. But then suffer an attack of superstition so decide to deliver a few more. An extra one or two votes may be enough to pull me past the winning post. I have the same feeling at 6.30, 7.00, and 8.00 and finally finish at ten past.

I head back to the Harris' caravan for a bite to eat. They're not around for a gossip because they're down in Dagenham for Peter's own campaign so I decide to settle down for a refreshing forty winks.

Friday 9th June 2017

I had set the alarm for 10 pm last night with a view to arriving at the town hall not later than 11 and just after the ballot boxes had been collected.

I slept through that alarm. The time is now 12:48 am. Shit.

I quickly iron the collar, cuffs and top front section of a shirt, missing out the rest. Being a fogey, and thus an enthusiast for waistcoats, has its advantages.

Speeding along the empty roads, the victor's speech is formulated. I'll finally be able to dust-off that quote from the 1980s horror film that wasn't used at the Euros back in 2014.

Arriving at 1.30, there's a parking space right outside the front door. A good omen? No.

Allah does not will it.

Branch Chairman Tony greets me.

'We were worried that you weren't coming. It's not looking good.'

John Wrigley says hello.

'It's not looking good.'

Mary Newton shakes her head.

'It's not looking good.'

I do a few interviews and candidates and agents are then called over to assess the spoiled ballot papers. Unlike at London counts, there are none featuring cartoons of ladies' bosoms or willies with all jizz coming out the end which are always a highlight of the evening.

One's marked 'Don't Worry' in Conservative Giles Watling's box. Munificently, I tell him that I'd have been happy for that one to have been added to his score. It's obvious that it wouldn't make any difference.

There are also a pair of papers which are presumably from the same household, both scrawled across and marked 'Taxation is theft' and 'Ron Paul'.

'Sound,' I say. 'Those are clearly meant for me. But I won't make a fuss as it changes nothing.'

Labour candidate Tasha Osben is nonetheless incoherently incensed.

'But. . . but. . . tax is investing in, er, public, services. . . and. . . and. . .'

At precisely 3 am, being, again, that Devil's Hour of legend when demonic powers are at their height, we march on to the stage for the announcement.

Just as we're lined up, my phone starts ringing. I ignore it. Then the thing rings again. I pay it no heed but both David Grace and Robin Tilbrook, who are flanking me, peer disapprovingly.

The damage is:

Conservative	27,031	(61.2%)
Labour	11,203	(25.4%)
UKIP	3,357	(7.6%)

Crestfallen, I return to the car. The irritating caller was south east Kipper Tim Scott.

'Tut tut,' I say to him. 'Ringing me when I'm on the stage for the declaration indeed.'

'Yes. I was watching you live on the TV and was hoping you might answer. A bit cheeky I know. But couldn't resist it.'

Friday 9th June 2017. Again

Yup, I know it's the same day as the previous entry. Having spent some time in the Tesco hypermarket on the way back from the Town Hall to buy lots and lots of wine (as a thank you to the Harris family, not to drown my sorrows), I've managed about thirty minutes of fitful sleep before the alarm goes off again. This time, I don't snooze through it. That counts, more or less, as a new day.

Last night BBC Essex had requested an interview first thing.

'Could you get to our office in Chelmsford for 8 am?' they'd asked.

'Not unless you're hoping that your lead story will be: "UKIP candidate killed in pile-up after dozing off at the wheel". Send a radio car.'

They have. Usual questions, usual answers: 'sick as a parrot'; 'we wuz robbed'.

'But are things over for UKIP though?' I'm then asked.

'In this, as in so many matters, we may seek comfort from the words of Obi-Wan Kenobi in Star Wars. "If you strike us down, we shall become more powerful than you can possibly imagine." So: No.'

I sit in the garden browsing the horrorshow news stories on the web when Peter appears having spent the rest of the night, such as it was, in a Dagenham hotel. He, too, has been trounced, coming a poor third behind Labour and the Tory runner-up. He received 3,246 votes or 7.1%. There's some relief in this. He was an established candidate with local links so my own disastrous showing probably had nothing to do with me being a fancy-London-counsel-carpetbagger.

There was something in the air which none of us could have done anything about. The worst result of all was Tory Craig Mackinlay increasing his majority in Thanet South in spite of the fact he's now facing criminal charges. Mass madness or what?

Anyway, we've both kept our deposits at least.

My phone rings. It's Oakden. We run through some of our more notable disasters of the evening on speaker but he's then, very mildly, a little impatient.

'Paul. NEC business. Can we have a word in private?'

We do.

'Nuttall's going to resign. I can't persuade him otherwise.'

'Oh, crap. Shall I have a try?'

'Go ahead. I doubt you'll have any luck. On the assumption that he's off, the NEC needs to appoint an interim leader. Alan Bown's proposing Steve Crowther. Are you prepared to second him?'

I don't have to give it very much thought.

'Definitely.'

Nonetheless, I try to dial Nuttall a couple of times. His phone rings off and he doesn't call back.

CHAPTER FORTY-TWO

Time to Relax? Er—no

Monday 12th June 2017

NEC MEETING, AND A MUTUAL DE-BRIEF on the election. There are tales of terror from around the nation and nothing, nothing at all, that we could have done about it.

We then run through and decide upon the options for the leadership election. Nominations will open on 23rd June, which happens to be the first anniversary of Independence Day. The result will be proclaimed at party conference on 29th September. A long while, but we're heading straight into the holiday period and there's no point declaring the result in July or August.

Paul Oakden announces a short break and accosts me as I leave the room.

'Jonathan Arnott.'

'What about him?'

'He's resigning as General Secretary. Largely, but not exclusively, because of the Integration Agenda. Do you want to take his place? Can't think of anyone better.'

Well. I narrow my eyes in suspicion.

He goes on.

'There's a lot of work involved. You'll be dealing with a string of inane complaints which members insist on making about each other. And, needless to say, the role's unpaid.'

'Oh,' I say. 'Sounds wonderful. Go on then.'

The rest of the NEC vote upon it and I'm condemned to take over.

Tuesday 27th June 2017

Peter Whittle is hosting a launch for Douglas Murray's book, *The Strange Death of Europe*, at his New Culture Forum in Tufton Street. It's had excellent reviews, even in the *Evening Standard*, and I'm looking forward to reading it. If, indeed, that is the expression, as it's said to be a most depressing account of how western culture is to be defeated by fundamentalist Islam.

The meeting's full, and I have to stand at the rear with many others.

Murray delivers an excellent speech and then there are questions. Mine is the best.

'As you look ahead, are there any optimistic signs? Or, like the Roman, do you seem to see the river Tiber foaming with much blood?'

Everyone laughs.

'Oh. I see what you did there,' he answers.

He has little optimism.

At this, a hand grabs my shoulder. It's Paul Nuttall. Wearing a baseball cap.

'Do you fancy a quick drink?'

I do. We head for the MOG.

'What's with the hat?' I ask. 'Hope you're not following the sartorial stylings of William Hague.'

'Naw, I'm just sick of people giving me grief when they recognise me in public. It's one of the many down-sides to having been leader.'

Maybe so, but we're grateful that he'd put aside his personal preference for a quiet life and battled as our leader for the sake of the cause. Admirable.

Tuesday 11th July 2017

My dedicated email address for the Clacton campaign has proved useful once more, albeit from beyond the grave. Something nice for once? No. A solicitor called Gerald Shamash from the firm Steel and Shamash has used the account as a point of contact, presumably because I'm now UKIP General Secretary.

The General Secretary of the Labour Party is responsible for employing staff, campaign and media strategies, running the constitutional and policy committees, organising Party Conference, liaising with the Party of European Socialists, ensuring legal propriety and preparing campaign literature. They are also a Registered Treasurer under the Political Parties, Elections and Referendums Act.

Shamash evidently hasn't realised that the General Secretary of

UKIP does none of these things.

I'm aware of him and his firm. They represented Labour's Phil Woolas in his unsuccessful court battle against Lib Dem Elwyn Watkins for making false statements in an election. Woolas stood down as MP for Oldham East as a result and a by-election followed.

They were also solicitors for Labour MPs Jim Devine, David Chaytor and Elliot Morley who were all ultimately jailed over the parliamentary expenses scandal.

The firm's website proudly states that Shamash himself has been a solicitor to the Labour Party for over 20 years.

The letter refers to the successful libel action which their MPs Barron, Champion and Healey had brought against our MEP Jane Collins and then goes on.

> 'After a close analysis of the documents provided it is apparent that UKIP agreed to commit a substantial financial contribution to this litigation, namely £50,000 plus VAT. We attach a clip of the relevant correspondence referring to a decision to do so by the UKIP NEC. It is clear from this correspondence that UKIP had a political interest in this case and sought to gain a political advantage by instructing the then representatives for UKIP, RMPI, not to settle this matter until after the 2015 General Election.
>
> 'We are satisfied that this is evidence of UKIP's attempt to frustrate this litigation which has caused our Clients to incur costs that otherwise would not have been incurred had the Defendant settled when presented with the opportunity to do so.
>
> 'We therefore invite you to agree to be adjoined to these proceedings as a non-party for the purposes of costs.'

Jane hasn't paid all the costs so these people are now going to chase the Party for money. I've no knowledge of the legal background as all this took place before I was elected to the National Executive myself.

UKIP is kept going by a handful of large donors and by subscriptions from rank-and-file members, many of whom get by on low incomes. They haven't libelled these Labour MPs but these solicitors are now looking to them for a payoff.

Repugnant cunts.

Sunday 16th July 2017

Nigel Farage has given an interview to the *Sunday Politics* in the Westminster Arms about the prospective choices for leader.

'If UKIP goes down the route of being a party that is anti-'the-religion-of-Islam' then, frankly, it's finished. I don't think there's any public appetite for that. Some, but it's tiny.'

He doesn't mention her by name, but it's obvious who he means.

Monday 17th July 2017

I have to speak to Nigel after his piece yesterday. I've no problem with Anne Marie Waters as an activist, or even as a councillor, AM, MP or whatever. We should celebrate the rich diversity of UKIP. But having her as leader?

Farage is right. A victory for Waters might destroy the party and, much more importantly, Brexit itself. However unfairly, the press would portray us as Islam-obsessives and discredit our main cause on the back of it.

As there are going to be seven or more candidates, she might sneak through the middle. However, if Nigel endorses an alternative then the members will do as they're told and vote for that person instead as I now tell him.

'Probably,' he says, 'but I haven't decided yet. I'm going to give it another week, week and a half, until nominations close before deciding.'

I try some arm-twisting.

'What of Whittle? He's not quite as exciting as you but he is a safe pair of hands. Even if he ticked off the MEPs with the Integration Agenda.'

Nigel's arm is untwistable.

'There's another issue. It might be inappropriate for me to endorse anyone at all. I'm still thinking about it.'

Hope he makes the right strategic choice.

CHAPTER FORTY-THREE

Buggins' Turn

Thursday 10th August 2017

PIERS WAUCHOPE, Returning Officer for the leadership election, has asked me and Steve Crowther to help him interview the candidates. There're eleven of them. Yes. Eleven.

We're in a room in the Farmers' Club in Whitehall Court. The applicants have had their social media accounts assessed. They've each been members for the requisite 2 years. They've paid the extortionate application fee. That monetary mountain was supposed to weed out the no-hopers. It hasn't.

First before our stern scrutiny is David Allen, a 70-year-old activist from Tunbridge Wells.

'Why,' asks Wauchope, 'are you wasting £5,500 by standing in this election?'

'I have a vision.'

Which is, broadly, electoral reform. Fair enough. Oddly, he's not keen on us adopting proportional representation for this very leadership election, the idea having been mooted by several of the NEC to avoid the winning candidate also losing their deposit.

'Where should we go?' queries Piers.

'Forward.'

There's nothing objectionable about the man and he's through if he wants it. While shaking hands with him as he's leaving, Allen adds something.

'In the next week I'm making a significant announcement. It came to me at 4.30 in the morning.'

We smile politely. The door closes behind him.

'Perhaps,' I ponder, 'he has discovered that he is the rightful heir to the throne.'

'Indeed,' says Crowther. 'I am always worried about visions which are revealed at that hour of day.'

Next up – Henry Bolton. Nope, no idea either. A soldier from the age of 16, he served in Central Croatia and Western Slovakia. On leaving the forces he joined the police and was decorated for bravery after a rescue from a burning home. He apparently stood for UKIP to be a Police Commissioner and lost his job as a consequence. And Farage is his political referee.

'If he wants to openly support me it will be up to him,' he says.

Yet you can tell that Bolton is simply not going to ask Nigel to do this for him.

As he leaves, I have to ask him.

'Have you, or are you writing your memoirs?'

I'm not kidding. The man's a superlative candidate. But he will not be leader of our party.

It's then the turn of David Coburn MEP. Coburn, is, well - Coburn.

'Someone's got to write the Conservative Party manifesto so it might as well be me.'

He's a bit threatening about the possibility of PR for this ballot.

'I wouldn't go for that if I were you. I'm not mad about it.'

David Kurten comes in and the room darkens. But only because the sun goes behind some clouds, of course.

Kurten has caused controversy over the past couple of days. A Christian, he has answered a questionnaire from a pro-family group which is loosely affiliated to UKIP. The questionnaire covered issues around homosexuality. *Pink News* found out about his answers. They didn't like them. Predictably (it is Kurten after all), Suzanne Evans condemned him. There's been friction between he and Whittle about it too.

Of more concern is the fact that Arron Banks and Leave.EU have been openly backing David. Piers warns him.

'There can't be any third-party campaigning on your behalf or there'll be a penalty. Although it won't take force against the funders themselves but against your vote. Do not forget that.'

As he's leaving, I grimly give my own warning.

'Be careful David, or it will be curtains for Kurten.'

Ho ho ho.

'But don't forget,' he replies. 'They call me Iron Kurten.'

Har har har.

'They do not,' I admonish. 'They actually call you Beef Kurtens.'

Tee hee hee.

Now John Rees Evans. This takes time. Crowther has severe forensic questioning for him. JRE's commercial interests include organising adventure treks and mountain climbing. Steve has a lot to work with.

'I understand there's a difference between puffing yourself as part of your business and being open in a political CV. But there are lots of discrepancies in your online history.'

These concern his military record in general and with the Parachute Regiment in particular. JRE ums, ahs and ponders. Eventually the story pulls together, but Crowther is a friendly interrogator. If John as leader were to be cross examined by Andrew Neil or even, frankly, a BBC weathergirl, it would look shifty and dodgy.

There is however one aspect at which he bounces back. This concerns his involvement in something called the 'European Man of Steel' which is some sporting jamboree or other. Although JRE is said to have taken part in this with Ranulph Fiennes, he doesn't appear in any of the event's videos.

John laughs.

'The reason I'm not in the footage is because I was the one who filmed it. You can see the cameraman's arms in some of the shots and those arms are mine. Cross-check the freckles.'

Yet Steve gives him some hard advice. In fact, it's not advice. It's an instruction.

'By this weekend. You will have a proper, thorough and accurate CV on your leadership website.'

Anne Marie Waters has been sitting outside the room on a neo-gothic oak bench which lacks any upholstery at all for the last thirty minutes, poor lamb.

Although Piers is chairing this assessment, Crowther leads again. Properly-so given his extreme experience of all aspects of fuck-uppery within the party over many years.

'Do you see any issues with having a former BNP member, Jack Buckby, on your campaign team?'

'Yes, I do. But we must challenge this. He's a decent chap. He's condemned the BNP many times. He should be allowed to move on.'

'You're challenging our rule on admitting former BNP members. You'd sweep away that rule if you came to power.'

'I wouldn't. Jack as an individual has denounced the BNP and I wouldn't open it up to him.'

Forceful formerly, she is penitent now. Neither Steve, Piers nor I believe her for an instant. Mind you, it doesn't matter at all because the leader can't change the Party Rules or the Constitution without the agreement of the NEC or party as a whole, respectively. Crowther moves on.

'Let's turn to today's article about you in *The Times*. If you were blocked from standing, would you start a new political party?'

'If UKIP stopped me from standing I might start a new party.'

'And – be honest – would you rather be banned by us from standing for leader at all or stand for the leadership and lose?'

'I'd rather go for it and lose.'

'Pshaw' the three of us think as one.

Time for me to have a go. I'd been having some thoughts about this as the person who'd had the most contact with her and apart from Islam, she's never spoken passionately to my knowledge about anything else at all.

'What are your priority policies in order please?'

'Law and order. A strong economy. And Brexit together with immigration. Brexit and fundamentalist Islam are the same thing to me. We must stop North Africa from coming here.'

Third priority. Third. Insert thought by which I take the Lord's name in vain here.

'Nothing as mundane as sovereignty? The immense cost of the EU? The creation of a superstate?'

'That's not fair. All these issues are on my website.'

It probably isn't fair because I haven't looked at her website but have heard her speak in person. Never, ever has she bashed Brussels in the froth-mouthed and gripped-fist fashion that's required. Nothing wrong with being a monomaniac, but that obsession must be related to our primary purpose.

Crowther then questions her on what she'd do with run-of-the-mill, non-devout Moslems. Would she advocate deportations? There's a long, long discussion about this and she denies that's her position. As this is going on, I remember that press piece when she'd stood for us in Lewisham. I borrow Piers' laptop and find it.

'This is from the *Daily Mirror* in 2015. You'll remember, because I had words with you at the time. Is this fake news or accurate? "A lot of people need to be deported. Many mosques need to be closed down. It really has to get tough".'

'Yes, that's probably accurate.'

We have to come to an end because our room booking is about to finish. Anne Marie volunteers this.

'I can just feel that I'm getting some sympathy from two of the members on this panel but none at all from the third.'

'Do you mean Steve?' I ask.

'Yes.'

'Let me tell you something. When you set up Pegida with Tommy Robinson, Nigel wanted you kicked out of the party straight away. It was me and Steve who persuaded him not to. I suspect Crowther's now changing his mind.'

Out of her comfort zone again, Waters says nothing about this maceration of her pure, certain and inalienable misconception.

Friday 11th August 2017

NEC Meeting. Despite concerns about one or two candidates – actually, one – actually, Anne Marie Waters - all applicants for the leadership of UKIP are approved to stand.

It is for the members to decide who rules this party, not us.

Wednesday 16th August 2017

Branch meeting tonight at the Greenwich Tavern. I've asked Peter Whittle to say a few words. Not because it's a leadership event, but simply as he, too, is a member. Besides, I don't want any of the other candidates muscling in and demanding to speak as they'd be entitled to if it were a formal hustings. Peter Lello has accordingly sent out the notifications to our people alone.

But: on arrival, I see a familiar face at the other end of the bar. Why, it's leadership wannabe Henry Bolton!

How peculiar. He's not one of us and Lello hadn't invited him. Nonetheless, I welcome Henry and ask him to address the branch too. We head upstairs to the first floor and the meeting commences.

While Bolton's talking to us, someone else walks up the stairs. Goodness, it's another contender for King of UKIP, Marion Mason! She's not been invited either.

'Good evening, Marion! How lovely to see you.'

She grunts.

'It's a real struggle to get down to this place. And I couldn't even find the pub when I did.'

The meeting draws to a close, all three leadership candidates having impressed us with their aspirations. Lello, Whittle and Oakley have a huddle.

'So who asked them along?'

'I think I've an idea,' says Whittle. 'I'll make enquiries.'

'And what is it with Marion's grumpiness?' I add. 'Whenever I speak at an outlying branch I always tell them it's great to get away from London and into civilisation. Be like Bonio out of U2: "Scunthorpe – we love you!"'

'Oh, she was like that at every meeting we've been to over the past few weeks. Marvin the paranoid android.'

Thursday 24th August 2017

Oakden needs to speak to me.

'There's going to be a legal challenge to having Anne Marie Waters on the leadership ballot.'

Tut!

'Let me guess. David Coburn. He was quite lairy during the candidate assessments.'

'Actually, no. It's Henry Bolton. Unconfirmed rumours are that he's backed by Nigel. And Freddy Vaccha says you've been telling everyone about it.'

News to me.

'Eh? Freddy's not called me for a while and I never call him or I know I'll lose an hour of my life. There were some mumblings about a challenge after Whittle's leadership launch the other night but I don't recall Freddy being there. And even though I'd Had Beer this stuff about Bolton is news to me.

'Well,' says Oakden. 'Apparently the attack is real enough. I'll give Freddy a call to find out precisely what he's been saying.'

I think for a second.

'It's no news that Anne Marie would be a disaster as leader. Perhaps we could be, well, a little "Medici" about this. And fight any such challenge – poorly.'

In that case all of the opprobrium falls on Bolton and not the NEC. Oakden laughs.

'And, of course, as Directors of the party you'd have the duty not to expose us to litigation we were bound to lose. Let's talk about this again.'

Being a bit Florentine, I've realised this. If Bolton successfully blocks AMW by using a judge who's an Enemy Of The People, he'll be cursed out by the membership at large. He won't benefit personally.

Whereas my lad Whittle, mighty author of the Islamosceptic 'Integration Agenda', certainly will as he scoops up Waters' votes.

Surely that ought to be obvious to Henry?

Friday 25th August 2017

A solicitors' letter has wended its way to the party. It comes from a two-man-firm whose offices are next to the 'Fone Shop' in Folkestone town centre. They're acting on behalf of Henry Bolton.

> 'We now have our client's instruction to invite the National Executive Committee to purge itself of the error that it has made by listing Ms Anne-Marie Waters as one of the eleven candidates for the upcoming leadership election and remove her from the list of candidates.
>
> 'We would request that this matter be dealt with as one of utmost urgency as we have our client's instructions to seek court injunction to enforce the provision of the Rulebook.'

If Bolton does issue a claim there's no doubt that Anne Marie will ask the court to be joined as a third party. That request will be granted although she might not be impressive if she appears as an Irritant-In-Person.

Then at lunchtime Stuart Agnew, our Eastern Area MEP, announces he'll back her financially with full legal representation in any such case. This will definitely get messy and the party's skint again so litigation's the last thing we need.

Saturday 26th August 2017

Paul Oakden has had a quiet word with Henry Bolton. Henry Bolton decides not to proceed with his action.

Oakden really is good value.

Tuesday 29th August 2014

Freddy's chairing his leadership hustings at the Vibast Community Centre in Old Street. Ten candidates are there, save that Bill Etheridge is appearing on behalf of John Rees Evans. The seating positions have been drawn by lot which has had an interesting outcome as Henry Bolton is right next to Anne Marie Waters.

Candidates open from right to left and then it's AMW's turn.

'Good evening, everyone. What a relief to be here. I almost wasn't because once again my candidacy was called into account. Isn't it a shame that those who oppose me very rarely oppose me on my views on the NHS for example.'

Henry sits with his fingers bridged in front of his face and a small smile behind them. His turn, he ignores the uncomfortable seating arrangement and opens with an anecdote.

'I was in a bar in Brussels. I fell into conversation with two local Belgians, one was an amateur military historian, and the other one said - you know, I wouldn't be too sure that Britain will leave the European Union. It's all a lot of fuss about nothing. But the other one said - you know, I wouldn't be too certain about that. There's a Lion in Britain. Twice it's come to the aid of little Belgium. For some years now it's been lying quietly.

'But it is a British Lion and it is stirring. And when the British lion stirs the rest of us would be sensible to sit up and listen.'

Hmm. Good cheese, but I would have served it up properly.

We come to questions. These have been texted in to Freddy's phone so that he can, sensibly, weed out the speeches disguised as queries. They're also read out without divulging the name of the questioner.

'Here's an interesting one from a very senior national officer who I spotted in the room,' He announces.

Whittle turns and looks at me straight away.

Freddy continues.

'Will the candidates commit to Brexit above all? Do they appreciate that if they get sidetracked and it is betrayed they will be just as deserving of the lampost and the piano wire as Blair, Starmer and . . . I'm not allowed to say Gina Miller so I won't. Yes or no?'

One-time Liberal Democrat activist Henry Bolton is first.

'With the one condition. . .'

The audience howls and Freddy interjects.

'Woah woah woah woah woah. Yes or no?'

'The nation comes first. Britain comes first. Yes.'

'Britain? Yeah,' says an unconvinced Freddy. 'But come on. Does Brexit trump any other policy?'

'Yes.'

That was hard work. Well done Fredward.

'Anne Marie?'

'It's point one. So without it everything else fails.'

She's been learning. But I don't quite believe her.

CHAPTER FORTY-FOUR

Henry Who? Phew

Monday September 4th 2017

DUNNO WHY, but there's another London leadership hustings in less than a week, this time at the Emmanuel Centre. Paul Oakden had asked if I'd chair it but I declined in order to avoid allegations that I was favouring Whittle. Which, of course, I would.

Peter seems to have lost all enthusiasm. But then, so have we all. And Henry Bolton decides to deliver exactly the same anecdote about the Belgians and the British Lion which he'd told a few days previously before largely the same audience.

As the meeting winds down, I pop outside to talk to Towler. He's woebegone.

'I very much hope that Anne Marie doesn't win.'

'Doesn't everyone?'

'No, it's more than the obvious. I'll be sacked as head of press.'

Dang.

'But you could go somewhere else quite easily couldn't you? Look at Michael Heaver. He's never off the telly now that he's set up that Westmonster thingamy.'

'Maybe, but. . .'

We don't get any further. The Emmanuel Centre has also been hosting an antiquities auction this evening. At this very moment, Tim Wonnacott – yes, him off of *Bargain Hunt* - descends the stairs next to us. Our hero, we have to talk to him.

Wonnacott knows who we are too, or, at least, the party. Something occurs to me.

'You've said one or two things over the last few years which have got me thinking. Are you, could you be, one of us?'

He peers at us in silence for a few moments.

'Do you know. I rather wish that you could mention certain matters on the BBC without being sacked.'

He adds nothing more but smiles before he walks away. Told you he was a top fellow.

Then, obviously, we're drawn in the direction of The MOG and who do we fall into step with, but George Cottrell!

That stint in a federal prison seems to have done him a world of good as he's lost at least a stone in weight and looks tanned and healthy.

'But I'm out of front-line politics forever. And I will never, ever, trust a journalist again,' he tells us, before buying me that pint.

The MOG's busy with the usual suspects but attendance gradually thins out as the evening winds down. Henry Bolton turns up. I want a quiet word.

All obvious Kippers having finally left, we sit down.

'Chatham House rules, Henry.'

His first-rate CV refers to diplomatic experience so this won't have to be explained. Presumably.

'I'm still backing Whittle for leader but you need to be a spokesman and Defence is the obvious choice.'

'Thank you,' he says.

'So I just want a chat. Because you may know a lot about Clausewitz but it seems you know fuck-all about Machiavelli.'

'Oh?' He frowns.

'Your legal case. Fine and dandy to threaten such a claim but you should have used a patsy rather than do it yourself. And your solicitors? They're a high street firm, not specialists in this sort of thing. I generally crush such non-specialists in the course of my practice. The NEC were laughing at your choice.'

'They were laughing at me?' he asks, sharply.

'Not you. Your choice of solicitors. If you're going to do that sort of thing you need a big firm of vicious beasts.'

'Well, maybe. But I couldn't afford more expensive lawyers and I wouldn't have gone through with it anyway. I just wanted the NEC to cave in.'

'Not good enough. If you draw your sabre it must taste blood.'

Friday 8th September 2017
Freddy Vaccha forwards an email for information. He's quite properly removed the name of its author.

> 'A snippet I heard last evening:
> 'After the Gillingham hustings, Paul Oakley went up to Bolton and told him to "be careful or I will crush you".
> 'Bolton himself told this to my (very much trusted) source.'

I wasn't at the Gillingham hustings and on the very rare occasions when it's necessary for me to crush someone, never give advance notice. They will not see it coming.

'Crush'. That's a very specific word, and a word which only one person has heard me say in this general context. But not in this specific context.

Not impressed.

Friday 22nd September 2017
Prime Minister May has dragged UK journalists off to Florence for some reason in order to debase herself before the EU and propose a further 2-year transitional period after Article 50 becomes effective. The Brexit Betrayal continues.

Farage is all over the media with a righteous sneer and Arron Banks Trumps off on Twitter calling for the UKIP leadership election to be halted and for Nigel's return.

Well, we can't do the former. But the latter? Hmm.

Saturday 23rd September 2017
Anne Marie posts the following Tweet to the world at large.

'Let me be clear, if I win the UKIP leadership, I will not stand aside. Happy to work with Farage. Ball is in his court.'

As if he would.

Sunday 24th September 2017
Given, 'developments', since May's Florence speech I need to have a chat with Banks about the possibility of Farage's return.

'Actually,' Arron admits, 'Nigel isn't very happy that I said this.'

'Let's say Waters wins,' I speculate. 'If she's sidetracked by Saracens and feeble on Brexit we just need nine members of the NEC to back a no confidence motion under the constitution.'

'Really? I'll have a word with him about that tomorrow.'

'Only problem is, there would need to be an Emergency General Meeting of the party afterwards. And Nigel would need to be waiting in the wings to take over or else it'd be pointless.'

Tuesday 26th September 2017

Getting ready for Party Conference, something serious comes to mind so I speak to Farage.

'Are you coming down to Torquay and if so do you fancy wetting a line on the Princess Pier? I'm bringing a pair of rods.'

'Nice idea,' he says, 'but I'm going to have to pass conference entirely because I've got a funeral on Friday.'

I'm sorry to hear this but his absence would, probably, be a good thing and avoid the media focus falling on him in Torquay. That will be so even if we elect a sensible new leader and especially otherwise.

'Hope we don't get a disastrous result,' he adds.

I tell him about my chat with Arron and the possible Nine Members 'way out' of any 'difficulties'.

'I'm not going to do anything at all along those lines,' he says. 'Just going to wait and see what happens.'

Wednesday 27th September 2017

Alex Forsyth of Radio 4's *Today* show records an interview with me in the MOG which will be broadcast before party conference begins on Friday morning. She's also going to speak to Crowther and Oakden but they'll be 'live' so up at the crack of dawn on the day itself. Unlike me. Har!

I puff Whittle of course and she asks some fair questions.

After the microphone's switched off, presumably that is, for I remain careful, we talk further about Anne Marie. Alex has been interviewing as many of the leadership candidates as she can, but Waters has proved elusive and hasn't responded to any contact.

'That's a longstanding problem. You can never get hold of her,' I say.

I dial her number myself in front of Alex. It rings off and I leave a message.

'Could you give Alex at the *Today* programme a call? I know she's been trying to get in touch with you. Don't worry – she's not going to bash you over.'

Forsyth later confirms that she received no call back.

For someone who plans on leading a national political party, such elusiveness is, frankly, stupid.

Thursday 28th September 2017

I don't arrive in Torquay for conference until 10 pm, having left London at 4, thus heading straight into rush hour traffic on the M4. Idiot. There's a pitstop stop just outside Bristol to do LBC with Clive Bull and I'm put on immediately after Farage which is cool. Again, to promote Whittle although it makes not the slightest difference now as the vote closed this afternoon.

I meet Lello, McIlvenna and Alan Craig in a dull pub near to my hotel. Everyone's heading off to bed, for they are old and lightweights, so I amble towards the Riviera conference centre for the remainder of Paul Oakden's famous karaoke. It's rubbish and the room three-quarters empty, so I decide not to treat the dregs to my amazing rendition of God Save The Queen and instead go to the Imperial Hotel to plot. Sadly, as I'm not a guest there it's not possible to buy any drinks because it's now after-hours. Instead, and unsadly, others have to buy drinks for me.

The most important issue is that of resignations in the aftermath of a Waters win. Many of our elected representatives have already been whispering that they'll be sodding off if she grabs it. The first of my MEP targets is there, Yorkshire's Mike Hookem, and I take him to a quiet table to explain the Nine Members proposal. Whether or not that made any difference, I'm pleased to hear that he won't be resigning.

Friday 29th September 2017

There being no visible 24-hour kebab shops in Torquay, I eventually slump into bed at 4 am after a short drive to McDonalds on the outskirts of town. Yum.

Up at 8, and straight to the conference for more skulduggery and, in particular, to target our elected representatives. Counting of the leadership ballots is taking place this morning at the offices of Electoral Reform Services in North London. Most candidates are, as you'd expect, in Torquay so they're permitted to have a representative at the Wood Green premises to confirm that all's above board. Those representatives will have their mobile devices confiscated by Returning Officer Piers Wauchope and the result relayed to Oakden at 5 pm for an announcement to conference 15 minutes later.

Yeah. That'll happen.

I sit with David Kurten AM during an excellent speech by Bishop Michael Nazir-Ali on 'Christianity and the Roots of our Civilisation', Kurten too will be staying in post even if Waters Wins. Good.

Following Crowther's final stately oration as Interim Party Leader, the word 'Interim' leaving me with some sense of loss, lunchtime approaches. The Whittle posse hire a brace of Taxis to visit the 'Green Ginger' Wetherspoons (of course) in the town centre. I'm squeezed next to Peter in the back seat of one of the cabs and he asks me to help put the yellow conference security bracelet on his wrist. Although he's already been into the conference hall, everyone obviously knows who he is so he hasn't had to flash it before.

The fine Wetherspoons establishment being full, we settle on the half-empty Revolution bar next door. Peter asks me to come outside while he takes tobacco.

'How are you feeling old chap?' I ask him.

'I don't know. I really don't know.'

He pauses for a moment.

'Do you like being General Secretary?'

'Yes – it's fine although more of drudgery than an accolade. There's a big complaint from Wales at the moment about one of the Assembly Members. It's vague and rambling. I tried to give the complainant some pointers about how to tidy it up but he's started a big email chain to all and sundry and has accused me of being "hysterical". Mouth-breathing wanker that he is.' I grin.

Peter's obviously thinking about the makeup of his team should he win. I'll be happy to carry on as GS should he want me to.

Just then, a man politely interrupts us.

'Are you at the conference?' he asks.

'Yes,' says Peter with a smile.

'Do you know what time the afternoon session starts?'

'I think it's at a quarter-to-two.'

'Oh, thank you.' He introduces himself, shakes ours hands, and then asks Peter a question. 'And who are you?'

Oh dear.

We wander inside and Whittle takes his rightful place at the head of our table while we recount the rumours. I'd seen Andrew Price from the JRE team in the garden of the hotel opposite my own first thing this morning. Andrew had shown me a message sent to him in the early hours. This said Bolton had won by a few dozen votes. Ho ho ho!

Freddy Vaccha is zooming down from the London count to Torquay as we speak and has texted several people around this very table to inform them that Whittle has won, together with a strange analogy about a pistol and *The Godfather* film.

That result sounds far more realistic than a Bolton victory. There are more rumours but none involve the election of Ms Waters.

There are some grizzled old hacks at this lunch who know an awful lot about the party. As well as Peters Whittle, Lello, Harris and McIlvenna there's Roger Gravett and his brother Gerald. What we don't know about our people isn't worth knowing. So the round-table consensus around this square table is this.

1 Whittle or Waters
3 JRE
4 Kurten
5 Bolton
6 Collins
7 Powlesland

We decide to walk back to the Riviera Centre in order to work off the flesh and fries. A small crowd has gathered outside the Crazy Golf cabin. Goodness! It's Anne Marie and her retinue. So she's finally turned up.

As we arrive at the conference hall there's some Leftards to be seen. UKIP have been very generous to them because as well as offering ourselves to be pilloried, we've also invited Dr Hugh Bronson to speak. He's a member of the Berlin State Parliament for the AfD party and thus, obviously, a fascist. Pfft. Notwithstanding our munificence, there's a disappointingly-tiny contingent of Trots. Many Kippers are hanging around to smile and peer at them, including Davy Coburn and his clansmen. I take him aside to explain the Nine Members proposal and also to plead with him, as a mate, to make things up with Whittle. He does.

'As long as you give me a free hand in Scotland leading up to the next election. And as long as there's no more rubbish about "throwing money over Hadrian's Wall", I'll back you Peter.'

They shake hands.

My NEC Colleague Katie Fanning is resplendent in a purple JRE costume on the bench next to the protestors. Paula Walters is with her, and concerned. Katie's nibbling her fingernails and bouncing her crossed-leg up and down.

'What's up?' I ask.

It takes some nagging to get her to open up.

'I'm just so worried that I've helped kill the party.'

'How so?'

'By letting Anne Marie on to the ballot paper. Have we really fucked it up?'

Paula's having none of this.

'Even though she'd be awful, we did the right thing. The members decide.'

I agree.

'If anything, it's down to Reeve, Whittle and me. If they hadn't suggested her and I hadn't endorsed her as a Lewisham candidate in 2015 there'd be no problem. We're the plonkers, not you.'

We head back inside. We should be listening to speeches from Bickley, Hookem and Agnew but have more pressing things to discuss. Shortly, Roger Gravett tells me his brother's still outside and has been texting.

'Anne Marie's heading in now. There's a massive pack of journalists with her and she's got a big smile on her face.'

Shee-it.

It's only half-three. Knew the result was going to leak early. This is a catastrophe if true. Don't want to sound like a fainting damsel or nothing, but my heart starts thumping hard and I phone Oakden and Crowther, neither of whom pick up.

Then I see them at the front of the stage and march over. A hand pulls at my jacket. It's Paul Nuttall in his baseball cap (again).

'Listen mate,' I say. 'It looks like the result's been leaked and it may not be good. I'm just off to find out what's happening.'

'Bollocks. Off you go then.'

I reach the big men.

'I hear it's bad news.'

'In a way,' Steve tells me. 'Peter's surprisingly far down the list.'

'But the worst bit?'

'Don't worry, Anne Marie's second.'

'Then who on earth has come top?'

'Henry Bolton.'

'Bolton?' I query.

'Bolton. And, yes. We know.'

I grab their shoulders with disappointment and relief and head off to find Whittle.

Freddy Vaccha accosts me as I'm still searching.

'Now. You're a fan of the *Godfather* aren't you? Well. . . .'

'Freddy. . .'

'You'll remember the issue of the gun. I'm not sure. . .'

'Freddy. . .'

'I'm not sure if some of your other compatriots got the point, you see. . .'

'Freddy! Enough! The result's just going to be announced.'

'No it's not. It's not being revealed until 5.15.'

'Yes. It is. Right now.'

I march off.

At a quarter to four the Party Chairman takes to the stage.

'Starting in seventh place with 85 votes and nought-point-six-five percent of the vote share: Aidan Powlesland.'

Poor Aidan. He'd needed 100 people to nominate him and hadn't even managed to get all of those to vote for him.

'In sixth place, with 566 votes and 4.4% of the vote share, Jane Collins.

'In fifth place, with 1,413 votes and 10.9% of the vote share, Peter Whittle.'

There are coos and oohs. People are genuinely surprised. I am, metaphorically, exenterated.

'In fourth place, with 2,021 votes, 15.6% of the vote share, John Rees Evans.

'In third place, with 2,201 votes, or 17% of the vote share, David Kurten.'

Now the important bit.

'In second place. With 2,755 votes, 21.3% of the vote share, was: Anne Marie Waters.'

At this the noise is deafening. Mixed yells of anger and relief and hand-hurting claps both from those who backed her and those who couldn't think of anyone worse as leader. I keep my own hands in my pockets.

Oakden concludes.

'Ladies and gentlemen. Making his way down from upstairs, so it may take him some time, please give an appropriately lengthy cheer and round of applause - with 3,874 votes and 29.9% of the vote share - the new leader of our party. Henry Bolton!'

I wait politely for his speech but then leave the hall with the crew. Whittle deserves a drink and we need a hostelry which won't be filled with a throng of senior citizen Kippers who'll overhear us. The noisy Sports Bar it is.

Things are sombre.

'I have to give matters some consideration now,' Peter tells us. 'I'm fifty-six years old. Do I have it in me to give it another go or just give up?'

He tears off his conference wristband and throws it on the table-top. The consensus is that giving up must be off the table for him.

We have more ale and additional Kippers join us outside while I'm having a chat with Nuttall. One of those who ambles over to us is a former squaddie himself.

'I've had a look at that Henry Bolton's CV and his postings abroad. The shit may have hit the fan in those places but by the time he'd arrived there the fans had been turned off. Not his fault of course.'

I've no idea if this is true or not.

Saturday 30th September 2017

Whittle delivers his briefing on London to conference just after 10.30. He's swallowed his disappointment, beams at the crowd and makes a point of warmly congratulating our new leader.

There's then a full list of other speakers. Reeve. Kurten. Collins. Reid. Etheridge. Coburn. Crosby. After lunch there are to be scheduled debates on branch motions for an hour and a quarter. Then there are awards for services above-and-beyond which have been rendered by activists. After that, we're going to have afternoon tea and then, finally, Henry Bolton will deliver a full leader's speech at 4.30, just before close of play.

Yet there's a problem which hasn't been considered by the conference organisers. It's a pretty-obvious one too; we're in Torquay which is miles from anywhere. Most of our activists do not live locally. Scores of them have already gone and scores more are leaving early to reach their homes at a reasonable hour. If the listing remains as-is, Bolton will be addressing a near-empty hall. The media will lap that up.

I deliver a discrete suggestion to Paul Oakden.

'Yes,' he says sharply. 'OK!' And strides off.

Accordingly, at 2.05pm a denuded delegation of attendees take their seats in the hall to hear our new leader earlier than advertised.

His speech of twenty minutes or so is perfectly adequate and I'm off as soon as he finishes and before the ovations conclude. I'm heading straight to Tidal Tackle to pick up some lugworm and then onto the pier for an extra couple of hours fishing before I, too, have to drive home.

That prospect had nothing whatever to do with my earlier suggestion to the Party Chairman that Bolton's slot be brought forward of course. Nothing!

Ahem.

And: I would have gotten away with it, too, were it not for that pesky Kirstan Herriott. She taps my arm as I'm heading out.

'Paul,' she asks. 'Are you driving back to London now?'

'Um, yes,' I lie, suspiciously. 'Why?'

'We were just wondering if you could give Dr Bronson a lift?'

Our Alternative für Deutschland guest is right behind her, sporting a winning smile.

'Certainly. With great pleasure,' I lie. Again.

My surliness was wholly-unwarranted. Bronson proves to be excellent company with many first-rate anecdotes to relate on the four-hour drive back. Furthermore, he proves to be a stentorian snorer when he dozes off from time to time. Top chap!

CHAPTER FORTY-FIVE

Reign of the Badger-Strangler

Saturday 14th October 2017

WELL. OUR NEW LEADER'S BEEN IN POST for a couple of weeks, but not much is happening.

Whittle sends out a round-robin.

'Friends, could we meet to discuss the general situation on Monday evening, 6pm, at The Bridge Lounge pub on Tooley Street just behind City Hall?'

Sunday 15th October 2017

Henry Bolton is getting media attention at last. He's on Niall Paterson's *Sky News* show.

'I know you like plain speaking in UKIP but like many other people, until recently, I hadn't heard of you,' observes Paterson. 'So we've been trying desperately to get to grips with you. I discovered this morning thanks to the *Sunday Times* that in an interview with *Russia Today* you said that you could strangle a badger with your bare hands.'

Henry takes the question well.

'Ah. They gave me a few options as ideas for an initiation ceremony into the leadership of UKIP. And the one that was probably most suitable for me was chasing a badger across Dartmoor, capturing it and then breaking its neck with one's bare hands which was a slightly unusual thing, but. . .'

'Yeah,' Paterson concludes. 'And possibly the strangest question I've ever asked.'

So what? If it takes silly stunts to raise Henry's profile that's fine by us (Dear Liza, Dear Liza). I Tweet about it.

'Unlike the feeble old parties, only UKIP has a leader who is mighty enough to kill a badger with his bare hands.'

The *Daily Mail, Daily Express, Evening Standard, Metro, New Statesman* and 'i' all pick up on my silliness about Henry's silliness. Good. Anything to create a buzz around our new leader. Within reason.

Monday 16th October 2017

There's me, Whittle, Lello, McIlvenna and Mark Quinlan. The main purpose is beer and the subsidiary purpose to work out what, if anything, is going on. By this time in 2013, we'd already started campaigning for the local elections and there's also the small question of Theresa May's continuing Brexit betrayal.

'We're going to get utterly destroyed in the council polls at this rate,' says Whittle. 'What on earth is our policy platform?'

The rest of us look at our feet: Don't Know Miss.

'If the party's over, perhaps we could all defect to another one?' offers McIlvenna.

We all snort mirthlessly.

'What, Labour?' asks Lello. 'And you can forget about the Tories. They won't touch any of the cultural issues.'

He's talking about the muslamics of course.

My thoughts are sought.

'It may be too late already. If Henry mucks things up then he must resign in May. But we can't do anything to help him on his way. We've had more than enough leadership contests recently.'

Saturday 28th October 2017

NEC meeting at Piers Wauchope's chambers in Temple. His conference room is cramped and I end up sitting on the window ledge behind Henry. This is his first full meeting with us since being elected. He briefs us on the roles for his new spokesmen and, more significantly, electioneering.

'I would like,' he tells us, 'to look at planning and campaigning processes for general and local elections. I think we ought to have a lot more depth and sustainability in terms of its impact. That planning will feed into regular updates.'

Excellent news.

Peter Staveley, both in his posts as a London Regional Organiser and latterly as National Nominating Officer, is fond of reminding activists of the precise periods before imminent elections. In fact, he usually starts his nagging the very day after each specific election is held, his eyes on the next one. That pedantry's rubbed off on me. It's now only 187 days until the 2018 council polls. Sounds like a long time but it really isn't and we need to be campaigning right now.

Monday 27th November 2017

NEC meeting again. Henry's been a busy bee. He's set up a Leader's Group, a Shadow Cabinet, a Communications Group, an Events Group, a Fundraising Group, a Membership and Recruitment Group, a Campaign Planning Support Team, a Save Our Services team, a Brexit Planning Support Team and an Elections Planning Support Team.

The NEC will certainly look forward to receiving reports from the members of these groups, whoever they may be, in due course.

As an afterthought, we also discuss the local elections. Bolton's view is firm and resolute.

'For me, the practical campaigning issue is the key point. Some branches do not have a couple of hundred quid, but members should be campaigning already.'

Indeed they should Henry. None of the promised updates have yet emerged though. 157 days and counting. . .

Monday 1st January 2018

Henry Tweets a cryptic new year's message.

'Myself and Jo Marney nearly run over by George Osborne in Covent Garden. We were a bit sharper than he was though - no surprise there.'

What – another assassination attempt on a UKIP leader? Never heard of this Joe Marney. Perhaps he's a new member of Bolton's staff. Best get hold of his contact details.

Wednesday 3rd January 2018

Ooh! That's nice! After a three-month delay, the leader of UKIP has got around to emailing the members about his activities for the very first time.

'Tomorrow morning, some of you may find yourselves reading the *Sun* newspaper. If you do then inside you might find a piece that's been written about me, specifically talking about my private life.

'The potential story is going to confirm that in recent weeks, I've had a change in my relationship status.'

Good to know. I suppose. Anyway, he signs off appropriately, and only three days too late:

'Here's to a successful 2018 and a very Happy New Year!'

Thursday 4th January 2018

The tabloids have been at work. Henry's 'relationship change' is that he's now snuggling up to a lady, called Jo Marney, who's various-ly-described as being either 25 years old or 25 years his junior. It's not clear.

Anyway, he's 54 apparently. Never knew that. Thought he was old-er.

Sunday 7th January 2018

We're getting lots of media coverage at last. Henry's wife Tatiana tells the press that he dumped her by text message on Christmas Eve and she's still breastfeeding one of their children.

Monday 8th January 2018

First NEC meeting of the new year. We've just settled down when Nigel's adjutant Dan Jukes sends me a text.

'Rewind *Daily Politics*. He talks about Bolton.'

I have my laptop open but am obviously not going to play the show out loud so look for the headlines instead.

'Appearing on the *Daily Politics*, Mr Farage said: 'While short-term, it may be uncomfortable for him, the truth is, people now know his name. It's up to him what he does. At least he's being talked about now.'

I nudge Bolton, who's at my left. He reads the piece and for some reason decides it's a good idea to nudge Elizabeth Jones, who's to his own left, with a smile. She scans it with a face of flint. Ye gods, Henry.

The leader tells us what he's been up to. Professionally, that is.

'Before Christmas I did a tour of the regions. I'm getting very good feedback from that. I've spoken to thousands of members and in one meeting I was on my feet for 6 hours. We're still doing very well in certain areas, such as Thurrock. The focus now is to get the working groups and policy forums up and running.'

Great! What else?

'The elections campaign isn't functioning due to internal issues. Lisa Duffy resigned from the group and there's been little work done. But I'm going to take a personal grip of that situation.'

Crimony! 115 days. . .

There are some cursory questions to him and then Fiona Mills gives the leader a very hard stare.

'Henry, that's fine. But we really need to talk about the elephant in the room.'

We do, in detail. Nobody's supportive of what he's done but some are more vociferous than others. There are several calls for him to resign but Katie Fanning, MEP Jonathan Arnott, Steve Crowther and Andrew Moncrieff are more concerned about the fact that we can't afford another leadership election, either financially or politically. Oakden tells us that Alan Bown, absent from the meeting, shares this view.

As for me?

'I don't care about your personal life but a lot of members do care and that bothers me. But I won't be supporting any calls for you to stand down.'

Elizabeth Jones formally proposes that there be a Vote of No Confidence. It can't be considered today but has to be at a future meeting. I very much doubt that Liz will be able to garner the Nine Members she needs to oust him.

Meeting over, we head to Henry's Bar although there are fewer of us than usual. Bolton tries to schmooze those who've turned up, although creakily. I'm not sure he's persuading the women in particular that he should stay in post.

'Hopefully, it'll blow over,' I tell him. 'And Jo's less than half your age, is she?'

He nods, with a pensive look.

'Well, I'd never say this in front of the ladies, but — you lucky bastard!'

He grins and guffaws.

Later that evening Oakden sends out an email to every UKIP member.

'At an NEC meeting today members discussed the recent press coverage of our Leader, Henry Bolton.

'It was agreed to defer the discussion to a special NEC meeting, which has been called for ten days time.

'No further comment will be made on this issue by the central party, or any NEC member until that meeting has concluded.'

That won't close it down. The reason for the adjournment is bound to leak.

Tuesday 9th January 2018

Dedicated email addresses of everyone on the NEC were published in the last issue of the party's 'Independence' magazine. This was to give every Kipper a direct line of contact to us. Members have started using the channel. I've received many messages about Henry's escapades, all critical.

I reply with a standard piece of blandness.

'Many thanks for getting in touch.

'As you will know from the email from Paul Oakden, the NEC will be holding a meeting on Sunday when recent matters will be considered in detail.

'The thoughts of members are always welcome and we're here to take them into account.'

Thursday 11th January 2018

Gawain sends a text first thing.

'What Ho. Henry wants to develop a policy in which there are increased statutory tariffs - like for hate crimes - for those such as taxi drivers and police officers and carers who have power over others. Could you call and discuss?'

I've got a hearing at 10 so don't call back until later when having the car cleaned at my favourite illegal immigrant hand-washing station. They do a great job.

Towler's curt.

'Sorry,' he says. 'I've got a lot to deal with at the moment.'

He hangs up and I don't realise why until I'm back in front of the PC.

Nigel's been interviewed about Brexit on *The Wright Stuff*.

'My mind is actually changing on this. What is for certain is that the Cleggs, the Blairs, the Adonises will never, ever, ever give up. They will go on whingeing. And whining. And moaning. All the way through this process. So maybe, just maybe, I'm reaching the point of thinking that we should have a second referendum on EU membership.'

Whuh?!? Never! Never! Never!

Towler calls back.

'Sorry about earlier. Had to get the press release sorted.'

He has:

'Henry Bolton has reiterated his and his party's opposition to a second referendum, "UKIP policy on a second referendum remains unchanged. The party opposes a second referendum".'

Good work Henry. Even better work by Nigel for giving our current leader the opportunity to slap him down over this nonsense. Crafty. At least, I presume that was the idea.

Friday 12th January 2018
The trains are down so I'm driving to Romford County Court. Oakden calls as I'm about to hit the Blackwall Tunnel.

'It's evenly-balanced. In fact, about fify-fifty. But my guess is that Liz Jones won't get the Nine Members she needs to pass the vote.'

'Good. But he still has to handle it carefully. There's no point trying to sway Fiona Mills but it's worth him having a word with Paula Walters.'

'Agreed. Bickley's definitely unpersuadable as well.'

'That's odd. John knows better than anyone that we've no money. He's usually sensible so I can't work out why he's so vehement that Bolton should go.'

'I can help you there. At the Newton Abbot Christmas lunch Henry slapped him down in front of everyone when discussing budgets. He said that he wasn't taking advice from him as he'd plenty of experience dealing with multi-million aid funding. John didn't like that.'

'Ah. Makes sense.'

'Anyway, look. The reason I'm calling is this. As you know, the members are blaming me for just about everything and I'm bored being Chairman. If Henry's to survive, he needs to make radical changes. I've suggested that he might think of installing you in the post instead. Can we discuss it on Tuesday morning in person? I'll be in town.'

I drive into the tunnel and we're cut off.

Saturday 13th January 2018
4.29 pm. Oakden calls.

'Another story about Henry's squeeze is going to hit the *Mail* tomorrow.'

I breathe out. Heavily.

'This is becoming tedious.'

'Yes. But it's far more serious this time and I need your help. She's been saying that Prince Harry's fiancée Meghan Markle will 'taint' the royal bloodline.'

Stupid, stupid, stupid. Anyhow, surely that's a good way of repairing the endemic inbreeding between the royal households of Europe? He goes on.

'I'm told there's more and it's worse so I'm going to suspend her this afternoon.'

'Have you spoken to Henry? When's their deadline?'

'Yes – and in half an hour.'

He sends me a draft which I tweak in line with the constitutional provisions and it's sent to Marney at 4.48.

'I write to you because it has come to my attention that you have allegedly sent messages in which views are expressed that are inconsistent and incompatible with the values of our party as set out in Clause 2.4 of our constitution.

'These alleged messages include, when talking about Meghan Markle:

"and her seed with [sic] taint our royal family"

'As a result of these allegations I am using the emergency powers granted to me under Clause 11.9 of the Constitution to suspend you from the Party for 14 days.'

11.55 pm. I see the coverage of the full exchange from Ms Marney on *Mail Online*.

'I wouldn't with a negro.'

'What's wrong with black people?'

'Ugly.

'Not my thing.

'They don't turn me on.

'Harry's marrying. God.'

'She's black.

'A dumb little "actress" that no one has heard of.

'This is Britain, not Africa.'

I only ever telephone people after 9 pm if it's absolutely critical. So I dial the party leader's number at precisely midnight.

'Henry. Really sorry to call you so late but this cannot wait. You have to ditch her. This is imperative. Right now.'

'Oh, I know,' he replies. 'Jo's at breaking point with all this coverage. She's really, really contrite.'

'I'm sorry about that but man to man this needs to end. I'm still not going to support a vote of no confidence in you but that's only because the party can't afford it.'

'OK. I'll do it. Thanks Paul.'

CHAPTER FORTY-SIX

The Assassination of Henry Bolton

Sunday 14th January 2018

MISSED CALL FROM FARAGE at 8.53 am. He's doing his LBC show with Alastair Campbell and Lord Adonis this morning about the ongoing Brexit betrayal. Really rather good and exactly the sort of thing we should be focussing on instead of the adventures of Henry Bolton's penis.

I call him afterwards.

'Great show!' And it was.

'What did you think of the guests?' asks Nigel. 'I still reckon Andrew Adonis is a fucking weirdo.'

'Agreed, although Campbell seems fun even if he talks crap. I could see myself having a beer with him.'

Ah. I belatedly remember that Campbell's a recovering alcoholic. Yet the sentiment remains.

'Anyway, can I just ask you if you'd be willing to come back if Henry can't hold on?'

'No, I really, really couldn't. I've had quite enough. It's not my party any more. And Suzanne Evans would walk it now if she stood for leader.'

'But what if we were to agree to the abolition of the NEC? I think it's the wrong choice but we'd do it for you. The cause is all.'

'Well, maybe, just maybe. But the chances are really remote.'

Can Arron Banks be more persuasive of Nigel? I try his number but can't get through. He calls back pretty much straight away from South Africa.

'OK,' he says. 'I'll try to give it a go but really can't promise anything. We might have to start a new party from scratch.'

Yet another one? That's gonna work.

'Well, maybe if everything goes tits-up you could swoop in like a vulture capitalist and take over the bones of UKIP. That'd be easier.'

He doesn't seem enthused.

'Maybe we will, and maybe we won't.'

So neither are going to bother then. This is deflating. It's not just me who's been pestering Nigel to do a ''68 Comeback Special' and it's probably bored him but—well—perhaps his time has passed after all.

Monday 15th January 2018

For reasons best known to himself, Henry's decided on a media blitz. *BBC Breakfast*, the *Today* programme, *Good Morning Britain*, LBC and Talk Radio. This would be wonderful if it had happened a month ago and he was making the case for Brexit. Maybe that was his plan, but it shows gross naivety because every journalist is, obviously, focussing on his private life. The details are embarrassing and it would only take the addition of some DNA and lie detector tests to make his posturing indistinguishable from other daytime telly shows.

As the morning progresses, my inbox becomes clogged with un-amused emails from Kippers so I have a blunt chat with him at half-five.

'Look Henry, this is getting worse. The vast majority who're getting in touch with me want you gone or they say they'll resign.'

'Yes, but I'm receiving an awful lot of support from members, too, you know. Lots and lots of emails and telephone calls.'

This may be true, but the fact remains that his groupies are more likely to be contacting him than his detractors. That's just the way things are.

'Would you perhaps consider standing down? Something along the lines of you having become the story when the real issue's Brexit?'

'No. I can bring this round. I'm not going to give up.'

Our chat was perfectly amicable but it's left me mildly-drained and I send Farage a text message.

'Nigel – just so you know, I don't think there's any way of saving him now.'

He replies.

'I know.'

Thursday 18th January 2018

The Press have another scoop. Bolton was seen in public with his floozy in the National Liberal Club last night despite his promises to ditch her.

The National. Liberal. Club.

Kai!

Friday 19th January 2018

Our current leader has been observing radio silence with the NEC. Yet today we receive a lovely email from him at last which has also been sent to random other people. A total of 65 recipients in fact, some of whom have apparently flounced off from UKIP in sympathy with Anne Marie Waters. Way to go when it comes to keeping things private Henry!

His position is: some bigger boys did it and ran away.

'The NEC is intending to make decisions on Sunday regarding the wrong person/s. Rather, the NEC should be protecting the integrity of the party by shutting down this insurgency. Instead the NEC is looking increasingly as though it is colluding with it.'

Saturday 20th January 2018

John Bickley calls to ask me to come off the abstention fence and join the rebel alliance. He's persuasive but I haven't decided.

Then Alan Bown rings. He has changed his mind and will now vote for Bolton to go. He's asked head office to keep a tally of members who are leaving because of Henry. There are lots.

Much more importantly, there's the string of members who've been contacting me directly to express disgust. Far more than there are supporters of Bolton. The NEC is supposed to represent the rank and file. It would be bad form to ignore them.

There's one minor, personal issue. I'd find it very hard to stand by a leader who stands by a partner who believes that 'Negros' are 'Ugly'. But that's easily-resolved. I can just doff my plumèd pickelhaube for the last time. Resign as General Secretary, step down from the NEC and jack-in the branch chairmanship. My personal distaste doesn't mean Bolton has to go.

Anyway, I'm still thinking about things.

Sunday 21st January 2018

The Vote of No Confidence in Henry Bolton is being considered to-day and I'm hosting it at our Chambers. I drive, listening to Rammstein and, specifically, "Waidmann's Heil". On repeat.

'*Auf dem lande auf dem meer, lauert das verderben. Die kreatur muss sterben!*'[1]

Nearing Temple, I see a figure in a tan coat at the junction of Bouverie and Tudor streets and wind down the window.

'Jump in Henry.'

'Thanks Paul,' he says. 'I'd probably have struggled to find it otherwise.'

He probably would.

The rest of the NEC have located the building quite easily and we all settle comfortably within. And Lo: I am seated at the left hand of the Leader.

Adam Richardson speaks up.

'I'm going to have to type the minutes of this. Does anyone mind if I record the proceedings?'

Nobody does.

Henry opens and reads a lengthy statement. A lot of that statement, an awful lot, is concerned with a dirty plot to oust him by an unofficial UKIP faction.

'Two members of the NEC, possibly three, are members of this Indigo Group and I consider that there is probably a conflict of interest there. There is no compulsion that I can exercise of course, but I can only ask them to withdraw from the Vote of No Confidence.'

'I myself have done absolutely nothing to bring the party into disrepute. It is others that have exploited this situation to do so that need to be blamed.'

Everyone's given the chance to comment or question the leader in turn. Steve Crowther's observation is by far the most cutting.

'Henry, you put up a very spirited defence, as one would expect. There's an old saying that "just because you're paranoid it doesn't mean to say they're not out to get you".

'I think there's another saying - "just because they're all out to get you it doesn't mean you haven't fucked up".'

All issues having been canvassed, it's time to decide. I'm content for Henry to remain in the room but most members want him out in order to have a private discussion.

I transport him across the stairwell to the other side of Chambers. As we walk past the front window, we can see a cluster of people in the Brick Court car park. There's a distinctive red scarf. Journalist Michael Crick has found us, the cunning little tinker, and has Tweeted.

---

1 'Waidmanns Heil', Ramstein, 2009. Trans: 'On the land, on the sea/Decay lies in wait/ The creature must die!

'UKIP NEC finally tracked down to chambers at 1 Essex Court where UKIP General Secretary Paul Oakley is a barrister.'

I plant Bolton at my desk. The room's freezing and I don't know how to turn the heating on. The only items for his amusement are a photograph of Winston (Churchill that is) and my First World War French army helmet.

'You can have a play with that if you like, Henry. But it's little more than a tin can and would have given minimal protection.'

I walk back to the conference room, trying to keep as far away from the front window and telephoto lenses as possible.

We have our discussion and it's clear that it's going to be unanimous. Apart, presumably, from Bolton himself who'll have a vote of his own. We consider whether Henry should be offered the chance to resign before the formal show of hands. Then a nice press release, thanks for all his efforts, etc. Oakden's amenable.

'I'd suggest that Paul comes with me. We'll have a quiet word and give him the opportunity to stand down as he's about to get trounced. I'm suggesting Paul because he knows where he is.'

There's a further issue to consider of course. Even if the NEC vote against him, that won't finish matters. The leader is then entitled to appeal to an Emergency General Meeting of the entire party. Needless to say, this will cost a lot of money. Needless to say, UKIP has no money. Again. Henry knows this and will surely do the decent thing as an officer and a gentleman.

We near-twins wander over to the other side of the building and shut the door. We explain what has happened and what's going to happen.

'Will you resign, Henry?' I ask.

He seems somewhat choked and takes a moment to compose himself. And there's no shame in that.

'No. I will not.'

The three of us return and Oakden proclaims the proposal.

'This is calling the official vote of no confidence in Henry Bolton as the leader of UKIP. Proposer: Mick McGough. Seconder: Katie Fanning. All in favour? Fourteen. Against? One. Henry — if you want to go back with Paul please?'

I guide Henry to my car. The press have disappeared, save that a van door opens and a bright camera lamp suddenly glares at us, dazzling me as I reverse. I don't run the Pap over but it would've served them right.

As we head out of Temple and towards Blackfriars station I try to coax him again.

'You know, Henry, I still think you'd make a great Defence spokesman. Step down to do that and all of this will soon be forgotten.'

'Well, I'll certainly think about it.'

'And another thing. If you want to make a formal complaint about this Chief Plotter you're concerned about, I'd be happy to consider it.'

'Maybe I will,' he says. 'Do you know something? You're decent. You really are.'

Having dropped him off, I join the others at the Old Cocke Tavern in Fleet Street. Rather fitting really. Gawain's there.

'I've just spoken to Crick. He says that whoever decided to hold the meeting in Temple was a genius. The security staff threw all the journos out.'

Monday 22nd January 2018

Rumours are that Henry's going to be calling a press conference at 4 pm when he'll stand down. I put the telly on and he keeps us waiting until eleven minutes past when he finally emerges from the Grand Hotel in Folkestone. I have a lot of sympathy for him as this can't be easy.

He reads from a prepared statement.

'I shall respect the next steps in the constitutional process and will therefore not be resigning as party leader. I shall repeat: I will not be resigning as party leader.'

'The NEC as presently constituted is unfit for purpose. And has severely handicapped the party's progress and political delivery for some years as recent UKIP leaders can attest. It has not only lost the confidence of me, as the party leader, in its ability to act objectively as the party's governing body, it has also lost the confidence of a large proportion of the party's membership.'

'In a single phrase, it's time to "Drain the Swamp".'

I be-Tweet, calmly and without comment, a picture of Garfield the cat sighing which Peter Walker at the *Guardian* picks up on. My internal musings are more akin to Tony Montana's phone-smashing conversation in Scarface: You wanna fuck with me? You wanna go to war? I'll take you to war.

UKIP are now going to have to find a five-figure sum to hold an EGM at our current leader's insistence. Because he's worth it. In his opinion.

It gets to 7 pm and Bolton's the guest of honour on Nigel's LBC show. To be fair, Farage punches him in the guts straightaway.

'A close colleague who I've worked with for years in UKIP said to me that in a short space of time you, Henry Bolton, have turned this into a soap opera and in doing so have brought the party into disrepute.'

His response is a-mumbling and a-stumbling.

'I wouldn't agree with that, Nigel. I, um, interestingly at the NEC meeting, yesterday, uh — there wasn't one charge, er, laid against me apart from, uh, the, the, the biggest charge and the most clearest of, the, the only allegation was that I had left my wife, um, and apart from that no other specific, er, charge was, er, levelled against me. Erm, so.'

Eeh! The lying git! I pull out my phone.

Our current leader carries on with a load more crap blaming everyone but himself for the present situation and the NEC most of all. Farage doesn't give him an easy run.

'Henry, I want to get this absolutely right. Are you suggesting that you will draft and present a new constitution for the party in the next, well, four weeks?'

'I am Nigel, yes. There are two things that need to happen. We have to reform the party and that requires a new constitution. We need to reform the NEC which again comes out of the constitution.'

LBC call back. Nigel's going to have me on. I remove the dog from my lap, place him in the bedroom with the missis and shut the door. I go downstairs to the lounge, make sure that this door is firmly closed, too, and recline on the chaise longue with the phone at my ear.

The adverts finally finish. Tantara! Tantara! Da Da Da!

'And on the line is Paul Oakley, he's a national executive member of UKIP and he's the General Secretary. So you were one of those who unanimously voted to say that he should stand down as leader. Can you explain to us — what has he done wrong?'

I do, in detail, and then the missis comes into the lounge followed by the dog. I wave her away but she doesn't understand. She's busy tidying and fussing because her cousin's about to come round for a chinwag. The hound jumps up and lies on my tummy. She shuts the door on us. Farage continues.

'Do you think, Paul, in your opinion as UKIP's General Secretary that he's brought the party into disrepute?'

'Personally, no, but that doesn't really matter. I mean you and I have had discussions in the past about reforming the NEC. . .'

At this, the front doorbell goes off and the hound goes off in reply, kicking me in the balls and barking like a nutdog. Nigel deals with the interlude in a far more professional manner than my pet has done and we move on.

'Could there, Paul Oakley, be something good that comes out of this EGM. That we start to have a proper debate about UKIP's management?'

'No. And I'll tell you why. It doesn't bode well for Henry that he hasn't even read the constitution. Because if an EGM is called in a leader that is the only issue which is going to be on the agenda. Now, if he was going to do this seriously I'd have backed him in this. He should have done it four months previously. He's done nothing at all apart from get on *Russia Today* with that "badger-strangling" quote.'

'Paul, listen, if he turns up at that EGM and he hasn't produced a new constitution and a new plan - he is toast! And he said today. . .'

I interrupt.

'He's toast anyway Nigel. When chaps like John Tennant, whom I know you know well, and all of his fellow activists in the north east give up the ghost because of Henry Bolton, you know that this guy is doing badly. It's outrageous that he's come out today and said this. The problem is his. He should go. It really is as simple as that.'

Tuesday 23rd January 2018

More bullshit from Bolton hits *The Sun*. The guy's not hanging about.

'UKIP refusing to pay under-fire boss Henry Bolton in bid to starve him out.'

'Under UKIP's rules, a generous salary can be paid to its leader from party funds. But Mr Bolton told a friend: "The party Treasurer is one of those trying to get me out, so he has stopped me receiving any salary. It will not work, because I am determined to do this job out of public service not personal advancement".'

John Bickley, the Party Treasurer in question, gives me a call as soon as he sees it.

'Can I sue?'

Of course he can. There never was a salary available for the leader as the party's brassic. Bolton knows that full well.

'It would take ages to trundle through the courts John and although *The Sun's* worth suing, Henry isn't. I'll ask Harry Cole to speak to you. A rebuttal is better value.'

The resignations continue. As of today, 14 spokespeople have sodded-off in disgust at our current leader. These include Whittle as well as Batten and Bickley. David Meacock has even resigned twice to underline his anger although Gawain unkindly tells me this was because nobody noticed when he did it first time.

Jonathan Arnott MEP has left the party altogether. Like his forebears, it's also slipped his mind that he should step down from his seat on the back of it.

Henry Bolton is oblivious to all this. Perhaps he believes that he is some kind of Jeremy Corbyn. But he is not.

Friday 26th January 2018

The Sun pulls through.

'KIPPER CASH: UKIP leader Henry Bolton given £10,000 expenses in the last month – but now claims he's skint.

'Party treasurer John Bickley confirmed he has been given thousands since September 29. Mr Bickley told *Sun Online*: "Ukip has paid him expenses and living allowances. It's incontrovertible he has had his expenses and living allowances paid. The party has been doing everything to try to help him. The party isn't undermining him".

'Mr Bickley also ruled out claims by Mr Bolton he had stopped him from receiving a salary. He added: "It was absolutely clear at the leadership election the role did not come with a salary. Mr Bolton knew there was no salary".'

Sunday 28th January 2018

If Bolton's ousted, the party will have to install an interim leader until there can be an election. Paul Oakden has been calling me and Steve Crowther about the issue and myself and Steve have in turn been calling Oakden and each other.

'You should be interim leader.'

'No, my dear chap, it has to fall to you.'

'Nonsense. You are the plain and obvious choice.'

The role is, of course, unpaid. Steve has already done his time in this regard and neither Oakden nor Oakley can live on thin air although Henry Bolton apparently believed that he could.

We'll give this further thought. In the interim, I decide to check who the bookies think will be the next leader. Coral have David Kurten in pole position, followed by Nigel. Whittle has the next-best odds, then there's a clutch of individuals at 25/1. They are: Paul Oakden, Arron Banks, Suzanne Evans — and Paul Oakley.

Gnarly!

Wednesday 31st January 2018

Very, very early hours. I've heard rumours that the Mighty Peter Harris is thinking of leaving UKIP and joining the Dagenham Conservatives. I send him a quick message to which he replies almost immediately.

I dial his number and we have a lengthy conversation. The Tories are nothing like us and Peter's talents will be squandered if he goes.

Hope this worked.

Tuesday 6th February 2018

Henry's homunculus and one-time leadership candidate David Allen (who bottled out of the race) posts an interview with Bolton on Youtube.

'Did any member of the NEC give you a reason as to why they were going to propose a vote of no confidence?' asks Allen.

'One said because I'd left my wife. Another one criticised my knowledge of economic theories.'

'And that was it?'

'And that was it.'

In certain circumstances and on certain occasions I figuratively step back, give myself a shake and ask these questions:

'Am I being stupid? Or are they being stupid?'

To help me make up my mind in this instance, I speak to Adam Richardson.

'Could you get a copy of the recording of the No Confidence meeting over to me?'

'No problem.'

'Has anyone else asked for it?'

'No, but they're welcome to have one if they want.'

Over several years of practice at the Bar I've become used to the idea of disclosure and exchange. Both sides must be aware of each other's evidence before a trial for reasons of fairness. I'm just about to make a courtesy call when I remember that this isn't a trial.

I don't dial Henry's number after all.

He will not see it coming.

Friday 9th February 2018

Peter Harris has buggered off to the Tories after all.

That's right. Peter. Blinking. Harris.

Bolton has no idea how much of a loss this is. That man has done far more for the party than this ex-Lib Dem ever will.

And Henry has finally written a formal complaint about the person he holds responsible for leaking private information to the media with a view to ousting him. On the face of it, there's a case to answer. The next step is for me as General Secretary to ask the Respondent for their comments but the EGM is in just over a week so we've little time. I ask Oakden what he wants to do.

'What I'd like,' he tells me, 'is for the NEC to be asked to suspend his membership pending a disciplinary hearing. I suspect you'll easily get the majority you need.'

Fine. The emergency powers to be exercised are those of the Chairman, but it won't hurt to have our backing. Tactically, this will allow us to show that Henry's belief in a conspiracy between the NEC and the Indigo Group is a bunch of bollocks. Detailed consideration of the issues can be pushed back until after the EGM. If swift action isn't taken, then our current leader will refer to and rely upon this in attack. I'm not minded to give Bolton the ammunition. Suspension it must be.

Tuesday 13th February 2018

People are asking me about the current leader's draft constitutional reforms. No idea because I've not seen them. Ha — but then I do. An email from 'Henry Bolton, UKIP Leader' has gone straight into the junk email folder. Most fitting.

Wednesday 14th February 2018

The current tally of NEC members is that seven support suspension of Henry's foe and three are against. Two have yet to say.

We all then receive an email from the Respondent himself. As this issue is supposed to be confidential, someone's been leaking to him. Moron that he (or possibly she) is.

'As one of the most vocal critics of Mr Bolton I am sure that he would very much like me not to be there, but suspending me because of my opposition would be unwise and politically very damaging to UKIP.

'If I do not receive notification within the next two hours of my ability to vote at the EGM I will be going to the High Court to get an order prohibiting my exclusion.'

Will you now? Go on then.

Nonetheless, I need to discuss this with the chairman.

'Paul – is it worth me having a private word with the guy about his suspension? He wants Henry gone, too. Surely he can see that this will kill collusion rumours? Won't he take a thrashing for the good of the school?'

'No. He's incapable of seeing the big picture. Don't waste your time.'

Fair enough. Adam Richardson has already drafted the notice of suspension. I cast my eye over it. For form's sake, I still need to hear back from two NEC colleagues so chase both. Otherwise, we have a majority. Let's pull the lever and do as Henry asks.

Thursday 15th February 2018

Mr Justice Warby, High Court Judge, delivers his ruling in the case of Barron, Healey & Champion v Jane Collins & UKIP. It's a lengthy judgment but the worst bit is this:

'I have concluded that a limited costs order should be made against UKIP, to reflect the impact on the action and its costs of the Party's deliberate and calculated decisions of late February and early March 2015, to ensure for Party political and specifically electoral reasons that the claimants' action should not be settled before the General Election.'

'A limited costs order' against the party doesn't sound too bad. Yet I know from my professional experience that it's not going to be pennies but, instead – well – a shitload of money. The exact figure will be calculated by the Judge at a later date.

Returning to current internal party matters, the Respondent hasn't taken us to court as he threatened to do yesterday afternoon.

I've had long chats with the two people who hadn't yet made up their minds. One's in favour and one against, so they cancel each other out. The majority to suspend remains and now's the time to act.

But then. . .

Bolton thinks it a good idea to send a legalistic email to Paul Oakden. It's not from solicitors but has been written by the current leader himself. A rambling diatribe of nearly four pages, the core is this.

'If by 4:00pm on Friday 16 February 2018 you have not suspended this person or produced a valid and well reasoned explanation for not having taken that action I will consult solicitors to make an emergency application for an injunction stopping the EGM taking place on Saturday 17 February

2018 pending the outcome of a Judicial Review by me against the failures of you and the NEC in failing to take said actions.'

Henry Bolton may be a barrack-room lawyer but Adam Richardson's a real one. His reaction is immediate and pithy.

'Judicial review only applies to an arm of the state. HA HA HA HA please let him do it!'

Now now, Adam. That's bad form. If Bolton actually instructs solicitors they might be able to find something substantive to bash us with. Can't think what though. I'm still minded to undertake the suspension as Henry's asked, but it's time for me to cook the dinner so this can wait.

Peter McIlvenna sends a text just after 9 pm.

'Well done on getting your picture into Nigel's "Support-For-Henry" article in the *Daily Telegraph*.'

He emails me the link to the piece which has just been published. Farage concludes with this.

> 'I believe it would be better to allow Mr Bolton, with all his faults, the chance to turn Ukip into an electoral machine again. The alternative is for the party to carry on down the path of self-destruction into irrelevance. It may be too late to save Ukip, but you never know.'

Dagnabbit Nigel! You weren't supposed to be making a decision until tomorrow!

I'd been planning on phoning him beforehand with my persuasive powers turned up full. Not to condemn Bolton (he wouldn't) but to ask that he keep his hooter out. I hadn't got round to it. On the other hand, the endorsement isn't glowing and, more importantly, the piece has a photo of me with Farage. In a national broadsheet. Ace.

That distraction over with, I return to considering the current leader's request, no: demand, for stern action against his foe. Proudly pig-headed, I rarely change my mind so am astonished to discover that Bolton has made me do so. I get in touch with Oakden at 10.30 pm.

'I am sharing these thoughts only with you. Fuck Henry. Let's call his bluff.'

Friday 16th February 2017

Our current leader hasn't taken us to court as he threatened to do yesterday afternoon.

Oakden gives me a ring while I'm in Bromley to buy a new shirt for tomorrow's EGM from Marks and Sparks. Bit pushed for time as the store's about to close.

'He says he's not going to sue us,' Paul tells me. 'But he's muttering about something else and implying he'd be backed in whatever that is by Arron Banks. Have you heard from Arron? And can you think of anything he might be able to do? In the legal sense?'

I ponder for a moment while also walking in the wrong direction and away from the men's section. I hate shopping.

'Not spoken to Banksy for a few weeks and honestly can't think what Bolton's on about.'

After we hang up I conclude that it might just be this:

'I will do such things. What they are, yet I know not; but they shall be. The terrors of the earth.'[2]

Saturday 17th February 2018

I'm awake at 5.15 to get spruced up in time for the car that's arriving at six. Mornings, eh? Aren't they rubbish? Sarah Montague is interviewing me about this afternoon's EGM on the *Today* programme. It was initially to have been at 7.50 but the scunners have brought it forward to 7.30.

Gawain, bless him, has offered to meet me at the studio to give a briefing before I go in. He sends a string of texts.

'Sorry'. 6.49 am.

'Bugger bugger bugger'. 6.54 am.

'I'll be there but with only a couple of minutes to spare.' 6.56 am

'Do you have papers etc?' 6.58 am.

It gets to 7.18 am. And:

'Sitting in the studio is the General Secr etary of UKIP, Paul Oakley, Good morning to you. And what is your case, what case will you be making today?'

'Well I have no interest whatsoever in his personal life it's basically, for me, the fact that he's done nothing as leader. He's not making the case for Brexit. A particular problem is we've got local elections in May. This time in 2014 we were already well down the campaigning route and we've done nothing.

'He was elected five months ago. He goes before the members today. If they say, "Look, we want him to stay", do you go?'

'Yes, the NEC will be standing down. But: big thrill. We're having

---

2 William Shakespeare, *The Tragedy of King Lear*, act 2, scene 4.

NEC elections now anyway. I will be standing again because Henry will be out after the local elections if he isn't out today.'

7.26 am and I'm finished. I receive another text from Gawain.

'Outside BBC now. Hardly seems worth it. Will advertise and listen.'

He then sends out a Tweet telling people to tune in to hear Oakley on the wireless.

We meet for a coffee and then he heads up to Euston to catch a Birmingham train. My BBC car has been booked to drive me to chambers. In fact, it takes me to the McDonalds in Fleet Street first for breakfast.

I've never been in chambers this early before but it gives me time to start thinking about this afternoon's speech. I'll be junior counsel to Steve Crowther who's lead prosecutor.

Haven't really got into it yet when Emmett Jenner arrives so I grab my laptop and a set of earphones as he's driving us up to Brum. Rudely, I sit in the back, listening to the recording of the Vote of No Confidence meeting and jotting down notes about the complaints that were raised. It looks like there were eighteen concerns although some are inter-related. That's in addition to his skirt-chasing.

We arrive at the International Convention Centre before noon. The doors haven't opened yet but there's already a mob of members at the bottom of the escalators leading up to the auditorium.

I accost Gawain and demand access to a quiet place to finish off my speech. He takes me up in the private lift to the press room where I deposit myself at the far end of the large table and away from the journalists. Shielding the work with the left arm as if in a maths exam, the thing's cut down even further as I'm only allowed to speak for five minutes.

There's then an NEC briefing in the Green Room behind the stage. I pass Bolton on the stairwell and insist on shaking his hand.

'Nothing that I'm going to say is personal Henry.'

He takes it in good sport.

'May the best side win.'

His eyes are hollow and red-edged. One of his retinue mutters something about ditching the NEC as I walk down the stairs.

The NEC are VIPs and given reserved front row seats in the auditorium. I squeeze myself between Paula Walters and Steve Crowther. Proceedings are delayed because of the huge mass of attendees, all of whom need to be accredited and given a watermarked ballot paper.

Eventually, we begin. Crowther opens on behalf of the Crown. He takes a long time to emerge on stage and the anticipatory applause dies to silence. Has he been kidnapped? Ah. Here he is. The clapping rises again.

'Tell us how this is not about you. Tell us about all the brilliant things you intend to do to make this party great, but haven't had a chance to start yet. Tell us that all of this is a trumped-up charge, a storm in a teacup that has been exploited to persecute you. Tell us it's everybody's fault but yours-the NEC, the MEPs, the spokesmen, the donors, the UKIP Lords, the media, you name it.

'Give it your best shot.

'Or, take a deep breath and, I'm sure not for the first time in your life, do the brave, honourable, decent thing. Bow out gracefully, and give this party at least a fighting chance of survival.'

Then - a shock which wasn't in the draft speech he'd sent to me.

'There needs to be a scalp and that scalp will be mine. Today, I will be resigning from the NEC.'

Henry's called. He too takes some time to reach the stage and Crowther's returned to his seat before he appears. I whisper to him.

'Why did you take so long to arrive? Was it for comedic effect?'

'Not at all. The route is by dog-leg and labyrinth. It takes a while.'

Aha. Here's Henry. He immediately attacks Elizabeth Jones for proposing the vote of no confidence and me for the comments on Radio 4 first thing.

'Some members have engaged on a subversive campaign to attack me.

'They are the enemy within.

'They are self-serving.

'Their behaviour is divisive and despicable.'

He's actually very persuasive. As Nigel is open about his contempt for the NEC, many party members are equally revolted by its very existence. Skilfully, Bolton plays on this. The fact that it has nothing to do with the reason for our attendance today is irrelevant.

'They have even attacked my career record.

'And NEC members have colluded with the mainstream media and the tabloids.'

Oh – and he does just about remember to apologise for his personal behaviour too. Overall, an excellent effort. Backed into a corner, he fights majestically. He might even pull it off.

Keen to avoid delay in reaching the podium for my own speech, I'm already standing by the door ready to move backstage as soon as

Bolton's finished. He does, and I can see the beginnings of a standing ovation for him before passing through.

Crikey, five minutes really isn't enough. I need seven, maybe six at a push. Let's see how quickly I can speak without garbling.

'Henry. On the day after the vote of no confidence you told Nigel Farage on his LBC show that the only allegation against you was that you'd left your wife.

'Which is an odd thing to say for someone who knew the meeting was being recorded. In the course of that 2 hour, 13 minute and 35 second recording, we did indeed mention your personal life. But there was a lot more.'

I run through a curtailed list of ten issues.

'And in your "non-resignation" speech of 22 January you said that the NEC needs urgent reform.

'But it can't be that urgent because you'd never mentioned it to the NEC in your three meetings as leader. And members can check the minutes of those meetings are on the website.'

Only because I'd finally gotten round to having them posted there a couple of days ago. Hee hee hee.

'Your new constitution proposes a huge power shift away from the members and to you. Perhaps you'll be a benign dictator. But we've already had a taste of what the brave new UKIP will be if you get your way, haven't we?

I read from his solicitors' letter about Anne Marie Waters. There are gasps from the audience.

'In our party it's people like these who decide who can and cannot be leader, not you Henry Bolton.'

I sweep my arm across the crowd.

'The members. Never, ever presume to take that right away from them.'

As intended, I receive prolonged applause for this. Oakden interjects.

'Thirty seconds Paul!'

Darn it. I'll have to hurry.

'And there was more on Thursday wasn't there? Because you said you'd take us to court to stop this very EGM unless we suspended your nemesis.'

I quote from Bolton's weedy email and am now over time.

'Well, we called your bluff Henry. We will not be bullied.'

Crap speech. Rushed. Missed out the bit where I'd have told him that we would have suspended the member were it not for his threat. And my closing flourish which was to rip off Senator Lloyd Bentsen's famous put-down, replacing Henry for Dan Quayle and Farage for Jack Kennedy.

Paul Brand of ITV news is forgiving of me nonetheless and Tweets:

'UKIP's Paul Oakley allegedly "eviscerating" Bolton. Huge applause for him in the room as he accuses Bolton of legal threats against those who've criticised him.'

The lovely Viv Evans from *UKIP Daily* is kind, too, in her live feed:

'"We stood up to him", says Oakley to thunderous applause. Oakley stuck the knife in good and proper.'

And West Midlands MEP Bill Etheridge is particularly charming in a text which hits my phone as I sit back down.

'Well done mate. You were fucking awesome.'

Other speeches from members for and against the motion are chosen from a bucket. None of them are as good as they could have been, and that goes for both sides.

The NEC have Paula Waters to close their case. Henry's also entitled to a Seconder to finish off on his behalf. He chooses himself for that role which says a lot. Anyway, the reference to the recording of the NEC meeting has annoyed him as it was meant to.

'I challenge the General Secretary to produce a copy of that recording!'

Oakden has warned us about heckling but I can't resist. At the top of my voice from the front row, which Henry can certainly hear even if the rest of the audience cannot:

'If you'd bothered to ask Adam for a copy he'd have happily given you one!'

Oakden rightly tells me to shut it and I do.

Then Bolton metaphorically pulls the pin on a fragmentation grenade but forgets he's supposed to throw it at the enemy and not keep hold of the thing.

'If you vote me out today. There will be consequences!'

That sort of warning might work well on new recruits to the Army Cadet Force. It's hard to think of anything worse he could say to the mob of bellicose deplorables who are the members of UKIP.

The shouts, jeers and whistles which ensue make it obvious, even to Bolton, that he's just signed his own death warrant.

The cacophony doesn't stop and Bolton can't finish. Oakden calls for order and demands that one lairy man at the back of the room is ejected from the premises.

'I've told you already,' Paul berates the crowd. 'This won't be tolerated. Henry - I'm giving the chance to repeat what you've just said. And it'll be heard without interruption.'

He does repeat it, but you can see that his spirit has left his body.

Formal proceedings over, Oakden announces the procedure for voting.

'I know that many of you have to head back to distant reaches of the country so you can go after you've put your ballot in one of the boxes. However. If you do leave the room you won't be allowed back in. I hope that's clear.'

So Katie Fanning and I decide to escape via the fire exit at the back of the stage to make a trip to the wine bar. There are 1,500 people here so the voting and the counting will take some time.

Upon our return, the NEC have another swift briefing in the Green Room. It's agreed that Gerard will take over as interim leader. Elizabeth Jones believes that we should do more and one or two colleagues seem amenable to her proposal.

'Henry Bolton,' she says, 'must be immediately suspended for bringing the party into disrepute.'

My lip curls.

'Absolutely not. I refuse to kick a man when he's down.'

Richardson, Wauchope, Bown and Crowther concur. The idea's dropped.

The press have finally been allowed into the auditorium and the Party Chairman makes the formal announcement.

'Votes cast by those who supported the motion of no confidence: 867 or 63%.

'Votes cast by those who opposed the motion of no confidence: 500 or 37%.

'As a result, Henry Bolton has been removed as Leader of UKIP.'

Peter Jewell has arranged for the NEC and party staff to have drinkies at his club which is a short cab ride away. There are many speeches from the departing chairman, the departing former chairman and others. The farewells are almost as overlong as those in the final film of the Lord of the Rings trilogy.

Sky News gets in touch.

'Keen to have you on live on *Sunrise* tomorrow morning to discuss what next for UKIP and your hopes for the party's future. I can send a camera to you.'

Kinell. I'd been hoping for a bit of a lie-in. I'll go to them. The house is a tip what with all this politicking over the past few weeks.

The evening dies down as I'm waiting to be picked up by Emmett. We're then unexpectedly treated to several Nocturnes from the piano in the corner of the room. It's the new leader.

'I didn't know you could play, Gerard?'

'Very few people do.'

CHAPTER FORTY-SEVEN

Oh—Tommy, Tommy!

Sunday 18th February 2018

The car takes me to Sky News in Millbank first thing. I'm shut into a remote studio to be interviewed by Stephen Dixon who's in a different studio but still in London. Odd, but not mine to reason why.

'Are you glad he's gone?' Dixon asks.

'I'm saddened he's gone. I don't think he's a bad man. He's personable but he's not a politician. But seriously, if the public want to know about personal issues like that they're going to watch The Kardashians. They ought not to be having this from the leader of a national political party and in that respect I'm pleased that we're no longer going to be focussing on this when people talk about UKIP.'

I don't really expect the tone of the interview to reflect the comment made by William Etheridge Esq to me yesterday, but it's irritating when Dixon swiftly moves on to his real interest. I praise the new leader's record and he jumps in.

'Gerard Batten who was talking, not very long ago, less than a year ago, about Islam in a way which many people found very concerning?'

'Gerard's entitled to his opinion and I don't necessarily share all his opinions. But we ought to be able to have a debate about this and he certainly shouldn't be silenced. He will not be "banging on about Islam" over the next few months. He will be focussing on Brexit. His views on Moslems and radical Islam are a complete irrelevance.'

'They're not an irrelevance though. . .'

I cut across him.

'Yes. They are.'

I'm delivered back home and continue watching Sky News with a nice hot cuppa. Gerard himself is now on. It's an outside broadcast under a beautiful blue sky. Cold, leafless trees stand behind him. By sheer force of will I instruct their branches to burst into bud before our very eyes just as they did in the closing scenes of John Boorman's *Excalibur* movie. They ignore me of course. At least for now.

Niall Paterson gets straight down to it.

'Do you still believe that all Moslems should sign a charter of understanding, a code of conduct, which demands that they renounce violence and certain passages from the Koran?'

Gerard is prepared.

'Thank you for asking me about it. I thought you might do that and I've got the little offending piece of paper here. Some years ago I commissioned a document from a former sharia lawyer, who rejected Islam, to lay out all of the texts in the Koran which allow people to justify violence and extremism. And what we did at the end of that document, which was my idea, was a little affirmation in which we asked people to reject those violent texts.

'They are things which are intrinsic to a literalist, radical interpretation of Islamic texts and I don't think it's unreasonable for people who come and live in our country to reject these dark age ideologies which many of them bring with them.'

Paterson carries on.

'OK. So you DO still think that Moslems should sign this charter of understanding.'

More of the same and more of the same and more of the same. Tiresome. Batten sums up.

'We don't want to go in fear of terrorist attacks or violence or intimidation by people who follow a particular ideological belief. Who wants to live in that kind of society? I certainly don't and I doubt that you do either.'

Gerard Batten is one of our clearest thinkers on the actual process for leaving the EU. Four years ago he'd even written a book about it called *The Road to Freedom*. If the Tory government had bothered to read it then Britain would have been spared much of the hand-wringing and caterwauling it's had to endure post-referendum.

Not that this matters to Paterson and his pals in the mainstream media because they really are utterly obsessed with Islam.

Tuesday 20th February 2018

Morning start at the MI + ME café in St Pancras station. I meet Lawrence Webb under the vast glass canopy. It's definitely worth coming because the leader of UKIP is buying us croissants.

Paul Oakden has decided to retire as party chairman and he knows why we're having this discussion today.

'Go for it,' he urged. 'This party needs you in that Chair.'

I'm of two minds. If I take on the role it'll be full time, and then some. I'll need to suspend my legal practice at the Bar and that will suspend my income. Problem is that the party was skint anyway and it's now even poorer after Henry Bolton decided that the five-figure cost of holding an EGM was money well spent.

'Gerard,' I say. 'I would be honoured to take on this role, but I'd need to be paid. I'm happy to accept a lower salary than Oakden's but just can't do it for free. Hope you understand.'

Monday 26th February 2018

Gerard confirms that the new party chairman will be Tony McIntyre from South-West Region. He's retired and on a pension so doesn't need a wage. I don't know the man but have heard good things about him.

He's introduced to the party officers at Anil's restaurant which is undergoing renovations. The place is basically a builders' yard at the moment. No matter. UKIP have worked effectively on bombsites many times before. In any event, McIntyre seems to be an excellent choice.

Although Batten would like to be focussing on the battle for Brexit, the Jane Collins court claim is a distraction because he'll have to waste a lot of effort on fundraising. From past experience and in happier times we know that the best way of doing this is by sending letters to members. Emails do not elicit the same response for two reasons. Firstly, many of our members don't have internet access. Secondly, it's common knowledge that emails are often unread, whoever the sender and whoever the recipient may be.

However, distributing that many letters will cost a whopping £22,758. The party doesn't have this cash to spare and it's unlikely that any firm of printers will give us credit. Yet Gerard has already worked out a solution.

'I will fund this from my own savings. I'll want the money back if we reach our target but to be honest – if we don't – then it won't matter.'

Mike Hookem MEP interrupts in his usual blunt fashion.

'No, you won't be funding this, Gerard. You'll be funding half of it. Because I'll be happy to make up the other 50% myself.'

Wednesday 7th March 2018

Although UKIP have engaged solicitors to deal with the High Court costs claim, Gerald Shamash writes a letter directly to Gerard Batten.

> 'Following today's news stories regarding UKIP officials, including you, admitting that UKIP may become insolvent in the next few weeks, we write to remind you and all UKIP National Executive Committee members of their duties as directors of UKIP.
>
> 'As you will be aware, our clients in the above-mentioned claim were successful in obtaining a costs order against UKIP relating to the 2015-2017 Jane Collins UKIP MEP defamation proceedings, on 15 February 2018. The costs that UKIP will be liable for have not yet been finalised but it is likely that UKIP will be ordered to pay a six-figure sum, Indeed, the interim (and not the final) costs payment we seek to obtain is £263,808.08. In light of this, we remind the UKIP directors that as they are aware of UKIP's insolvency risk they must take every step to minimise potential loss to creditors, namely this firm and its counsel William McCormick QC.
>
> 'Under sections 214 and 246ZB of the Insolvency Act 1986, if UKIP continues to trade as normal once UKIP directors know that there is no reasonable prospect that UKIP will avoid going into insolvency, any Insolvency practitioner for UKIP can seek a declaration from the courts that the directors personally contribute to UKIP's assets.
>
> 'We would not hesitate to assist the court in such proceedings should the occasion arise.'

Sunday 18th March 2018

Idiot that I am, I've alighted from the Tube on autopilot at Green Park, having forgotten quite how far away this station is from Speakers' Corner in Hyde Park. There's a large crowd as I eventually arrive and I notice some of those artificial green garden canes discarded on the ground. It's odd because there are no plant beds in the vicinity and it's too early in the season to grow tomatoes anyway. The canes are the type made of plastic-coated steel rods.

There are murmurings about some kind of altercation. Strange, as everyone in the vicinity seems to be a normal-looking Brit. No characters with pink hair and masks or Saladin lookalikes are to be seen.

I turn to the Afro-Caribbean bloke who's standing next to me.

'Has something happened?'

'A gang of about twenty Moslems were here. But they were persuaded to leave.'

It's surprising they'd be interested in today's event which is dry and specialist. Fresh-right luminaries Lauren Southern, Brittany Pettibone and Martin Sellner had arranged to hold a free speech event here this afternoon. However, the UK's Home Office had denied them entry to the country a few days ago so somebody else is going to read out Sellner's words in a symbolic fashion.

That somebody is Mr Tommy Robinson.

Eventually, the man himself arrives and gets started. I'm only about twenty feet away from him but can hear barely a thing as he doesn't have a microphone and there's a background hum. Nobody is being intentionally rude as he speaks but there are excited exclamations and murmurings from the closely-packed mob which are just loud enough to drown him out.

In any case, Robinson is a smart cookie and has produced printouts of Sellner's speech which are passed through the crowd. There are only a few copies, but I manage to grab one.

It's quite a long lecture but he eventually draws to a close with this:

'The battle, our battle for freedom of speech, has just begun. And Speakers' Corner will become a symbolic place in that struggle. When you go home know I want you to bring the spirit of Speakers' Corner with you. Every single person who raised his hand because he could relate to this moment of fear, when he did not dare to speak his mind. Promise me, promise yourself this: Next time I will overcome my inner fear. Next time I will speak up.'

I assume that's what Tommy's saying anyway because he still can't be heard so I'm reading the handout.

Everyone starts to disperse, peaceably and in a good-natured fashion.

Then I see somebody else I know from UKIP. Elizabeth Jones is here too.

'Oh. Hello Liz,' I say. 'Didn't know you were coming. Did you enjoy it?'

'OutSTANDing,' she exclaims.

We chat for a moment and then George Cottrell appears. Jones moves nearby to talk to someone else.

'Raheem's about,' he tells me.

Kassam duly-joins us too. They've arranged to have a drink with Tommy.

'Coming?'

Obviously, but perhaps a few more might want to tag along?

'Er,' I offer, 'Liz Jones is, er, hanging around. Um, shall we, er . . .'

'No,' says Cottrell.

'Absolutely not,' adds Raheem. 'Come on. Let's go.'

We march off quickly in the direction of the Edgware Road which is nicknamed London's 'Arab Street'. Shariah banks, hookah bars and middle-eastern restaurants abound.

'I can't normally head up this way without being harassed as an apostate,' Kassam confides to us.

Today is different. As the rally is dispersing to all corners of the capital, he is stopped several times by departing participants who want to shake his hand or take selfies. Good heavens. He's become famous without me even noticing! To be blunt, I should have noticed. That group photograph of him standing with Gerry Gunster, Arron Banks, Nigel and Andy Wigmore has become a classic of our age. Especially as it also features President Donald J Trump giving a thumbs-up.

Nonetheless, I'm wondering where we're going to find a pub at which we're going to avoid a pestering. Not by teetotal jihadists, but by any of their Leftard apologists who, coincidentally, might be having a quiet pint at the same venue.

'Don't worry about that,' says George. 'It's round here.'

We head down a side street and walk along a little way before coming upon your classic English boozer. Low lighting, wood panelling and an excellent range of beers. It's called. . .

Actually, I'm not going to say. That's because Tommy arrives just after we do and receives a warm welcome. There's no need to draw unwanted attention to this hostelry and thereby damage its business.

This is the first time I've met him in person although we've been following each other on Twitter for a while. Turning on my New Age

Sensors, I observe no wickedness within him. He's your typical working class English lad of the type so despised by the metropolitan establishment. Tommy is full of smiles and energy and pleased to natter to everyone around our small table at the pub.

I am a little wary though. As the hard-left and our dim-witted intelligentsia regularly warn, Robinson is a 'facist'.

Indeed, it's a well-known fact that the Führer of Germany from 1933 to 1945 had very extreme views on Islam himself. He believed that Moslem-occupied and shariah-run medieval Spain was an example to the world. He was frustrated that Charles Martel had won the Battle of Poitiers because Europe would otherwise have been an Islamic continent. Practising what he preached, his blessing was then given to Heinrich Himmler to set up Moslem Waffen SS regiments for deployment in the Balkans.

As far as I can make out, Robinson agrees with none of this. So he is, at best, a shit Hitler.

Tommy records a brief video message which is posted online straight away. This will receive millions of hits as he is now popular right across the globe. My party has recently realised the sheer power of internet blogging and will soon be moving into the field as well.

So someone suggests that Tommy should consider joining UKIP.

'No – not my thing,' he replies.

CHAPTER FORTY-EIGHT

A Good Day to Bury Bad News

Monday 19th March 2018

A COURT ORDER IS SERVED on UKIP. Mr Justice Warby has considered the written submissions made by the lawyers and calculated that the appropriate interim costs payments are two sums of £125,000 and £50,000. That total figure is £88,808.08 less than Steel and Shamash were seeking, but it's still a colossal amount for UKIP to pay.

Solicitor Gerald Shamash is quoted in the *Guardian*.

'The MPs have been through nearly four years of litigation. UKIP has to pay £175,000. The party has put the MPs through misery and if the result of that is that UKIP no longer exists, then UKIP no longer exists.'

There being an imminent bank holiday, the party has to find this money in just over a fortnight and certainly not later than 3rd April.

Wednesday 22nd March 2018

Our chap David Kurten puts a formal question to Labour mayor Sadiq Khan in the London Assembly.

'Are you making plans to mark the occasion when London, as capital of the UK, leaves the European Union on 29th March 2019?'

The query is perfectly reasonable. Khan's reaction? Not so much.

'If your party's still around next year I'd be curious to see what ideas you have. Maybe there'll be a bucket going round for the legal fees they've got to pay in the next couple of weeks. I'm looking forward to seeing which party you represent next time there's mayor's question time. Maybe we'll mark that day with a celebration when UKIP's finally abolished.'

Just pause to think about that for the moment. The Labour party presents itself as a kind-hearted organisation which values fairness above all. It's fine for them to disagree with UKIP and to seek to defeat us at elections. No problem with that. Yet here there is gloating and lusting that a political party, an outlet for the voices of millions of people, will be destroyed forever. Not at the ballot box, but after every penny it has is squeezed into the pockets of lawyers.

Labour are lower than vermin.

Sunday 25th March 2018

Gerard confirms that, as a result of his frenetic fundraising, he's managed to raise a mammoth chunk of cash so far. This has come not only from members but from true democrats in the wider world. In other words, we can now pay off the Labour Claimants in full. And damn their impudence.

This is being kept quiet for now. It'll piss off the Leftards when they discover that we haven't been liquidated after all.

Tuesday 27th March 2018

Notification is sent to the members about the imminent leadership election. The requirements have been tweaked once more.

'On 19 March 2018 applicants must have been a member of the party, in good standing continuously for at least five years. (In the case of MEPs the term good standing is to include regular payments to the party in compliance with the MEP's charter). Applicants must also have held office within the party (as a branch officer or higher) AND have stood for parliament for the party.'

A hundred signatures are needed again, but this time assentors can back as many candidates as they please. That will make the process a little easier for all aspirants. The tithing requirements will make the process a little harder for some MEPs because many of them have 'forgotten' that they're supposed to donate to the party and have been keeping their hands in their pockets. The level of the deposit has been raised to £7,000. That'll have a neutral effect. Any candidate who will struggle to raise that sum would have found the previous figure of £5,000 equally intimidating.

Nigel Farage will have no difficulty complying with any of these criteria. As the British government is continuing to betray Brexit, now must be the time for his return.

Tuesday 3rd April 2018

Today's the very last day for UKIP to pay that £175,000 to the Barron/Healey/Champion lawyers. If we do not, then steps will be taken which might close the party down forever.

I've been on tenterhooks and am finally able to announce something to the world on Twitter: Alive and kicking. Accompanied by that iconic still from the film of Barry Hines' book, Kes.

In fact, we paid them every single penny last Thursday. Eat shit and die, Steel and Shamash.

Saturday 14th April 2018

UKIP issues a press release.

'We are pleased to announce that as of 5.00pm today, Gerard Batten MEP is the new Leader of the UK Independence Party.'

'Returning Officer Piers Wauchope confirmed that no applications for the leadership had been received by the deadline.

'Mr Batten, therefore, assumed the Leadership after an uncontested election.'

Ach. So Nigel hasn't gone for it.

Nonetheless, Gerard tells us that he'll only remain in post for a year. He's a reluctant leader after all.

Thursday 3rd May 2018

Council elections are taking place today. I am standing in Downham ward under the UKIP flag. A new organisation is on the ballot paper too. It is the Democrats and Veterans Party aka the DVP aka the 'Gay Donkey' party. This was set up by that former candidate for UKIP leader, John Rees Evans, who is an advocate of a concept called 'Direct Democracy'. He is rumoured to have abandoned UKIP on the very day of the leadership announcement on 29th September when the members had, for the second time, directly and democratically rejected his campaign for the post. And we scornfully call it the 'Gay Donkey' party because JRE had once delivered an anecdote about a homosexual ass which tried to rape his horse.

One of the DVP candidates is Massimo DiMambro who also remains a member of our local UKIP branch. Strictly-speaking, as he's challenging my own mighty struggle to be a councillor for Downham, his expulsion from our party should be automatic.

I pretend not to have noticed but will have firm words with the silly beggar at a later date.

Friday 4th May 2018

My phone beeps in the dead of night. At 6.46 am to be precise. A text message has been received.

'Hi Mr Oakley, Tom Smithard here from Radio 4 *Today* programme. We're keen to speak to you on today's show between 8.30am and 9am about the election results. Would you be available?'

I call Gawain who remains on the party payroll as part-time press officer. He gives it the green light.

'Do the best you can. It's been a disaster.'

The telly is turned on and it transpires that UKIP have already lost 92 councillors and had only run a quarter of the candidates that we'd put up in 2014 to boot. The smirks of the presenters as they pronounce the death of the party are galling. And Suzanne Evans has been no help with her piece to the BBC.

'If UKIP does crumble I think you could still arguably make the case that it's been one of the most successful political parties in history.'

No. No. NO! This obituarial narrative needs to be stamped on right away.

I'll need a soundbite. A mighty one which will cut down this story like weeds, sweep those weeds into a bucket and empty that bucket over the fence of next-door's garden where its contents shall be forever forgotten.

Something along the lines of 'we'll be a phoenix rising from the ashes.' Not this of course – I don't deal in clichés.

I've overdone the Star Wars analogies recently so that's no good. What about Napoleon's heroic escape from Elba?

Except. He was then squashed at Waterloo and was a Corsican proponent of a European empire in any case. No - that'd be silly.

Think, boy. Think!

I glance at the pile of books on the bedside table for inspiration.

Naomi Wolf? Naw.

Ron Paul? Too dry.

Matt Bracken? Ha – best not.

Philip Ziegler? Now. That might just work. Dare I? I do so dare.

I'm more than happy to take one for the team and any consequential criticism from our enemies won't trouble me at all. Besides, I've nearly finished writing my own book and a touch of 'The Filth and The Fury' will be a useful boost when it's punted to publishers.

The BBC call up and leave me on hold. I can hear presenter Nick Robinson wittering away in the background. Then he comes to me.

'Isn't it time to say it's all over for UKIP? You did your job, I mean, you'll have a very large chapter in a rather important book about the history of Britain, but: it's over.'

'No, it's not over at all. Think of the Black Death in the middle ages. It comes along and it causes disruption and then it goes dormant. And that's exactly what we're going to do. Our time isn't finished because Brexit is being betrayed and there's a lot of anger in the country about that.'

'Can I just clarify? As General Secretary of UKIP you've just compared your party with the Black Death?'

'Absolutely. What's wrong with that?'

I hang up. Every TV bulletin, every radio bulletin and, indeed, the internet itself immediately explode and keep on exploding for the rest of the day. Nailed it.

CHAPTER FORTY-NINE

Stop the Khanage

Tuesday 8th May 2018

THE LABOUR MP FOR LEWISHAM EAST, Heidi Alexander, informs her public that she's standing down from parliament even though she'd only been re-elected to her seat eleven months ago. Sadiq Khan has offered her the role of deputy London mayor with responsibility for transport.

Sadly, this means that taxpayers will have to cough up for the cost of holding a by-election and other political parties will have to fork out for the cost of campaigning in it. This can't be helped.

Those 'other parties' are likely to include For Britain, whose leader Anne Marie Waters has flounced off from UKIP. They might also include the 'Gay Donkey' party.

If these vanity factions do stand in the by-election, this will squeeze UKIP's vote, perhaps to an embarrassing degree.

There's a positive side though. Heidi Alexander's salary is about to rise from the threadbare £77,000 she currently receives as an MP to a far more reasonable £130,000 in her new post at City Hall.

Wednesday 9th May 2018

As the constituency is covered by our branch, I've made a number of calls to see who can be 'volunteered' into standing as the UKIP candidate. Whittle's not interested. Hoong Wai Cheah and Keith Forster are ambivalent. Peter Lello might, possibly, raise his hand but he's not sure. I cannot be effed either, but will do it if nobody else steps forward.

Saturday 12th May 2018

Gerard has a word with me about the possible candidates and I tell him about our three lukewarm options. Batten favours a fourth choice: London Assembly member David Kurten. This being a by-election, the selection will be undertaken by the National Executive Committee and that decision will be taken tomorrow. Nonetheless, I email the branch members to ask for their thoughts to pass on. I get on very well with David myself, but have a sneaking suspicion that some of my boys may not be so happy.

Sunday 13th May 2018

Kurten is chosen as the UKIP parliamentary candidate for Lewisham East.

Tuesday 15th May 2018

There are new elections for the National Executive Committee and my term's expired so I'm standing again. It's an honour to be backed by a strong list of proposers and assentors: Paul Oakden, Peter Whittle AM, Mike Hookem MEP, David Kurten AM, Alan Craig, Vivian Evans, Peter Staveley, Dan Jukes, Mary Newton and Peter McIlvenna.

Candidates' supporters are listed within *Independence* magazine to help members cast their votes. And believe you me, our people take careful note of those endorsements. The form also includes a space to set out past party activities. I just about manage to squeeze it all into the box and – blimey – even impress myself when reading it back. Although, to be honest, that's not hard to do.

The application is filed with Head Office without certainty but with high hopes.

Thursday 17th May 2018

Conclave of UKIP Greenwich and Lewisham. The members are meeting David Kurten and we're planning the campaign along with assistance from the neighbouring crews in Bexley and Bromley.

Several of our fellows have discrete words with me afterwards. This is because, for entirely random reasons, a very great number of my branch activists are – well – 'good with colours'. Do you follow?

No? Alright. They 'dive straight into the mosh-pit at Kylie gigs.' Get it?

OK. Let me put it another way. The branch laughingly self-identifies as a Nest of Pooves.

One of them is particularly-plain.

'I cannot in all conscience as a gay married man support this candidate. So I'll not be campaigning or offering any support to the party during this by election.'

I fully-understand.

'I won't hold that against you at all. All our activists are volunteers and give up their valuable free time for the party, a fact that I never forget. Wouldn't dream of twisting anyone's arm over an issue like this.'

It goes without saying that none of the chaps are going to blab to the media about this either. Golden boys.

Friday 18th May 2018

PR Week publishes an article: 'UKIP's "Black Death" comment: PR gold?' It's a positive piece and concludes with these thoughts.

> 'The key message was maintained. Though ripe, the analogy was clear.
>
> 'Though damaged, the party could well rebound and act as the democratic disruptor that it has so successfully been over the past few years.
>
> 'Mission accomplished. It'll be the only thing anybody actually remembers from the local elections.'

The author is somebody called 'Gawain' who, obviously, I've never heard of. Nonetheless, his analysis is correct.

Monday 21st May 2018

Lewisham council release the list of nominated persons for the by election. One of those is Massimo DiMambro who is standing as candidate for the DVP and thus against David Kurten.

That cannot be ignored. Regretfully, he is expelled from UKIP.

The campaign team is then finalised by Kurten. It's Batten, Oakley, Forster, Grainger, Goodliffe, Waters (Ryan that is), Tucker, Vachha, Braine, Craig and Towler.

Tuesday 22nd May 2018

We've agreed on a layout for the leaflet which will be delivered to all voters by the Post Office. The design is very hush-hush. Richard Braine explains.

'Gerard wants the leaflet to have some impact when it lands on postal voters' doormats starting this Friday. He's concerned that sharing it online could cause it to be leaked by accident. It would be a good idea to hold off on social media until the leaflet starts arriving, at which point it's not impossible that all hell will break loose.'

Thursday 31st May 2018

Mayor Sadiq Khan is, effectively, the London Police and Crime Commissioner through the MOPAC committee. Notwithstanding his powers, there's been a rising toll of knife crime in the capital. The greatest concentrations of stabbings and slashings are in the London boroughs which have Labour councils and Labour MPs. Nothing to do with them though, guv. It's all the fault of the Tory government, they explain.

Whether it's impotence or incompetence, as far as UKIP are concerned there's no point in voting Labour if you want to see a reduction in the number of kids being sealed into wooden boxes.

Our secret leaflets deal with this. They're now being delivered, late as usual, by the Post Office and have been discovered in turn by the media. They depict the outline of a knife with the slogan 'Stop the Khanage'.

Lewisham Deptford's Labour MP, Vicky Foxcroft, clutches her pearls and speaks to the *Evening Standard*.

'This is a nasty leaflet full of lies which trivialises the serious problem of violent crime across the UK. In Lewisham, we celebrate our diverse community and we are confident that people here will reject this nonsense.'

Foxcroft really can't help the fact that she's pale, stale and female and her lecture to David Kurten, a proud black professional, is well-intentioned advice from her position of privilege. However, he is disinclined to 'celebrate' any sector of the community which thinks it's fine to stab a fellow human being.

Saturday 2nd June 2018

A photo is taken of Team Kurten. David himself is standing right in the middle of the shot as you'd expect. It's posted online just before we head off to campaign in Bellingham ward.

The picture is electronically-grabbed by an organisation called 'Far Right Watch' and re-posted by them. We already knew that they were as thick as pig shit, but this is extreme bell-endery even for them.

David Kurten is very amused by the caption they've added.

'UKIP in Lewisham today, a solid white male gammon fest . . .'

Sunday 3rd June 2018

John Hamilton of People Before Profit sends out details of the hustings event that he has organised via 38 Degrees together with an online flier.

'Labour,' he adds, 'still hasn't responded to the invitation and I have been told that they don't intend to attend in case Janet Daby makes a cock-up. Tory also not coming, but at least he has told me. All other candidates have confirmed attendance.'

I send a copy of this out to the members and then have a quick browse of Google to see which other local groups are publicising it.

There's this on Facebook from those arseholes of South London Anti-Fascists:

'Anne Waters, (Sharia Watch, Pergida) who was too extreme even for UKIP, has promised to organise a "Mass Leafletting" on the 9th and 10th June in Lewisham East.

'She has also mentioned a public meeting being planned at an unspecified "community centre" in Downham on Friday the 8th June and a strong presence at the scheduled hustings on the 12th June at the Salvation Army Hall in Catford.

'There is a coordinating meeting to oppose this being held by a range of local groups and TUs being held on 5th June, 8 pm, at 43 Sutherland Road, Forest Hill London SE23 2PS. All Welcome.'

43 Sutherland Road? Where's that I wonder?

I have however heard of 43 Sunderland Road. That address shares exactly the same postcode as this mysterious location and also happens to be the official headquarters of Lewisham West and Penge Labour Party. I'd love to pop along but suspect that the coda 'all welcome' isn't really true.

CHAPTER FIFTY

Clowns to the Left of Us

Monday 4th June 2018

I'D LEFT A MESSAGE with my own local police officer to ask for contact details for the Inspector of Rushey Green district where the hustings will take place. There was no response so I've now delved through the Metropolitan Police website and discovered that the proper officer is one Inspector James Weston. There's an online report form which will be directed straight to the man concerned and I complete it.

I email both Anne Marie Waters and Massimo DiMambro to suggest that they do likewise.

Wednesday 6th June 2018

The police finally respond.

'Inspector Weston has now moved away from Lewisham Borough and will therefore be unable to deal with your request. Inspector Yaxley is the current Safer Neighbourhoods Inspector.'

Great. The request hasn't been passed on to Inspector Yaxley though so I have to complete the online form once more.

And it transpires that the reason Janet Daby is refusing to attend the hustings isn't because she's scared. Oh no. This is a moral issue for her and she's actively refusing to share a platform with For Britain. It's probably never occurred to Daby that her own philosophy is equally repugnant to Anne Marie. Waters is a bit more grown-up than her about it though.

Saturday 9th June 2018

More campaigning for Kurten in Lewisham East. On returning home I see that the Metropolitan Police have roused themselves at last and are creaking towards action.

'We have sent your query to the relevant department, who will be in touch with you in due course.'

In your own time, officers. . .

Monday 11th June 2018

The hustings are tomorrow. Sergeant Biddle contacts me and I repeat my concerns yet again, also adding this:

'As you may be aware, "Antifa" groups of this kind often resort to violence and intimidation and, as a consequence, breach Section 2 (1) (b) of the Public Order Act 1936.'

This statute remains in force. However, there don't seem to have been any recent prosecutions under it as far as I know. The fascists of Antifa are largely left alone these days, usually dressed in uniform black, often carrying big sticks and invariably wearing masks. This is puzzling, as the Act was introduced all those decades ago to tackle people of precisely their kidney. It isn't hard to decipher:

> '**Prohibition of quasimilitary organisations**.
>
> 'If the members or adherents of any association of persons, whether incorporated or not, are organised and trained or organised and equipped either for the purpose of enabling them to be employed for the use or display of physical force in promoting any political object, or in such manner as to arouse reasonable apprehension that they are organised and either trained or equipped for that purpose; then any person who takes part in the control or management of the association, or in so organising or training as aforesaid any members or adherents thereof, shall be guilty of an offence.'

The sergeant's reply is reassuring.

'I can assure you that Lewisham Police and the Metropolitan Police Service are aware of the hustings this week.

'I can also assure you that there will be a proportionate policing plan and response covering the event. I will forward this on to Inspector Yaxley.'

Tuesday 12th June 2018

I take the bus to Catford for the Lewisham East hustings and alight by the theatre which gives me a few minutes to get there before the event begins. It's a short walk to the Salvation Army Hall on the north of the South Circular road. Presumably, the Leftard protestors will have been instructed by police to stand on the grassy wasteground on the other side of the street. This is right next to Mecca and the ideal place for them. It's a large, safe area in close, clear sight of the venue and they can squeal and squawk there as much as they choose to.

Oh – 'Mecca' is the local bingo hall by the way.

As I get closer, it turns out that the police have given no such instructions. In fact, the Leftards have been allowed to cluster right in front of the venue itself and encroach on the entranceway. That's unacceptable in itself.

What's even more unacceptable is that they're blocking people from coming in. They are jostling attendees. Prodding them with the hefty sticks they're being allowed to carry (which have inane placards stapled to them for a secondary purpose). Screaming at them. Threatening them.

'You should be ashamed! Ashamed!'

'Fucking wankers.'

'Racist scum, racist scum, racist scum.'

'Shame on you shame on you shame on you!'

What are the police doing in response? Bugger all that I can see. It's not as if they're short-handed; there are about thirty Bobbies on duty on the pavement and in a row inside and several meat-wagons parked up. Soooooo... What the heck is going on?

On reaching the gateway I'm happy to force my way through the demonstrators. This will probably mean I'll need a shower when I get home later, but so what? I start to edge in.

'Where are you going sir?' asks a female officer.

Have they reduced the educational requirements for entry to the College of Policing I wonder?

'In there. To the meeting.'

'We can't allow that sir as we can no longer guarantee public safety.'

'I'm not asking you to guarantee anything. I'll take my chances.'

'No, we can't let you. You'll have to stay here.'

I look to my left and I look to my right at the mass of coppers who aren't very busy.

'Or,' I offer, 'You lot could do your job and push these demonstrators back. Let law-abiding members of the public listen to their candidates and make an informed choice. That sort of thing?'

She ignores the suggestion.

So. I'll just loiter here until the Plod finally get around to pulling their fingers out of their arses and start earning their wages. Then I can saunter inside. While I'm waiting, Alan Craig and Peter Lello also arrive. At least this means I can have some adult conversation to drown out the screeches of the shrew in a headscarf who is cawing crap through a megaphone. Then Anish Patel joins us. He abandoned UKIP to join Waters' new party but we're still pleased to see him.

'Did Anne Marie arrive safely?' I ask him.

'No,' he says. 'She hasn't come.'

'Understandable,' I reply. 'I really wouldn't want her to get hurt.'

'It's not that', he says. 'She has security but the meeting's been shut down.'

Has it? That can't be right. I've been here for a quite some time and there's no sign of the other candidates exiting the hall.

'When did you hear that?' I ask him.

'Oh, a little while ago. The police told her.'

That makes no sense.

We chat for a while, but the communists are still convulsing. A 'lady' right in front of us spits over the shoulders of two police officers at a man standing behind them.

'Stop it,"'one of them tells her, with all the power and gravitas of his uniform.

What? 'Stop it'? This revolting skank has just committed an arrestable offence and they watched her do it. Perhaps they might think about, well, arresting the creature?

She does it again. And is told to 'stop it' again. And that's all.

There's a bigger commotion outside the hall. People are now starting to exit the building. The Maoists ramp up again.

'Whose streets? Our streets."

'Racist scum.'

Blah blah blah. You get the picture. Their vitriol is especially vicious when directed at older or more vulnerable people I notice. Then Kurten appears, all-smiles as usual. Their vehemence seems to decline a little bit when faced by our man in person. Maybe this is because they have realised that if David had to, say, utilise a right hook in self-defence they'd certainly know about it. Rather – they would not – as they'd be out cold in an instant.

Keith Forster's giving David a lift home. His car's parked in a side road further along the South Circular, just to be on the safe side. Even though this is in the other direction from the nearest Wetherspoons, a few of us are going to accompany them, just to be on the safe side.

'Spill the beans,' I ask David. 'We've been stuck outside the whole time.'

'It was quite funny,' he replies. 'I was talking about the Customs Union when a grey-haired elderly lady stood up to give a rambling rant about racism. She was white.'

'You're a racist are you? The mad old Gammon,' I interject.

He tells us more.

'The audience jeered over her. The police eventually led her out although it took two of them even though she wasn't resisting in any way. Then John Hamilton announced that the police inspector was closing the hustings down for public safety.'

'Did he give the inspector's name?' I ask.

'No', says David.

'Wonder if it could have been that Inspector Yaxley,' I ponder.

'I really don't know,' he replies.

Wednesday 13th June 2018

Having sought Gerard's approval, I write to Inspector Yaxley in an official capacity as General Secretary on behalf of UKIP. We'd like a detailed explanation for last night's bewildering police operation. 'Please note', I conclude, 'that both this letter and your reply, or lack thereof, are not to be considered either private or confidential.'

Friday 14th June 2018

I didn't even set off to the town hall for the count until 11.30 last night having assumed that it would be just as slow as it normally is. Yet this time Lewisham Electoral Services have been much more efficient than usual and the result's nearly ready by 12.30 am. That there's been a pitifully-low turnout at just 33% of eligible voters has helped speed the process along.

We Kipper boys are enjoying a blether with the supporters of the Democrats and Veterans, the Libertarian Party and of course the Monster Raving Loonies and their legendary candidate, Howling Laud Hope. In a generous gesture, the Council has also made hot drinks and biscuits available for us. The defector from UKIP and DVP hopeful, Massimo DiMambro, is ill so won't be coming. We can't see Anne Marie Waters or anyone else from her new For Britain party either.

The Labour placewoman is victorious. Yawn. She receives just 11,033 votes, a fall of 17.7% from their level of support in last year's general election. When it comes to the interesting parties, our lad David polls 380 votes or 1.7%. Lost deposit. Anne Marie has 266 or 1.2%. Lost deposit. Massimo receives 67 and Sean Finch of the Libertarians has 38. Lost deposits.

The candidates coalesce on the dais for the result to be officially proclaimed and Anne Marie's there after all, sporting a sad smile.

The sole speech is from the winner. It's boring. The only good part is when she pledges to resist a hard Brexit, at which I boo politely from the audience.

Everyone starts to leave and I stroll over to pass the time of day with Miss Waters.

'How you doing Anne Marie? Not seen you for a while. You're well, I hope?'

Oh dear. She's in a bad mood and speaks through part-gritted teeth.

'Fine. Thanks.'

I utilise some more inanities but she's not reciprocating.

'You managed it Paul. You succeeded. You all forced me out.'

Eh?

'But our branch backed your candidacy for this seat with the national party last year.'

'Yes,' she replies, 'But only to destroy my leadership campaign.'

Eh?

'But the NEC approved your candidacy for leader.'

'Yes,' she retorts, 'but you only let me stand so I would fall.'

Eh?

'You came second.'

She ignores that and changes tack.

'And you Paul, of all people. You told me to stay away from Tommy Robinson. You! Yet that photograph of the pair of you together was all over Twitter a few weeks ago.'

At this, I am tempted to gaze at the ceiling and start whistling in a tuneless fashion but resist the impulse.

'Anyway,' she goes on. 'It's not happening.'

'What's not happening?' I query.

'I'm not coming back to UKIP. Even if you beg me on your knees, I'm not going to do it.'

That's not why I wanted a chat. I don't tell her this and neither do I inform her that Gerard's already had her membership record marked 'Do Not Renew'.

'Good night, Anne Marie. Hope you have a safe journey home.'

CHAPTER FIFTY-ONE

Jokers to our Right

Friday 6th July 2018

Inspector Yaxley finally galvanised himself on Monday to write a short letter which has arrived by second class post today.

'Regarding your correspondence of 13th June 2018, please note that we do not discuss operational intelligence, planning or decision making with non-statutory stakeholders.

'If you wish to make a complaint about the conduct of any specific officers on the day, please see our website for information on how to do so or, alternatively, please contact the Independent Officer for Police Conduct directly.'

Oh. So a political party has no 'stake' in a disrupted democratic process. That's us told, and no mistake. And it would be impertinent to require any anonymous senior officer who took the shutdown decision to justify it. As for the grunts on the front line, how do we identify them? 'The fat placid ones?' A complaint would be pointless.

I fish out the debut album by NWA from the CD rack and play track two on loop for a while. That makes me feel better.

Saturday 7th July 2018

The postie delivers the latest *Independence* magazine and I open it straight away to see the other NEC applicants who have had the effrontery to stand against me.

Alas. This time, the full list of assentors isn't printed next to the candidates' names and the party CVs have been completely omitted. Cock-up though, not conspiracy.

Friday 27th July 2018

UKIP announces the results of the elections for its National Executive Committee. Six people have been successful and none of them is your Dear Author.

My phone starts receiving calls. On top of the lack of CVs within Independence, the consensus is that many members confused me with Paul Oakden who, apparently, is not quite so popular within the party at large as he is with me.

Too bad. The people have spoken and I must suck it up. Anyway, I'm still General Secretary and will carry on attending NEC meetings, even if only in an advisory role.

Sunday 5th August 2018

Been listening to Nigel's radio show on LBC while slapping a coat of emulsion on the bedroom walls. Just before it comes to an end, a listener calls in. A Kipper, but not one I know. He gives Farage a bit of an earful about how he's abandoned the party and become part of the establishment himself.

I phone in to Nigel as well but wait until the show's over before doing so.

'I'm hearing this a lot from the members. That guy isn't unique. If you seriously want to come back as leader next year then it'd be a good idea to build some bridges.'

To be plain, if he were to stand at this moment it's my view that he'd no longer be a slam-dunk victor.

'Oh, I'm certainly going to do that,' he soothes. 'I've just been confirmed as speaker at the conference dinner in September.'

Phew.

Monday 6th August 2018

A malodorous story oozes over the internet. There's a group called 'Make Britain Great Again' which is directed by a young UKIP member called Luke Nash Jones. He's an aspiring fresh-right internet vlogger and has posted several guerrilla videos featuring he and others engaging in japes while wearing Trump-style red caps. All a bit wanky to be honest, but fairly harmless.

A new video is online which was filmed on Saturday. This time the 'harmless fun' is an invasion of a left-wing bookshop in Bloomsbury called 'Bookmarks'.

Nash Jones enters the shop and is followed by around a dozen supporters who march inside while tolling a bell.

'We love Trump! We love Trump! We love Trump.'

Nash Jones buttonholes a shop worker behind the counter to berate the man and there are shouts from the others.

'Traitor!'

'Paedophile lovers! Fucking paedophile-lovers!'

'Scum!'

'Fucking traitors!'

'I hope your shop burns down! I hope it burns down! Fucking disgusting!'

A poster is destroyed and several books taken from the shelves to be exposed to what is, frankly, ignorant critical analysis.

Although this onslaught must be incredibly alarming, the assistant remains calm and cool throughout.

'Kindly leave the property. I'm asking you to leave.'

He gently touches Nash Jones to guide him off the premises. Others proffer what is, frankly, ignorant legal analysis.

'That's assault! That's assault!'

The man would be perfectly-entitled to use reasonable force to eject LNJ. To be honest though, few people would think the worse of him if he'd broken his jaw and then dragged him out of the door by his wispy ginger beard.

Although a proud swivel-eyed right winger, my sympathies are entirely with the shop worker. So what are normal people likely to think if they see this? That's blindingly-obvious. Book-burnings and Kristallnacht. Yet Luke Nash Jones is supposed to be a great social media expert. Not that I can see.

The party undertakes a hurried investigation. On its face, the footage seems to show that, as well as Nash Jones, two other Kippers were involved, that is, Martin Costello and NEC member Elizabeth Jones.

Tony McIntyre contacts all three.

'I am writing to you to say that I have taken the exceptional powers afforded to me as Party Chairman to suspend you forthwith for bringing the party into disrepute. You were present and involved in an altercation that took place on Saturday 4th August at The Bookmarks bookshop in London which was filmed and then the film was put in the public domain.

'You have been suspended under the following rules in the constitution: Rules No 11.9 and 11.11. You obviously have the right to appeal this decision.'

This escapade is the sort of thing that the far left engages in. We haven't yet noticed any media coverage of the disciplinary proceedings brought by Labour or Momentum over the thuggery at the Lewisham hustings; perhaps we've just missed it. However, UKIP must always show itself to be better than the fascist left because UKIP is better than the fascist left.

Tuesday 7th August 2018

Costello and Elizabeth Jones have so-appealed. The former admits he'd gone into the shop but had left as soon as things turned ugly which was, effectively, immediately. He offers an unreserved apology anyway. She in turn claims not to have gone in at all. Investigations of the footage and other sources are undertaken which corroborate their accounts.

I relate my views to Tony McIntyre and Gerard Batten.

'I've spoken to Adam. We're agreed that if there's no evidence Liz was involved in the actual altercation then she must be exonerated. No question about it.'

She is, and her suspension's lifted straight away.

Martin Costello remains sanctioned and his case will be heard by the disciplinary committee of the NEC at a later date.

Luke Nash Jones has also tendered written submissions. These are rather more – vigorous. There are veiled references to legal action although he himself is not a lawyer. Adam and I take this in a magnanimously-mellow manner. Somewhat, we imagine, as boxer Tyson Fury might do if ever menaced by a two-pint 'Mike Tyson'.

He will also have the opportunity to put his case before the committee.

Sunday 19th August 2018

The disciplinary panel of the NEC are hearing the appeals of Luke Nash Jones and Martin Costello against their suspensions. Adam Richardson is present as Legal officer along with me as General Secretary. The two voting members are from the NEC itself and have been chosen because they've had no prior dealings with either appellant.

The cases are heard separately and the men make oral submissions before being questioned. Regarding Costello, the committee retire for a few minutes to consider their decision and then call him back in. He is to receive a short suspension. When that suspension is set against time 'already served', it is lifted immediately.

As for Nash Jones, the members wish to reflect and reserve their judgment.

Tuesday 21st August 2018

The committee have reached their decision and Adam Richardson posts a letter to Luke Nash Jones.

> 'The panel, given the high degree of personal culpability, the lack of genuine mitigation and the damage done to the Party and potential future harm, unanimously form the view that you are to be expelled permanently from UKIP.'

Wednesday 5th September 2018

Nash Jones submits an appeal against his expulsion, as he is fully-entitled to do.

Thursday 6th September 2018

Out of the blue, an article appears on a semi-official UKIP website:

> 'UKIP's National Executive Committee will this weekend consider giving party members the power to decide if Tommy Robinson should be allowed to join UKIP, Kipper Central can exclusively reveal.'

News to me. It goes on.

> 'The motion calling for Robinson's recruitment to the party, which Tommy's supporters hope will be debated and voted upon at UKIP's national conference in Birmingham later this month, must first be given the go-ahead by the party's Chairman – Tony McIntyre, after he has consulted the party's ruling body, the NEC, this Sunday.
> 'The motion's been proposed by Alan Craig. Oh, come on mate! What are you playing at?

Tony McIntyre gives me a call.

'More leaking,' he says. 'It's extremely unhelpful. Should I have the debate? It's my decision, but seeing as this is my first conference as chairman I need to take some advice on Sunday.'

Sunday 9th September 2018

We're in the bar after the NEC meeting. Mike Hookem is fuming and grousing about resigning from the party.

'We shouldn't even be having the fucking debate in the first place. It'll dominate the whole conference. There's no fucking point me giving my speech on Friday about fisheries. It'll be wiped off the news. Why the fuck should I bother even turning up?'

'Disagree,' I offer. 'The "Tommy" issue won't be considered until the Sunday. You'll already have had your own blanket media coverage on the Friday. Don't stay away.'

'I'll think about it,' he says, 'But I wouldn't piss on Robinson if he was on fire.'

Guess what? Gerard doesn't share Mike's opinions. It's impossible to say if he'd go to quite the length of pissing on Tommy if he were on fire but our leader is definitely a votary.

'The decision needs to be left to the members though,' he says. "And I'll accept their ruling either way.'

My own position is precisely in the middle of these two MEPs. Having actually bothered to read Robinson's book and then undertaken an exercise in compare/contrast with his portrayal by the liberal media, I've concluded that he isn't Abbadon incarnate after all. Nonetheless, that is the authorised and authoritative opinion of polite society. Cliff Richard's fans had to 'lump it' for a while. Tommy Robinson's fans will have to do the same.

It is for this reason that Tony McIntyre approaches me with a request.

'Can I ask you to speak against the motion at conference?'

He can indeed. The flavour of the speech will be easy enough. It'll be along the lines of:

'I like Tommy. But.'

I'm certainly not going to be rude about Robinson or, even more importantly, those of our members who support him. However. Brexit has still not been achieved. UKIP is the only force which has consistently, and rationally, made that case for departure. The federasts would like nothing better than to divert public attention away from those arguments and focus on our 'racism' against the religion of Islam instead. That might help to betray Brexit itself and keep us chained to the EU. If this happens, Farage's warning of three years ago that the migrant flood to Europe is peppered with jihadists will loom large. That's because the potential terrorists among them may have every right to settle in Great Britain under the laws of free movement. In other words, allowing Robinson to join UKIP at this, of all moments, would intensify the threat from fundamentalists, not reduce it. Just my opinion anyway.

And it has to be cause and party before personal ambition. Every time. Particularly as he didn't even seem interested in joining a few short months ago.

I bring Nigel up to speed later on.

'Motion's going to be debated, with regret. I'm the opposing speaker. We'll beat it.'

Farage isn't happy.

'OK. I must think.'

Tuesday 11th September 2018

I'm busy with a trial at court so the phone's off. Come lunchtime, I see some missed calls from Graham Eardley of the Bruges Group. I ring him back.

'What's this about the Tommy motion being dropped?' he queries.

'Dunno who told you that. Tony definitely approved it,' I tell him. 'And I'm speaking. Looking forward to it in fact.'

Baseless gossip is incredibly irritating. I turn off my phone again and return to court.

Trial over, my phone's back on and Chairman McIntyre needs to talk.

'I've decided, on reflection, not to consider the motion at conference. Technically, it's been submitted too late and in any case it wasn't proposed by a full branch as it should have been.'

'Oh, for Heaven's sake Tony,' I reply. 'Why on earth didn't you do that on Sunday then? Have "words been had"?'

'Yes. They have.'

'This makes us look stupid. You should have stuck to your guns and we'd have closed it down quickly. Now it'll fester.'

'I'm sorry.'

'Well, even though you're: a) Party Chairman and b) a big monster who could snap me in half if you felt like it, consider this a telling-off.'

'And I accept it,' he closes.

CHAPTER FIFTY-TWO

So Long. Farewell

Friday 21st September 2018

'A "Birmingham Speech", I say to the audience. 'On immigration? At UKIP conference? What could possibly go wrong?'

This is quite a technical oration. Its primary purpose is to showcase our new policies but I'll also attack the government's record and have a dig at the United Nations too. I relate some facts and figures and am just about to disclose what's in the new mini-manifesto.

'So. What's to be done?' I ask rhetorically.

A shout comes from the crowd.

'Send them back!'

There are a few chuckles and some sparse applause. I smile, but: fucking numbskull.

'No,' I retort.

It had been my intention to use the following words as a closing flourish but I bring them up now instead.

'To begin with – to begin with I'm going to tell you what's not to be done. And that is to tyrannize people who came here at the invitation of the then-government fifty years ago.

'The persecution of the Windrush generation by Theresa May and Amber Rudd was one of the shabbiest, ugliest and nastiest episodes in our recent domestic history.

'Now everybody knows that the Conservatives are trying to swindle voters into supporting them by ripping off our policies.

'But let us tell them this: Not in UKIP's name, Conservative Party.

'Anybody who has made this country their home by legal means and has contributed to our society remains welcome. And that's not going to change.'

That receives an extremely enthusiastic reaction from the crowd. The vast majority of our members are neither cruel nor idiots.

The big finale having been deployed prematurely, the speech fizzles out as I'm too slow and dim to think of anything equally amazeballs to replace it with.

'Thus endeth the lesson.'

Tony Macintyre has asked that I introduce the Party Leader immediately afterwards. No notes needed.

'Six months ago we were in this very building at the ICC. We were holding an Emergency General Meeting about the escapades of our then-leader – er, old "what's his face" - who thought it was more important to go round the chat shows talking about his private life than to make the case for Brexit.

'That practically killed this party. Membership was nose-diving and on top of that we were facing a £170,000 legal bill.

'At the worst possible time this man, Gerard Batten, stepped into the breach. Gerard has turned this party around in six months. Membership is rising; it's up to 24,000. We have paid off the lawyers who were chasing us for the £170,000 and, in passing, I very much hope that they choke on it.

'And, at long last, we are making the case for Brexit again. So. Without further ado, may I introduce the leader of our party? The MEP for London. Mr. Gerard. Batten.'

I mean every word. But please, Gerard. Rein back on the muslamics a bit.

It's lunchtime when Batten finishes. I'm heading to my hotel to book in, helped on my way by backslappings and handshakes for my own speech and, in particular, the response to the heckler. One fellow smiles broadly.

'You won't remember me,' he says, 'but I was a member of For Britain and saw you speaking to Anne Marie at the Lewisham count. After listening to you both I've resigned from her party and joined UKIP.'

Finally ensconced in my room, the suitcase is unpacked and I then Google myself about this morning. For I am vain.

There's a lengthy, rambling dissing by *The Independent* which concludes that Oakley has 'all the studied grace of the captain at your local EDL golf club.' That's so ridiculous that I really like it.

The Financial Times also quotes me about our rising membership and the *Daily Mirror* has something to say, too, and, in particular, about the heckler.

'He asked: "So what's to be done?"'

'One audience member shouted: "Send them back!"'

'Mr Oakley did not respond . . .'

The Daily Mirror are liars.

EVENING

Former leader Nigel Farage delivers a speech to the conference dinner. It is excellent.

Then current leader Gerard Batten delivers a speech to the conference dinner. It is excellent.

Farage walks out of the room while Batten is in the midst of speaking and does not return.

September 26th 2018

The Earl of Dartmouth, one of our MEPs, writes a resignation letter to the party leader.

'I cannot in good faith continue to be a member of a party whose Leader continues to make abusive and offensive comments on Islam and the prophet Mohammed. There are also the homophobic comments publicly stated by your appointee as UKIP spokesperson on the family, which, as you know, I also deplore.

'I will continue to serve as an Independent MEP representing the South West and Gibraltar according to the principles on which I was elected. I will not be joining any other political party.'

'The prophet Mohammed'? Didn't realise he was one of the faithful. Although perhaps I've just misread it.

Batten tells him to 'get bent'. He uses statesmanlike language, but it's still 'get bent'.

> 'Thank you for your letter of resignation. I have received this without regret, and I am sure that my relief in receiving it exceeds your relief in sending it.
>
> 'As an Earl and a gentleman I trust that you will now do the decent and honourable thing and resign your seat and hand it to the next person on the UKIP Southwest List, Gawain Towler.
>
> 'Your seat was provided for you by the selfless efforts and generosity of UKIP members and donors and your seat morally belongs to UKIP not to you.
>
> 'Toodle pip!'

Tuesday 2nd October 2018

Bill Etheridge MEP says goodbye to UKIP too. Batten isn't bothered. As it happens, the pair have been chuntering at each other for a long while about matters wholly-unrelated to Stephen Yaxley-Lennon. At least those problems are now to be considered as resolved.

Sunday 7th October 2018

UKIP Chairman Tony McIntyre is standing down from the role. It's an intense job in any event but the stress inculcated by the Tommy Robinson difficulties have made things worse. Being blunt, his doctor has told him that if he carries on in the post it will kill him. This is serious, and not a strop.

Personal health must trump both cause and party every time. We're extremely grateful to Tony for all his work but also pleased that Gerard has chosen the fearsome Kirstan Herriot to be his successor.

Wednesday 10th October 2018

Appellant Luke Nash Jones eventually paid his £500 appeal fee some three weeks late. The Party decided to ignore that tardiness and treat the case as substantive. There have however been additional problems in that he's been lobbying NEC members directly and indirectly and made accusations of bias against others. So it's been difficult to find a completely independent panel but we've now achieved this.

I write to inform him of the date of the appeal which is set for 18th November and to ask for copies of any documents he wishes to submit. These, with the party's own papers, will be collated and sent to him in a numbered bundle before the hearing.

Sunday 14th October 2018

Nash Jones sends me an email.

'Mr Oakley

'Before you trouble yourself to consider addressing a letter of expulsion to me, consider myself to have sadly resigned, due to your hostility, from your party. The appeal route you have offered is a blatant sham, with a foregone conclusion, and thus expropriation of funds under false pretences. I await the transfer of £500 to my bank account, which you hold records of, and I shall be seeking legal advice.'

He then rambles-on for several pages. The NEC has it in for him and there's stuff about the Star Chamber, Luke 6:42 and Montesquieu. There's also said to be some kind of conspiracy involving Freemasons.

Most irritating of all, he mentions alleged infractions by other party members, officers and an MEP. They are the ones who should be castigated, not him.

Mr Nash Jones hasn't appreciated that Vichy-style snitching butters no parsnips with me. Especially as that list includes someone else:

'You yourself, Paul Oakley, called UKIP the "Black Death" - resulting in rather awkward news headlines indeed, putting you in no position to judge myself.'

Dear oh dear. It's not me who'll be judging him and, contrary to the rumours, this silly little boy does indeed know fuck-all about 'Shock and Awful'.

Monday 15th October 2018

Having had far more important things to deal with yesterday, like washing the car and trimming the hedge, I finally send a short response.

'Thank you for your email which raises many grave and

intricate allegations. It is observed that you nonetheless "re-sign" from the party, even though you have already been excluded, and that your appeal is withdrawn. In the circumstances, we need not rebut the assertions you make.

'The party is happy to refund your £500 appeal fee. We note that you sternly-threaten us with legal action, again, over a right to interest. In order to avoid such a prospect and without any admission of liability, UKIP will pay this to you. The current Bank of England base rate is 0.75% so this amounts to an additional 14 pence. The matter is now closed.'

Tuesday 30th October 2018
Professor Matthew Goodwin has just published a new book with co-author Roger Eatwell. It is called *National Populism: The Revolt Against Liberal Democracy*. Peter Whittle hosts a launch for the work at 55 Tufton Street.

In the eight elections to the EU Parliament since 1979, voter turn-out in the UK has been as low as 24% and never higher than 38%. This past history demonstrates that most Brits couldn't give a toss about the European project. Indeed, from 1999 onwards a great proportion of those who did bother to vote were actively-opposed to the federast dream. That was the election in which UKIP first returned MEPs. Voters also began to mark their crosses for the pseudo-sceptic Tories as well as other, minor, anti-EU parties in increasing numbers.

As the decades passed, many Britons concluded that democracy, sovereignty and national self-determination are incompatible with EU membership. As far as we're concerned, the concepts are unarguable. No different from the Chartists' crusades, the 19th century Reform Acts or Votes for Women. We hold these truths to be self-evident. Surely no sensible person could disagree?

And yet.

The Brexit referendum has uncovered an ugly side to our country. The internationalist intelligentsia have finally revealed their contempt for the mass of mainstream Britons who were insolent enough to reject the approved *Weltanschauung*.

This new Eatwell/Goodwin study seeks to explain the phenomenon which has not only given the world Brexit but also Trump, the AfD, Victor Orban, the Sweden Democrats and other naughty people who make the metropolitan liberals swoon.

The United Kingdom will leave the European Union at some stage.

That is certain. What is also clear is that new and different exertions will be needed after our departure to return our country to a happier course. Our work is not yet done. This is undoubtedly why the audience for Goodwin's lecture this evening includes not one, not two but three former UKIP leaders. That is to say, Pearson, Farage and Nuttall.

Nigel has to leave early but Nuttall takes me to the MOG afterwards.

'We can harass Goodwin face-to-face and pick his brains.'

CHAPTER FIFTY-THREE

Oh—Gerard, Gerard!

Sunday 18th November 2018

Another meeting of the National Executive Committee. There's a fervid discussion about a certain matter which must and will remain entirely confidential.

Tuesday 20th November 2018

Tommy posts a video briefing online. He'd been planning to hold one of his marches on 1st December but for various reasons has decided to postpone it. His protest will now be on Sunday the 9th, shortly before an important parliamentary vote on Brexit.

He's slouched on a settee, the cameraphone footage jerking about as he speaks to the punters up close.

'This isn't a Tommy Robinson protest at all,' he tells us. 'This is the great betrayal protest. As I said last night, I sat and waited for Tory Brexiteers. I sat and waited for Nigel Farage. I sat and waited for someone to organise or orchestrate and bring people together - for something. And no-one was. So to all the Brexiteers out there and to anyone who feels frustrated and feels like they're being sold out on the biggest democratic vote of our country's history: it's now the 9th. Please spread that.'

He pauses and then continues.

'Gerard, I know you don't do the livestreams but we're saying hello.'

The lens pans around to a familiar figure on the other side of the table who takes off his glasses and chuckles. It's the Leader of UKIP.

'It's a novelty to me. Well, this is the "Brexit Betrayal March" as you've described it but it's also the "Brexit Means Exit" march. It's about what Brexit should mean—a full, clean unencumbered exit from the European Union.'

Thursday 22nd November 2018

The Leader sends out his usual round-robin to the UKIP membership at large. At its end are these comments.

'I promised to update you on what happened at the NEC meeting on Sunday 18th November. I put a motion to the NEC asking that they allow a ballot of the Members on whether or not Stephen Yaxley-Lennon (aka Tommy Robinson) be allowed to join UKIP.

'The NEC declined to allow the motion but passed an alternative motion saying that if he applies to join this matter be deferred until after 29th March 2019. I have spoken to Tommy and he fully understands and accepts the NEC's decision. Meanwhile, I have appointed him as my Special Personal Advisor on Rape Gangs and Prison Conditions and Prison Reform."

I finish reading it and cup my chin in my palms for a few moments.

'Why, Gerard? Piers' motion was a brilliant way to calm things down until after Brexit Day. You could still have taken advice on the quiet from Tommy. In fact, everyone kind of expected you to. This sleight of hand isn't subtle; it's sticking a middle finger up to the NEC.'

'That wasn't my intention,' he assures. 'He's only a personal adviser to me and not to the party as a whole.'

Friday 23rd November 2018

Our former leader has been speaking to the *Daily Telegraph*.

'Mr Farage said he had not "given up" on UKIP and that he would lead the fight to get rid of Mr Batten saying he would be writing to the party's 15-strong National Executive Committee to urge them have a vote of no confidence so "we get rid of him".

'He added: "I will be meeting the UKIP MEPs, those that haven't already resigned in Brussels on Wednesday next week. We are going to have one last go at getting rid of somebody who as leader is dragging us in a shameful direction".'

Tuesday 27th November 2018
Patrick O'Flynn MEP makes an announcement as well.

'At this vital stage of the battle for Brexit, Gerard Batten has appointed Robinson as his policy adviser and announced a plan for UKIP to be centrally involved in a mass demonstration being planned by Robinson on the issue of Brexit. This is despite the last two street demonstrations attended by Gerard ending up with some demonstrators engaging in very ugly scenes.'

He is thus abandoning The Kip and signing up to the barely-breathing Social Democratic Party. As is now customary, it has slipped his mind that he should resign his seat in the EU parliament.

Having said this, we're now very close to 29th March so it makes little difference. In any case, the two of us have enjoyed many connoisseur discussions about classic music and, in particular, the oeuvres of Weller/Buckler/Foxton.

'Disappointing decision Patrick. Effectively, you've renounced The Jam and joined The Style Council.'

I'll leave it at that.

Gawain then wants a word about the 9th December. The far left intend to put on a counter-demonstration. Their vows have been warlike. Perhaps the football lads and forces' veterans on 'our' side will give them what they want. The soyboys might then realise that one should always be careful when it comes to wishes — but that would be disastrous too.

'It's very troubling,' I say. 'But Gerard tells me that Tommy's crew will self-police his crowd. Videos will be rolling and all malefactors handed straight over to the Five-Oh.'

Doesn't really matter to me personally as I'm not planning to go along. It's not an official UKIP demo and we've got family stuff organised for the day. Besides, I'm a lover, not a fighter.

The former leader of UKIP then sends that heartfelt appeal to the NEC and we party officers.

'I am certain that if the proposed march takes place on 9 December, with our leader still in good standing, it will be the end of UKIP as an effective electoral force. It will be the last straw for many of us. Even more seriously, this event could have disastrous consequences for Brexit itself.

'Currently, the House of Commons vote on the final Brexit proposal is expected to be held within a couple of days of this march taking place. Judging by past events attended by Tommy Robinson and his followers, we can confidently expect violence and yobbish behaviour.'

I dearly, dearly hope that Nigel's wrong. Yet even if Gerard is ousted, he will certainly still attend and speak. And even if it's not a UKIP event, many of our members will be there to hear him. And if the day descends into disorder, the mainstream media will lay the blame firmly upon this party no matter what. That's what they do. We're stuffed every way.

Wednesday 28th November 2018

The Leader of the UK Independence Party and Member of the European Parliament for London sends a summons to his General Secretary.

'I'd like to invite you to speak at the Brexit Rally on 9th December on immigration and the UN Global Compact. The rally will be on major aspects of the Brexit Betrayal and we're finalising speakers now.'

Ah.

Rumination is required. I ponder the problems once more but there are other arguments.

Firstly, this is a courteous request. It comes directly from the man who heads our party and asks for my support.

Secondly, if the offer is accepted, I will certainly not be banging-on-about-Islam during any speech that I deliver. That might help to knock the intended narrative of the mainstream media off course and keep the heart of our party pumping. Moreover, if things kick off while I'm actually speaking, I'll try my best to exercise on-stage crowd control as Jimmy Pursey was forced to do at all those Sham 69 recitals.

Thirdly, a crowd of thousands is expected. This will be the biggest gig I've ever done.

Gerard: you're on.

Thursday 29th November 2018
Kirstan Herriott has a message for the party officers.

'I am writing to inform you that I have received the following motion proposed and seconded by Richard Ford and Mick McGough respectively:

'That the NEC has no confidence in Gerard Batten as Leader of UKIP.'

'The Leader has waived his right to 7 days notice and requested that this item be covered first on the agenda of the meeting on 2nd December.'

Later, a post appears on the official UKIP Facebook page to advertise Brexit Betrayal day. Attached is a poll: 'Tattoo wars. Which is better?' Readers are invited to pick their preference between an inking of Tommy Robinson and one of Nigel Farage. Tommy is currently leading by about 70-30.

Friday 30th November 2018
I and others are still confused about the status of the forthcoming rally so I check with Chairman Kirstan.

'Is this an official UKIP event or is it just something that we're attending and, if so, who are the organisers?'

'It's not an official UKIP event,' she tells me. 'Gerard is just there as a key speaker. From what I can gather, it's being organised by the football lads and the veterans. Gerard's having a planning meeting with them today.'

Later, our leader posts a team photograph of that very meeting online. There are eleven people present including Gerard, Tommy, Lawrence Webb, Peter McIlvenna, Kris Hicks and Liz

Phillips but I don't know the others.

Saturday 1st December 2018

The Daily Telegraph does know one of the people around the table in yesterday's family photo. He is said to be Danny 'Tommo' Thomas and there's more:

'It can be revealed Thomas, a father of four, was jailed two years ago for the attempted armed kidnapping of a man in Hampshire.'

After this, Jonathan Bullock gets in touch with me again.

'The mood amongst the MEPs and members I speak to is very grim having lost Patrick and Bill. We should be at 15 to 20% in the opinion polls but can't even make double figures even though the Tories have sold out Brexit. The publicity is awful; if this march turns violent there'll be political trouble too. Batten has to go. Otherwise you'll lose more MEPs and members. It's all very upsetting.'

CHAPTER FIFTY-FOUR

The King is Dead

Sunday 2nd December 2018

I'M JUST ABOUT TO HEAD IN to hear the Motion of No Confidence in Gerard Batten. I won't have a vote, but do have a wily suggestion about how all this unpleasantness might be ended with the least possible fuss. I've already mentioned this to Gerard and I'm now going to propose it to the NEC as well.

I finally get to speak to Nigel by phone just as I'm ascending the stairs to the front entrance of the venue.

'Batten's got to go,' he insists. 'We can't stand any more of this.'

'Nigel – I just don't think there's the hunger for yet another leadership election amongst the NEC.'

'Then they should listen to the members. We've already lost scores of hardened activists in South East Area.'

South-East is his own region. He knows his people well and mentions a few by name who are teetering right now. I'd be appalled to lose them too.

'I don't doubt that at all, but it's mixed. My branch are split. Clacton invited me to speak a few weeks ago. They're solidly-Robinson and that surprised me. Then there's Elizabeth Jones and her Lambeth lot. I've heard they want to tear up the proscribed list completely.'

'Yes,' he observes. 'But she's a fucking weirdo.'

Ouch!

'There's a potential solution to all this but I don't know if it has traction.'

'You've got to get it done today,' he insists. 'Otherwise UKIP risks turning into the British National Party.'

'Well, if something isn't sorted today we'll resolve this later. It will never become the BNP though. Never.'

I have to head in as the meeting's starting and the dreaded Motion is top of the bill.

I take the elevator and have a think. If Gerard's ousted within the next hour, what then? As many of our MEPs have also left the party itself, they simply cannot stand for leader under the Constitution. And is Nigel actually, finally, at long last planning to return himself? He didn't say. Farage is a keen amateur military historian so it's surprising that he's mentioned no follow-up strategy. He has his Operation Overlord firmly in place but there's no sign of an Operation Goodwood to follow. Not the best analogy perhaps as it might suggest that Gerard is Literally Hitler. Which he isn't. But you can see what I mean.

So is Nigel just hoping that UKIP will completely collapse? I'm not having that.

I deeply respect both Farage and Batten who, in different ways, have proved their commitment to leaving the EU through decades of hard work. Nonetheless, my greatest urge at this precise moment is to clasp the left ear of Gerard Joseph Batten and then to clutch the right ear of Nigel Paul Farage. And bang both their heads together. All of this was totally unnecessary.

As for the meeting? It's another 'Emotional' one. I'll tell you everything that happened when I write my memoirs. Not these memoirs, silly! Later ones. When I'm really old. You'll have to wait.

Light is however shed on one issue as people gather their things when the pow-wow's over. Nate Ryding has some words with Gerard.

'I've been told that Kris Hicks posted that poll on the website about the Tommy and Nigel tattoos. That was totally unprofessional and you need to pull him up on it.'

Gerard looks him in the eyes.

'I told him to do it. I'm sick of being attacked by Nigel Farage. It was my idea. It was a bit of fun and we should lighten up.'

Anyhow, the Party sends out a press release before 6 pm.

'Today, the UKIP NEC voted overwhelmingly against a motion of no confidence in the leader Gerard Batten.'

The NEC also decided the following:

'The party does not endorse the appointment of Tommy Robinson in any advisory role. He is not a UKIP member and through his associations he is barred from joining UKIP.

'The planned march on 9th December was not organised by UKIP but members are free to attend should they wish.'

I'm walking to the railway station when a text message is received.

'Hi Paul, hope you're well. Would you be available for a phone interview with Nick Ferrari on LBC at 8:20am tomorrow to discuss the NEC's decision today?'

I check with the Leader.

'I've already turned them down,' Gerard says. 'The news is the motion failed. All Ferrari will do is try and unpick it. Don't worry about being polite; we don't owe the MSM anything. They all have their own agenda. Don't go on unless it helps ours. Resist the limelight.'

Aw.

'Very good,' I reply. 'I do enjoy LBC but will make a regretful excuse. I'll pretend to be busy with a trial but have a nice lie-in instead.'

Monday 3rd December 2018

Gerard posts a Tweet about Nick Ferrari's morning show while it's actually on-air and covering the aftermath of yesterday's failed Vote of No Confidence:

'The propaganda war against UKIP is in full cry. Farage trotted out along with a Professor to say we are going down a "far right" path, and apparently we are now "Islamophobic" and "anti-semitic". The establishment gloves are now off. Join us now. Fight back'

Tuesday 4th December 2018

Ferrari finds out about this Tweet and broadcasts a lengthy rant on today's show. He lists a number of occasions when Gerard has been asked to appear on the programme but has failed or refused to do so.

'So let's go back to yesterday when you declined again to speak to us. When you declined, we spoke to your Deputy Leader Mike Hookem. He declined. We spoke to the party General Secretary Paul Oakley. He declined. We then spoke to NEC member Mick McGough. No response. We then spoke to London spokesperson Peter Whittle. He declined. We then spoke to the UKIP party press office from which there was no response. So rather than sitting sadly, presumably in your back bedroom, Tweeting about how the propaganda war is on and Farage is trotted out along with the professor, why don't you accept this Mr Batten? That you were offered the opportunity to go on the programme.'

Nick isn't pleased. Snigger.

Tuesday 4th December 2018

Nigel Farage MEP has resigned his membership of the UK Independence Party.

I'll repeat that. Nigel Farage has resigned from UKIP.

Kirstan gives the party officers an exhortation.

'It's possible you may be contacted by the media to give a comment or statement. The press are not our friends and I would urge you to direct any queries to Kris Hicks. However, if you choose to engage, please do so with extreme caution.'

Nonetheless, LBC demand my attendance on Nick Ferrari's show tomorrow morning at 7.40 am sharp to explain ourselves.

'Gerard,' I say. 'I'd better do it or else they'll claim we're a bunch of pussies. Don't worry though, I will be astonishingly bland.'

'Well, alright then,' he says. 'And do you know what? You can tell him that the reason I don't go on his show is because I hate the bloody thing.'

'I will too. That'd be funny. Have to say though that I do enjoy Ferrari. I only turn off LBC at 10 am in the week. Can't bear listening to all that bile and hatred which comes through the speakers afterwards.'

Wednesday 5th December 2018

12.15 am. A worried NEC member has a plea for me.

'Paul, please consider "calling in with a sicky" on Sunday. You're a good man, and a very busy lawyer. You don't need to be seen taking part in a rally which isn't approved by the NEC and which may get you bad publicity. And talking alongside a doubtful character who's been on the wrong side of the law may not be a wise professional move.'

This has a chilling echo of the Letter to Lord Monteagle in 1605. What rumours have they heard? None are mentioned, but, although genuinely touched by this concern, I reject the advice. If the prophecies of Nigel Farage and others are fulfilled then at least I'll be able to say that I was there when it all collapsed. Whitehall, London, 9th December 2018 will resonate through history in the same way as Winterland, San Francisco, 14th January 1978 already does.

7.10 am. Gerard wishes me well for Ferrari's programme.

'Oh,' he adds. 'I've had second thoughts. Do not mention what I said to you about the reason I don't go on. He'd only make another story out of that.'

Doggone. And I've already worked out the soundbites. Never mind.

7.40 am. I appear before Mr Nicholas Ferrari and am, as planned, as flavourless as a broth concocted from skimmed milk and water.

Come the evening, and it is touching and humbling to discover that I've received an award! Lefty magazine *The New Statesman* publishes its 'A to Z of the political year' and I'm there under 'B' for Black Death. There doesn't seem to be a prize though. Tightwads.

CHAPTER FIFTY-FIVE

Never Mind the Bollocks.
Here's the Brexit Betrayal.

Thursday 6th December 2018

I EXPRESS MY REGRET TO NIGEL about his departure from the party. Whether he is right to leave or wrong, I am categorically not going to criticise him in public. Ever. Yet I think he is wrong and feel the loss already.

'Batten is destroying it,' he observes.

'To be fair, he's said he'll take full responsibility if Sunday goes tits-up. Anyway, as Alan Bown says, the damage is already done.'

'It sure is.'

Then the news comes in that Uncle Mick, who helped beguile me into the arms of The Kip in the first place, has also abandoned us.

Friday 7th December 2018

The Head of my Personal Bodyguard conjures every ounce of his strength to protect his tetrarch.

'Wow. Nigel, Mick McGough last night, now Paul Nuttall gone. The ship is letting in water fast. It may be taking on more passengers but who seriously joins a sinking ship? Coburn and Julia Reid have gone too. Time to start reaching for a lifebelt yourself. Before it's too late and the party becomes too toxic, and you can't escape infection. I'd seriously think about quitting if I were you. Jump. Now.'

My ears are closed.

The Leader tells me about the arrangements for Sunday's march and rally.

'You're third on the speaking list and will have a five minute slot. We need to keep to this to get everyone in, leave the crowd gagging for more, and get them all away by 3 pm. Be ready to speak by 1.30 although it'll be about 1.50 pm when you're on.'

The first two on that lengthy speakers' list are to be Gerard himself, followed by Robinson. Crikey. I'm ahead of several others on the bill including Lord Pearson of Rannoch, Stewart Agnew MEP, Sargon of Akkad and Neil Hamilton AM. That's a very flattering running order.

Come lunchtime, Batten issues a press release. He's standing down.

'UKIP Leader Gerard Batten MEP has announced that he is leaving the Europe of Freedom and Direct Democracy (EFDD) European Parliament Group.

'Mr Batten said, "I hereby resign membership of the EFDD Group with immediate effect. It is not possible for me to remain in the Group when the President of the Group Mr Farage launches continual attacks on me and UKIP in the UK media."'

Just to be clear – this is just some arid arcanery of the EU parliament. He very much remains party leader.

The number of resignations from spokemanships and even from the UK Independence Party itself continues. I receive the latest of several phonecalls from my old Tory pal and current UKIP MEP, Jonathan Bullock.

'I can't carry on in the role of Energy Spokesman,' he tells me. 'And I'm thinking of leaving the party itself.'

'Don't. Look – we're all a bit too "moral" in UKIP. Just remember how the other parties deal with this sort of thing. Why aren't dozens of Tory MPs standing down over May's Brexit Betrayal? And Corbyn's former frontbenchers are still Labour members even though they failed to oust him. Stick with it.'

'I've heard Steve Crowther isn't renewing his membership,' he tells me.

'Do not follow his example.'

'And I've also been told that Gerard has applied for an EU parliamentary pass for Robinson.'

I don't know what to say to that.

Just finished speaking to Jonathan when Tom Rayner from Sky

News gives me a call. Have I heard of any more people who are thinking of leaving UKIP?

'Nobody. Sorry,' I say.

'What about you?'

'Me? No. The very blood in my veins runs purple. I'm not going anywhere.'

'Please tell me if you hear any rumours,' he asks.

'I certainly will,' I assure him.

I certainly won't.

Anyway, where would I go? Back to the Conservatives? I can't match the calibre of prospective Tory politicians. To start with, I'm hobbled by the facts that my school was a bog-standard Comprehensive and I didn't go to Oxbridge. That Oik-ery is an old problem, which can be dealt with. Much worse than that though, the new crop of wannabe MPs are far superior to me when it comes to their sex. Or race. Or sexuality. Or fondness for *The Guardian*. Or all four. Maybe I'd be graciously permitted to deliver leaflets for them while wearing a muzzle, leash and ankle monitor but that'd be it.

The variety of vanity parties set up by former Kippers are also unattractive. Except, possibly, for 'The Henry Bolton Party', Our Nation. Perhaps I could defect to them and then oust Henry as leader once more. Just for a laugh this time.

Naw, only kidding.

Sunday 9th December 2018

Today is the march and rally. I can't go to the former because we're having relatives over later and I have to run some errands first.

Jonathan Bullock MEP tells me that he's leaving UKIP just as I'm leaving home. Nobody will notice that departure today.

I arrive at the destination by 1.15 pm. The west end of Whitehall has been barricaded off and a stage erected. There is nobody to stand on that stage and nobody to listen to them. Where the flip is everyone?

I call Gerard and Peter McIlvenna to see what's going on. They don't pick up. Uneasy, I head into the Red Lion for a swift one and chat idly to some tourists. Has everything descended into riot and alarum already? Of course, if I possessed a smartphone it would be easy enough to find out. But I do not.

Outside, the street gradually begins to fill, which is some relief.

Batten calls at 2.09 pm

'You close? My phone was disabled.'

'Where the hell have you been? I was worried.'

'No need. The march was bigger than we thought and it took a while to head off. There's been no trouble at all with our lot although we've heard that the hard left are attacking the police.'

The UKIP Leader delivers the opening speech.

> 'Over the years we have been lied-to time and time again. And at the heart of the problem there was always this issue. Are we going to be governed from Brussels? Or are we going to be governed by our own democratically-elected parliament and government?'

I listen with care and trepidation but he says not a single word which could be interpreted as a mullering of Mullahs.

> 'Our message today, plain and simple, to Parliament is: Dump the Deal! Brexit means exit. And exit means "Now". Under our steam, not how the European Union tells us it can be done. Please help us and UKIP to make that happen.
>
> 'Some of my colleagues tell me that I should be concentrating on Brexit. Kind of overlooking the fact that that's exactly what I've been doing while some of them have been lining their pockets in Brussels. Well I tell you what I've done. Not even am I concentrating on Brexit but I've even got Tommy Robinson to talk about Brexit. That's an achievement isn't it?'

Then it's Tommy Robinson. He, bless him, bangs on about: Brexit! Yet he humbly defers to the experience of Gerard and Lord Pearson in this. There's one particular phenomenon he's noticed though.

> 'For too long I've got excited about the elections in Sweden or in France or in Holland as we've watched the populist parties grow. The election in Austria. The election in Italy. And for too long we get excited about other countries. It's our turn and this country is ready.'

Then he's rather cheeky.

> 'I know you've spent your money coming here. I know it's two weeks 'til Christmas. I want to ask as many of you to join

me with what I'm about to do. I'd like to ask you to go on your phones. The only way that there can be a political option is for the public to support it, back it and join it. So I've got my phone out and I'll go on UKIP's website. It's £4 a month. It's the price of a beer—the price of a beer in London anyway— and join as a member of UKIP.

'Do you know what? Gerard put his head on the line. There's been, I believe, resignations all week from UKIP. To all the people in UKIP who were worried? Don't worry, be- cause the cavalry has arrived.'

He then spends about seventy seconds fiddling with his smartphone. Nearly there. . .

'Now it's the final frame before I put my bank details in.'

Nearly there. . .

'Declined! Gerard, that's something you're gonna have to sort out mate.'

Hmmm. . .

And: Oakley's on.

'What a joy it is to look out on this crowd. . .'

The mob respond immediately and forcefully.

'Can't hear ya.'

'Speak up.'

'Can't HEAR you.'

Alan Craig is good enough to help adjust the microphone. I continue.

'Look at this crowd. People of all ages. People from every economic background. Health workers. Teachers. Service- men. We have people here, brothers and sisters from the old Commonwealth, whose families came generations ago. We have people here from the new Europe who have made this country their home. Every person here has one thing in com- mon. They share the new consciousness which is emerging in the West. They share the new consciousness which is emerg- ing in Europe. And it has nothing to do with loyalty to the European Union, let me tell you that.'

In the aftermath of the shocking murder of Jo Cox MP, the left adopted one of her sayings as an anthem. Namely, that we have 'far more in common than that which divides us'. This is certainly true when it comes to the basic necessities of life. It is not at all true when it comes to the core philosophies of life.

Perhaps their preferred future will be a happy one. Regional blocs with global free movement supervised and directed by the United Nations. A minimum wage, if wage at all, which is also a maximum wage. Those monies to be spent on whatever products the trillionaire corporations inform us that we need. 'Facist' speech outlawed and 'Facist' thought discouraged because that kind of divergency is not to be celebrated. Alien clan rivalries will settle forever and definitely not reignite in European cities before a perplexed local populace. Gay bars and mosques will nestle beside each other along every high street. Men will be able to transition to women and adopt a niqab of a new-found faith while all sing an 'Ode to Joy'. And the lion shall eat straw like the ox. Perhaps.

The foes of Brexiteers often tell us that we wish to return to the 1950s. Not I. As per the millennial warcry: 'I wasn't even BORN then'. The world of today, though flawed, is exciting enough. East European catholic conservatives have recent experience of the weight of a superstate. Sikh daughters were the very first victims of Moslem grooming gangs. Indian Hindus are knowledgeably wary of their northern neighbours. West Africans understand the weaknesses of artificial countries and the strengths of Boko Haram. Jews are fearful once more as religious and political antisemitism vomits forth again. Kurds. Pakistani Christians. And more.

New friendships and new alliances are evolving right now and our convergency is our strength. Which side are you on, boys? Which side are you on?

Enough of the deviation already. Back to the speech. I cover the imminent horrors of the UN's Migration Compact and then return to our core purpose and my core purpose. Leaving the EU.

'The risk is, we're now going to get a second referendum. Tony Blair has said . . .'

'Bastard!'
'Boo!'
'Fucker!' These words come from the crowd, not me. I carry on.

'. . . that if there is a second referendum, that will settle matters for once and for all.

'Oh. No. It. Won't.

'We will never accept continuing membership of the European Union. Let me tell you this. At times of national crisis it is customary to refer back to the giants of our culture. Henry the Fifth. Horatio Nelson. Winston Churchill.

'And with this in mind I say: Beware, Remoaners. For our strength and our courage come from the example of:

'The Terminator.'

With that are recycled here, today, before this crowd of many times the magnitude, the selfsame words used in my first speech as a UKIP freshman nearly seven years ago. They apply now more than ever.

Those who wish to betray Brexit are proud to flaunt a (self-assessed) intellectual superiority over those who choose freedom. Yet over the past quarter-century, I have discussed this cause with hundreds, if not thousands, of such 'inferior' souls.

Those who wish to betray Brexit have not had these conversations. Certainly, if our nation is sucked back into the EU as they plan, then most of those who voted to Leave will swallow the swindle and move on. That's just what happens in time of the breaking of nations.

Many will not give up. Under any circumstances.

It hasn't occurred to the Brexit betrayers that they're presenting that small group, and half-a-billion EU citizens at large, with a clear and logical statement of fact. Namely: it is impossible to leave the European Union by peaceful, democratic means.

The naivety of that arrogance is terrifying.

Bella, horrida bella.
Et Thybrim multo spumantem sanguine cerno.[1]

---

1 Wars, horrid wars, I view—a field of blood,
  And Tiber rolling with a purple flood.
— Virgil, *The Aeneid* lines 86–87 (translated by John Dryden); Sibyl's prophecy to Aeneas.
— Cf. Enoch Powell's 'Rivers of Blood' speech.

CPSIA information can be obtained
at www.ICGtesting.com
Printed in the USA
BVHW071029020519
547199BV00004B/34/P